DECADENCE AND INNOVATION

DECADENCE AND INNOVATION

Austro-Hungarian Life and Art
at the Turn of the Century

EDITED BY

ROBERT B. PYNSENT

Reader in Czech and Slovak Literature
School of Slavonic and East European Studies
University of London

WEIDENFELD AND NICOLSON

LONDON

ISBN 0 297 79559 7

Photoset by Deltatype Ltd, Ellesmere Port, Cheshire
Printed in Great Britain by
Butler & Tanner Ltd
Frome and London

Contents

Notes on the Contributors

Steven Beller is Research Fellow in History at Peterhouse, Cambridge. His main academic interest lies in the role of the Jews in Viennese culture at the turn of the century, on which he has published several articles.

Magda Czigány is the Librarian of Imperial College, London. She was educated at London University. She has published articles on modern art and is the author of a bibliography of English translations of Hungarian literature.

Monika Glettler is Professor of History at Munich University. She has also taught at Columbia. She is the author of several books on ethnic minorities and on emigration.

Nicholas Goodrick-Clarke was educated at Oxford. He is the author of *The Occult Roots of Nazism* (1985). Since 1982 he has followed a number of interests, including banking. He now lives in Berlin and Oxford and is increasingly involved in film and television.

Allan Janik is Visiting Professor at the Brenner Archive of Innsbruck University. He was educated at Anselm College and at Villanova and Brandeis Universities. He has published books and articles on Wittgenstein, Offenbach, practical reasoning and Viennese culture.

André Karátson is Professor of Comparative Literature at the University of Lille (III). He has published books and articles on Franco-Hungarian cultural relations, Symbolist verse and on twentieth-century Modernist prose.

Jiří Kudrnáč lectures on Czech literature at Brno University. He has published numerous articles, mainly on Czech *fin-de-siècle* literature.

Kevin Mulligan is Professor at Philosophy at the University of Geneva. He previously taught at the Universities of Graz and Constance. He has published mainly on Austrian philosophy.

J. C. Nyíri is Professor of Philosophy at the University of Budapest. He is author of *Gestalt und Gefüge: Studien zum Entstehen der Philosophie Wittgensteins* and *Am Rande Europas: Studien zur östereichisch-ungarischen Philosophiegeschichte*.

Robert B. Pynsent was educated at Cambridge. He is Reader in Czech and Slovak Literature at London University. He has published books and articles, mainly on Czech literature.

Edward Timms, is Fellow of Caius College and Lecturer in German at the University of Cambridge. His publications include *Karl Kraus – Apocalyptic Satirist: Culture and Catastrophe in Habsburg Vienna*.

Petr Wittlich is Reader in the History and Theory of Art at Prague University, where he was also educated. He has published articles and books, mainly on Czech art and architecture at the turn of the century. Recently he has published *Česká secese* (1982, second edition, 1986).

Ferenc Tibor Zsuppán is Lecturer in Modern History at the University of St Andrews. He has published articles mainly on Hungarian institutions and on the 1919 Hungarian 'Soviet' Republic.

Prefatory Note

This volume comprises a small selection of papers from a large international conference on Austria-Hungary at the turn of the century, held at the School of Slavonic and East European Studies at the University of London in December, 1986. The School and the editor would like to express their gratitude to the Austrian Institute, the British Academy, the British Council, the Czechoslovak and Hungarian Embassies in London, and the (West) German Academic Exchange Service for their generosity, which made the conference possible.

The editor apologises for the Czech bias in his Conclusory Essay, and for his narrow knowledge of Austrian-German and Magyar culture. He would also like to thank primarily Dr László Péter of London, but also Dr Brušák of Cambridge, Mr Peter Sherwood of London and Mrs Sonia Kanikova of Sofia for their critical comments on the Conclusory Essay, and Dr Péter for his help in compiling this volume. He is also grateful for the painstaking proof reading of his colleague, David Short.

The Conclusory Essay began as an Introduction but so many themes suggested by the chapters selected turned out not to have been treated in any large detail that a broad introduction appeared necessary. The introduction became so broad that it would have become not so much indelicate as crude to place it at the beginning of the book. I call it a conclusory essay, but it does not come to conclusions. I hope it does, however, suggest further paths of research.

The 1986 conference had the following academic 'manifesto', which was composed by the editor of this volume:

In Europe the perception of civilisation in terms of decay rather than progress goes back to the Romantic movement. Philistine materialism appeared to intellectuals to be usurping the pursuit of beauty and the promise of the Enlightenment. In western Europe a sense of decay was evident from the middle of the nineteenth century.

Matthew Arnold saw 'the predominance of thought' in the nineteenth century as having 'produced a state of feeling unknown to less enlightened but perhaps healthier epochs – the feeling of depression,' the feeling of *ennui* ('On the Modern Element in Literature'). Critics considered Baudelaire and Moreau to be products of the failure of the 1848 revolution to create a new society, as well as what they clearly saw as the social degeneration brought on by the restoration of the French monarchy. Only after 1870–1, however, did Baudelaire's influence become all-pervasive in French and west European art. Verlaine described himself as the Empire in its decadence and thought of the 'barbares blancs' who would come with a new 'civilisation'.

In Austria 1867 had a similar effect to that of 1870–1 in France. The main cultural centres of the Monarchy, Vienna, Prague and Budapest, began to go their own separate ways. Initially the Hungarians were content with the Dualist system, but the intellectuals turned their eyes to Munich and Paris, not Vienna. The Czechs turned first to Moscow, but then, finding no inspiration there, to Munich, Berlin and Paris. The nature of intellectual society in Vienna changed just as radically once the Jews began to dominate cultural life: Viennese Jewish intellectuals also looked to Germany and France. Cultural centres on the peripheries of the Empire, Cracow and Zagreb, however, turned not only to Berlin and Paris, but also to Vienna and Prague. The sense of decay in the Monarchy was more intense than in western Europe because the intellectuals of the Monarchy no longer had a single unifying cultural centre at home. On coming to Paris or Berlin, more rarely London, these intellectuals found their counterparts there despairing of the decay of their own culture and looking for the 'New'. For the intellectuals of the Monarchy Paris or Berlin was by no means in a state of decay, and so they naturally came to consider their native regions as miasmic backwaters.

This sense of decay also had a political background. After 1867 the Monarchy itself appeared fragmented. The emergence later of mass political parties seemed further to fragment the Monarchy. No serious work has been done to compare the sense of cultural and political decay in the main national centres of the Monarchy. The Conference was intended to initiate such comparative studies.

The papers given at the conference were as follows. An asterisk indicates that a version of that paper is included in this volume.

Introduction

Professor Norman Stone (University of Oxford): The Metaphysics of Anti-Metaphysics.

Professor Soloman Wank (Franklin and Marshall College): Österreich ist ein Trummerfeld': Pessimism in the Austrian 'Establishment' at the Turn of the Century.

Metropolis

Professor J. P. Stern (University College, London): The Czech View of *fin-de-siècle* Vienna.

*Dr Edward Timms (Caius, Cambridge): Images of the City: Vienna, Prague and the European Avant-Garde.

*Dr Monika Glettler (University of Munich): Minority Culture in a Capital City: the Czechs in Vienna at the Turn of the Century.

Dr Emil Brix (University of Vienna): The Language Question in the Habsburg Monarchy at the Turn of the Century. Assimilation and Integration.

The Impact of Wagner and Nietzsche

Professor Hugh Macdonald (University of Glasgow): Wolf's Adulation of Wagner in the Vienna Press.

Professor Peter Kampits (University of Vienna): The Significance of Critics of Language and the Reception of Nietzsche by Fritz Mauthner.

Culture and the Army

Dr Alan Sked (The London School of Economics): Social Attitudes as Evinced in Army Life in the Monarchy.

Dr Susan Wimmer (University of Vienna): The Influence of Military Life on Austrian-German Writers at the Turn of the Century.

Jews and Austrian Culture

*Dr Steven Beller (Peterhouse, Cambridge): The Role of Jews in Viennese Culture and Society at the Turn of the Century.

Dr Michael P. Steinberg (University of Chicago): The Catholic Culture of the Austrian Jews.

Politics and Culture

*Dr Jiří Kudrnáč (University of Brno): The Political Meaning of Czech *fin-de-siècle* Criticism.

†Professor Tomasz Weiss (University of Cracow): The Politics of Culture in Galicia at the Turn of the Century.

Professor Rene Lovrenčić (University of Zagreb): The Influence of Critics in Vienna and Prague on Cultural Development in Croatia at the Turn of the Century.

Philosophy in Austrian Culture

Mr Brian McGuiness (Queen's, Oxford): Ernst Mach and His Influence on Austrian Intellectuals.

*Dr Kevin Mulligan (Universities of Constance and Graz): The Expression of Exactness: Mach, the Brentanists and the Ideal of Clarity.

Dr Barry Smith (University of Manchester): Austrian Philosophy and the Brentanian Heritage.

*Professor Allan Janik (University of Innsbruck): Weininger and the Development of Psychiatry.

*Professor J. C. Nyíri (University of Budapest): The Concept of Tradition: Mach, the Brentanists and the Early Musil.

Dr J. Zumr (Prague): Ladislav Klíma: An Absurd Existence in the Absurd World.

Decadent Relations
Dr Stanislaw Eile (School of Slavonic and East European Studies)
Decadence in Galicia: K. Tetmajer and F. Przybyszewski.

Dr Jacek Baluch (University of Cracow): Polish-Czech Relations at the
Turn of the Century.

Dr Ewa Miodonska-Brookes (University of Cracow): Wyspiański in the
Light of Contemporary French and German Art Theory.

Innovation in the Fine Arts
*Dr Petr Wittlich (University of Prague): The Self: Destruction or
Synthesis: Two Problems of Czech Art at the Turn of the Century.

Dr Irit Rogoff (London): The Self and Others: Kokoschka, Schiele,
Gerstel.

Dr Ilona Sarmany-Parsons (Vienna): From Pantheism to Social Radicalism:
Hungarian Schools of Painters at the Turn of the Century.

*Magda Czigány (University College, London): Imitation or Inspiration:
The Reception of Cubism in the Habsburg Monarchy, 1910 –15.

Vladimír Šlapeta (Prague): Czech Architecture 1900 –14.

Publishing and Politics
Dr Robin Okey (University of Warwick): The *Neue Freie Presse* and the
South Slavs of the Monarchy: The Limitations of a *Weltblatt*.

Dr Murray Hall (University of Vienna): The Literary Publishing Business in
Vienna between 1900 and 1914.

Innovation in Literature
*Professor André Karátson (University of Lille III): Les Paradoxes des
adeptes hongrois du symbolisme et du decadentisme au début de xxè siècle.

Professor Mihály Szegedy-Maszak (University of Budapest): Tradition and
Innovation in Early Twentieth-Century Hungarian Prose.

Professor Maria Podraża–Kwiatkowska (University of Cracow): Die
Katastrophische Einbildungskraft in der Literatur des 'Jung-Polens'.

The Darker Side
Professor Péter Hanák (University of Budapest): The Perception of Death
in Budapest and Vienna.

*Dr Nicholas Goodrick-Clarke (London): The Modern Occult Revival in
Vienna 1880 –1918.

Music

Dr Paul Banks (Goldsmiths College London): The Perception of Mahler by Contemporary Artists.

Dr Alfred Clayton (Hamburg): 'Lebendig müssen die Märchen werden': An Approach to Alexander Zemlinsky's *Der Traumgörge*.

Dr T. Tallián (Hungarian Academy of Sciences): *Bluebeard*, the Realism of Dissonances: Bartok's Musical *Weltanschauung* in his First Maturity.

Patrick Carnegy (Faber and Faber): The Inter-relationship Between Schoenberg and Kandinsky.

Dr Michael Musgrave (Goldsmiths College, London): The Second Vienna School.

The New Politics

Professor Fritz Fellner (University of Salzburg): Josef Redlich 'Das österreichische Staats-und Reichsproblem' – Politics and Scholarship in the Years of the Dissolution of the Habsburg Monarchy.

Professor Karl Stadler (University of Linz): Renner and Bauer on the Crisis of the Monarchy up to 1914.

Professor J. W. Boyer (University of Chicago): The Affinities of Viennese Mass Politics: Christian Socialism and Social Democracy.

Dr Reinhard Knoll (University of Vienna): The Austrian Fabians: Scholarship, Social Reform and Politics at the Turn of the Century.

Professor J. M. Bak (University of British Columbia): Politics, Culture and 'Counter-Culture' in Ervin Szabó.

Dr György Litván (Hungarian Academy of Sciences): The Social Role and Readership of *Huszadik Század*.

Professor Pierre Kende (Ecole des Hautes Etudes en Sciences Sociales): Oszkár Jaszi's View of Hungarian Society, 1900 –14.

*Dr Tibor Zsuppán (University of St Andrews): The Reception of the Hungarian Feminist Movement, 1904–14.

The conference was jointly organised by G. F. Cushing, László Péter, Trevor Thomas and the editor from the School and by Norman Stone from Oxford and Martin Swales from University College, London.

R. B. P.
June 1988

1

Images of the City: Vienna, Prague and the Intellectual Avant-Garde

EDWARD TIMMS

From earliest recorded history the city has formed one of the magnetic poles of human existence. But the growth of great metropolises during the nineteenth century gave an unprecedented urgency to this theme. Around 1900 the city became the focal point for an intense debate about the dynamics of technological civilisation. The urgency of this debate was signalled by the Futurist Manifesto of 1909, which identified the city as the preeminent theme of modern poetry and painting. This challenge was taken up by avant-garde writers and artists in every capital city of Europe, with regional and social variations which have been analysed in a recent collection of essays entitled *Unreal City*.[1] The present chapter is designed to show how that 'Unreal City' *motif* emerges from the work of writers and thinkers in Vienna at the turn of the century – and (more briefly) in Prague. It aims to show, if only in outline, how radically these writers challenged traditional conceptions of society – developing their own alternative visions.

My *leitmotiv* derives from T. S. Eliot's poem *The Waste Land*:

> Falling towers
> Jerusalem Athens Alexandria
> Vienna London
> Unreal

It may seem paradoxical to represent Vienna as unreal. The city, even today, seems so solid and unchanging. It is an enduring monument to the grandeur of Habsburg civilisation: an inner city of Baroque churches and town-houses on the bank of the Danube, circled by the magnificent Ringstrasse, with its main thoroughfares radiating out through solidly constructed residential quarters into the leafy suburbs and the surrounding Viennese woods. When Eliot's lines about the 'unreal city' were published in 1922, the Austro-Hungarian Empire had just collapsed as a result of defeat in the First World War. In *The Waste Land* Vienna thus exemplifies the precariousness of imperial power, indeed of western civilisation as a whole; it foreshadows the decline of London. But in 1900 Vienna was still an 'imperial city', enjoying unprecedented power and affluence. The great public buildings of the Ringstrasse outshone those of London and Paris as emblems of imperial splendour and cultural achievement. The paradox to be explored in this chapter is that even in that period of apparent stability a significant number of Viennese writers were already portraying the city as unreal.

The architectural opulence of Vienna was one of the primary sources of that sense of unreality. Vienna was (still is) so evidently a Baroque city, a city of the seventeenth or early eighteenth century. Even the great public buildings of the nineteenth century were all constructed in earlier historical styles. Vienna, indeed the Austro-Hungarian Empire itself, seemed like a grandiose attempt to stop the clock. Rapid demographic change was not accompanied by a corresponding modernisation of social institutions. But while Austria-Hungary slumbered, convulsed by occasional eruptions of military conflict and civil strife, dynamic changes were occurring else-where. And suddenly around 1900 people in Vienna woke up, rubbed their eyes and looked around them in amazement. They were still living in that traditional Baroque city, although its old ramparts had been transformed into spacious boulevards. But they recognised that in other great cities there had been a qualitative change. As principal city of central Europe, Vienna had been overtaken by the dynamic growth of Berlin. Technologic-ally, the small craft industries of Vienna could no longer compete with the sophisticated products of Paris and London. And an awareness of the skylines of Chicago and New York made the domes and spires of Vienna seem anachronistic.

The 'Shock of the New' is the title which Robert Hughes has given to the transformation of attitudes towards art and architecture which occurred around 1900.[2] In Austria that shock took an extreme form. Vienna in 1900 was a city riven by the conflict between tradition and modernisation. The terms of this conflict were more extreme in Austria-Hungary than in other parts of Europe. On the one hand there was an essentially medieval model of society, based on the Christian moral order, the authority of the Catholic Church and the infallibility of the Pope on questions of doctrine, the divine right of kings, the principles of multinational empire and dynastic allegi-ance, the predominance of aristocratic and military castes, and the loyalty of a quasi-feudal peasantry. On the other, there was the sudden and disruptive impact of twentieth-century civilisation with its factories and urban slums, its mass political movements and rapid means of communication, bringing into prominence a new capitalist bourgeoisie of manufacturers and bankers (many of them Jewish in origin) and secular creeds like liberalism, scientism, racialism and especially antisemitism. In Austria the process of adaptation to modern industrial society was not spread over two centuries, as it was in England, leaving time for a gradual assimilation of disruptive social forces. In Austria, as in Germany, this process took place within a single lifetime, and the medieval and modern orders collided head-on. It was (as Karl Kraus put it) a 'techno-romantic' civilisation, where modern industrial forces were still decked out in the trappings of imperial tradition.[3]

This view of Vienna was shared by Kraus's friend, the architect and designer Adolf Loos. In their different spheres they conducted a campaign against a common enemy: the anachronistic cultural institutions of Habsburg Austria. Their aim was the demolition of façades. This theme was announced in Loos's essay, 'Potemkin's City' (1898), in which he derided the pretentious façades of the Ringstrasse. The Russian General Potemkin had constructed whole villages out of cardboard and canvas, in order to deceive Catherine the Great into believing that progress was being made in the Ukraine. The façades of the Ringstrasse (Loos argues) are equally spurious, since they are designed to make modern apartment blocks look like the town-houses of aristocrats. To satisfy the vanity of the *nouveaux riches*, ornamental façades have been nailed on to imitate Baroque stucco or Tuscan stone. But in fact they are made of cement. In other essays Loos extended this argument into a comprehensive critique of Austrian design. In every sphere, from leatherwork to plumbing, he insists on the need for practical efficiency rather than ornamental design. The beauty of a practical object (he concludes) can only exist in relation to its function.

Loos had visited London and spent a year in Chicago. He knew what a dynamically modern city looked like, and it was this that inspired his functionalist principles. Reacting against the anachronistic clutter of Vienna, he declared ornament to be a 'crime'; but the functional elegance of his buildings so affronted Austrian tastes that he received relatively few commissions. For he was too principled to compromise with the prejudices of his day. He confronted the imperial opulence of Vienna with an alternative vision of a functionalist society. He even dreamed of an era when the 'the streets of the cities will shine like walls of whiteness. Like Zion, the sacred city.'[4]

This tendency to construct alternative cities of the mind can be seen on an even grander scale in the designs of Otto Wagner (1841–1918). Wagner was the initiator of functional architecture in Vienna. But where Loos was a purist, Wagner was a pragmatist. He was willing to make the concessions necessary to secure commissions for important public works – the Metropolitan Railway (*Stadtbahn*) and the regulation of the Danube Canal. His functional designs are encrusted with classical or *Jugendstil* embellishments which reflect the changing fashions of his day. Yet even Wagner's vision had a utopian element. He too was caught between the traditions of old Vienna and the dream of a purely functional city, which finds expression in his influential writings, *Moderne Architektur* (1895) and *Die Großstadt* (1911). Wagner's plans for the expansion of Vienna have a geometrical severity which is out of keeping with the character of the city. He seems to be dreaming of that ideal city which was later to be invoked in Musil's novel *The Man Without Qualities*:

a kind of super-American city where everyone rushes about, or stands still, with a stop-watch in his hand. Air and earth form an ant-hill, veined by channels of traffic, rising storey upon storey. Overhead-trains, overground-trains, underground-trains, pneumatic express-mails carrying consignments of human beings, chains of motor-vehicles all racing along horizontally. (*MQ*, I. 30).[5]

This reads like a parody of Wagner's architectural ideals; and Musil's novel emphasises how remote this model of the metropolis was from the retarded tempo of life in Vienna.

Wagner's plans were not mere pipe-dreams. He accurately identified the dynamics of metropolitan development. Indeed, visions dreamed up in *fin-de-siècle* Vienna have shaped the life of the twentieth century in spectacular ways. This is particularly true of the work of political visionaries. Theodor Herzl, founder of modern Zionism, was literary editor of a Viennese newspaper. His blueprint for the foundation of a new Jewish state, *Der Judenstaat*, was greeted with incredulity and ridicule when it appeared in 1896. But only twenty years elapsed between the launching of the Zionist movement and the Balfour Declaration which gave it political reality. Herzl's vision offered hope to a beleaguered generation of Jews, although few were fortunate enough to reach the Promised Land.

For there was another political dreamer who dreamt the opposite dream. Adolf Hitler came to Vienna in 1908 as an aspiring student of architecture. His five formative years in the city left an indelible stamp on his personality. In *Mein Kampf* he describes the corruption of the metropolis in lurid terms: unemployment and destitution in the doss-house, the miseries of slums and building sites, the glaring contrast between rich and poor, the growing power of the masses, the corruptness of the press, the decadence of bohemian life and the lure of prostitution. Hitler may have stylised his account (he was not actually as destitute as *Mein Kampf* suggests), but the horrific impact of the metropolis on a young man without contacts or resources clearly shaped his political vision.

Hitler attributed the evils of the city to a single factor: the Jews. It was the Jews who were responsible for the lies of the press and the decadence of modern art, the socialist creed that was corrupting the workers and the miscegenation which was polluting the lifeblood of the German *Volk*. For Hitler antisemitism had the power of a religious revelation. Suddenly the chaos of the metropolis made sense, as a battleground between good and evil, German and Jew. He was clearly seized by a kind of paranoia. But so widespread was the revulsion against modern civilisation which Hitler epitomises that he was able, twenty years later, to impose his paranoid vision upon millions of German and Austrian followers.

Hitler's revulsion against the city had sexual undertones. He was haunted by images of lecherous Jews debauching innocent German maidens. One of the most emotionally charged passages in *Mein Kampf* describes his evening walks through the Jewish quarter of Vienna, where he was overwhelmed by the spectacle of prostitutes and pimps. The sexual displays of the city were indeed deeply disturbing, as is clear from Stefan Zweig's memoir of Vienna before the First World War, *The World of Yesterday*: 'The present generation has hardly any idea of the gigantic extent of prostitution in Europe before the First World War . . . . The sidewalks were so sprinkled with women for sale that it was more difficult to avoid them than to find them'.[6] Prostitution formed a dimension of the unreal city which only came to life after dark, but in the daytime lurked beneath the threshold of consciousness.

This was the domain of Sigmund Freud. His archaeology of the emotions probed beneath the surface of urban social life to uncover a turbulent realm of sexual appetites. 'If I cannot move the higher powers, I shall stir up the underground river of Acheron' is the motto of his *Interpretation of Dreams* (1900). He unquestioningly accepted the 'higher powers', the superstructure of Austrian society, leading an amazingly conventional middle-class life as physician, professor and paterfamilias. But beneath the frock-coated respectability of the Viennese bourgeoisie he revealed an animal only partly tamed and vulnerable to eruptions of unsublimated instinct: sexual desire, aggression, the impulse towards death and destruction. In an essay of 1908 he identified 'civilised' sexual morality as the source of 'modern nervousness'. And in *Civilisation and its Discontents* (1930) he even suggested that society as a whole may have become 'neurotic'.[7]

Freud's work radically undermined traditional conceptions of 'reality'. The stable self vanishes into a vortex of conflicting impulses which strain against social cohesion. This questioning of stable identity was all the more subversive because it was supported by the findings of other psychologists: not only the members of Freud's own circle but also the philosopher Ernst Mach. Mach's contributions to physics influenced the early work of Einstein. In psychology his seminal work was *Die Analyse der Empfindungen* (The analysis of sensations, 1885). Where Freud explores the workings of the unconscious, Mach analyses conscious sense-impressions, radicalising Kant's model of the subjectivity of perception. What our senses of sight and sound, time and space convey to us is not reality, but an unstable sequence of sensory stimuli. Consciousness is composed of a multiplicity of chance impressions and memories. The notion of a stable and unified self is therefore untenable: 'Das Ich ist unrettbar' (The self cannot be salvaged.[8]) When this provocative claim, coalescing with the ideas of Freud, filtered through into general intellectual debate in Vienna after 1900, its impact was incalculable.

This questioning of received 'reality' becomes one of the central preoccupations of Austrian and Czech writing. The coffee-houses of Vienna (and to an extent of Prague) were the meeting places for groups of exceptionally gifted writers and thinkers, artists and musicians. Each leading figure had his own circle, which might regularly meet at a particular coffee-house or on a specified evening: Freud's Wednesday-evening gatherings of psychoanalysts, Schoenberg's group of avant-garde composers, Schnitzler's circle (which included high-minded authors like Hofmannsthal), Kraus's clique of iconoclasts (which included Adolf Loos), the painters around Klimt and the Social Democrats around Victor Adler. At certain points the circles intersected, which ensured a rapid circulation of ideas and a fertile interaction between different art forms.

Among such a diversity of talent it is hard to identify common factors. What is striking, however, is the paucity of realistic representations of social life and of the city itself. Led by Gustav Klimt, the painters of Vienna developed an exotic idiom for the exploration of inner states, coloured by sensuous eroticism (Klimt) or extreme nervous tension (Kokoschka and Schiele).[9] The poets and novelists were equally cavalier in their disregard for social realism. There is no Viennese equivalent of Dickens, Balzac or Fontane. The work of Arthur Schnitzler comes closest to reflecting the social life of the city. His novel *Der Weg ins Freie* (The path to the open, 1908) and his play *Professor Bernhardi* (1912) portray the ideological conflicts of the day, particularly the emergence of antisemitism and the clash between scientific scepticism and the clericalism of established institutions.

Schnitzler's fundamental attitude is revealed in a passage from his autobiography (written during the First World War) which looks back on his own carefree existence as a young doctor:

> Did he not have a homeland from which to draw strength and life, a fatherland of which he was a citizen, with or without pride? Wasn't there history, world history, which never stood still and which blew around one's ears as one raced through time? Of course there was. But homeland was a place to cavort in, wings and backdrop for one's private fate; fatherland was a creation of chance, a totally indifferent administrative affair.[10]

Although this passage refers to younger days, it epitomises the disjunction between social environment and individual sensibility which characterises Viennese art and literature around 1900. Social life is perceived as the 'backdrop' (*Kulisse*) against which to play out individual emotional dramas.

In Schnitzler's writings the artificiality of life in Vienna seems to be taken for granted. The most sophisticated exploration of the divorce between social environment and individual sensibility is to be found in Musil's novel *Der Mann ohne Eigenschaften* (*The Man Without Qualities*). Although not published until 1930–3, the first two volumes of this novel give definitive expression to the inauthenticity of life in Habsburg Vienna.

Robert Musil was trained as an engineer, but he was a man of literary and philosophical inclinations, and in 1902 he fell under the spell of Ernst Mach (on whom he wrote a doctoral dissertation). About the ideas of Freud he was more sceptical, although his early story *Törless* (1906) is a study of adolescent emotional ambivalence which echoes some of the findings of psychoanalysis. After living through the collapse of Austria-Hungary, Musil set about the task of writing a kind of alternative history of that historical crisis, in a fictional form which bears clear traces of Mach's influence.

Set in the final years before the First World War, the novel explores the ideological turmoil of Vienna and the impending collapse of Habsburg institutions. But Musil does not dwell on political factors, such as Slav nationalism or the rivalry between Britain and Germany. His focus is on the instability of the human mind and the turmoil of thoughts and feelings which animate it. Life in Vienna exemplifies that 'intellectual revolution' which occurred with the onset of the twentieth century:

> The contradictions . . . were unsurpassable. The Superman was adored and the Subman was adored; health and the sun were worshipped, and the delicacy of consumptive girls was worshipped; people were enthusiastic hero-worshippers and enthusiastic adherents of the social creed of the Man in the Street; one had faith and was sceptical, one was naturalistic and precious, robust and morbid; one dreamed of ancient castles and shady avenues, autumnal gardens, glassy ponds, jewels, hashish, disease and demonism, but also of prairies, vast horizons, forges and rolling-mills, naked wrestlers, the uprisings of slaves of toil, man and woman in the primeval garden, and the destruction of society. (*MQ*, I, 59)

This ideological turmoil is explored through the personality of Ulrich, Musil's hero. But 'personality' is the wrong word. For Ulrich is a man 'without qualities', a Machian hero whose character dissolves into a multiplicity of divergent selves:

> For the inhabitant of a country has at least nine characters: a professional one, a national one, a civic one, a class one, a geographical one, a sex one, a conscious and an unconscious and perhaps even too a private one; he combines them all in himself, but they dissolve him . . . Hence every dweller on earth also has a tenth character, which is nothing more or less than the passive illusion of spaces unfilled . . . an empty, invisible space with reality standing in the middle of it like a little toy brick town, abandoned by the imagination. (*MQ*, I, 34)

The disjunction between reality and self could hardly be more radically formulated. Ulrich lives his life 'hypothetically', guided not by his 'sense of reality' but by the 'sense of possibility' (*MQ*, I, 12).

The novel begins realistically enough. We are plunged into the streets of Vienna in the rush hour, with cars intersecting the bustle of pedestrians and a hundred different sounds converging and fragmenting around us. Braking sharply, a lorry swerves and knocks down a pedestrian. But Musil is not concerned to analyse the cause of such an accident (as Brecht does in a well-known essay).[11] Musil's focus is on the responses of the onlookers. A sentimental lady feels a paralysing sensation in the pit of her stomach. But her companion responds with the pragmatic observation: 'These heavy lorries they use here have too long a braking-distance.' This technical analysis is intended to be reassuring, especially as the gentleman adds: 'According to American statistics there are over a hundred and ninety thousand people killed on the roads annually over there'. (*MQ*, I, 5–6)

These contrasting responses express the problem which preoccupies the whole novel: how to reconcile scientific exactitude with spiritual truth, 'facts' with 'eternal verities' (*MQ*, I, 295). We are living in a civilisation created by scientific precision and statistical analysis, where (as Musil seems to have anticipated) the computer will soon be king – the symbol he invokes is the slide-rule (*MQ*, I, 38). How can this urban technocratic civilisation accommodate the claims of emotional and spiritual life? The problem is explored from a multitude of different narrative angles with immense intellectual verve and stylistic subtlety. The solution which Ulrich aspires to is a synthesis of science and spirituality. It is adumbrated in the novel through his relationship with his sister Agathe, a kind of mystic union which guides them towards the realm of 'the other condition' ('der andere Zustand'). The novel begins with the screeching of brakes on the streets of a recognisable city. It ends, or rather peters out (for Musil's sprawling manuscript remained incomplete), in a realm of disembodied intellectuality. The real city, in short, is reduced to 'a little toy brick town abandoned by the imagination', while the narrative moves into that 'empty, invisible space' where all contradictions may be reconciled.

The sense of a loss of reality is related to a loss of confidence in language. The inadequacies of language form one of the recurrent laments of Austrian writing, from Hofmannsthal then to Peter Handke today. The work of the philosopher Ludwig Wittgenstein is centred on precisely this problem. But few imaginative writers shared Wittgenstein's confidence that language can be reduced to an orderly system. One passage from the *Philosophical Investigations* even suggests that language can be mapped in a way one would map a city: 'our language can be seen as an ancient city: a maze of little streets and squares, of old and new houses, and of houses with additions from various periods; and this surrounded by a multitude of new boroughs with straight regular streets and uniform houses.'[12] Wittgenstein's analogy for lexical accretion is too static to accommodate the problems encountered by Austrian imaginative writers of his generation. New words in a dictionary may be like new houses on a city plan. But the lived experience of the city eludes linguistic expression.

There are few Viennese writers of this period who seem securely at home, either in the city where they lived or in the language which they wrote. They felt themselves to be living among 'sleepwalkers' – people unaware of the vacuum on which the social consensus rested (*Die Schlafwandler* is indeed the title Hermann Broch gave to his ambitious novel on this theme, published in 1931). Their dilemma is summed up in Elias Canetti's novel *Die Blendung* (1935), an allegory of the intellectual who takes refuge among his books from a city with which he has lost rapport. The fire which finally engulfs him and his great library is reflected in the novel's English title *Auto-da-Fé*. But the folly of this enterprise of trying to construct a stable intellectual edifice amid the turmoil of the city is more appropriately reflected by the title under which this novel first appeared in America: *The Tower of Babel*.

Of course there were minor poets in Vienna, like Anton Wildgans, who wrote about the city in a more traditional and homely idiom. Most notable among them was Josef Weinheber, a poet who came from humbler social origins and wrote vernacular poetry which echoes the rhythms of Viennese dialect. The poems of his *Wien wörtlich* (Vienna in its own words, 1935) celebrate the tranquil suburbs and wine villages, where the thirsty soul may find refreshment even if they offer no solace to the exacting mind. But the more rigorous authors of the Austrian avant-garde were spiritual exiles in their own city, long before they were, like Musil, Broch and Canetti, forced into exile by political events.

In Prague the sense of estrangement was even greater. The historical context has been reconstructed in *The World of Franz Kafka*.[13] Prague is another city where time seems to have stood still. A beautiful but haunted cityscape of medieval lanes and Baroque palaces converges on the banks of the Moldau under the dominating presence of castle and cathedral. Rapid industrialisation generated an extensive sprawl of new suburbs in the late nineteenth century. But the buildings of the old city remained more or less intact. They are still there today, crumbling as magnificently away as they did then. In 1900 the air of unreality was even greater. For Prague was a German outpost in a Czech hinterland. Czech nationalism had left the German-speaking urban élite stranded in a turbulent sea of Slavs. It was a relationship of master and servant, in which the Austrian–German ruling class was still supposedly in command but the educated Czech populace were already flexing their muscles. For the Czechs this meant cultivating the art of survival under an oppressive régime and awaiting the moment when the political tables could be turned. This situation is reflected in the relationship between Czech servant and Austrian–German master in Jaroslav Hašek's great unfinished picaresque novel, *The Good Soldier Švejk* (1920–3). Švejk's earthy realism enables him to survive the First World War, while the Austro-Hungarian system is falling apart around him. Whatever the crisis, Švejk can always be counted on to take refuge in a reassuring anecdote or a cosy pub round the corner.

In Kafka's writings, by contrast, the city dissolves into a penumbra of insecurity. It is often argued that as a German-speaking Jew living in the Czech capital Kafka suffered from a double alienation, and that this explains the existential anxiety of his writings. But it must be remembered that Kafka was only one of a whole group of Jewish writers who contributed to the brief but spectacular efflorescence of German literature in Prague. And it is against their work that his responses must be measured.

The central figure was the ebullient Franz Werfel. It is not adequate to argue that Kafka wrote as he did 'because he was a German Jewish writer living Prague.' Werfel, too, was a German Jewish writer living in Prague, yet he wrote in a style that is the exact antithesis to Kafka's. The relation between urban environment and imaginative response must not be simplistically conceived. Werfel's early poems, published under the title *Der Weltfreund* (Friend of the world) in 1911, express a joyous global philanthropy. He celebrates the multifarious activities of modern urban society in a manner reminiscent of Walt Whitman. His vision of brotherhood forms the positive counterpart to the apocalyptic mood of German Expressionism and is given particular weight in the later, more optimistic sections of the anthology *Menschheitsdämmerung* (The twilight of mankind). Werfel's all-embracing humanism is the converse of Kafka's vision of inescapable solitude. But each in his own way transcends realistic representation. Werfel's joyous band of brothers are as remote from actual social relations in the city as Kafka's desolately isolated outsiders.

German Jewish writers thus responded to the situation in Prague in divergent ways. But there is little doubt that a specifically Jewish predicament contributed to the intensity of their writings. With the growth not only of Czech nationalism but also of a particularly virulent antisemitism among the Germans of Bohemia, the Jewish communities did feel exceptionally vulnerable. But this insecurity expressed itself in a diversity of ways: in Max Brod's Zionism and Martin Buber's revival of the Hassidist tradition, as well as Werfel's compensatory optimism and Kafka's quiet despair.

Kafka certainly did not lack the gift of realistic observation. His stance in the early volume *Betrachtung* (1912) is that of a solitary man 'with a window looking on to the street'. As he stands idly at his window-sill, 'the horses below will draw him down into their train of wagons and tumult, and so at last into human harmony' (*KS*, 384).[14] The prose sketches of *Betrachtung* are so sharply observed that the English title might well be 'Observation' rather than 'Meditation'. They are snapshots of urban experience with existential undertones:

On the Tram

I stand on the end platform of the tram and am completely unsure of my footing in this world, in this town, in my family. Not even casually could I indicate any claims that I might rightly advance in any direction. I have not even any defence to offer for standing on this platform, holding on to this strap, letting myself be carried along by this tram, nor for the people who give way to the tram or walk quietly along or stand gazing into shop windows. Nobody asks me to put up a defence, indeed, but that is irrelevant . . . (*KS*, 388).

Under Kafka's gaze, the routine experience of the city commuter becomes an existential challenge. And the passenger's sense of insecurity is intensified by the contrast (in the second paragraph of the same sketch) with the young woman who seems so amazingly self-assured as she prepares to alight from the tram. Existence has to be justified – though by what authority?

Kafka does not create a dream city, as Alfred Kubin did in the fantastic novel *Die andere Seite* (The other side, 1907). Kafka's art makes the mundane mysterious. He starts with the most familiar of situations, like waking up for breakfast or rushing to catch a train:

Give it Up!

It was very early in the morning, the streets were clean and deserted, I was on my way to the station. As I compared the tower clock with my watch I realised that it was much later than I had thought and that I had to hurry; the shock of this discovery made me feel uncertain of the way, I wasn't very well acquainted with the town as yet; fortunately, there was a policeman at hand, I ran to him and breathlessly asked him the way. He smiled and said: 'You asking me the way?' 'Yes,' I said, 'since I can't find it myself.' 'Give it up! Give it up!' said he, and turned with a sudden jerk, like someone who wants to be alone with his laughter. (*KS*, 456).

From these small-scale vignettes of alienation in the city and among the crowd Kafka moves on to his classical exploration of urban insecurity in his masterpiece *Der Prozess* (The Trial, 1925). His language modulates so that 'asking the way' ceases to be a practical inquiry and becomes an existential quest.

The compelling power of his novel derives from these transitions between real and surreal. He starts (as he puts it in his own note 'On parables') with 'the cares we have to struggle with every day' (*KS* 457). But we cannot deny the impulse to 'go over' into some 'fabulous beyond'. Anxieties arise out of a recognisable social environment: an apartment block, a neighbour's bed-sitter, a lawyer's office, an artist's studio or a corridor at the bank. But we never know whether the door will open into an adjacent room or an existential void. The flow of images between social environment and subjective response is all the more bewildering because it is a two-way process. The novel acquires a hallucinatory quality when the urban milieu assumes shapes which reflect the hero's anxieties. It doesn't really matter which part of the city he visits in his quest for self-vindication. For his haunted mind will find a court sitting in judgment 'in almost every attic' (*KN*, 125).

There is a further source of Kafka's exceptional power. His image of the city synthesises elements from the work of other critics reviewed in this chapter. It is usually Musil's novel that is praised as a monumental work of intellectual synthesis. But *The Man Without Qualities* explores the conflicting ideologies of the age at a level of intellectual abstraction. In Kafka's novel they are assimilated more subtly and imaginatively, so that they form a subtext in which the reader becomes inextricably enmeshed. Kafka synthesises Mach's emphasis on the unreliability of perception with Freudian eruptions of unconscious impulse; Kraus's satire on bureaucratic obstruction and misinformation with the clutter of claustrophobic interiors which Loos sought to sweep away; Herzl's and Buber's articulation of specifically Jewish aspirations with Hitler's rabid underworld of assassins who arrive at night. Kafka's individual sensibility fuses the aspirations and anxieties of his age into a remarkable imaginative synthesis.

A journey through these cities of the imagination is likely to leave the reader with ambiguous feelings. These feelings become particularly acute when we actually visit Prague or Vienna after having read Musil or Kafka. The city seems so solid. It has vitality and charm. If offers congenial creature comforts. But from within the city we can hear two incompatible voices. Near at hand is a vernacular voice – the voice of Weinheber or Hašek. This voice reassuringly says: 'That reminds me, there's a pub just round the corner. Let's go in and have a drink!' But we can also hear the voices of Musil and Kafka. Their vision directs our gaze towards a more distant horizon, towards the hills that surround Vienna or the Castle which floats so enigmatically over the rooftops of Prague. Their words are equally powerful. Authentic life (they say) is not to be found in the city. It can only be glimpsed if we 'go over' into that 'other condition' which is 'beyond'. But the castle (as in Kafka's second great novel) seems to recede, the more we strive to approach it. The quest is ultimately for a spiritual city which is by definition unreal.

NOTES

1. *Unreal City: Urban Experience in Modern European Literature and Art*, ed. Edward Timms and David Kelley, Manchester, 1985. The present chapter is an adaptation of Chapter 15 in that volume and is reproduced by kind permission of Manchester University Press.
2. Robert Hughes, *The Shock of the New*, London, 1980.
3. For a more detailed analysis, see Edward Timms, *Karl Kraus – Apocalyptic Satirist: Culture and Catastrophe in Habsburg Vienna*, New Haven and London, 1986.
4. Adolf Loos, *Sämtliche Schriften*, Vienna, 1962, pp. 153 and 278.
5. Quotations from Robert Musil, *The Man Without Qualities*, trans. Eithne Wilkins and Ernst Kaiser, 3 vols. (London, 1953) are identified by *MQ* followed by volume and page number.
6. Stefan Zweig, *The World of Yesterday*, London, 1943, p. 72.
7. Freud, Standard Edition, IX, pp. 177–204 and XXI, p. 144.
8. Ernst Mach, *Die Analyse der Empfindungen*, 2nd edition, Jena, 1900, p. 17.
9. See Peter Vergo, *Art in Vienna 1898–1918*, 2nd edition, Oxford, 1981.
10. Arthur Schnitzler, *My Youth in Vienna*, London, 1971, p. 234.
11. Bertolt Brecht, 'Die Strassenszene', *Gesammelte Werke in acht Bänden*, Frankfurt am Main, 1967, VII, 546–58.
12. Ludwig Wittgenstein, *Philosophical Investigations*, trans. G.E.M. Anscombe, Oxford, 1953, p. 8.
13. F. W. Carter, 'Kafka's Prague,' in *The World of Franz Kafka*, ed. J. P. Stern (London, 1980), pp. 30–43.

14. References are to *The Penguin Complete Short Stories of Franz Kafka* (Harmondsworth, 1983), abbreviated as *KS*; and *The Penguin Complete Novels of Franz Kafka*, London, 1983, abbreviated as *KN*.

2

The Role of Jews in Viennese Culture and Society at the Turn of the Century

STEVEN BELLER

People of Jewish descent played a large part in Viennese high culture around 1900. The products of an emancipation and assimilation which lasted barely a hundred years provided the greatest names in the various cultural movements, from Freud to Wittgenstein. Tradition has it that the audience for this culture was also Jewish, at least the more prominent part.[1] The main problem for historians has been what to make of all this. On the one hand someone such as George Steiner would stress the Jewish aspect to the virtual exclusion of all others.[2] On the other, there has been a tendency to play down the Jewishness of *fin-de-siècle* Vienna. This is exemplified by Carl Schorske, whom I take to be saying in his book that the Jewish aspect is at base unimportant: Jews were the same as other Viennese, to be regarded as Viennese liberal bourgeois rather than Jews.[3] One has to ask which view is the sounder.

In the Viennese context George Steiner can provide a long list of the most important cultural figures who were of Jewish descent. Although an equally long list of non-Jewish figures could be produced, it is certainly true that they would neither be concentrated in the same cultural fields as their Jewish counterparts, nor would they have quite the same aura of intellectual innovation.[4] At the same time, however, when we look outside the Viennese context, at Europe as a whole, it is evident that other cities and countries, where the Jewish presence was much smaller, were also creating the 'modern world'.[5] Even in supposedly Jewish fields such as linguistic philosophy (*pace* Steiner) there were always people such as Bertrand Russell and Gottlob Frege, and above all Nietzsche. It should be remarked here that looking at the wider perspective not only puts a specifically Jewish contribution in doubt, but also severely limits many of the claims that have been made for the unique quality of the part played by Vienna in 'modern culture' (though not all of these claims). It is not a coincidence that it was a play by Oscar Wilde which was performed at the *Kunstschau* in 1908.[6] The cultural geography of Viennese culture is something which needs far more research if we are to understand in what way Vienna really was special.

This is by the way. It is clear that Vienna and the Viennese Jews were part of a general European cultural movement. This does not mean that the Jewish aspect can be ignored, just as it would be inadvisable to ignore the Viennese context. If we assume that there was a specifically Viennese contribution to modern culture, then the sheer size of the Jewish part in that contribution would suggest that it was only a matter of common sense to see how the ideas involved could have arisen from the Jewish context, within the Viennese one. This is so even if those ideas are universally applicable and tenable, and derivable by other ways, as must have been the case, if we look at modern culture as a whole.

The Jewish role in Viennese culture creates all kinds of questions. To start with, we should look at the extent of the problem with which we are dealing. How large was the Jewish part in Viennese modern high culture? If we look at the various cultural groups which made up 'Vienna 1900', then the simple answer would be something like: from a half to two thirds of the personnel of the culture, although it varied greatly. The group around Freud was almost exclusively Jewish.[7] The Vienna Circle of logical positivists, apart from the two German imports, Schlick and Carnap, was mainly Jewish, as was the group of socialist theoreticians known collectively as the Austro-Marxists.[8] On the other side of the 'liberal' political spectrum even the Austrian school of economics, from which Jews had been effectively excluded, was, by the inter-war years, led by a Jew, Ludwig von Mises, and his private seminar was comprised of something in the order of eighty percent of people of Jewish descent.[9] Over two thirds of the writers' group 'Young Vienna' was Jewish by descent, as was the later generation of writers, Musil notwithstanding.[10] Musil, in fact, received support precisely because, as a non-Jewish writer, he was regarded as something special.[11] In music, there stood at the centre of the transition from chromaticism to the twelve-tone scale the figures of Mahler, Zemlinsky and Schoenberg, all three of Jewish descent.[12]

It is also the case that Schoenberg's most famous pupils, Berg and Webern, were not of Jewish descent; nor, at the other end of the spectrum, were Bruckner and Brahms. Such facts are a healthy reminder that not all Viennese culture was Jewish. This is especially true in the visual arts. There were painters of some importance of Jewish descent, such as Richard Gerstl and Emil Orlik, but the great names, such as Klimt, Kokoschka and Schiele were not.[13] The same is true in architecture: Otto Wagner, Josef Olbrich and Adolf Loos were not Jewish (though Oskar Strnad and Josef Frank were).[14] A paucity of Jews in this sector might well be traced back to the traditional animosity to idolatry in the Jewish religion.[15] On the other hand, if we look at the consumers of this art, the patrons and supporters, a different picture emerges. Although state patronage was of great import-ance to modern art in Vienna, it was the private patronage which showed the social audience for the new art. If impressions are anything to go by, then a large majority of the private patrons of the *Secession* were Jewish.[16] Robert

Waissenberger commented that the supporters among the younger genera-
tion were also mostly Jewish.[17] It was families like the Bloch-Bauers, the
Gallias, the Mautner-Markhofs, the Lederers, the Wittgensteins and the
Waerndorfers who provided the private support for modern art in Vienna.[18]
The sponsor of the *Sezessionsgebäude* is said to have been Karl
Wittgenstein, Ludwig's father.[19] The man who commissioned Adolf Loos to
design the 'Looshaus' on the Michaelerplatz, *the* symbol of Viennese
modernism, was Leopold Goldman, a Jewish tailor.[20] Behind the scenes,
then, there was also a large Jewish presence in the visual arts, as there was
throughout modern culture in Vienna.

How is this huge presence to be explained? The 'intellectual pre-
eminence' of Jews has invited many explanations: a common, but not
particularly helpful, notion appears in its more sophisticated form as a
special gift of Jews for radical, analytical thought, and, in a more
straightforward manner, as the claim that Jews are just cleverer than the
rest. There are many problems with such a view, not least of which being
that, as Peter Gay has put it, there were stupid Jews too.[21] We should also
remember that, when talking of the cultural élite of Vienna, we are talking
about a very small group, of the exceptional. Can generalisations about the
Jewish racial character apply to these exceptions? There is another
explanation for the prominence of Jews among intellectuals, which
concentrates on the marginal nature of the Jewish individual entering
Western society and culture. Having left the certainties of Jewish tradition,
but without being totally absorbed into Western conventional culture, the
'renegade' Jew has no cultural home, but neither does he have any cultural
baggage to weigh him down. This is where intellectual innovation,
necessarily antagonistic to received thought, can burst forth.[22] This certainly
appears to be an attractive cultural explanation for the large Jewish presence
in cultural innovation.

The problem is that elsewhere there was the same innovation, the same
antagonism to received thought, without Jews. All modern culture, to a
certain degree, had this nature. This could be explained fairly neatly by the
fact that there are alienated outsiders in any society, especially European
society at the turn of the century. The question is, then, why in Vienna,
where Jews comprised less than 10% of the population, were most of these
outsiders Jewish, and why was there no one else to rival them in this role. It is
plain that the second sort of explanation, concentrating on the consequences
of assimilation, is far superior, methodologically, to ideas of an innate gift of
Jews to think radically. If it could be shown that it was indeed mostly Jews
who were the alienated outsiders in Vienna's cultural élite, then this would
make any idea of innate gift or tendency redundant. That is what I hope to
do.

We need first to construct a model of what we take to have been the social
foundation of modern high culture. If the model is correct, as I believe it is in
the main, then the cultural position of the Jews can be largely explained as a

function of their social role in the city. Let us adopt, in its albeit vague terms, the model which Schorske suggests for the base of *fin-de-siècle* Vienna. It is not particularly controversial: an 'educated, liberal bourgeoisie' was 'alienated' from political power in the late nineteenth century by the rise of mass politics, most notably in the form of antisemitism, which was most successfully articulated in the Christian Social party. The result was modern culture.[23] There are thus four criteria which members of Schorske's base group would have to satisfy: they would have to be 'liberal', 'bourgeois', 'alienated' and 'educated'.

If we leave the last category to one side for the moment, then we can see that, for the other three, almost all Jews in Vienna would qualify. As Ivar Oxaal and Marsha Rozenblit have both pointed out, Jews in their social structure in Vienna were eminently bourgeois, being in the vast majority either self-employed or salaried employees.[24] Furthermore, one can make a convincing case of saying that the Jewish tradition itself was inherently 'bourgeois' in its attitudes to society.[25] Jews in Vienna were in addition almost automatically supporters of the German liberals, and later the socialists, for it was only the 'progressive' parties which safeguarded the emancipation.[26] Moreover, Jews were political liberals almost regardless of social position, and this was more so the more assimilated and 'Westernised' they were.[27] Further, Jews were plainly the group most alienated by the successes of antisemitic mass politics at the end of the century, which hurt even more because of Jewish hopes that the liberal era would finally end an alienation which had lasted many centuries, and which was still present in relations with the Habsburg Establishment.[28] Jews therefore qualify for Schorske's group very easily, not as much for social as for ethnic reasons.

This cannot be said for Vienna's non-Jewish population. Fitting social groups to the criteria is problematic. The analytic efficacy of the term 'bourgeois' allows us to exclude the mass working class of the city at one end, and the aristocracy at the other. (Aristocrats supported high culture, but not, generally speaking, the liberal or modern variety.)[29] We are still left with the taxing question of how 'liberal' Vienna's 'bourgeoisie' was. According to John Boyer the answer to this by the late 1890s would be: hardly at all. The vast bulk of the artisan class was voting anti-liberal and antisemitic by the 1880s; and by the election in Vienna in 1895 so was the majority of teachers and officials, among other groups which had formerly been part of the extended liberal coalition.[30] Vast swathes of the 'bourgeoisie' voted for the Christian Socials, so much so that Boyer sees the party of Lueger as reconstructing a unitary middle class.[31] It is true that not by any means all of the non-Jewish electorate voted for the Christian Socials, and this is especially the case with the higher bureaucracy, where Josephinist traditions meant the survival of a form of liberalism.[32] On this point it might be asked how powerful this Josephinist tradition still was, and whether the mentality associated with the Habsburg bureaucracy is quite what is meant

by 'liberal bourgeois', culturally.[33] Moreover, if we look at the high
bureaucracy in the light of our third criterion, 'alienated', we might ask
whether a high bureaucracy can be called alienated which, with the
succession of *Beamtenministerien* of the first years of this century, took over
real political power when the parliamentary system ground to a halt.[34] The
anomalous nature of this clique at the top of the Austrian bureaucracy
should be recognised, and this might call into question the advisability of
constructing such monolithic models of the social reservoir of cultural élites,
pointing to the need, perhaps, for a more pluralistic approach. Nevertheless, it does seem that, whatever Schorske himself says, the bureaucrats
were not prime material for an alienated, liberal bourgeoisie.

It would seem, then, that the core of the social reservoir of the cultural
élite reduces to a capitalist bourgeoisie, and its 'superstructural append-
ages': commercial independents and semi-independents, financiers, manufacturers, lawyers, physicians, journalists, and *rentiers*. It so happens that
Jews were vastly over-represented in these groups. In the liberal professions, for instance, by 1890 Jews made up half of Vienna's physicians and
lawyers; in 1909 well over half the members of the press club *Concordia* was
of Jewish descent.[35] Much of Vienna's private banking was in the hands of
Jews.[36] Yet, if we are to believe the census figures of 1910, although there
was a massive over-representation of Jews among commercial independents
and salaried employees, Jews still only accounted for about a third of all
male independents, and for slightly fewer of the salaried employees in the
fields of commerce and transport – hardly what one would call a predominance.[37] The figures for industry produce a much smaller number.[38] In other
words, although Jews were greatly over-represented in just those categories
which were the core of the key sector identified above, they were still not
predominant. The Jews' position in society in general does not explain the
cultural situation.

If we now introduce our fourth criterion, 'educated', the picture changes
dramatically. It is a matter of some debate quite where to draw the line
between who is 'educated' and who is not in Vienna at the turn of the
century. If we are looking for a measure of the educational base of the
cultural élite, I would suggest that the best place to look is in Vienna's
central *Gymnasien*. The *Gymnasium* held a special place in the Austrian
educational system. Until 1904 only those who had passed their matriculation at a *Gymnasium* could go to university.[39] The *Gymnasium* was also the
only form of secondary school which offered an education in the classics,
while the *Realschule*, more practically orientated, offered only modern
languages. A good knowledge of Latin and Greek was, however, a
prerequisite for a man of culture in nineteenth-century European civilisation.[40] It is no surprise, therefore, that most of the major intellectual figures
of Vienna were educated at a *Gymnasium*. Hermann Broch, who went to a
Realschule, is the exception that proves the rule; he held a grudge against his

father for not allowing him to go to a *Gymnasium* so that he could follow his academic inclinations.[41] If the *Gymnasium* is not an exhaustive measure of the educated élite, it is its centre and representative of the whole.

In a sample of the matriculation candidates of the nine (out of eleven) *Gymnasien* in the central nine districts of Vienna still to have records, the following remarkable picture emerges.[42] It is known that slightly under a third of all *Gymnasium* pupils in Vienna were Jewish.[43] The percentage in the sample, taken over the period 1870–1910, was slightly higher, but almost exactly right for the nine schools involved.[44] (The exclusion of the aristocratic *Theresianum*, because of a lack of records, is the main reason for the disparity between the general case and my sample.)[45] If we now look at the table below, we can see where this very large percentage of all pupils came from. The table shows the distribution of son's religion against father's occupation. It therefore shows the social background of those already in the educated élite, and of those aspiring to enter it. Jewish fathers represent over eighty percent of all fathers in commerce. They are large majorities in finance and industry, and very substantial minorities in the professions of law, medicine and journalism. If all groups in the key sector described earlier are taken together, then Jews comprise 65.3% of the group which we take to have been the social base of Vienna's modern cultural élite.

Distribution of Father's Occupation against Son's Religion (and/or Ethnic Descent) among the Maturanten of Vienna's Central Gymnasien 1870–1910 (Sample).

Occupation	Jew.	Cath.	Prot.	Other	Total	%	Jew.	Cath.	Prot.	Other
1. Commerce	318	53	16	4	391	21.6	81.3	13.6	4.1	1.0
2. Finance	34	17	6		57	3.1	59.6	29.8	10.5	
3. Industry	68	37	11	1	117	6.5	58.1	31.6	9.4	0.9
4. Handicrafts	19	96	2		117	6.5	16.2	82.7	1.7	
5. Public employ.	23	297	12	3	335	18.5	6.9	88.7	3.6	0.9
6. Private employ.	62	112	12	2	188	10.4	33.0	59.6	6.4	1.1
7. Railway employ.	14	52	2		68	3.8	20.6	76.5	2.9	
8. Lawyers	37	49	3	1	90	5.0	41.1	54.4	3.3	1.1
9. Doctors	44	38	7	1	90	5.0	48.9	42.2	7.8	1.1
10. Journalists	7	10			17	0.9	41.2	58.8		
11. Teachers	34	87	13		134	7.4	25.4	64.9	9.7	
12. Misc. Profs.	16	29	12	2	59	3.3	27.1	49.2	20.3	3.4
13. Hausbesitzer	6	14	1		21	1.2	28.6	66.7	4.8	
14. Agriculture	2	47	1		50	2.8	4.0	94.0	2.0	
15. Private income	39	33	2	2	76	4.2	51.3	43.4	2.6	2.6
Total	723	971	100	16	1,810	:100:	39.9	53.6	5.5	0.9
(+/− converts)	(707)	(982)	(101)	(20)			39.1	54.3	5.6	1.1
Group A	547	237	45	9	838	46.3	65.3	28.3	5.4	1.1
Group B	176	734	55	7	972	53.7	18.1	75.5	5.7	0.7
Group A*	88	97	10	2	197	10.9	44.7	49.2	5.1	1.0

(Group A = 1–3, 8–10, and 15. Group B = 4–7, 11–14. Group A* = 8–10.)

Even if my analysis, my model of the social base of the culture, is mistaken, the huge concentration of Jews in this key section would go a long way to explaining many of the traditional ideas about the Viennese liberal bourgeoisie's being Jewish, for in the educated élite of the capitalist classes such ideas were a reflection of the true situation. If my model is correct, then it shows that the predominance of people of Jewish descent in the cultural élite is mathematically predictable from the level of secondary education onwards. Jews were not more intelligent than non-Jews, but they dominated the educated sector of the social base from which the culture of *fin-de-siècle* Vienna is supposed to have sprung.

This result leaves more questions than it answers. Why was there this huge over-representation of Jews among *Gymnasium* pupils and especially among the sons of merchants and the like? Part of the answer must have something to do with the different stratification of Jewish and non-Jewish society. In the set of matriculation candidates we are dealing with a very small number. All eleven schools, from 1870–1910, only produced something in the region of 12,300 matriculation passes, in a population approaching the two million mark by 1910.[46] It only needs a relatively small group at the assimilating margin of Vienna's Jewish population, perhaps following a Jewish, but secularised, tradition of education, radically to change the balance of the *Gymnasien* figures. Behind this, however, is still the thought that, however marginal, the differing attitudes of a Jewish and a Roman Catholic merchant to education could well have played a role in creating such a Jewish over-representation in the key sector of the educated élite.

This raises the question of the influence of Judaic traditions on the contribution of Jews to Viennese culture. Did the Jewish element provide certain attitudes which would otherwise not have been present, or at least not so evident, in 'Vienna 1900'? I can offer tentative suggestions by way of an answer. First, the fact that so many sons of the capitalist classes received an élite education is probably derived partly from the Jewish tradition of respect for learning. It was this flood of Jewish merchants' sons which meant that Vienna was given a much more intellectually powerful, and powerfully alienated, base for modern culture than one might expect from a purely Roman Catholic Austria. This very intensity of 'Vienna 1900' might well rest on a secularised Jewish tradition.

Secondly, the assimilated Jews in Vienna were a creation of the German Enlightenment, much more than they were culturally in any sense Austrian. They had been emancipated by a German liberalism which, until 1867, saw the frontier between Germany and Austria as a result of reaction, and artificial. Those Jews who assimilated into Western culture in Vienna did so primarily as Germans, whatever that may have signified. As such they tended to be more convinced by the ideas of the Enlightenment, more liberal, more orientated towards the West, and more culturally indebted to

Germany than many other groups in Austria, for it was the former which had created them, the assimilated and emancipated Jews, not the latter. Vienna was for them still a 'German city'.[47] Perhaps because of this, Viennese culture was much more turned outwards, and northwards, than might otherwise have been the case.

Thirdly, Jewish attitudes to intellect, *Geist*, and also to the ethical responsibility of the individual differed markedly from Austrian Baroque Roman Catholicism, and could identify much more with a German and Protestant tradition. The admiration of German culture not only resulted from the history of emancipation, but was also implicit in much of Jewish tradition in the first place. Vienna proved, by the late nineteenth century, to be anything but a German city in this sense, with the overwhelming triumph of a not only Roman Catholic and corporatist, but also overtly antisemitic political movement. Cannot much of Viennese culture be viewed as a Jewish reaction to this paradoxical and disturbing state of affairs? Perhaps this is why Viennese modern culture, from Freud to Schoenberg, is so redolent of an ethical reaction to an aestheticised environment, to an aestheticised, and hence evaporated self?[48]

What I would like to suggest is that, ultimately, the special contribution of Vienna to modern culture is the puritanical rejection of modern 'decadence', in favour of a radical vision of the ethical possibilities and duties of the individual. Was not Vienna's innovation essentially a reaction to decadence rather than decay? If this is Vienna's great contribution, then I would further suggest that the fact that the culture's leaders were Jewish is vitally important to understanding how it was Vienna, of all places, which could produce such ideas.

NOTES

1. For example, Stefan Zweig, *Die Welt von gestern*, Berlin, 1944, 1982, p. 37; Julius Braunthal, *Auf der Suche nach dem Millenium*, Vienna, 1964, pp. 20–1.
2. George Steiner, *Vienna: The Crucible*, televised lecture on the *South Bank Show*, LWT, 16.06.1985. For similar views see Norman Stone, *Europe Transformed*, Glasgow, 1983, pp. 407–8.
3. See Carl E. Schorske, *Fin-de-siècle Vienna: Politics and Culture*, London, 1979, pp. 7, 148–9.
4. I am grateful to Sir Ernst Gombrich for reminding me about the non-Jewish contribution in a discussion on 8 May 1985.
5. For example, se M. Bradbury and J. McFarlane (Eds.) *Modernism, 1890–1930*, Harmondsworth, 1976; H. Stuart Hughes, *Consciousness and Society: the Reorientation of European Social Thought, 1890–1930*, Brighton, 1979.
6. Schorske, *Fin-de-siècle Vienna*.
7. Dennis B. Klein, *The Jewish Origins of the Psychoanalytic Movement*, New York, 1981, p. vii.
8. On the Vienna Circle I rely on a list of members published in the pamphlet *Wissenschaftliche Weltauffassung*, reproduced in Otto Neurath, *Empiricism and Sociology*, Dordrecht, 1973,

p. 318. The genealogical information is thanks to Paul Neurath, Eckehart Koehler, Professor K. R. Fischer (all in Vienna) and Renate Heuer, Frankfurt am Main. On the Austromarxists, see Hans Mayer, *Aussenseiter*, Frankfurt am Main, 1981, p. 438; William M. Johnston, *The Austrian Mind: An Intellectual and Social History, 1848–1938*, Berkeley, 1972, pp. 99–111.

9. This claim is based on a list of the seminar's members in Ludwig von Mises, *Erinnerungen*, Stuttgart, 1978, p. 65. The genealogical information comes from Renate Heuer, Frankfurt am Main; Dr H. Jaeger-Sunstenau, Vienna; and Professor Martha Steffy Browne, New York. On the exclusions of Jews before then, see Erich Streissler, *Die Wiener Schule der Nationaloekonomie*, in P. Berner, E. Brix, and W. Mantl (Eds.), *Wien um 1900: Aufbruch in die Moderne*, Vienna, 1986, p. 80.

10. This is based on the analysis of two lists: the first by Schnitzler in 1891, in B. Zeller, L. Greve, W. Volke (Eds.) *Jugend in Wien: Literatur um 1900*, Stuttgart, 1974, p. 119; and the second in Ernst Lothar, *Das Wunder des Überlebens*, Vienna, 1966, p. 38.

11. Interview with Stella Ehrenfeld, Surrey, 25 March, 1984.

12. Zemlinsky's descent is confirmed in the register of births of the Jewish community of Vienna of 1871.

13. Harry Zohn, 'Fin-de-siècle Vienna: The Jewish Contribution,' in J. Reinharz and W. Schatzberg (Eds.), *The Jewish Response to German Culture: From the Enlightenment to the Second World War*, Hanover, NH, 1985, p. 146.

14. See Sigmund Kaznelson (Ed.), *Juden im deutschen Kulturbereich: ein Sammelwerk*, Berlin, 1962, index.

15. For example, see the speech by Rabbi Leopold Goldschmidt, 'Die Stellung der Juden zur modernen Kunst,' in *Die Neuzeit*, 26 April 1895, No. 17, pp. 177–9.

16. See James Shedel, *Art and Society: The New Art Movement in Vienna, 1897–1914*, Palo Alto, 1981, p. 61.

17. Interview with Dr Robert Waissenberger, 24 February, 1984.

18. On the Bloch-Bauers, interview with Bettina Ehrlich (Adele Bloch-Bauer's niece), London, 4 January, 1984. On the Gallias, interview with Frieda von Hofmannsthal (Gallia), London, 31 May 1984. On the Mautner-Markhofs, C. M. Nebehay, *Ver sacrum, 1898–1903*, Munich, 1979, p. 90. On the Lederers, C. M. Nebehay, *Gustav Klimt*, Frankfurt am Main, 1976, pp. 142–3. On Waerndorfer, lecture by Peter Vergo at the Edinburgh Festival 1983, 23 August, 1983. Also see Schorske, *Fin-de-siècle Vienna*, p. 264; Oskar Kokoschka, *My Life*, London, 1974, p. 35.

19. Allan Janik and Stephen Toulmin, *Wittgenstein's Vienna*, New York, 1973, p. 172.

20. Burkhardt Rukschcio, *Wien, Adolf Loos und das Haus am Michaelerplatz*, in the catalogue to *Traum und Wirklichkeit, Wien 1870–1930*, Vienna, 1985, p. 443.

21. Peter Gay, *Freud, Jews and other Germans: Masters and Victims in Modernist Culture*, Oxford, 1978, p. 99.

22. For a representation of this view, see Paul R. Mendes-Flohr, 'The Study of the Jewish Intellectual: Some Methodological Proposals' in F. Malino and P. Albert (Eds.), *Essays in Modern Jewish History*, London, 1982, pp. 142–66.

23. Schorske, *Fin-de-siècle Vienna*, pp. 7–9.

24. Ivar Oxaal and Walter R. Weitzmann, 'The Jews of pre-1914 Vienna, an Exploration of Basic Sociological Dimensions,' in *Leo Baeck Institute Yearbook* XXX (1985), pp. 424–8; Marsha Rozenblit, *The Jews of Vienna, 1867–1914: Assimilation and Identity*, Albany, 1983, pp. 47–70.

25. See Julius Carlebach, 'The Forgotten Connection: Women and Jews in the Conflict between Enlightenment and Romanticism,' in *Leo Baeck Institute Yearbook* XXIV (1979), pp. 113–17.

26. See W. B. Simon, 'The Jewish Vote in Austria,' in *Leo Baeck Institute Yearbook* XVI (1971), p. 104 ff.

27. See Joseph S. Bloch, *Erinnerungen aus meinem Leben*, Vienna, 1922, pp. 20–1.

28. For example, Sigmund Mayer, *Ein jüdischer Kaufmann, 1831–1911: Lebenserinnerungen*, Leipzig, 1911, p. 289.

29. For example, see Kokoschka, *My Life*, p. 25; also Sigmund Mayer, *Die Wiener Juden: Kommerz, Kultur, Politik 1700–1900*, Vienna, 1918, pp. 296–8, 364–5, 396–403.

31. Ibid., p. 416 ff.

32. I am grateful for this point to Professor P. G. J. Pulzer, All Souls College, Oxford.

33. See Johnston, *The Austrian Mind*, pp. 17–19, 45–50.

34. See Shedel, *Art and Society*, p. 60.

35. Hans Tietze, *Die Juden Wiens*, Vienna, 1935, p. 232. My claims for *Concordia* rest on an analysis of the list of members in Julius Stern, *Werden und Walten der Concordia*, Vienna, 1909, pp. 239–258.

36. Tietze, *Die Juden Wiens*, p. 232.

37. The census figures are reproduced in Ivar Oxaal, *The Jews of pre-1914 Vienna: Two Working Papers*, Hull, 1981, p.60.

38. Ibid., p. 60. The figure for male independents in industry is 11% Jewish.

39. Gustav Strakosch-Grassmann, *Geschichte des Unterrichtswesens in Österreich*, Vienna, 1905, p. 321.

40. Ibid., pp. 249 and 276.

41. Manfred Durzak, *Hermann Broch*, Reinbek, 1966, p. 23.

42. The records for the other two schools, the *Theresianum* and the *Elisabethsgymnasium*, were destroyed during the Second World War. Information of the Schools' headmasters.

41. Calculation from the *Statistisches Jahrbuch der Stadt Wien, 1886–1911*, section on *Mittelschulen*. Also Rozenblit, *The Jews of Vienna*, pp. 102–5.

44. The sample has a Jewish proportion of 39.1% (by religion), against an expected 38.8%.

45. With the *Theresianum*, the proportion of Jews for the eleven *Gymnasien* is 32.2%, without it, for the remaining ten, it is 36.7%.

46. Calculation from the schools' *Jahresberichten*.

47. This phrase constantly recurs in the 1890s in Vienna's major newspaper, *Die Neue Freie Presse*.

48. For further on this theme, see my article 'Fin-de-siècle Vienna and the Jews: The Dialectics of Assimilation.' in *The Jewish Quarterly*, Vol. 33, No. 3 (123) 1986, pp. 28–33. It will be explored in more depth in my forthcoming publication with Cambridge University Press.

3

Weininger and the Science of Sex: Prolegomena to Any Future Study

ALLAN JANIK

Otto Weininger saw himself as a scientist. My thesis is that Weininger was indeed a scientist. Furthermore, I insist that he can neither be understood nor evaluated unless we take this claim seriously. I must make it absolutely clear from the outset that I do not say this to legitimate his views, but, rather, to aid their demystification. It is necessary to emphasise this in the face of the common misconception that the family of words including 'science', 'scientist' etc., are commendatory as well as descriptive. Moreover, it would seem to imply the dubious proposition that science is all of a piece, rather than a highly diversified, continually evolving set of activities based on different paradigms, research programmes or ideals of natural order, as most methodologists would today view the matter. Indeed, in the wake of what, for want of a better term, I call the Kuhnian Revolution in the philosophy of science, understanding what is scientific involves grasping how a certain sort of experimentation or theorising fits into a given research programme, that is, a wholly *contextual* enterprise, whose chief assumption is an historical relativism of a certain type. But to explain that further would take us far afield. I just want to make it clear from the outset that I take my approach to Weininger to be rooted in a practice-oriented philosophy of science. The principal practical consequence of this approach for under standing and evaluating Weininger is that outmoded science has a way of looking ridiculous. To see this we need only reflect upon, say, the notion that the earth is flat. It is the merit of the historical approach to science that it emphasises how it was that, once upon a time, there was a radically different way of understanding our world, which was compatible with a different sort of astronomy and cartography than ours but no less deserving of the description 'science' than ours. Briefly, it is the data and reasoning – or to put the matter slightly differently, the status within the scientific community – rather than the substance of what is claimed which is relevant to determining what has status as science. This is what I propose sketchily to reconstruct with respect to Weininger's search for a science of sexuality.

I have termed these remarks prolegomena because Weininger is so badly understood that I have to begin by explaining what I mean by 'Weininger'.

Otto Weininger enters into the history of ideas in at least two radically different ways. First, as the deadly serious, gifted young man (something everyone who knew him admitted), who wrote *Geschlecht und Charakter* (Sex and Character) in response to Nietzsche's plaint, 'who among philosophers was a psychologist before me?' (*Ecce Homo*, 'Why, I am Destiny').[1] Secondly, he is a figure who typifies a certain tendency, at once purist and morbid, in *fin-de-siècle* Vienna, who exercised enormous influence on central European culture. Concern with Weininger stems almost exclusively from the latter. Thus, we know much more about Weininger's influence than we do about his views. But the curious fact is that there is a sense in which the reception of Weininger is almost independent of Weininger's own work. Weininger's influence rests as much, if not more, on posthumously published essays from his papers, i.e. on *Über die letzten Dinge* (On last things) and the *Taschenbuch* (Commonplace Book), than on what Weininger himself published. Thus, the *Wirkungsgeschichte* of his corpus, which, doubtless, is, in the end, more interesting than Weininger's own work, will be radically incomplete until we know the extent to which he has been correctly understood both by friend and foe in the eighty odd years since his suicide. As disconcerting as the thought may be, it may well be that the most influential of Weininger's works were precisely what he would have thrown away, had he lived.

Weininger's suicide has obscured almost everything about him. For friends it was a sign of his integrity; for foes of his fanaticism. Both ignore the huge difficulties surrounding the attribution of intention to suicides. More important for my investigation is that we do not know how he would have reacted to criticism of his work. This, as Sir Karl Popper (interestingly a not unsympathetic reader of Weininger) has tirelessly pointed out, is the measure of rationality, i.e., willingness to change one's mind in the face of contrary evidence. We simply do not know what he would have done. It is possible to advance a bold claim only to abandon or modify it later. Eduard von Hartmann is a good case in point. His initial claim in his *Philosophie des Unbewusstseins* (Philosophy of the unconscious) that wisdom dictates the collective suicide of the human race, is, if anything, even more bizarre than Weininger's idea that acting morally precludes all forms of sexual behaviour. Yet, Hartmann lived to become a sober author of a multi-volume *Erkenntnistheorie* (Theory of cognition). Perhaps Weininger would have done so as well. (On Hartmann see F. Copleston, *History of Philosophy*, VII, 291–2. I am indebted to Heiner Rutte for calling my attention to Hartmann's contribution to late nineteenth-century debates in the theory of knowledge.) The point is that we just do not know. But what of Weininger himself?

One of the few things that we do know about Weininger with certitude is what he intended to do in *Geschlecht und Charakter*. It is not as if he spelled this out clearly once and for all in his book, but that his intentions can be reconstructed on the basis of the copious footnotes to the book, which, *pace* Lukács, are more than mere ostentation. Unfortunately, the English and American publishers of Weininger, apart from printing a bowdlerised translation, which Wittgenstein rightly regarded as 'beastly', did not see fit to include the 135 pages of notes and references, which make both Weininger's sources and intentions clear. On the basis of the context these sources, which clearly indicate *inter alia* that Weininger saw himself as writing a sort of commentary on the existing literature on sexuality, it is fairly easy to reconstruct his intentions. This project has informed my various researches into Weininger for the last decade. This sort of analysis yields at least four analytic 'moments' in Weininger's work: cultural criticism inspired by Nietzsche (whose critical influence on Weininger remains only hinted at in the literature), speculation on the biological foundations of sexual differentiation inspired by the research of K. W. von Naegeli, articulation of a peculiar, but by no means implausible, version of Kantian ethics based on the Heidelberg reading of Kant, in aid of developing a comprehensive account of the psychology of lived experience of the sort that Wilhelm Dilthey advocated. Because Weininger took the most pressing problems in his society to revolve around sexuality, this became the focal point for his research. Indeed, it is almost as if Weininger set out to provide a theoretical account of just how a world such as that depicted in Schnitzler's dramas was possible at all, on the one hand, and to determine *exactly* what was wrong with it, on the other.

Weininger's cultural criticism has two sides to it. One is the analysis of the psychological origins of narcissism, the cult of orgasm, in the psychological mechanism what we feel as wanting in our own personality onto others; the other is advocacy of certain social reforms. This second element in his social criticism is usually overlooked in discussions of Weininger's work. It will be my point of departure. In Chapter Five of Part One of *Geschlecht und Charakter* Weininger makes it perfectly clear that he favours reforms with respect to three current social problems: homosexuality, prostitution and education. He pleads for an end to laws against homosexuality and prostitution on the grounds that both are 'natural'. It is the burden of the 'scientific' part of his book to explain how this can be so. Weininger takes it to be the task of psychology to establish the reality and significance of individual differences. In this he takes his lead from the 'differential psychology' of William Stern – although he hopes to put what merely has a statistical basis in Stern's work, which in fact was pioneering in the field of intelligence testing, on what Weininger took to be a sounder foundation in the form of his theory of Ideal Types. Anyway, Weininger favours greater flexibility in education because he thinks that individual psychological differences demand it. No small part of his claim that *all* human beings are bisexual in varying degrees involves the claim that, contrary to the then current educational psychology, there is no single standard against which all children can be measured.

If we reflect upon Weininger's difficulties in maintaining that homosexuality was 'natural' for a moment, we can gain an illuminating perspective on this whole enterprise. Laws directed against homosexuality rested ultimately on the notion of Natural Law. To argue for the de-criminalisation of homosexuality, then, one had to argue that it was natural, i.e., that homosexuality was rooted in human biology. However, this was not enough; for modern biology recognises both environment and heredity as principles which can explain diversity. If homosexuality was environmentally determined, it could be in principle 'cured' by changing the homosexual's environment. This, Weininger points out, was in fact assumed by a certain Viennese therapist named Fuchs. The latter attempted to 'cure' homosexuals, first, by suggesting that they really desire heterosexual intercourse while under hypnosis, and, then, by sending them to brothels. It is not difficult to imagine that his patients were less than enthusiastic about their therapy. Now, if homosexuality was to be recognised as natural, it had to be established that it was an hereditary phenomenon. However, in the absence of Mendelian genetics, more specifically, of the notion of recessive traits, which do not appear in every generation, this was very difficult to maintain; for, as an astute observer remarked, homosexual children are rarely the offspring of homosexual parents. Weininger's infamous theory of plasms represented one way around this. It rested on two assumptions: first, that there is a distinction between gender and sex; second, that all humans are bisexual. Both were stock in trade of such sexual psychologists and social reformers as Havelock Ellis and Magnus Hirschfeld. Weininger's originality in developing his theory of plasms, which would account for homosexuality in terms of a plasmic imbalance, lay in its efforts, which were wholly wrongheaded, to explain the basis of sexual differentiation deductively from body chemistry. This effort was part and parcel of the enlightened liberal movement for social reform in the period. What one must see is the reasonableness of Weininger's perspective.

The first part of his book, which was, generally speaking, well received, even by critics, like that in Hirschfeld's *Zeitschrift für sexuelle Zwischenstufen*, endeavoured to explain individual psychological differences on the basis of a universal bisexuality, which would account for how personality could manifest itself in a well-nigh infinite variety of ways. If everybody was bisexual by nature, given the imperfection in natural populations, it was to be expected that here and there Nature would make a mistake or two, thereby producing creatures who were anatomically – and legally – male, but constitutionally, i.e., physiologically and psychologically, female. There is no reason why the reverse should not happen, so his denial that there are anatomical females who are in fact constitutionally male is not consistent with Weininger's theory. So runs the main part of Weininger's argument in Part One of *Geschlecht und Charakter*. His questions, for the most part, emerge from contemporary thinking about homosexuality. In context they are eminently reasonable. Even his ridiculous sounding Law of Sexual Attraction seemed more overstated than wrong-headed to so astute a critic as Charlotte Perkins Gilman when she reviewed the English edition in 1906. Part Two of the book, clearly recognised even then as more wildly speculative, nevertheless endeavours to answer a question which follows from the perspective in Part One. If there are no males or females in the world in any strict sense, what does male and female mean? This question was pressed upon Weininger, not simply from his advocacy of universal bisexuality, but also by a whole tradition of thinking about normality and deviance.

The dominating figure in this tradition was Cesare Lombroso, the father of modern Italian forensic medicine. Not only did Lombroso, along with Ellis, provide Weininger with empirical evidence about women, but the conceptual structure of Weininger's book – including its shortcomings – were determined by Weininger's relationship with Lombroso. The latter sought to put penal reform on a scientific basis. That meant erecting a penal code on the basis of biological principles. Thus, Lombroso proceeded from the assumption that there were two types of deviance, one which was determined by heredity, another by environment. Since Lombroso, like Spencer, believed in the retention and transmission of acquired characteristics, he sought to distinguish hereditary, and, therefore, incurable, criminals, from those 'occasional' criminals, who could be rehabilitated. As a scientist deeply rooted in the spirit of nineteenth-century Positivism his method for distinguishing the two was phenomenalist and mathematical. In tune with current conceptions of psycho-physical parallelism, whose echoes we find throughout Weininger's book, he assumed that the body was the key to the mind. Moreover, he assumed that normality and deviance distributed themselves in the population at large along a graph whose form was a bell-shaped curve. Head measurements were especially significant for Lombroso. Facial assymetry, strabismus and the like were particularly important in his researches. When people today occasionally speak of a criminal type with a low forehead and shifty eyes, it is a throwback to Lombroso. Saxe Rohmer and Bram Stoker both incorporated Lombrosan features in their embodiments of evil. In any case, Lombroso's efforts to distinguish the normal from the pathological on the basis of their bodily dimensions was the origin of the science of anthropometry.

To have amassed measurements was not, however, to explain the causes of deviance. In his search for the solution of that problem Lombroso enlisted what we know today to have been the two most dubious principles of nineteenth century biology: the Lamarckian belief in the transmission of acquired characteristics, which we have already discussed, and recapitulation, which we must now discuss. Recapitulation is the view that the embryonic development of the individual repeats *exactly* the stages through which the species has evolved. Thus, the slogan 'ontogeny recapitulates phylogeny'. Modelling himself on the findings of comparative anatomy according to which highly developed animals are examined anatomically with a view to casting light upon anatomical structures found in more primitive creatures, the social Darwinist, Lombroso viewed 'modern', 'liberal' 'Man' as the norm, which explained the 'primitive', the 'criminal', the congenitally sick (especially the epileptic) as-well as the 'genius' as deviants from the norm who could be used to cast light upon one another. In short, Lombroso's programme implied a whole philosophy of culture, which was ethnocentric to the point of being racist. At the same time it was anthropomorphic in projecting human qualities onto plants and animals as he sought to explain the biogenesis of antisocial behaviour among humans by comparison with the 'conduct' of 'drunken' bees and 'killer' plants. The cause of deviance was taken to be arrested development or atavism. It represented a reversion to the primitive. Thus, in the absence of a notion of recessive characteristics, and, generally, the conceptual repertory of Mendelian genetics, one could explain the reappearance of characteristics after an absence of one or more generations. But for Lombroso this was equally the key to cultural development. Thus, he explained antisemitism in liberal societies as a throwback to tribal instincts or medieval superstitions, which the Church continued to transmit. Similarly, tatoos found on modern criminals were taken to be throwbacks to an earlier stage of civilisation in which body decoration was normal – it is all too little known that Adolf Loos's argument in 'Ornament und Verbrechen' (Ornament and crime) depends entirely upon Lombrosan premisses. It must be emphasised that, whereas much of what Lombroso maintained had come under fire within the scientific community by the time that Weininger wrote *Geschlecht und Charakter*, it was only in 1913, when Sir Charles Goring began measuring the heads of Oxford students, that the Lombrosan programme finally fell into disrepute. At no time in Weininger's short life were Lombroso's credentials as a liberal challenged. But, lest it seem that I deviate too far from my theme, let me turn to Lombroso's view of women, where his connection with Weininger will become more apparent.

Women presented Lombroso with a number of problems. For a start, he could not understand how they could 'normally' combine such contradictory moral characteristics as pity and cruelty. Similarly, their tendency to lie was something that he thought required explanation. Generally speaking, he took women to be more excitable, less inhibited and, above all, more vain than men. Most mysterious of all was the low incidence of crime among women. All of these things demanded a theory of femininity from Lombroso. He advanced just such a theory in his book, *The Female Offender*. Unsurprisingly, Lombroso revealed what Kant once referred to as 'woman's secret' to be nothing less than her atavistic nature. Woman was nothing but a male whose development had been arrested. This 'triumph of observation' as Lombroso was wont to refer to it, was derivable in purely phenomenal terms. Woman was smaller in every respect than man: therefore, she was an inferior version of the male. To defend the scientific nature of this claim Lombroso cited Darwin's observation that males were more varied than females among lower animals; this was enough for him to conclude that they were on that account less perfect.

Lombroso explained that woman's intellectual inferiority was rooted in the fact that she had smaller sense organs. This indicated that she must receive fewer and less intense sensations than the male. Now, citing Aristotle's principle that there is nothing in the intellect that was not first in the senses, he concluded that women were intellectually inferior, i.e., because their inferior mode of sense perception made them incapable of universalising sufficiently to perform basic logical functions. Moreover, insensitivity led in its turn to atrophy of her sense of self. Once having established that, it was reasonably easy to deduce the rest of her characteristics. Her weakness of intellect explained weakness of character. She could, then, be both more merciful and more cruel than man. It was also part of the explanation of why she was more prone to lying. In fact, Lombroso cites eight reasons why women lie. They are interesting both as background to Weininger's conception of the irrational woman and as clues to the way in which Lombroso's theory transformed social stereotypes into scientific facts. In his view women lie on account of:

1 weakness
2 atavism
3 menstruation – the 'glandular' explanation was the most powerful for him
4 shame (taboo among lower races)
5 the battle of the sexes
6 the desire to be interesting
7 suggestibility – Lombroso cited Lotze as maintaining that women do not distinguish true from false
8 the maternal obligation to conceal the 'facts of life' from her offspring

From today's perspective it is difficult to see how a man who was a serious scientist and social reformer could make such naive errors in the name of science; but that may be our limitation more than his, for we often forget how difficult it is to begin a scientific investigation of anything. It is impossible to miss Lombroso's emphasis on woman's sexuality as a factor in the explanation of her tendency to lie. This is a reminder to qualify an assertion that I made earlier on Lombroso's behalf; namely, that woman's organs are smaller than man's. This does not apply to her sex organs – and that is for Lombroso the decisive factor in explaining 'feminine' behaviour. Women are dominated by their sexuality in a way that men are not. Further, if intelligence varied inversely with reproductive fecundity, as Lombroso thought it did, woman's larger sex organs explained everything – including why she was less prone to crime. This was because the female equivalent of crime was a half-hearted affair, what we would today call a victimless crime, prostitution. Woman cannot control her own sexuality. That lies in the hands of the man who desires her. Woman's decadence was, therefore, a product of masculine exploitation of her maternal urges – I think it is worth noting the confusion of sexual and reproductive urges which occurs here. In short, woman's sexuality was in fact a function of man's character. Males were the villains in more than one sense: first, because they took sexual advantage of females, but also because they simultaneously created a myth around woman's saintliness. In the end, women were less criminal because they were less moral constitutionally.

Thus, we arrive at a picture of woman with scientific credentials which prefigures Weininger's conception of women almost totally. Indeed, all the main features of Weininger's approach to the question of the relationship between sex and character are rooted in Lombroso – a fact which helps to explain why it should be that his work was so well received in Italy.

The considerations which played such a crucial role in Lombroso's analysis of deviance, especially, its inherited character, became the cornerstone of the nascent, perhaps misbegotten, science of sexuality. Later sexologists, like Havelock Ellis and Magnus Hirschfeld, as well as Weininger, adopted Lombroso by no means uncritically. Nevertheless, his determinist account of deviance remained the point of departure for thinking about, say, homosexuality. Thus Ellis could be convinced of the congenital nature of sexual abnormalities without being committed to their atavistic origin. Similarly, the critics in Hirschfeld's *Jahrbuch* could accept his determinism while rejecting the crudities of his version of psychophysical parallelism. Once more, Ellis could view himself as improving upon Lombroso's skimpy empirical base in setting a pattern of carefully recording statistics relating to sexual behaviour, which has formed the core of the empirical study of sexuality, from his day to ours, as his work was improved upon by figures like Kinsey, Masters and Johnson, Hite and Bornemann. I suggest that Weininger aimed at just the kind of theoretical integration of the study of sexuality with general psychology, the lack of which today makes sexology a dubious science. To be sure, his work was based on hopes which were premature. Nevertheless, it was rooted in a legitimate scientific tradition and raised important conceptual questions within that tradition. It was left to Sigmund Freud to develop the sort of descriptive and analytic framework Weininger vainly sought. Freud often proceeded from the same sources as Weininger, but he carefully rethought both the significance of his data and his principles of explanation as he went along. If Freud's work marks an advance on the tradition I have been discussing, it is precisely because it incorporates a radical reinterpretation of sexual experience, i.e., what Kuhn once called a paradigm shift, whose significance was only to be appreciated long after Weininger's death. In this context it is worth reminding ourselves that Weininger was one of the very few to appreciate the value of Freud's researches from outside Freud's own circle, as Ludwig Wittgenstein was wont to emphasise.

A final point should be mentioned in this chapter as far as the scientific status of Weininger's work is concerned. I have suggested that Weininger was, in effect, the end point of a certain way of conceiving of human behaviour. Many of the scientific ideas he espoused were already under attack at the time he was writing. Moreover, the discovery of Mendelian genetics and its linking with evolutionary theory, which had been fully accomplished by the end of World War I established firmly that nothing of the biological element in Weininger's thought was tenable. The superiority of Freud's approach to understanding sexuality was becoming apparent at roughly the same time. Thus, in the inter-war years what had been a rationally defensible, if speculative, even flawed, contribution to a science of sexuality took on a wholly ideological character (which it seems to have had in Italy from the start). But this, too, is another story. I shall consider myself successful if I have been able to make it at least plausible that these are two stories, the story of the genesis of Weininger's thinking and that of the reception of his ideas, and that they must be kept distinct (I do not say separate) if we are to understand both Weininger and the reception of his work.[1]

NOTE

1. I have discussed some of the ideas in this chapter in my book, *Essays on Wittgenstein and Weininger*, Amsterdam, 1985, and in my essay, 'Therapeutic Nihilism: How Not To Write About Otto Weininger.' *Structure and Gestalt.* Ed. Barry Smith, Amsterdam, 1981.

4

The Expression of Exactness:
Ernst Mach, the Brentanists and
the Ideal of Clarity

KEVIN MULLIGAN

Clarity and cognate terms such as rigour, exactness, analysis, truth, precision, univocity, distinctness, analysis recur again and again in the highpoints of Austro-Hungarian theoretical and artistic production around the turn of the century, in the writings of philosophers as well as artists, of novelists as well as economists. Clarity was, it seems, an end in itself and a value that, during the last two decades of the nineteenth century, came increasingly to preoccupy Austrian minds. The well-known and well-documented obsession with exact expression was powered by a preoccupation with exactness itself. Again and again exact expression is opposed to *Phrasen* (empty phrases), to *Geschwätz* (blether), to vacuous ornamentation etc., in the name of exactness or clarity. The attention paid in recent work on Austro-Hungarian culture to the importance of critiques of language and of other types of expression has meant that the fact that the concern with exact expression was itself a function of a concern with exactness or clarity *tout court* has been overlooked. We ought perhaps to take literally what Kafka says when he writes that what he seeks is total clarity, and Husserl when he tells us that he cannot live without complete clarity, and Ehrenfels when he writes of the importance of total clarity. And the examples could be multiplied.

We need only consider the two or three years around the turn of the century.

Kraus writes in the preface to *Die Fackel* (his periodical) of his ambition to dry out the esteemed bog of empty phrases (*eine Trockenlegung des werten Phrasensumpfes*), an ambition thenceforth pursued by dissecting empty political and journalistic phrases.

Musil plans a novel about the life of a 'vivisector of the soul,' a vivisector who, as we know, went on to analyse and discard a variety of delusions that have in common their attachment to obscurity.

Klimt's 1900 frieze *Philosophie* led immediately to a debate between the professors who could make out only the representation of 'confused thoughts by means of confused forms' and his defenders who argued that it was the professors' prejudices that prevented them from seeing what Klimt had represented all too *clearly*. Loos announces that 'lack of ornamentation is a sign of spiritual strength' (*Ornament und Verbrechen*).

The importance of clarity was not felt only in Austria-Hungary. The Anglo-American Imagists were insisting in the first decade of the century on, in T. E. Hulme's words, 'absolutely accurate presentation and no verbiage'. (F. Flint quotes this phrase in his 'History of Imagism', *The Egoist*, 1915. T. E. Hulme, like T. S. Eliot, was fully aware of the similarities between his own interests and contemporary Austrian philosophy. See Hulme's *Speculations*.) A similar emphasis is to be found in Valéry. And in Cambridge G. E. Moore and Bertrand Russell were laying the foundations of an approach to philosophy which would put clarity and exactness onto the centre of the philosophical stage.

In this chapter, however, my concern is not with the many forms of the obsession with exactness and with the horror of its opposites in the Monarchy. I want rather to look at what is almost certainly the least well-known of all the Austrian preoccupations with exactness, although it is as systematic and pervasive as is the same preoccupation in the work of, say, Musil, Loos, Wittgenstein or Schoenberg. Austrian philosophy in the forty years around the turn of the century, the works of Mach, of Brentano and of his six gifted pupils – Marty, Stumpf, Twardowski, Meinong, Husserl and Ehrenfels – is characterised not only by its introduction of a new level of exactness into philosophising in German, a level unknown since Leibniz's day, but by a persistent effort to make explicit what exact philosophy, as opposed to the ever present temptations to obscure blethering, actually is. This attempt to say what exact writing in philosophy is has a number of different facets and strikingly resembles the thematisations of ornamentation and unclarity to be found elsewhere in Austria-Hungary. I shall set out some of the main features of this philosophical preoccupation with exactness and pay particular attention to its connection with the perception by philosophers of innovation and decay.

I do not wish to attempt to summarise the thought of Mach or of the Brentanians, nor need I go into the pervasive and – in the case of the Brentanians – subterranean and forgotten influence these philosophers had on twentieth-century philosophy as well as on such disciplines as linguistics, economics, psychology, particularly Gestalt Psychology, anthropology and sociology, an influence they exercised throughout the Monarchy, in Prague, Lemberg, Vienna, Czernowitz and Graz.

Brentano instilled in his pupils a definite conviction about how exact and scientific philosophy should be done, a conviction that was to stay with Twardowski and Ehrenfels, Meinong and Husserl throughout their immensely influential philosophical careers. This detailed picture of the way to achieve rigour included a taxonomy and indeed a theory of inexact philosophy.

In 1866 Brentano defended various theses (for his *Habilitation* in Würzburg). The two most famous theses were: 'Philosophy must protest against the division of the sciences into speculative and exact, and the justification for this protest is its very right to exist' and 'The true method of philosophy is no other than that of the natural sciences.' Brentano's brilliant defence of these theses immediately attracted a large number of enthusiastic adherents. During over thirty years in Vienna he continued to win over philosophers to his ideas. But it was not only Brentano's persuasiveness that announced itself in Würzburg. To his great amusement the door of the lecture-theatre in which he had defended his theses and in which it was normally the ideas of Schelling that were inflicted on students bore the word *Schwefelfabrik*, gassing or waffle factory. The identification of traditional German Idealism as one of the most dangerous forms of inexact philosophy was to remain a constant in the writings of Brentano and of all his pupils.

The taxonomy and theory of inexact philosophy is set out in Brentano's Four Phases theory. Brentano argued that three times in the history of philosophy a sequence of four phases could be observed. To the first phase, characterised by a purely theoretical interest and by a scientific approach, there belong Aristotle, Aquinas and then Bacon, Descartes, Locke and Leibniz. In each case a period of flourishing scientific philosophy was followed by a decline in three phases. First, a weakening of the purely theoretical interest, often in favour of purely practical motives – the Stoics, Duns Scotus, the Englightenment (Voltaire, Wolff). Secondly, a period of scepticism – Sextus Empiricus, Ockham, Hume. And finally, the triumph of speculative mysticism – Plotinus, Fichte, Hegel, Schelling. In this final phase of philosophical decadence,

> [t]he natural desire for truth, prevented from running its course by scepticism, breaks out in a violent form. With a pathologically exaggerated eagerness/zeal philosophers return to the construction of philosophical dogmas. In addition to the natural means with which philosophers worked in the first phase, quite unnatural modes of knowledge, principles devoid of any evidence, the immediate intuitive forces of geniuses, mystical exaggerations of intellectual life are conjured up, and soon philosophers are luxuriating in possession of what they think are the most sublime of truths, truths that are beyond all human capacities.

This influential account of the history of clarity and confusion in philosophy was not intended to yield any mechanical account of the history of philosophy, or allow any sort of prediction. Brentano simply thought that his description of the history of philosophy was correct and that the sequence of phases he had described could be explained or made plausible by 'considerations belonging to cultural psychology'.

Whether or not this is the case, it is apparent that the *Brentano effect* was itself a cultural phenomenon of the greatest importance. This effect consisted of the eager propagation of the Four Phases theory, its wide reception by the best minds in the Monarchy and the perception that, if

German Idealism belonged to a period of extreme decadence, then Brentano's scientific philosophy might mark the beginning of a new period of precision. It was a recognition that decay should be dealt with not just by any old innovation but by a quite specific sort of renewal. Scientific philosophy as it had been practised in the past was to be revived. But it was also to be found going on outside philosophy institutes. For one of the points stressed by Brentano was that exact philosophy was in fact being done, but by scientists such as Mach, Hering and Helmholtz. In this connection it is worth remembering that Brentano, Meinong and Stumpf were instrumental in introducing the discipline of experimental psychology into Austria and Germany.

To see just what the Brentano effect amounted to one must appreciate the extent to which the Brentanians went in for *cultivating* what was exact and scientific in the philosophical tradition and *condemning* and falling away from this idea. Philosophical figures exemplifying this ideal were the subject of detailed examination – Aristotle by Brentano, Descartes by Twardowski, Kastil and Kraus. Philosophers who exemplified the ideal in part received the same detailed treatment – Meinong and Husserl on Hume, Brentano on Reid. In every case the philosophers dealt with are regarded as contributors to a theoretical debate entirely removed from the mundane practical sphere, a debate in which one and the same problem can be formulated equally easily in Ancient Greek, twentieth-century German or eighteenth-century (Scots) English. Philosophy in other words is not the self-understanding of an age, (cf. the Brentanists' defences of absolute truth.) It is, however, on the Brentanian view in time that it makes progress, if very unevenly. This attitude to the philosophical clean lines exemplified here and there in the philosophical tradition has long been common in analytical philosophy – itself in large measure an Austrian product – at least insofar as this tradition has paid any attention to the tradition. But it was a new phenomenon in philosophy in German and is indeed still an attitude almost entirely unknown in German language philosophy (in which interpretation, history and practice still loom large and so explain the almost complete ignorance of the Brentanian tradition in contemporary German philosophy).

It is, however, the attitude towards philosophical decadents that is most revealing. Throughout the writings of the Brentanians, which are distinguished by an almost uniform sobriety – descending to the level of pedantic boredom only in the work of Marty, and then mainly in his (extensive) polemics (but then Marty, although a key Austrian philosopher, was Swiss by birth) – there runs a thematic line of vitriolic outbursts against the German Idealists and against Kant in particular. Brentano never tires of denouncing Kant's 'confusions' (*Verwirrungen*). Ehrenfels, who amongst other things provided psychology with the beginnings of Gestalt theory, writes in a still unpublished autobiographical fragment that, since he was predisposed by nature to be a passionate admirer of Wagner and his music, he would undoubtedly have succumbed first to Schopenhauer and then to Kant, had the great force of Brentano and Meinong not saved him from this deadly 'double embrace'. His debt to his two teachers is that 'I was spared the poison of the Kantian mode of thought from the beginning of my philosophical career, that the style which works with postulates rather than knowledge appeared to me from the very beginning as bearing the stigma of intellectual corruption'. Emil Utitz, who went to school with Kafka and attended with him the regular discussions of Brentano's philosophy in the Café Louvre in Prague writes about what impressed him above all in the work of the Brentanists, among whom he was soon to number himself: 'I became enthusiastic about their manner of proceeding, their elegant, sober, strict lack of empty phrases, their sense of semantic and moral responsibility to every concept, a responsibility expressed by demonstrating its origin in experience.' Husserl's remark, 'I have always hated everything connected with German Idealism', could have been made by any of Brentano's pupils. Kant introduced and was responsible for 'what are in their arrogance the most monstrous of philosophemes', as Brentano puts it. For 'arbitrary constructions' and an 'unnatural [notion of the] a priori' (*Über die Zukunft der Philosophie* [Concerning the future of philosophy], 1929, 12.).

Wittgenstein describes perfectly the attitude of the Brentanists – although his reasons for adopting it are not identical with those of the Brentanists: 'Let's have no transcendentalist blether when everything is as clear as a clip on the ear.'

It goes without saying that the anti-Kant tradition in Austria precedes Brentano. As early as 1798, in a report to the Court, Franz Karl Hägelin had argued that Kant's philosophy should not be taught in Austria. For although 'Leibniz and Wolff introduced no new terminology into the sciences . . . Kant has destroyed, without substituting anything solid; he has introduced a new terminology.' Were the Kantian philosophy to be introduced, 'the result would be that there would be a lot of gassing [*schwatzen*] about obscure matters and nothing would be understood of necessary things.' This tradition has been documented in part by Roger Bauer (for example, in *Der Idealismus und seine Gegner in Oesterreich*). It achieves its first notable expression in the patient and detailed criticisms of Kant by Bolzano and in their development and systematisation by the latter's pupil Příhonský in his *Neuer Anti-Kant.* If Bolzano speaks, as Brentano was to, of Kant's 'confusions', his term for what came later is 'gassing *à la* Schelling and Hegel' ('*Schelling-Hegelschen Geschwätz*', see Winter, *Der böhmische Vormärz*, p. 215.).

What was the method of doing exact philosophy that the Brentanians found in Aristotle, Aquinas, Leibniz and Descartes as well as in the work of contemporary scientists, but not in most contemporary philosophers, nor in any of the examples of philosophy in decline already mentioned? The Brentanians wrote on the philosophy of mind, the philosophy of language

and on metaphysics, and their writings all exhibit the following half dozen
traits, which together form, they thought, the marks of exact philosophy.

First, deductive arguments and definitions predominate. Stumpf writes in
his Autobiography of 'The method inherited from Brentano or Aristotle of
working towards a direct proof of one view by setting out a complete
disjunction of all possible views and eliminating all except the correct view'
(cf. Stumpf, 1925, p. 5), a procedure which is to be found not only
everywhere in Brentano and Stumpf, but also in all the Brentanians – in
Ehrenfels's elimination of different theories of value, in Husserl's forty-
page-long argument in LI V §§ 32–43, in which all possible versions of the
thesis that every mental event contains or is a presentation are set out, and,
with the exception of Husserl's own anti-Brentanian propositional theory of
judging, eliminated. This is one of the first extended rigorous arguments in
modern philosophy.

Another feature of Brentanian philosophy is its distinctive preference for
partial, point-by-point investigation of particular problems. Thus Meinong's
300-page-long *On Assumptions* is a relentless pursuit of the properties of a
single type of mental event. Twardowski's *Zur Lehre von Inhalt und
Gegenstand der Vorstellungen* (On the doctrine of the content and object of
conceptions) is concerned simply to establish the three-way distinction
between act, content and object. Ehrenfels launches the entire discipline of
Gestalt psychology by raising and answering one simple question: 'Is a
melody a sum or heap of tones?' Husserl's *Investigations* consist, as he
himself says, of seven loosely connected investigations which form a
'systematically connected chain but not really a book or work in the literary
sense' (Vol. I, xi–xii).

This preference for the punctual finds a pregnant formulation in
Wittgenstein's *Tractatus*: 'Although a sentence can be an incomplete picture
of a certain situation it is always *a* complete picture.' (5. 156) (This point is
also made by Meinong and Husserl but not as eloquently.) Provided a
sentence or theory is clear, *something* will always be clearly represented
even if many of the connections between this something and other states of
affairs remain unclear. Brentano describes in his Four Phases Theory (1926,
56) what happens when this point is not taken to heart: we find 'suddenly or
in the middle of a train of thought . . . the most daring assertions. One thinks
one can reach the most unattainable peaks; one even thinks one has got
there and one fills the gaps in one's knowledge with the most arbitrary
assumptions.'

A third feature of exact descriptive philosophy is a mental set that I can
best describe as that of a naive discoverer. Brentano had described the
periods in which exact philosophy had been cultivated as periods in which
'new questions are attacked', in which 'hypotheses are deepened', in which
'questions multiply and interconnect'. Now whether we look at Ehrenfels's
discovery of Gestalten, Twardowski's discovery of the act-content-object

distinction, Meinong's discovery of assumptions, or Husserl's discovery of the different types of sense and nonsense, or the discovery by nearly all the Brentanians of the category of states of affairs (a discovery that given a late but classic formulation in the opening lines of the *Tractatus*), in every case we find Brentano's descriptions confirmed and also a naive sort of glee that something solid has been discovered. This attitude is best expressed in a remark of Russel's about a discovery he had made with Wittgenstein: 'today we found a new beast for our zoo'. (That is Moore – although I do not want to suggest that Russell actually shared the mental set of the Brentanians, only that he has described it.) The fourth feature of work in this tradition is the appeal to examples. Examples abound in the work of the Brentanians and they are employed to do a number of different jobs.

This emphasis on examples also has a critical edge. In their anatomies of the confusions of philosophers such as Kant, one of the most frequent charges is that the use of philosophemes, that is to say of big words reverentially passed down from famous philosopher to famous philosopher without too much attention being paid to their precise meaning or extension, leads to a closed philosophical language. The first step in criticising the use of such a philosopheme, for example, Kant's use of 'form' – which is subjected to searching criticism by Brentano and Marty – is to ask what lower-order phenomena or examples the term could possibly subsume. Often the Brentanians' conclusion is that the philosopheme in question simply is not exemplified. This then provides *prima facie* evidence for diagnosing 'constructions' and slapping on one of the rich series of epithets reserved for philosophising that is inexact in principle: *Geschwätz*.

Finally, perhaps the single most important feature of exact Austrian philosophy, one to be found in different forms in Bolzano, Mach, Brentano, his pupils and heirs, and in Wittgenstein: the method of variation. The phenomenon under study is varied in different respects in thought, and the variations and constant connections observed are described. Descripton of this sort must precede all explanation. Hence the Brentanian term for their investigations in the philosophy of mind – descriptive psychology.

A good illustration of the way the Brentanian recipe for seeing and describing 'clearly' connects up with their attitude to 'decadent' philosophy is provided by their attitude towards Kant's ethical writings and his notion of a universalisable categorical imperative. Ehrenfels describes the latter as the expression of a 'metaphysical-mystical dogmatism', and similar strong condemnations by the Brentanians could be multiplied. Kant, they thought, had simply failed to describe clearly and fully the domain of acts of ethical evaluation and choice. His higher-order philosophemes simply failed to apply to any moral phenomena. In particular, Kant's diet of examples was restricted to norms and failed to do justice to, or even take into account, values. The moral life involves a variety of positive and negative attitudes to values of different sorts and these are only indirectly bound up with norms and actions. Kant fails to give any account of how individual acts of choice and emotional states, preference and pleasure, actually hang together – a deficiency the Brentanians attempted to remedy in their theories of value. This reaction to Kantian ethics is common. It is to be found in Musil: 'The categorical imperative and whatever has since then been taken as a specifically moral event, is fundamentally nothing more than a surly worthy plot intent on returning to feeling. What is, however, pushed into the foreground is something dependent and entirely secondary, something which presupposes instead of creating moral law: an auxiliary experience and by no means the central experience of "morality".' (Perhaps the different importance accorded norms and values in German and Austrian thought is not unconnected with the difference between a Roman Catholic and a Protestant culture.)

What, then, are the characteristics of the Brentanian tradition in philosophy that might be of interest to the historian of decay, innovation and the Austrian mind?

They are, I suggest, its anti-historicist nature, its perception of itself as innovatory, its readiness to appropriate parts of the tradition and damn other parts, its perception of itself as a case of philosophical renewal, its acute awareness of the threat of decay in contemporary philosophy, particularly as represented by German philosophy – an awareness that remained alive until the 1930s when we find Brentanians bravely struggling against the tide of Spenglerian and Heideggerian *Geschwätz*. Finally, its preference for clean lines.

There is a danger of misunderstanding here. Nowadays it is all too easy to see in the Brentanian tradition certain ideas and attitudes which have been made popular by the logical positivists and by analytic philosophy. This can blind us to important historical differences. It is true that the Viennese Positivists damned large parts of the philosophical tradition as nonsensical, like the Brentanians. But the positivist dismissal was extremely peremptory and often based on very little argument. The Brentanians, however, went in for detailed criticism, in particular *Sprachkritik*, before passing sentence. In this respect, as in others, the positions of the Viennese Positivists are mere caricatures of positions taken up much earlier in Vienna. Thus the unity of science programme was given a much subtler formulation by the Brentanians than by the Positivists.

One of Mach's favourite words is *Eindeutigkeit*, univocity, as in 'univocal determination'. But the particular twist Mach gave to the opposition between exactness and obscurity has itself become obscured, as has the Brentanian version of this opposition, as a result of the subsequent development of twentieth-century thought, and the tendencey to read back later theories into Mach's work.

It is invariably overlooked just how much the Brentanians had in common with the philosopher, physicist and psychologist Mach. Brentano and his pupils stressed often that, in spite of substantial philosophical disagreements with Mach, he was a good example of the exact way of doing philosophy. Brentano suggested experiments to Mach. Ehrenfels's Gestalt theory of perception takes ideas of Mach as its starting point. The doctrine of Mach's which had such a great influence on Viennese intellectuals, his claim that *Das Ich ist unrettbar* (the I is unsavable) was in fact first elaborated in detail in 1901 by Husserl in his *Logical Investigations*. And this doctine was defended by Stumpf and to a lesser extent by the early Brentano and Meinong. Mach also shared with the early Brentanians an attitude of optimism about the progress of science and society. All the marks of exact philosophy I have already mentioned are explicitly recognised as such by Mach.

Univocity, according to Mach, is to be achieved by subjecting the fundamental concepts used by scientists and philosophers to a remorseless investigation in which their lower-order, experiential bases are laid bare. Wherever a concept cannot be shown to have some phenomenal anchoring it must be dropped. Now this programme has been common to many empiricists and Positivists. Mach, however, actually carried this programme through in a manner which was all his own. And two features of the way he did this are of interest in the present connection.

First, the sheer thoroughness with which Mach went to work. Heat, light, causality, tones, absolute time and absolute space, perception, the ego, substance, all are examined for their experiential credentials and where these are to be found, as in the case of heat (felt warmth), or light (intensity of illumination), Mach attempts to show how the phenomenal concepts can do all the work needed for science; where they are not to be found as in the case of absolute space or the ego, Mach simply ditches the concepts concerned. In every case what we find is a concerted effort to strip away every sort of superfluous commitment. Husserl was to describe the essential feature of this method as follows: 'The sense of this method for men such as Mach and Hering lay in a reaction against the threat of groundlessness; it was the reaction against a theorising with the help of conceptual formations and mathematical speculation removed from intuition which brought no clarity into the correct sense and achievement of theories' (1962, p. 302).

The second feature of Mach's method to which I want to draw attention is his attitude to history. As Nyíri will show in his chapter, Mach was no traditionalist. His lengthy conceptual criticisms of the different physical concepts do, however, all contain deservedly famous historical accounts of the gradual evolution and differentiation of physical concepts. This historical sensitivity is at first sight puzzling. There can have been few famous physicists who have so frequently introduced historical considerations into their work. Now Mach's subtle historical investigations have a number of different functions. Only one of these is of interest here. Mach wanted to show that where breakthroughs had occurred in science, whether the scientists concerned were aware of this or not, these were a direct result of the fact that Mach's method of concentration on what is actually given and of elimination of all excess baggage was actually being applied. Wherever Mach saw that that his method was not being applied, as in Newton's account of absolute space, he thought he could identify bad science and bad philosophy. Only his method of doing science could guarantee clean lines.

I conclude, then, that the attitudes of the two most influential philosophical currents in the Monarchy towards philosophical and scientific innovation and decay overlapped considerably.

REFERENCES

Many of the claims made in the text are documented in detail in pieces by Mulligan and Smith listed below.

Bachmaier, H. (Ed.), 1989 – *Paradigmen der Moderne*, Amsterdam, forthcoming.
Brentano, F., 1926, *Die Vier Phasen der Philosophie*, Leipzig: Meiner.
Brentano, F., 1929, *Ueber die Zukunft der Philosophie*, Liepzig: Meiner.
Husserl, E., 1962 *Phänomenologische Psychologie*, The Hague: Niemayer.
Mulligan, K., 1986, 'Genauigkeit und Geschwätz' in Bachmaier, *op. cit.*
Mulligan, K., 1986a 'Exactness, Description and Variation: How Austrian Analytic Philosophy was Done', in Nyíri, *op. cit.* Mulligan K. (Ed.), 1986, *Mind, Meaning and Metaphysics: The Philosophy and Theory of Language of Anton Marty*, Nijhoff.
Mulligan, K., 1985, 'Franz Brentano's Ontology of Mind' in Smith, B. (Ed.), *Philosophy and Phenomenological Research*.
Mulligan, K., 1986b, 'Mach and Ehrenfels: the Foundations of Gestalt Theory', in Smith, *op. cit.*
Musil, R., 1983, 'Moralische Fruchtbarkeit', in (Hgb.) A. Frisé, *Essays und Reden*, Rowohlt.
Nyiri, J. C., (Ed) 1986 From Bolzano to Wittgenstein. The Tradition of Austrian Philosophy, Vienna: Holder.
Smith, B. (Ed.), 1982, *Parts and Moments. Studies in Logic and Formal Ontology*, Munich.
Smith, B. (Ed.), 1982 *Structure and Gestalt: Philosophy and Literature in Austria-Hungary and her Successor States*, Amsterdam.
Winter, E. 1956, *Der böhmische Vormäz*, Berlin: Akademie Verlag.

5

The Concept of Tradition:
Mach and the
Early Musil

J. C. NYÍRI

The usual view of the Mach-Musil relationship seems to be roughly the following. First, the young Musil was obviously influenced by Mach, albeit in a way difficult to fathom; at the same time, however, Musil was critical of Mach's philosophy of science, even if, according to his thesis supervisor, Stumpf, that criticism did not go far enough. Secondly, the later Musil, the author of *The Man Without Qualities*, turned from professed foe to covert disciple, accepted many of Mach's suspicions about the merely potential character of what is called 'reality,' and, particularly, accepted Mach's view of the ego: namely, that there is no such thing. Blackmore suggests that the very title of Musil's novel in itself shows an influence of Mach;[1] and the phrase 'a man without qualities consists of qualities without a man'[2] strongly recalls Mach's dictum that: 'The primary fact is not the ego, but the elements. . . . The elements constitute the I. I have the sensation green, signifies that the element green occurs in a given complex of other elements (sensations, memories). . . . The ego is not a definite, unalterable, sharply-bounded unity. None of these attributes is important; for all vary even within the sphere of individual life; in fact their alteration is even sought after by the individual.'[3] A possible corollary to, or a possible presupposition of, the received view described here might be the belief that, thirdly, Mach's doubts about the necessary constancy of world and ego were but a reflection of a well-founded premonition of impending, catastrophic social change, of imminent historical doom. Mach's creativity, his insights, are rooted, from this view, in a humus of decay; whilst Musil's reiteration of the same insights presumably testifies to a climate of innovation, of modernity, of progress. Parallelling all these ideas is the conviction that, fourthly and lastly, the later Musil was a nonconformist thinker, someone who, rightly or wrongly, was intent on showing the detrimental effects of those social bonds which in Mach's time had been real but on the verge of bursting, but were after the War just a sham, phoney, a fake to be got rid of. The image of Musil the nonconformist is dominant in literary circles, but even an Austrian professor of philosophy could, way back in 1960, write a paper called 'Der Mann ohne

Eigenschaften und die Tradition' (The Man without Qualities and Tradition) in which Musil is accused of an 'arrogant nonconformism with regard to any tradition',[4] an accusation which, among other things, implies that Musil's *Törless* and his later novel should be seen to be representing one and the same *Weltanschauung*.

I suggest that the view recounted here is thoroughly mistaken. I would maintain – taking the last assertion first – that the later Musil, far from being a nonconformist, in fact held traditionalist views. Musil writes in Chapter 5 of *The Man Without Qualities*: 'In his potentialities, plans, and emotions, man must first of all be hedged in by prejudices, traditions, difficulties and limitations of every kind, like a lunatic in his straitjacket, and only then will whatever he is capable of bringing forth perhaps have some value, solidity and permanence.'[5] And this is not an isolated idea within the work, or rather within the plan out of the wreck of which came the novel. In a draft chapter written in the mid 1920s the protagonist says to his sister: 'We are pursued by an impulse against the order . . . Love can grow out of spite, but it cannot survive on the basis of spite. It can only survive when linked into a society. It does not constitute a contents for life. On the contrary, it is a negation, an exception from contents for life. But an exception needs something to be an exception from. One cannot live only off a negation.'[6] As early as in the comedy *Die Schwärmer* (The enthusiasts), however, a piece written in 1921, a tale of Utopian-nonconformist revolt, the promise contained in the insight 'one man is a fool, two a new humanity'[7] remains unfulfilled, the moral of the story being that without what amounts to unjustified social beliefs, without 'that bright little spark of stupidity'[8] man cannot live and cannot create. This point of view is elaborated in some detail in the essays Musil wrote during the 1920s. Handed-down forms of feeling and thought are, he stresses, the constitutive basis of human existence. As he put it in 1923: 'The very shapelessness of his natural make-up forces man to adapt himself to forms and to assume the characters, customs, morals, styles of life and the whole apparatus of an organisation . . . For one can say that man becomes man only through expression, and this gains its own form in the forms of society.'[9] Man's development occurs 'under the guidance of tradition and by cautious adjustments of direction';[10] reason cannot replace tradition,[11] and even the spontaneity of an artist is inconceivable without handed-down forms and concepts.[12]

In science in particular, Musil points out, the work of previous generations plays an essential role. Inherited methods are taken over and further developed, so that it is 'in the ratio: individual/traditional that there lies the economy of practice'.[13] Even if Musil is reluctant to follow Spengler in entirely dissolving natural science into cultural forms, he is certainly convinced, by the 1920s, that facts are what they are only in an historical context. And so, too, with norms, values, and indeed the individual self. These are not non-entities, as Mach would have it; but nor, either, do they exist independently of specific forms of life, or of the motley of traditions and constraints which constitutes human culture.

There is a remarkable passage in Chapter 8 of *The Man Without Qualities*, where Musil, picturing himself as travelling on 'the train of events', goes on to say: 'What is flying past flies past because it can't be otherwise, but for all our resignation we become more and more aware of an unpleasant feeling that we may have overshot our destination or have got on the wrong line. And one day one suddenly has a wild craving: Get out! Jump clear! It is a nostalgic yearning to be brought to a standstill, to cease evolving, to get stuck, to turn back to a point that lies before the wrong fork in the road. And in the good old days when there was still such a place as Imperial Austria, one could leave the train of events, get into an ordinary train on an ordinary railway-line, and travel back home.'[14] Now if, as I have suggested, the later Musil was a traditionalist, then this passage is neither predominantly ironic, nor indeed without an ideological background. In fact, when Franz Theodor Csokor wrote that for Musil 'with the year 1918 his homeland really vanished. In *The Man Without Qualities* he re-created it,'[15] he was indicating a fact of profound theoretical significance. Far from being a nonconformist in an avant-garde age, Musil was a conservative living on memories of bygone times. His ideas were the theory of a nonexistent practice – as ideas invariably are. 'A tudat a bizonytalanság reakciója,' says the Hungarian poet and essayist Mihály Babits,[16] that is: consciousness is a reflection, a consequence, of uncertainty. And this brings me back to Mach, and to the third tenet of the received view described above by way of introduction, namely to the relation between, on the one hand, Mach's uncertainty as regards the objective structure of the world and the ego, and on the other, the uncertainty Mach and his contemporaries allegedly felt when contemplating the fate of Austria. And here I would like to suggest that this latter uncertainty hardly existed at all; indeed there could have been hardly any reason for it to have existed. True, there did prevail a climate of corruption, of the absurd, a climate, in particular, of linguistic dishonesty, of empty clichés. It would be wrong to take no notice of the moral tensions reflected in the writings of, say, Hofmannsthal, Schnitzler, Weininger, Kraus, or indeed Kafka, and Macartney is right when he regards it as being easy 'to find Cassandra cries enough in the diaries and correspondence of men in a position to see below the surface of things'.[17] But Macartney at the same time points out, correctly, that 'it would be quite erroneous to suppose the general life of the Monarchy during [the pre-war] years as overshadowed by a sense of impending and ineluctable doom'.[18] After all, it is trivially true that Hungary did not dissolve because it was unfit to exist, but that it was dismembered because it had lost a war, and I believe that the same is true, perhaps less trivially, of the Austrian Empire as a whole. As to our present concerns, that is as to Mach: his anarchism, in particular in the domains of the philosophy of mind and the philosophy of science, may perhaps bear testimony to a weak personality in complicated social surroundings, but it certainly does not bear testimony to a weak society. It seems that *fin-de-siècle* Austria was stable enough to carry the load of a philosophy of science entirely false and disruptive, whilst being at the same time extremely popular.

In Mach's philosophy the role of tradition, in society in general and in science in particular, is depicted in an overwhelmingly negative manner. Handed-down patterns, uniformity, Mach suggests, 'are excellent for soldiers, but they will not suit minds'.[19] Schools should not 'select the persons best fitted for being drilled'[20] and thereby suppress the 'powerful judgement' which 'would probably have grown [in children] if they had learned nothing.'[21] The 'aim of instruction' should be 'simply to economise on experience'.[22] Even though it is a fact that in science 'the majority of the ideas we deal with were conceived by others, often centuries ago',[23] that does not, according to Mach, represent an essential feature of cognition. It amounts only to an 'exquisite economy':[24] each individual could, in principle, think out everything for himself. Thus no 'mystery' is involved in the 'power' handed down by science: with respect to specific results, science 'yields us nothing that we could not attain, given sufficient time, without method'[25] – *ohne alle Methode*. That Mach is entirely blind to the social embeddedness, to the necessarily social nature, of the individual, becomes quite obvious from his last book, *Kultur und Mechanik*, a book whose very topic inevitably introduces, or so one would assume, sociological considerations. Reflecting, for example, on the conditions under which primitive inventions are likely to occur, Mach thinks of warm climates, say those of Africa: there, he writes, 'conditions [are] most favourable, and difficulties the least.'[26] 'False! Quite to the contrary!,' the psychoanalyst Sándor Ferenczi wrote into his copy of Mach when reading this passage. Ferenczi certainly had, even more than his teacher and friend Sigmund Freud, an eye for psychosocial relations; he was given to realising, as Mach did not, that the conditions conducive or not conducive to invention were social conditions, and it is precisely where Nature is unkind that an appropriate, i.e., more elastic, social organisation will come into being. Similarly, Ferenczi was bound to explode when, in the same study, he encountered Mach's argument to the effect that the growth of knowledge would be an easier and altogether smoother affair if men were not mortal. 'A group of eternally living individuals,' writes Mach, 'would make incomparably greater progress. Those countless hours lost in the reassuming, learning again, but also finding again of what had been lost would cease to be necessary. . . . Heredity is something analogous; it consists in the assuming and vital augmenting of experience and thus of cultivated or culture-determined capacities with the elimination of the individual.'[27]

Just occasionally, however, Mach does concede that the handed-down fulfils indispensable functions. Thus, in his 1883 Inaugural Address, he refers to 'fixed customary thought'[28] without which new problems will not become perceptible, to the 'importance and utility' of 'habitual judgment' and of 'prejudice'. 'No one could exist intellectually,' he writes, 'if he had to form judgments on every passing experience, instead of allowing himself to be controlled by the judgments he has already formed. . . . On prejudices, that is, on custom-based judgments, not tested in every case to which they are applied, reposes a fair portion of the thought and work of the natural scientist. On prejudice reposes most of the conduct of society. With the sudden disappearance of prejudice society would hopelessly disintegrate.'[29] Still, all the emphasis Mach places on psychological, sociological, even ethnological factors, on the relativity of 'the standpoint of our culture' (*Kulturstandpunkt*),[30] and all the importance he attaches to the historical variability of science, serves only to underline the primary character of facts theoretically uncontaminated. As the Lemberg physician and philosopher Ludwik Fleck was to point out in 1935, Mach simply did not fathom the extent to which the sociological dimension permeates the epistemological, and did not doubt that cognition was but a mere adaptation of thoughts to some given, extraneous facts.[31]

Mach played a crucial role in the intellectual odyssey of the young Robert Musil. 'Mach's popular scientific lectures,' Musil noted in his diary for 26 May 1902, 'fell today into my hands at just the right time to prove to me the existence of a reality that is largely understandable yet nonetheless of great significance.' Six years later he earned his doctorate in philosophy with a thesis on Mach which was critical of the latter's monism, phenomenalism, conventionalism and indeed of the whole programme of *Denkökonomie*. Taking a classical Realist position, Musil had no patience with Mach's psychologistic relativism and, incidentally, no eye for certain important rudiments of Realism in Mach's work itself, as revealed for example in the idea of *Gestalt*, an idea which, through several mediations, was to become quite essential to Musil later. It can indeed be said that in the years before the War Musil had even less appreciation of the role of tradition in science and society than had Mach. Soon, however, he came not only to discover a realm other than that of facts, laws, rules, and concepts, a realm he now terms that of the non-ratioid,[32] but also to see that life in this realm – the 'other condition', *der andere Zustand* – could never be more than a social and psychological exception. In summary, the young Musil to some extent was, but the later certainly was not, a Machian. The later Musil succeeded in grasping important historical and, may I say, philosophical, facts about the world in general, and about Austria in particular. Mach did not succeed in these two matters. His influence lives on.

NOTES

1. John T. Blackmore, *Ernst Mach: His Work, Life and Influence*, Berkeley, 1972, p. 189.
2. *The Man Without Qualities*, Ch. 39.
3. Ernst Mach, *The Analysis of Sensations*, New York, 1959, pp. 23f.
4. Erich Heintel in *Wissenschaft und Weltbild* 13 (1960), p. 194. 'Musil', writes Heintel in the same paper, 'steht in jenem Traditionsverlust des Abendlandes, der sich etwa von dem Zusammenbruch des Idealismus im vergangenen Jahrhundert über die Linkshegelianer, dann über Schopenhauer und Nietzsche auf unsere Tage erstreckt. Soziologisch handelt es sich dabei um die Auflösung der sittlich-politischen Substanz des Bürgertums.' p. 189.
5. Translation by Eithne Wilkins and Ernst Kaiser.
6. Robert Musil, *Gesammelte Werke*, Vol. 1–9, ed., Adolf Frisé, Reinbek, 1978, 5:1673.
7. *Gesammelte Werke*, 6:331.
8. Ibid., 6:361.
9. Ibid., 8:1374.
10. Ibid., 8:1369.
11. Ibid., 8:1081 f.
12. Ibid., 8:1250, from 'Der Dichter in dieser Zeit' (1934).
13. Ibid., 8:1409, from 'Die Krisis des Romans' (1931).
14. Translation by Eithne Wilkins and Ernst Kaiser. See note 5.
15. Csokor, 'Gedenkrede zu Robert Musils 80. Geburtstag', in Karl Dinklage (ed.), *Robert Musil: Leben, Werk, Wirkung*, Zurich, 1960, p. 354.
16. Babits, 'A magyar jellemről,' *Esszék, tanulmányok*, vol. 2, Budapest, 1978, p. 631.
17. C. A. Macartney, *The Habsburg Empire 1790–1918*, London, 1968, p. 754.
18. Ibid.
19. Ernst Mach, *Popular Scientific Lectures*, translated by Thomas J. McCormack, La Salle, Ill., 1943, p. 369.
20. Ibid., p. 370.
21. Ibid., p. 367.
22. Ibid., p. 191.
23. Ibid., p. 196.
24. Ibid., p. 198.
25. Ibid., p. 197.
26. Ernst Mach, *Kultur und Mechanik*, Stuttgart, 1915, p. 75.
27. Ibid., p. 84.
28. *Popular Scientific Lectures*, p. 227: 'a fixed habitude of thought'.
29. Ibid., p. 232.
30. Ernst Mach, *Die Geschichte und die Wurzel des Satzes von der Erhaltung der Arbeit*, Leipzig, 1909, pp. 25f.
31. Cf. Ludwik Fleck, *Entstehung und Entwicklung einer wissenschaftlichen Tatsache* (1935), Frankfurt am Main, 1980. English translation: *Genesis and Development of a Scientific Fact*, Chicago, 1979.
32. 'Skizze der Erkenntnis des Dichters,' 1918.

6

Minority Culture in a Capital City: The Czechs in Vienna at the Turn of the Century

MONIKA GLETTLER

In the 1860s clear changes began to appear to the geographical distribution of nationalities in Austria. Above all, there were distinct signs of an increased migration from the Bohemian Lands into Vienna and Lower Austria.[1] The attraction was economic: higher earnings, particularly in manual occupations. In 1890 at least half of the inhabitants of Bohemia were no longer in their birthplaces. The situation was similar in Moravia; horizontal mobility had already fundamentally changed the social structure of the Bohemian Lands before the turn of the century.[2] The attraction of the capital city was so strong that migration from the natural hinterlands took place although the population had a good standard of living.[3] The number of people who had lived in Vienna ten years or longer decreased, while the number of recent immigrants increased. Between 1880 and 1900 Vienna grew by 130%.

Contemporary official statistics recorded the person's language of communication, that is, either German or Bohemian-Moravian-Slovak, which was reported by the head of each household. This registration system bore with it many factors of uncertainty. The census of 1880 listed 60,000 Czechs in Vienna and the surrounding areas. In 1890, there were already 44% more Czechs than in 1880, and in 1900, 46% more than 1890. At the turn of the century the Czechs had reached their largest number – officially 103,000 out of the total Vienna population of 1,650,000. Unofficially, allegedly more than one twelfth of the inhabitants of the Crown Lands and one fifth of the population of Vienna were Viennese Czechs.

The concentration of Czechs searching employment in Vienna was considerably overestimated[5] by public opinion at the time because official statistics showed a higher birth rate among the Czechs than among the German-speaking population of Austria.[6] Nevertheless, the labour market was not flooded by migration.

Indeed, the exact number of the Vienna Czechs cannot be determined, not only because the Slovaks were included in the Czech category in the registration of languages, but also because the registration had at times been arbitrarily changed or influenced for political purposes on the part of the Austrian-Germans. The basic problems were two-fold. One was *assimilation*. With regard to national origin, approximately one quarter of the inhabitants of Vienna were of Czech or Slovak nationality; but with regard to nationality as determined by the census system of language, the figure was hardly one tenth. The second unknown factor was *fluctuation*.[7] Neither of these factors was taken into consideration in the local census. However, they contributed decisively to tensions between the Government, the city administration, the German-speaking population, the Vienna Czechs, and Czechs in the Bohemian Lands.

The number of Czech brickyard workers or construction workers, servants mostly in noble large-landowning households, apprentices, students, civil servants, artists and military men fluctuated, since such employment was temporary or seasonal. There was no way of separating these temporary groups from the Czechs who were permanently resident in Vienna.

Despite the fact that the censuses always took place in late December, at a time when the seasonal workers had already left Vienna, the fluctuating element decisively strengthened the backbone of both the Czech and German national movements. Since the constant coming and going – be it to the new German or the old Czech homeland – was balanced, the population base of the Vienna Czechs changed very little.

A comparison of the employment and class structure of Czechs and Germans in Vienna in 1910 shows that Czechs were disproportionally represented in the industry and trades sector and in the working class. The distribution by branch of employment was 74% in industry and (artisan) trades. (German figures: 46%.) The working-class section of the Czech population amounted to 79%; the comparable section of the German population comprised only 56%. Many Czechs worked in the small shops traditionally based in the capital of the Monarchy. In general, Czechs preferred the 'rag trade' (28% of the employed Czechs worked as tailors or as shoemakers) and in some areas the brickyards attracted Czech workers.[8] Actually, however, there was hardly a trade in which Czechs could not be found.

An analysis of the basic social statistics of the Vienna Czechs according to age and sex, and to economic and area distribution, gives only a superficial insight into the social conditions. It does not give any indication of the attitude of the individual towards his or her national homeland or of the motivation underlying individual decisions or actions. The Czechs 'on the Danube' expressed their national identity through cultural and religious societies, trade unions, sports clubs and political parties. Each of these organisations emphasised a special aspect of Czech identity.[9]

Discussion about the national identity of the Czechs was instigated by the question whether the Czechs in Vienna represented a native population (i.e.

with a right of abode, *Heimatrecht*) and whether the Czech language was, according to the Imperial Laws of 1877, 1880 and 1882, 'a language which was spoken in everyday use by a significant number of people'. To support their claim, the Czechs quoted official census material which showed that the Czech-speaking proportion of the national population remained constant. In addition to this they tried to demonstrate that they were a native group because of their common national consciousness, as expressed in their language and in a multitude of clubs, the full number of which was registered neither by government officials nor by the Vienna Czechs themselves.[10] The role the clubs played in forming national consciousness is described by Josef Karásek, the first historian of the Czech minority in Vienna, in 1895: 'The great importance of these institutions can be appreciated best if we say that the clubs are for us what the community and the state are for other peoples and nations. All we have been able to do, to accomplish up to now in a national sense, had its origins in the clubs.'[11]

Karásek's statement confirms that the clubs were one of the most important integrative elements for the Vienna Czechs.

Therefore, in analysing the significance of the organisations within the total complex of the Czech national community in Vienna, one should not reduce the problem to a question of ideologies or look at these organisations from a merely political standpoint.

The language question in education can be explained with an example of a club which was a national and political centre of the Viennese Czechs, the '*Komenský*-Schulverein' (Comenius School Association). The support of this organisation was an unwritten law for the establishment of all Czech clubs. All their efforts, political, social and economic, were more or less centred on it. The Comenius Association was created in Eastertide 1872 by the Czech-Slav Labour Club, which had been founded in 1868. In 1883 it had opened its first private school in the tenth district, where the majority of Czechs lived.

In 1885 a long series of vain attempts to get official approval to establish a regular council school began, that is, to obtain government support for such a school. Its requests were based on Article 59 of the state school legislation (*Reichsvolksschulgesetz*), by which a council school could be opened, provided that, over a five-year period, at least forty children of a certain nationality were registered as living within half a mile of the school building.

The language taught at the school was determined exclusively by the school board responsible. In those provinces with several nationalities, council schools were established in such a way that every nationality could be guaranteed an education in its mother tongue.

Three decisions of the Imperial Court (*Reichsgericht*) had guaranteed the establishment of council schools for Czech children in three villages in Lower Austria.[12] The Comenius Association made its applications on the basis of these precedents.

On the whole, the spokesmen of the Viennese Czechs proved to be substantially freer from ideological prejudice and more realistic than they appeared in German nationalist propaganda. Never, in the 1870s, the 1880s or shortly before the outbreak of World War I, did the Czechs demand education solely in Czech, nor did they consider knowledge of the German language some sort of national betrayal.

On the contrary, they only wanted their children to start learning in their mother tongue because most of them came from purely Czech-speaking areas and spoke no German at all. Beginning with the second year of school, they should then systematically acquire fluency in the language of the region, in the case of Vienna, German. This was nothing more than a gradual acclimatisation to Viennese circumstances. The Prague politicians' view of the matter is shown in the opinion of the managing director of the Czech Central School Organisation (ÚMŠ). In June 1910 he wrote the following in his report about the Comenius Association in Vienna:

> My inspection confirms my opinion that our efforts have had but little success. The children go to Czech schools only because their parents think there they would learn German quicker and better. In my opinion, we must first decide whether or not we should work for the maintenance of the Czech nationality in Vienna at all.[13]

The situation was similar in the leading political organisation of the Viennese Czechs: the Czech National Council of Lower Austria (*Národní rada dolnorakouská*).[14]

There were two reasons why the Czechs of Vienna founded the National Council at the turn of the century. First, it was to be a counterpart of the German peoples councils (*Deutsche Volksräte*) which came into existence around the same time; and secondly, it constituted a reaction of the Czech minority to the most important statement of German nationalist politics in the pre-war period, the so-called Whitsun Programme (*Pfingst-Programm*) of May 1899.[15] This programme demanded for Lower Austria a legal statement that the German language should be the only language in all schools, whether these schools received government support or not.

Thus, it is certainly not accidental that the secretary of the Comenius Association, Josef Urban, was proposing the formation of a large organisation that would be empowered to represent the interests of all Vienna Czechs. Such a political organisation, however, did not meet their needs. In Vienna Czech office workers and shopkeepers were not politically organised, and the traditional cultural association, founded in the mid-1860s, insisted on their political neutrality. Although the Czech National Council in Vienna had solicited funds for years from Czech banks in Vienna, it no longer received financial support from these sources. The Council claimed, however, to be the only national organisation to look after 'the widest variety of interests of the whole Czech nation on the Danube, being far above all narrow-minded party political standpoints'.[16]

Its programme included district committees, organised agitation on the school issue, on census and franchise issues, as well as negotiations with the Slovaks. The programme, however, stood in sharp contrast with the practical result of its effort. In March 1914 the Association's chairman, Josef V. Drozda, informed the central office in Prague that at the latest elections in the tenth district, in which 18,500 Czechs lived, only 160 votes were cast for Czech candidates. Such facts bring into question the conclusion reached in both Czech and German sources: that the Czech National Council in Vienna was the most important centre of Czech influence, that it was the leading force of the whole Czech national movement in Vienna, or even that it was created by Prague and not by the Vienna Czechs themselves.[17]

Writing on the lack of effectiveness of Czech organisations in representing the interests of the community, Hanuš Sýkora, the editor of the nationalist party's *Česká Vídeň*, stated in a leader dated June 1913:

> We have to admit it: there is no organisation which links the Czech people here in Vienna. As a result of this unsatisfactory state of affairs we have suffered such losses over the last years that it could almost be said that we are witnesses of a great Czech funeral in the middle of a huge Czech cemetery.[18]

According to Sýkora, whom I have here quoted as a representative of Czech nationalists in Vienna, the leading intellectual circles had to bear the full responsibility for this state of affairs.[19] The members of the Czech intelligentsia living in Vienna were prepared neither to use their numbers nor to change their attitudes in any way which might help unify the hundred thousand officially registered Bohemians, Moravians and Slovaks into one Czech national bloc. This had very little to do with their own pride of place or lack of trust in their fellow-countrymen, for in most cases Czech intellectuals only spent a limited period of time in Vienna before returning to the Bohemian Lands to take up prominent positions.[20]

If, however, they wanted to stay in Vienna or had to do so, they soon found themselves victims of discrimination. They were discredited as nationalist exponents of Czech minority ideas. At the very least they were thrown into a dilemma between professional aspirations (assimilation), cultural heritage, and leading positions in an ethnic minority.

But there are further reasons why most Czech immigrants could not escape the process of adaptation and acculturation. Two hostile social systems confronted each other – on the one hand the aspiring industrial society of Vienna, on the other the constant stream, usually peasant, of Czechs pouring in from the Bohemian Lands in search of employment – and one system was bound to dominate the other. First of all, the industrial city, with its metropolitan milieu, demanded the rapid and passive adaptation of the Czechs, a kind of 'Get on your bike' or *accommodation*.[21] Secondly, pressure was put on them to integrate in the sense that they were made to accept external concepts and apply them in their own households.

In effect, this meant that if Czech newcomers succeeded early enough in adapting their attitudes to those of the German-speaking Christian Social majority, they might come to believe that they had freely chosen to accept the norms decreed by the city government under the office of the mayor, Karl Leuger, and to recognise the 'German character of the city of Vienna', as the law demanded.

The penalty for refusing to do so was social, economic[22] and psychological degradation.[23] The new city bye-law (*Gemeindestatut*) introduced by Lueger on 28 March 1900 was a combination of *patriarchal* sentiment and nationalistic arrogance. Until then the law of 19 December 1890 had been applied, according to which it was only necessary for a person to make some sort of declaration of loyalty to the city to be granted citizen's rights.[24] Each applicant had to swear an oath to the mayor 'that he would conscientiously fulfil all the duties of a citizen in accordance with the city bye-laws and do his best to further the interests of the city'.[25] Since the new bye-laws had come into force, however, every Czech who applied for citizen's rights had to swear an additional oath that he would '*do his utmost to preserve the German character of the city of Vienna*'.[26]

This brings us to the issue that forms the root of all the political disagreements concerning the Czechs in Vienna, an issue that was also to have a substantial effect on the whole of their national and political ideas: were the Czechs who wanted to, or for career reasons had to, become citizens of Vienna prepared or even obliged to take an oath of loyalty veiled in such terms? Viennese 'of Bohemian descent' were, for example, expected to swear that they did not belong to any kind of Czech association and that they did not intend to form such organisations, although this would have been perfectly legal according to the Austrian national constitution. A Czech migrant knew that if he refused to swear the oath he would not be granted right of domicile and would suffer social and occupational disadvantages and be subject to other forms of reprisals. If he took the oath to avoid these sanctions, he could be punished for perjury or even for 'causing Czech provocation' if he simply engaged in lawful activities in which only Czechs were involved, such as the foundation of a Czech loan-fund. Refusal to swear the oath would have meant that Czech civil servants who had been employed in Vienna for years and other Czechs, like Czech businessmen or shopkeepers, would have had to abandon everything they had built up over the years and would have lost the whole basis of their existence.[27]

The question we have to ask is whether the rigorous policies of the mayor and the city council were in fact successful. The political reality of life for the Czechs in Vienna was far less influenced by nationalistic and social aggressiveness than by factors compelling social adaptation and assimilation.[28] Nevertheless, if Lueger was to be given credit for achieving a *de facto* reduction in the size of the so-called Czech problem by means of his successful social policies – that is, increased assimilation as a result of economic prosperity – then a clear distinction must be made between his effectiveness as a flexible politician and his rigorous ideological intentions. Still it was this oath compelling the acknowledgement of the German character of the city that had been one of the impulses for the growing volume of Czech protest since the turn of the century.

It was, however, only occasionally, though somewhat more frequently after 1910, that the voices of protest united to form anything like a national movement.[29] The surrender of the Czech cultural political leadership in Vienna does not have its origins only in the trend towards assimilation which resulted from socio-economic conditions.

In view of the countless number of clubs and societies, the idea of a Czech power vacuum in Vienna was hard to accept, but there simply was no social upper class or even any kind of ethnic consensus among Czechs in Vienna. There was, however, an 'establishment' – if this term is used in the sense that Ralf Dahrendorf has given it, i.e. that it is, that 'buffer zone of modern social structures' in which customs, claimed to be the result of conscious decisions, are stubbornly defended. A good example here would be the long tradition of holding Czech-language services in Vienna churches.[30]

Even worse than the comparatively low socio-economic status of the Czechs in Vienna were the constant public insults which reminded them that they were not welcome in the capital of the Monarchy. There were the minor inhuman acts of everyday life, such as tenants being given notice to vacate an apartment because they listed their nationality as 'Bohemian' rather than 'German' in the census forms.[31] There were also the more important inhuman acts inflicted on them by institutions, like the compulsory registration of Czech children in German schools after their own schools had been closed. To this the authorities added the demand that the parents should be punished for registering their children in a Czech school.[32] The consequences of this situation were, on the one hand, protests, on the other, passivity or integration, whichever was more expedient.

In accordance with their political status as a minority, the more actively nationalist sections of the Czech population of Vienna took on the passive role of heroic martyrs. Feeling themselves to be pioneers working for a promised land in which subsequent generations would no longer be underprivileged, they considered justice and the future to be on their side.[33] In order to draw attention to their own suffering they were constantly finding new experiences in a wide variety of situations, which would support the 'justice' of their cause.

Their position in relation to Austrian-German society could be generally characterised as indicating the predetermined 'inferiority' of the Czech element in Vienna, for example in the Austrian Germans' pointing out that the Czechs regarded themselves as 'a nation of domestic servants'.[34]

At the same time the nationalists felt themselves to be the representatives of the whole Czech people. And it hurt them all the more that they were not only the victims of the Austrian Germans' scorn[35] but that their Bohemian fellows also played out 'a perfect comedy' with the Czech minority in Lower Austria and did not hesitate to send them into the lion's den.[36] For the development of their self-perception, it was of considerable importance that they realised that in Vienna they were no longer part of the Bohemian nation. At the beginning of the 1890s Josef Svatolpluk Machar, a Czech poet in Vienna, first used the expression 'opuštěná větev' (forlorn branch) a *motif* that does not only pervade the writings of the Viennese Czechs prior to 1914, but is still to be found in 1946 in Antonín Machát's 'Naši ve Vídni (Our Compatriots in Vienna).[37]

Jan Auerhan, the Czech expert on minorities who was the correspondent of the foreign section of the Czech National Council in Prague, explained that the 'forlorn branch' was in fact an 'offshoot', for the Vienna Czechs were destined to put down their own roots *detached* from the main stem.[38]

The more assimilation occurred, the more superlatives were produced that were supposed to prove the opposite. This constant assertion of the group's own potential superiority, which was based on what it had achieved and which was intended to act as a stimulus for what it still hoped to achieve, played an important role among the Vienna Czechs. In answer to the Czech Social Democrats' proud claim of 'We are the nation!' the bourgeois parties proclaimed: 'We are proud to declare ourselves the champions of the Czech ideal in Lower Austria.'[39] Memories of the sufferings and achievements of past generations of Czechs in Lower Austria were revived in an attempt to increase their own self-esteem. For this reason support was lent to the printing of pamphlets in Czech and German which described the extent to which Lower Austria had been affected by Czech or Slav influences.[40]

The bourgeois Vienna Czechs declared that 'patriotism or nationalism' did not mean privately boasting that one was a member of a nation but openly fighting for the nation against 'the enemy'.[41] A clear line must be drawn between the enemy without and the enemy within. While the continuing existence of the enemy without, that is, the Austrian Germans, was a precondition for national identity, the enemy within could split their ranks. By failing to attempt to bring about the ideological integration of the great majority of the Czech population, that is, the Czech Social Democrats, the nationalism of the bourgeois Czech leaders in Vienna proved predictably to be an unsatisfactory concept. To quote the *Vídeňský denník*: 'Especially for us Czechs, internationalism means exactly the same as German culture for the Slavs. The main enemy inside our Czech body, the enemy within, is the idea of internationalism, which is just as much of a danger to our survival as a nation as any efforts to Germanise us.'[42]

Hence there were two opposing interpretations of the nature of the Czech question in Vienna and of the solutions to it. In bourgeois circles the nationally inspired struggle against assimilation was of foremost importance, whereas the Social Democrats devoted their attention to social injustices such as discrimination and the Czechs' lack of equality with the Austrian Germans. Bourgeois morality with its self-satisfaction had no time for deviants. Antonín Hubka, a National Social deputy and strong critic of the leadership of the Vienna Czechs, called the Czech 'renegades', the 'detritus of a morally corrupt Vienna'.[43] The members of the bourgeois Czech leadership also looked upon their Social Democrat fellow-countrymen as renegades with whom they had basically nothing in common.

A brief analysis of at least a few elements of nationalism among the Vienna Czechs shows that the nationalist ideological system was only externally intact; internally it lacked the ability to constitute an interacting force. Beneath a surface which seemed to indicate that Czechs in Vienna had found some kind of national identity, the basic problems remained unresolved.

The reasons the Czechs in Vienna failed to develop an adequate form of national consciousness are manifold. One point that contributed to their assimilation was the way in which they settled in the city. They were scattered throughout the various districts of Vienna and it was only in the tenth district that almost every house contained Czechs who knew each other from their place of work or because they were neighbours. The process of integration was also accelerated by living in a comparatively open social structure. The Austrian socialist, Otto Bauer, who propagated the idea of national assimilation as a modern means of class formation, came to the conclusion that the 'middle strata', i.e. apprentices, craftsmen, self-employed workers, small entrepreneurs, servants, and industrial workers, were the most easily assimilated. The social structure of the Vienna Czechs fulfilled all these conditions.[44]

Transition to a new way of life placed a further burden on the Czechs seeking employment in Vienna: the loss of their homes, which they left voluntarily and, in many cases, permanently. From the psychological point of view Czech migration from the Bohemian Lands meant their removal from the centuries-old framework of their culture. Their experiences, their sense of security, and their knowledge of their surroundings no longer influenced their lives; they were alienated from their native values. It is essential to realise that this process of their losing their 'home' played a significant role in this history of the Vienna Czechs.

'Home' in this case did not only mean the geographical area of Bohemian Crown Lands but also a system of norms and values.[45]

The more their old 'home' faded into the past, the more the Czechs resorted to the small circle of their compatriots in the various clubs and groups – as the only support that they could reply on in their new world.

Nevertheless, one symptom of the advanced stage that assimilation had reached was the ineffectiveness of Czech organisations, whose functions duplicated non-ethnic organisations. The organisation representing the interests of the 54,000 Czech tradesmen in Vienna, for example, had only fifty members,[46] whereas social clubs, and drama and choral societies, were much more popular, since they catered to the tradition of Czech theatrical and musical performances, a welcome change from everyday life in Vienna. Economic integration and cultural distinctiveness were the two poles of Czech life in Vienna.

The generation gap also played an important role. The second generation remained only partly adjusted to their new surroundings. School children characterised their situations as follows: 'Nejsem Němec, nechci býti Čechem, jsem Vídeňák a vy jste Češi' (I'm not a German; I don't want to be a Czech; I'm Viennese and you're Czechs).[47]

In addition to the two extremes – on the one hand the nationalists, on the other the 'renegades' – a large proportion of the Viennese Czechs must be assigned to the so-called floating ethnic group which had no definite preference for either the new or the old culture. This helped to foment the claims of both nations, made for close contacts between them as well as conflicts.

Ethnologists have indicated that there is a number of stages in the process of ethnic alienation. One of those, in the case of the Vienna Czechs, was bilingualism. Many of those Czechs claimed to use German for the purposes of everyday communication but in spite of that they felt themselves to be Czechs.

In conclusion, Vienna provides us with an example of an important phenomenon that has all too frequently been ignored. There was obviously an overwhelming difference between the historical importance and the political consequences of national consciousness and the minor role which it played in the private lives of the Vienna Czechs. Sometimes it can and must be the task of the dispassionate historian to defend an ethnic minority in great social difficulties against the extreme postulates of its own political ideology. The Vienna Czechs represented chiefly their own legitimate social interests and in no way followed any of the non-Vienna Czechs, or the notional Vienna Czechs' overblown nationalistic slogans.

NOTES

1. Monika Glettler, *Die Wiener Tschechen um 1900. Strukturanalyse einer nationalen Minderheit in der Großstadt*, Munich and Vienna, 1972, pp. 32–44.

2. Heinrich Rauchberg, *Der nationale Besitzstand in Böhmen*, 3 vols, Leipzig, 1905. Erika Fischer, *Soziologie Mährens in der zweiten Hälfte des 19. Jahrhunderts als Hintergrund der Werke von Marie von Ebner–Eschenbach*. Diss., University of Leipzig, 1919.

3. Gustav Otruba, L. S. Rutschka, 'Die Herkunft der Wiener Bevölkerung in den letzten 150 Jahren', *Jahrbuch des Vereins für Geschichte der Stadt Wien*, 13 (1957), pp. 227–274, here, p. 230.

4. Of interest is the officially confirmed percentage of Czechs in several Lower Austrian villages in 1900: Bischofswart, 95.5% Czechs; Unterthemenau, 93.3%; Oberthemenau, 92.8%, i.e. remaining settlements of Slovaks and Croats from the reign of Maria Theresa and

Joseph II. See Anton Schubert, *Ziffern zur Frage des niederösterreichischen Tschecheneinschlags*, Vienna, 1909, pp. 51–62. Vienna belonged administratively to Lower Austria until 1920.

5. Otto Wittelshofer, 'Politische und wirtschaftliche Gesichtspunkte in der österreichischen Nationalitätenfrage', *Preussische Jahrbücher*, 76 (1894), pp. 445–601, here p. 491.

6. Rauchberg, *Der nationale Besitzstand*, I, p. 193, p. III, charts V; VII; VIII.

7. Glettler, *Die Wiener Tschechen*, pp. 31–62.

8. Ibid., pp. 60–72.

9. Monika Glettler, 'Das tschechische Vereinswesen in Wien um 1900.' In: *Bericht über den 14. österreichischen Historikertag in Wien, veranstaltet vom Verband österreichischer Geschichtsvereine in der Zeit vom 3. bis 7. April 1978*, Vienna, 1979, pp. 74–96. Monika Glettler, 'The Organization of Czech Clubs in Vienna circa 1900: A national Minority in an Imperial Capital.' *East Central Europe*, 9, Parts 1–2, 1982, pp. 124–136.

10. Glettler, *Die Wiener Tschechen*, p. 75.

11. Josef Karásek, *Sborník Čechů dolnorakouských 1895*, Praha, 1895, p. 179.

12. Glettler, *Die Wiener Tschechen* pp. 90–111.

13. Ibid., p. 101.

14. Ibid., pp. 121–132.

15. Ibid., pp. 126, 299, 303.

16. Josef Hůrecký [Josef Drozda], 'O významu a úkolech Nár. rady'. *Vídeňský Národní kalendář*, 1 (1906), p. 43f.

17. Karl Gottfried Hugelmann (Ed.) *Das Nationalitätenrecht des alten Österreich*, Vienna and Leipzig, 1924, pp. 430, 438, 447.

18. *Česká Vídeň*, 25, 21.6.1913.

19. *Národní politika*, 23.2.1906.

20. Ibid., 13.4.1906.

21. Alexander Mitscherlich, 'Aggression und Anpassung'. In: Marcusel Rapoport/Horn (Eds.), *Aggression und Anpassung in der Industriegesellschaft*, Frankfurt am Main, 1969, pp. 80–127, here p. 109.

22. Glettler, *Die Wiener Tschechen*, pp. 232–240.

23. Richard Kralik, *Karl Lueger und der christliche Sozialismus*, Vienna, 1923, p. 231.

24. *Niederösterreichische Landesgesetze*, vol. 2, 'Gemeindestatut für Wien', Vienna, 1897.

25. Law of 19.12.1890, *Niederösterreichische Landesgesetze*, vol. 2, p. 16, para. 10.

26. *Gemeindestatut für die k.k. Reichshaupt– und Residenzstadt Wien*, Vienna (Verlag des Magistratspräsidiums), 1900, para. 10, Hugelmann, *Das Nationalitätenrecht*, pp. 444, 487.

27. Glettler, *Die Wiener Tschechen*, pp. 293–299.

28. On both terms see Mitscherlich, *Aggression und Anpassung*, pp. 80–127.

29. Glettler, *Die Wiener Tschechen*, pp. 265, 352, 375.

30. Ralf Dahrendorf, *Soziale Klassen und Klassenkonflikt in der industriellen Gesellschaft*, Stuttgart, 1957. See: 'Denkschrift des DONRČ an Ministerpräsident Gautsch, 28.11.1905', in Glettler, *Die Wiener Tschechen*, Appendix, p. 544.

31. Ibid., p. 369.

32. Ibid., p. 362.

33. *Vídeňský denník*, 77, 23.5.1907.

34. Various editions of the *Vídenský denník* appearing in 1907.

35. *Politik*, 5, 22.2.1907 and 25, 17.5.1907.

26. *Vídeňský denník*, 10, 28.2.1907.

37. Josef Svatopluk Machar, 'Opuštěná větev'. In: Karásek, *Sborník Čechů dolnorakouských*, 3. Antonín Machát, *Naši ve Vídni*, Prague, 1946, p. 10.

38. Jan Auerhan, *Československá větev v Jugoslavii*, Prague, 1903, p. 352.

39. *Vídenský denník*, 84, 1.6.1907, and 78, 24.5.1907.

40. Glettler, *Die Wiener Tschechen*, p. 426, footnote 61.

41. *Kalendář Čechů vídeňských*, 9 (1900) p. 65; 11 (1902) p. 39; *Vídeňský denník*, 24, 16.3.1907.

42. Ibid., 78, 24.5.1907.

43. Antonín Hubka, *Čechové v Dolních Rakousích*, Prague, 1901, p. 26.

44. Otto Bauer, 'Die Bedingungen der nationalen Assimilation', *Der Kampf*, 5 (1912), pp. 246–263, here p. 256.

45. Wilhelm Brepohl, 'Der Aufbau des Ruhrvolkes im Zuge der Ost-West-Wanderung', *Beiträge zur deutschen Sozialgeschichte des 19. und 20. Jahrhunderts*, Recklinghausen, 1948, p. 26.

46. *Vídeňský Merkur*, 8, 15.5.1905.

47. Josef Sulík, *Proč máme vychovávati své děti v českých školách?* Vienna, 1914, p. 13.

7

The Reception of the
Hungarian Feminist Movement
1904–14

F. T. ZSUPPÁN

Historians of the so-called 'Second Reform Generation' of Hungary have so far paid little attention to those socio-political movements which took place parallel to and in contradistinction from the movements associated with Oszkár Jászi, Gyula Alpári or Ervin Szabó. Yet, Hungarian historiography generally and the history of the Second Reform Generation in particular would greatly benefit from an historical investigation of Hungarian feminism, anarchism and pacifism between 1900 and 1914.

This chapter hopes to offer some observations about the ground in which feminism was able to take root and about the main factors which helped or held back the Hungarian feminist cause.

The 1890s heralded qualitative changes in Hungary's social and economic life. For our purposes, the urban developments are of interest: Budapest and another dozen towns swelled in size of population. Budapest grew by 45% between 1896 and 1913; most of the newcomers arrived from Magyar districts of the countryside. The formerly German-speaking Budapest became a Hungarian-speaking city; grown-up children of the Jewish Lipót and József areas of the city (perhaps the main recruiting ground of feminism) had learned to speak and write Hungarian. Rapid economic and demographic growth made living conditions worse: the cost of living rose by 35% between 1898 and 1909; the housing stock was not able to cope with the rapid population growth, since more than half of all self-contained accommodation units had only one bedroom. The growth in industry, banking, commerce, state and municipal institutions and utilities gave rise to an increase in white-collar workers and young professionals. These, at the lowest level of the pay scale, earned 1,000 crowns a year – an income which would have had to be tripled to allow marriage and life in a one-bedroom flat. It is, then, no surprise that Budapest had a lower percentage of married inhabitants than other sizeable Hungarian towns. The incidence of prostitution had also increased because of the large influx of female domestic labour.

Trained and semi-professional women became increasingly common as the universities opened their doors to women (1895) and other schools provided professional diplomas. 13,742 women teachers, 5,000 female telephone and postal clerks and 5,000 white-collar clerks in trade and industry were to be the potential recruits of feminism. Among these, the backbone of feminism was to be found in the Women Clerical Workers Association (founded in 1897, its membership reached 1,800 by 1914) and the closely linked political group, the Hungarian Feminists' Association, with 306 members at its foundation in 1904 (one fifth being male members), but still no more than 1,000 by 1914; its limited growth is characteristic of the fortunes of feminism at this time.

During the first decade of the twentieth century, predictable reactions (characteristic also of other negative attitudes to women seeking to organise themselves for any purpose whatsoever), though more covert in Budapest, emerged undisguised in Hungary as a whole: a feminist in Fiume (Rijeka) reports that it was held to be deeply disturbing there that 'feminism wished to uproot women from their true vocation'; a male headmaster, writing from Győr (Raab), warned a leading feminist that he had to 'tread warily in the question of feminism'; a female anti-feminist gleefully wrote, to the same recipient, from Csáktornya, that the notion of women's suffrage had become a source for jokes. Another report relates, significantly enough, that in the Social Democratic Party headquarters the response to the question of women's suffrage was a dismissive wave of the hand at this 'last straw' in the face of the 'other troubles' they already had. The attitude of the old-style leadership, toying with the idea of the necessity of a limited suffrage reform in the wake of the Russian Revolution of 1905 and of the parliamentary reform in Austria, is typified by Baron Dezső Bánffy's communication of 1907: 'The order of Nature has already determined the place of women . . . we would destabilise the foundations of the family and act against the entire being of society and state, if women were to get the vote.'

In this same period, although Hungarian feminism stood for all women's 'liberation as individuals and as citizens equal before the law', the provincial press, as well as public opinion still equated feminism almost exclusively with the urban middle classes, as well as with the anarchism which was seeking to bring about 'free love'. The superficial resemblance, for example, in dress (the press seemed particularly bewitched by the *pince-nez*, straight skirts and the wearing of hats rather than kerchiefs, sartorial aspects previously denoting a limited class or type), between urban feminists and the earlier Russian *narodniki*, must have contributed to the feminists' failure significantly to extend recruitment at this stage. Even more serious was the lack of accurate information in the press as to the feminists' actual aims (periodicals' frequent refusal to review translations of feminist works was characteristic).

Unlike, for example, Finnish and Czech feminism, Hungarian feminism did not succeed in transcending the limitations of its immediate political goal of woman's suffrage. It failed, for instance, to identify with any issues which might have taken it into a wider political current. The crucial issues of reform of the Bank, the Common Army, the demand for an independent customs area on national grounds, barely registered in the thinking of Hungarian feminists (although the General Association of Hungarian Women's Organisations, to which the feminists were affiliated, did voice patriotic aims, particularly in 1906, for the furthering of homework). Hungarian feminism in its early phase, thus, stood in isolation from what other people doubtless saw as the central issues of the day. In general, non-Magyars (anyway, as non-town dwellers, less likely to be aware of, or interested in, such an urban phenomenon as feminism) stood uncompre-hending before the image of feminism which, showing little interest in Magyar national political issues, manifested even less concern with non-Magyar concerns. The Rumanian member of the Budapest parliament, Sándor Vaida, offers a very rare exception, in his offers of support to the feminist cause.

As the women's question was beginning, reluctantly, to be accepted by the Magyar parties after 1904–5 as an unavoidable political goal, feminist fortunes were ineluctably tied to the fate of suffrage reform: in 1905, 1908, 1912–3, that is, preceding the introduction of the suffrage bills of those years, feminist fortunes temporarily improved, but at the same time they suffered the setbacks of the lower classes when the first two bills failed; feminism was truly slapped in the face by the fact that none of the three bills contained provisions for women's suffrage.

Feminism has had at best an uneasy relationship with the Social Democratic movement and with Communism in Hungary, right up to the present day. The broad reform movement that began in Hungary in 1900, with the first issue of the journal *Huszadik Század* (Twentieth century) felt little sympathy with the feminists' cause (as was generally also the case with reform movements in central and western Europe). In Hungary, the feminists and the Social Democratic Women's Organisations, in 1903, drew on the same potential pool of support; consequently, the fear that the feminists might capture the allegiance of socialist women, who were anyway few in number, was ever-present among the female militants of the Social Democrats (e.g. Mariska Gárdos). Oszkár Jászi and his Radicals similarly stood aside from the struggles of the feminists, just as Jászi, like the socialists, tended to believe that the 'woman's question' would solve itself through the inevitable arrival of socialism. (O. Jászi, *Beszélgetések a szocializmusról*).

Whilst in other countries in Europe, feminism usually enjoyed the backing of at least some major figures in the artistic or academic world, in Hungary the feminists could in general rely only on second and third-rank personages: Dezső Márkus (a High Court Judge) and Gusztáv Dirner (a lawyer) are notable exceptions. The support of, for example, Giesswein and Prohászka did not go beyond non-political, purely social aims – such as the desire for the greater education of women – within the feminist cause, (though it is fair to say that even this moderate support may have gone some way to restraining the attacks of the Christian Socials under Ernszt). Columnists and editors of periodicals like *Új Idők* and *A Hét* were more or less consistently hostile.

However many negative factors may have worked to retard the advance of feminism in Hungary, there were even weightier factors working to its advantage.

Unlike its German-speaking neighbours, the Hungarian half of the Dual Monarchy did not impose actual legal restraints on women's rights of assembly and association and consequently, after 1867, a vastly variegated assembly of women's mutual aid associations grew up, not to mention religious societies (among them many clubs formed by Jewish women). By 1908 there were as many as eighty-one women's organisations, by the reckoning of the Hungarian feminists.

Since a large component of the expanding Hungarian urban middle class was of non-Magyar, often Jewish, origin (families who retained their largely Germanic-sounding names), it is not surprising that the daughters, some-times working-class, but generally from the aspiring middle classes, those involved in trade, industry, commerce and the professions, took so readily to feminism in 1904. The correspondence of such central figures as Vilma Glücklich, Róza Bédy-Schwimmer, Szidónia Willhelm, Adél Spády, and Paula Pogány characteristically reveals both the immediacy and affection of a close-knit group. This factor must have helped Jewish women make decisive contributions to the Hungarian feminist movement.

Given its earlier philanthropic activity, Hungarian freemasonry was inevitably involved in social reform, especially following the initiative of French freemasonry in 1898. By 1906, Hungarian feminism was receiving a degree of active encouragement – though little money – from the Grand Lodge Symbolic. In particular, the Grand Lodge instructed its member lodges (the Kálmán Könyves Lodge, the Haladás Lodge and the Good Templar Lodge) to nurture the feminists' social activity in education reforms and in their efforts to gain the vote. There is evidence to suggest also that it was through freemasonry that the feminists developed contacts with opposition groups within the Hungarian Social Democratic Party (including Gyula Alpári), who urged their Party (never mind how unsuccessfully) to support women's suffrage. Masonic support was not, however, whole-hearted (as the feminists were aware): Oszkár Jászi's Radicals, for example, never ceased to campaign against them in the lodges.

Belief in the beneficial effects of the imitation of the 'civilised West' had been widespread in Hungary well before feminism became serious in 1904. As international contacts became more widespread, and as Dutch,

Austrian, German and American feminist leaders gave lecture tours in Hungary, we find that the establishment of branches in country towns was gradually becoming more acceptable to society as we approach 1910. Again, international contacts were paving the way to the acceptability of the feminists by the Magyar aristocracy: the Seventh Congress of International Woman's Suffrage Alliance in 1913, by the fact that it was held in Hungary, not only raised the Hungarian feminists' standing as against that of the Austrians (who were deemed to be unable to host the Congress), but even involved members of the Upper House of Parliament (Teleki, Haller, Pejacsevics).

In 1912 the '1848 Independence and Kossuth Party', as well as the '1848 Independence Peasant Party' accepted women's suffrage as one of the items on their platform, thus paving the way to political acceptability during World War I.

However hopeless, for the time being, it became to accept further concessions on male and female representation after 1913, by that time feminism had proved itself capable of political survival; further, its scope and interests had broadened: the establishment of institutions for the peaceful solution of world disputes and (during World War I) 'Wilsonism' became its main areas of concern, quite apart from suffrage. By then, feminism had a foothold in twenty-eight Hungarian towns.

Hungarian feminism was born and remained a radical political organisation for two reasons: its working class and unwealthy white-collar membership and the steadfast leadership of such as Vilma Glücklich and Róza Bédy-Schwimmer. Its class affiliation brought with it constant animosity with the Socialists but also, together with the strength of the leadership, ensured that the movement was never simply absorbed into other parties. This latter point is particularly important in that the feminist movement played a vital role in keeping alive the question of suffrage reform in general, even when other parties appeared temporarily to have lost interest. Similarly, even during World War I, Hungarian feminism made for one of those few elements in the International Woman's Suffrage Alliance that did not wallow or sink in patriotic fervour. It seems, therefore, that it did not deserve the crushing setback it suffered in 1919. Unlike some other reform movements in Hungary, however, feminism has still not received its due, at least in terms of research and scholarly interest.

8

Paradoxes in Hungarian Adepts of Symbolism and Decadence at the Beginning of the Twentieth Century

ANDRÉ KARÁTSON

In 1904 Dezső Kosztolányi was making his literary debut by publishing a story which manifested the conflict of his whole generation. It is the story of a father and his son; both of them are sculptors and both are called Károly (Charles). One day the father gives up his art and abandons himself to alcohol. His son, having returned from Paris transformed by his experience of the West, despairs at his father's downfall. He could show his father his reproductions of statues; he could extol energy, 'the creed of the modern age',[1] but his father does not react. As an old drunkard, he just enjoys being mediocre. The young man thinks up a cruel trick to try to revive his father. He buys two bicycles and promises his father champagne if the old boy succeeds in riding faster than he. A frenzied race takes place. Thanks to the superhuman strength drunkenness gives him, the father outrides his son but, because he loses control of his bicycle, he ends up drowning in the river which flows beside their appointed track. This last event or the parricide in disguise, fulfilled the functions of a manifesto by the author: with all the intolerance of his youth, Kosztolányi was proclaiming that no sacrifice was too great insofar as it might provide one's country with some sort of salutary dynamism. His story illustrated a general mental state.

Naturally enough, historians of Hungarian literature insist that an enormous intellectual and artistic renascence took place at the beginning of the twentieth century, a renascence whose hallmark was vehement opposition to what had gone before. For convenience's sake one may say that on the Right the retrograde, chauvinist bastions of feudalism, clericalism and 'academism' were taking shape while, on the Left, new forces were being mobilised which were trying simultaneously to put Hungary on the path to social change and to bring Hungarian culture up to date within the 'European' context. One must draw in here the innovators' main weapon, the periodical, *Nyugat* (The West). The vital position of this publication led to the period of innovation's being labelled the *Nyugat* Era.

Innovation and a breaking with the past appear to constitute the key concepts. One has, however, to ask what content and form we can assign to those concepts, and whether it was not true that there was something paradoxical in the fact that, actually, as far as newness was concerned, the contributors to *Nyugat*, including the author of the subversive story I have just mentioned, were defending the aesthetic values of the *Fin-de-siècle*, which were hardly values suggesting incentive to progress and which had already been rejected by the Avant-gardes and were no longer all that 'modern'. And did there not lie an even greater paradox in those authors' will to combat conservation in the name of the West on which, ever since the Middle Ages, the Hungarian 'tradition' had always fed? One might shed light on many aspects of the problem by ascertaining the movement's genesis within the national context. But since this book has given me the opportunity I shall try also to explore the cohesiveness of the 'Westernising' plan in the context of the Austro-Hungarian Monarchy. To avoid being diffusive, I shall consider first and foremost the cultural role of verse.[2]

From this point of view the first thing to remember is doubtless that the 'civic' character of the Hungarian Muse had been strongly emphasised by the Romantic period. If he desired to be fully appreciated the poet had to participate in contemporary public debates; he also had to represent or embody the moral conscience of the nation. The task of the poet had, before 1849, been relatively simple when it had been a matter of shaking off the Austrian yoke, but after 1849 it became ever more difficult to fulfil that task. While it increased Hungary's importance, its potential for exploiting the upsurge of liberal capitalism, the *Ausgleich* also safeguarded archaic feudal structures. The uncultivated, defenceless majority of the population, the peasantry, remained at the mercy of the large landowners. The peasantry had even lost the ideological support they had previously received from the 'glorious' 1840s generation who had conceived of their literature as being in the service of the peasantry. Once its political loading had disappeared, the peasant *motif* in literature had become sugared down to little more than that of the rural idyll. Academicism saw 'national character' in that and so did its best to perpetuate it. As a result of a major change in the path of civilisation, however, the demand of peasant idyllicism was deprived of all justification.

Much to the distress of the conventionally-minded, Budapest ended by presenting two faces. Having tripled its population since the *Ausgleich* (280,000 in 1870; 733,000 in 1900, 1,098,240 in 1910), this, the sixth largest city in Europe, certainly effected spectacular results in the securing of national consciousness. On top of that Budapest appeared to give authenticity to all the bold assertions of nationalism by its exceptional success in realising assimilation. Before 1848 two in three inhabitants of Buda and Pest were German-speaking. By round about 1900 Hungarian had completely established itself as the dominant language. In the last decade of the nineteenth century the confidently national idiom was beginning to express more or less cosmopolitan ideas. Furthermore, because they wanted to put themselves on the map the new burgeoisie had made themselves better informed about the fashions of Vienna, Berlin, Munich and Paris than they were in the ideals of their own 'deep' country. Actually, from a nationalist's point of view, the capital appeared at the same time admirable because of its outward flair and detestable because of its alienation from the cause. Now at last, even before the great ideological confrontations of the 1900s, the social crisis had been exteriorised as a crisis of culture.

Was Budapest really Hungarian? Should one not submit Budapest to the salutary influence of the provinces? The sort of insults levelled against the inhabitants of the capital and particularly against their Jewish component (and the Jews had been guilty of a particularly successful assimilation), the sort of insults which were to be heard from 1890 to the beginning of the Great War, were, 'degenerate souls', 'perverted morals', 'alien mentality' or 'international Sodom'. The Jewish stratum in the new Hungarian intelligentsia, because it wanted to be integrated, was not afraid of taking up the challenge. We just have to think of Ignotus (Hugo Veigelsberg, 1869–1949), a poet and essayist who took on the lion's share in the defence of Budapest. Responding initially to antisemitism he consistently upheld the idea that urban man had every right to express his experience in accordance with his special perception of things and that city-dwellers' competitive, individualist spirit had developed from national evolution itself. In his battle for the intellectual rights of urban man he came across a brilliant ally in the person of another assimilated non-Magyar, Aladár Schöpflin (1872–1950), the offspring of a magyarised German family. According to the patriotic arguments of both, the Hungarian soul had chosen to take up residence in the capital and the capital itself, because of its qualities as a civilisation, resembled more closely the West than the Magyar backwaters.

In the course of struggling to lend dignity to this 'modern' fortress, however, the intelligentsia was suddenly caught off guard by the immensely powerful voice of Endre Ady (1877–1919), a poet of provincial provenance whom a sojourn in Paris had made painfully aware of the accumulated backwardness of Hungary. In his *New Poems* (1906)[3] his astonished readers were faced with two deliberately contrasted chapters, one devoted to blessing 'singing Paris', the other to cursing 'the barren soil of Hungary'. It was an offensive comparison. On the banks of the Danube, where the poet found himself 'the laughing stock of demons', no future was offered to the souls of the élite. In this vision of an 'East without a sun' the opposition of metropolis and provinces had lost its *raison d'être*. Qualifying himself as 'a son of Paris', Ady had put the whole of his homeland in one bundle as 'this graveyard of souls' or as 'this uncouth Budapest', which he characterised as 'Necropolis' or as 'Curse-town'. As Georg Lukács later remarked, the Hungarians' conviction that they belonged to Western civilisation changed thus into a problem.[4] I would add that this belonging had not been demanded as a task to be accomplished by the Hungarians with the greatest possible urgency to any degree less persuasively in Kosztolányi's story.

After a little consternation the Hungarian 'progressive' intelligentsia aligned themselves with Ady's views whose tempestuous verse served as a preface to the first issue of *Nyugat* (1908).

The radical changes in Hungarian literature were, then, subsumed by the chauvinist conservatives and the innovators. The latter were stigmatised as renegades and anti-national thinkers. The periodical's scandalous Westernism would not have been enough to ensure it the audience it received all over the country. The decisive impulse came from the quality of the artists grouped in the new type of alliance between the modernists of the capital and those of the provinces, and absolutely no distinction was made between their ethnic origins. Ignotus, Miksa Fenyő and Ernő Osvát, who made up the editorial board, were assimilated Jews, and the group's principal patron, Baron Lajos Hatvany was also an assimilated Jew. As far as a programme or manifesto was concerned, *Nyugat* contented itself with its title, although Ignotus did add something to that in his reflections on the visit of a troupe of Finnish actors to Budapest. Entirely recognising that a small nation's efforts were limited and the results of their efforts imperfect and out of date, he added: 'The sun, humanity and history pass from the East to the West. Thus, if they have chosen that path, a people of the East marches forward under the same sun, is distinguished by the same humanity and forges the same history as the greatest of nations.'[5]

Once again Hungarian literature was in a position where it had to play the role of a civiliser involved in the fate of the nation. Close to the radical bourgeoisie who were fighting for parliamentary democracy, *Nyugat* did its best to protect the aesthetic domain from any political or doctrinal invasion. Absolute freedom should be assured to brilliant individuals. How then did these poets exploit 'artistic liberalism' in order to link themselves with the West? Historians have not yet examined this somewhat uneasy symbiosis. While the ruling classes were vigorously assimilating the nationalities, the members of the *Nyugat* school were assimilating or annexing what passed for representative of Western lyric verse from Edgar Allan Poe and Baudelaire to Rilke. One wonders whether the same politics of magyarisation was not involved in the two different areas. Both Endre Ady and Árpád Tóth included in their trailblazing collections translations from French verse.[6] Mihály Babits, Dezső Kosztolányi and Árpád Tóth all put together anthologies.[7] Those anthologies did not constitute simply some sort of literary information service. They chose 'spiritually excellent' texts which were meant to serve the victory of a new poetry. Because of that goal, the beauty of the Hungarian version was of greater importance than faithfulness to the original. Stimulated by the cult of individualism, the Hungarian translators, under the pretext of prosodical skill, produced *belles infidèles* by exploiting their highly personal styles. On the other hand, personal style could be developed in the course of their learning the art of adaptation. As a result of osmosis Western poets became naturalised Hungarian poets, while

Hungarian poets, in the way they explored their egos, became potential rivals of Baudelaire and Baudelaire's followers. Thus Westernism marked the end of big-city cosmopolitanism, which had, at the end of the nineteenth century, been singing the praise of the abstract 'dream' and 'ideal' of something non-material, something which was felt to be alien to the 'genius of the language'. Abandoning oneself to the joy of self-expression in a language as rich and graphic as that of the nineteenth-century masters of Hungarian verse ended up in reactivating the national tradition, in rendering autonomous the individuality of the artist in a culture which had believed itself to be threatened by individual autonomy and in celebrating this new alliance as a patriotic victory.[8]

Hence the paradoxes of this literary reception. Though lassitude, morbidity and artificiality characterised the adepts of Decadence, these deserters from a feudal world were keen to re-evaluate all values in a reinvigorated country, and so they also introduced vitalism and affirmed their complicity with modern renewal. *L'art pour l'art* as a doctrine did not serve only to provide the bourgeoisie with the qualities of aristocratic taste. As far as the middle classes were fighting for power, adherence to the notion of aesthetic excellence appeared to its defenders to be in the service of social evolution. The same thing went for Symbolism. Used as it was to a sensibility thirsty for the concrete, the quest for the essence of things, the goal of pure poetry (*poésie pure*) in the end put up with Impressionism, and the empyrean of Platonic Ideals was populated by ideals related to the present, the topical, ideals which forced readers to take sides. These poets inquired into the mystery of individual souls and lives, but these were on no account separable from a collective; implicitly or explicitly *Nyugat* Symbolism suggested Hungary herself, the ideal of a synthesis with the West and the always frail hope of realising that synthesis. For, if art already had at its disposal the means of prefiguring this synthesis, it remained an airy intention on the political and social levels. Let us take Ady. No one else in his generation propagated so fervidly fusion with the West and, at the same time, no one said so loudly that that goal was unattainable for his nation.[9]

At this stage I cannot fail to point out that in the *Nyugat* debates Hungary seemed to be playing out its fate in isolation although it was an integral part of the Monarchy. Furthermore it is striking to note that, when those intellectuals spoke of the crucial centres of Western civilisation, the name of Vienna was hardly ever quoted next to those of Paris, Berlin or Munich. The Westernist dream purposely obliterated contacts with Austrian civilisation which was palpably better placed to tap and adapt the experiences of 'modernity'. This phenomenon seemed all the more curious since, in contrast to the agitation for independence which was taking over the political field, the *Nyugat* writers never seriously sought to denounce the ties of Dualism. In fact, with hindsight, one could interpret their silence about Vienna as a part of a systematic strategy towards the ruling land in the

Empire. The fact seems to be that it was a nationalist strategy to which the promotion of Budapest offered some promise and whose outcome would paradoxically be guaranteed by *Nyugat*'s cultural plans. It might be best to consider the struggle for anti-feudal progress as having been set in motion by patriotic men of letters whose intention was to work for the elevation of national life and culture by means which were modern and more internationally competitive than those of their opponents. Apart from that the West was too far away and its reality too little known to instigate the idea of a true dialogue. What was actually at stake has to be seen within the context of relations in the Monarchy. Was it not certain that acquiring 'stable values' from the West would enable Hungary to catch up with Austria and would it not also support Budapest's claim to be in competition with Vienna and, given time, allow Budapest to wrest Vienna's privileges from her? Although otherwise so cool in his judgements, did not Aladár Schöpflin distinguish in the sounds emanating from the Hungarian capital 'the accents of the magnificent symphony of the nation's future, of national grandeur'?[10]

Above all the relative situations of the Austrian and Hungarian bourgeoisies can shed the correct light on the ambitions of *Nyugat*. Carl Schorske has shown to what extent the crisis of human values in 'Vienna 1900' was burned up with the anxieties of the bourgeoisie who, having experienced a brief and incomplete 'apogee', now felt themselves to be in decline. In contrast, at that time the Hungarian bourgeoisie were only preparing themselves for accession to political power. In Vienna the crisis of Austrian national identity, uncertainties about the future and apprehensions about a coming barbarism had created a favourable soil for a certain nihilism, a new questioning of art and of language itself. But even if the Hungarian bourgeoisie was already being harassed by their left wing, nihilism could barely have any place in their thinking for they did not share the same mistrust of the future. Even Georg Lukács, who was otherwise so critical of nationalist obsessions, admitted that in Hungary 'the over-lively, over-great energy of an over-young race' was opposed to indifference to 'artistic innovation'.[11] But this artistic innovation, particularly in poetry, was already old hat. Nevertheless it was very well suited to this intelligentsia eager for 'spiritually excellent' refinements of art whose efforts were concentrated on the perfecting of culture and who hardly admitted avant-garde subversion.

Thus belonging to Europe did not mean belonging entirely to actual modernity. In 1913, when Europe was threatening to turn into a powder-keg, Ignotus was still proclaiming a future world literature guaranteed by spiritual concord and propitious for individual national characteristics.[12] It is perhaps not out of place that postulating this harmonious union of distinctive elements had been directly conditioned by the structures of the multinational Empire. From this point of view could not Hungarian Westernism be defined as a fiction of Europe conceived in the image of the

Monarchy, of this Monarchy whose men of letters confident in the mission of their art were among the last to hope for a great cultural blossoming? In any case it is this dream of integration which, in spite of all paradoxes, assured the coherence of their cultural design. At a time when Hofmannsthal could confide in Leopold von Andrian that 'we have a native land but no mother country',[13] the contributors to *Nyugat* had no difficulty in founding national identity on historical discourse. Seeing their movement in the framework of the Monarchy enables us to define their aestheticism and their span of interests in foreign lands as an avatar of nationalism. It was in fact a nationalism in disguise which sought to adapt itself to the cultural possibilities of the Dualist system and to conform to its expectations. But in these fundamental aspirations it was not completely alien to the other side of nationalism. A certain resemblance was therefore to be seen beyond the rupture between the innovators and traditionalists. In conclusion I shall return to Kosztolányi's tale about the murderous generation conflict. It begins with these significant precise statements: 'Károly looked very much like his father. In body and soul they were one and only . . .'

NOTES

1. 'Kifele', which appeared in *Szeged és Vidéke*, 18th–23rd Sept., 1904, renamed 'Károly apja'. Cf. *A léggömb elrepül*, vol. I of *Kosztolányi Dezső összegyüjtött muvei*, edited by Pál Réz, Budapest, 1981.

2. For a more detailed examination of this see André Karátson *Le Symbolisme en Hongrie*, Paris, 1969, and *Edgar Allan Poe et le groupe des écrivains du 'Nyugat' en Hongrie*, Paris, 1971.

3. Endre Ady, *Új versek* (1906).

4. György Lukács 'Új magyar költők,' *Huszadik Század*, Nov., 1908.

5. Ignotus, 'Kelet népe,' *Nyugat*, 1908, I.

6. Baudelaire, Verlaine and Jehan Rictus figure in Ady's *Új versek* and Albert Samain in Árpád Tóth's *Hajnali szerenád* (1913).

7. Mihály Babits, *Pávatollak* (1920); Dezső Kosztolányi, *Modern költők* (1914), Árpád Tóth, *Örök virágok* (1923).

8. Cf. André Karátson, 'The Translation and Refraction of Symbolism: A Survey of the Hungarian Example,' in *The Symbolist Movement in the Literature of European Languages*, Budapest, 1982.

9. 'What's man worth if he's Hungarian?' This desperate question reverberates in Ady's 'Azős Kaján' (*Vér és Arany*, 1907), a poem inspired by Nietzsche where the chaotic, depraved, 'Dionysian' nature of the poet challenges his 'Apollonian' double who is irresistibly thrown in the direction of the Western scene. It is only apparently a rhetorical question. It actually indicated what was fundamentally at stake, what was seen at the time as the most concrete problem: how could one make sure that the values of Hungary were quoted on the European cultural stockmarket?

10. Aladár Schöpflin, 'A város,' *Nyugat*, 1908, I.

11. György Lukács, 'Új magyar líra,' *Huszadik Század*, Nov., 1909.

12. 'the world is sufficiently mature and united by intellectual concord to have a sense of community, to feel related with everything that springs from the human soul, no matter where that soul is. The world is in a position to assess interest whose warmth grows with the degree of

individual quality or – which, at the highest point on the scale of collectivity, means the same thing – with the degree of racial individuality in any product of the soul.' Ignotus 'Világiradolom,' *Nyugat*, 1913, I.

13. Letter of 1913, quoted by Michael Pollak, *Vienne 1900, une identité blessée*, Paris, 1984, p. 150.

9

Imitation or Inspiration:
The Reception of Cubism in the
Habsburg Monarchy, 1910–15

MAGDA CZIGÁNY

Cubism was a revolt of the young. Between 1907, the year in which Picasso painted *Les Demoiselles d'Avignon* and 1909, when he showed his Horta pictures in Ambroise Vollard's gallery, Cubism, as the new revolutionary movement came to be named, evolved as an instantly recognisable style. Both Picasso and Braque, and almost all the artists whose innovative interaction in the *Groupe du Bateau-Lavoir* formulated the first phase of Cubism, were still in their twenties; they were a group of ardent young men intent on creating an art 'relevant' to the new age. The artists of the Habsburg Monarchy who reacted eagerly to Cubism and embraced its principles were of the same generation. Most members of the 'Osma', the Prague 'Eight', and the artists who regrouped themselves in 1911 in the Group of (avant-garde) Artists, *Skupina výtvarných umělců*, were born in the first half of the 1880s. The architects who belonged to the group or were closely associated with Czech architectural Cubism were, even more remarkably, all born between 1879 and 1882. The Hungarian 'Eight', the 'Nyolcak', who were profoundly influenced by French developments although with the exception of one painter did not become Cubists, were also of the same generation and, finally, the somewhat younger men in Hungary who later emerged as the activists around Kassák were born in the same decade, between 1887 and 1890.

It is not surprising that these young artists, all still in their formative years, were trying to find a style which complied with their artistic aims; what, however, is surprising, is that while the emergence of new styles in France, a rapid succession of abrupt changes beginning with Post-Impressionism, were internal developments, the equally strong need for change felt by the artists of the Habsburg Monarchy urged them to seek salvation elsewhere, in Germany or France. The choice was wide and they were fully aware of that; only when a particular style was so all-embracing and powerful as the *Secession* in Austria, which held most of the young artists in its grip, was the lure of external influences negligible.

Beside the *Secession* or *Jugendstil*, the main trends of art in the Habsburg

Monarchy during the first decade of the twentieth century included waning 'academicism', *plein-air* painting, Symbolism and Expressionism. Academicism survived only as 'end-game' to nineteenth-century historicist painting, and in monumental sculpture, both of which still enjoyed public esteem. It survived also in the hashed-up neo-Baroque of the new buildings which were sprouting up in a quickly expanding capital like Budapest. It also continued to make its presence felt in the academies; because of the young artists' resilience and enterprising spirit, though they benefited from their thorough technical training, they soon escaped from the stifling atmosphere of the academies and enrolled in private schools or joined artists' groups which were often opposed to the art Establishment, for example, the *Hagenbund* in Austria or the *Mánes* group in Bohemia. Academic training in Munich, which was still fashionable during the last decades of the nineteenth century, lost its attraction; only the independent schools like Simon Hollósy's still attracted students, but even Hollósy was more involved with developments in Hungary than elsewhere; he became a founder member of the *Nagybánya School* and set up for his students a 'double-centred' curriculum based in Munich and in Hungary.

Against the pomposity and ostentatious monumentality of academic art a trend towards simplicity, directness and intimacy gained strength. This culminated in a belated empathy with Corot's Naturalism on the one hand and in a quiet withdrawal to Symbolism on the other. That induced artists to join the Nabis of France, as, for example was the case of Rippl-Rónai, or to share the melancholy 'mysticism' of Nordic painters, as, for example, in the sensitive paintings of Antonín Hudeček or Antonín 'Slavíček. In Hungary the break-through to Naturalism and *plein-air* painting led to the foundation of the *Nagybánya School* (1896); in Bohemia both trends were embraced by the *Mánes* group (1895). The *Mánes* group constituted a much broader movement; some of its members were committed to *Jugendstil* and later to Expressionism. Both the *Mánes* group and the Austrian *Hagenbund* represented diversity and simultaneity of styles, a receptiveness to the influx of new ideas; both helped to foster an attitude of circumspect selection and conscious choice when the urge for artistic renewal was awakened.

Even the *Secession*, the most distinctive and comprehensive movement in the Monarchy, offered a great variety of styles, from the flamboyant, sensuously curvilinear art of Alphonse Mucha or the richly decorative surface patterns of Klimt to the restrained architecture of Wagner, Olbrich or Loos, which was almost devoid of ornamentalism. Some cultural historians now even equate the busy surface decoration of the Vienna *Secession* with the survival of the spirit of Makart, implying that only the patterns and their deployment changed, but that the basic underlying need for surface elaboration remained.[1] Furthermore, it is claimed that where these patterns are spatial they are the three-dimensional equivalents of the playful geometric forms displayed all over the vestments of Klimt's figures, which may, indeed, superficially resemble the geometric-plane structure of Cubism, or even Constructivism, but should not be regarded as the predecessor of either.

The decorative elements of the *Secession* derived from diverse sources: from the common language of Art-Nouveau design, from folk art, or even from the revival of ancient, for example, Celtic *motifs*. Folk art especially lent itself to the creation of 'indigenous' schools; Ödön Lechner, the Hungarian architect, for example, wanted to establish a so-called 'Hungarian style' in architectural decoration, based on the study and application of folk-art *motifs*. The expression of national identity in art, however, went far beyond the use of decorative patterns and varied from the robust, Naturalistic depiction of peasant life (the *Hódmező vásárhely School* in Hungary or the work of Jóža úprka) to the continued interest in historical subject matter. (For example, the paintings of Körösfői-Kriesch of the *Gödöllő School* or the twenty monumental compositions of Mucha devoted to the history and mythology of the Slavs, which he painted after his return to Bohemia in 1910). The struggle for political, economic and, in the arts, spiritual independence within the confines of the Monarchy led to a double contradiction: on the one hand, to the artificial sustenance and resurrection of traditional, worn and outmoded themes which appeared again and again in new forms, and to the conscious acceptance of the national artistic heritage, especially of the Baroque in Bohemia, which was gaining recognition as a legitimate source of inspiration for the creation of a 'national' school of art. On the other hand, the same struggle led to the formulation of a slogan which advocated 'opening the doors to Europe', that is, welcoming alien influences because that would help to bypass Vienna. Vienna, the natural centre of the Habsburg Monarchy, reared relatively few artists; it was supplanted first by Munich, then by Berlin or Dresden. When the search for new ideas began to be focused on Paris, even the so-called 'central European cultural unity' was threatened and eventually destroyed; the expression of a resistance to the Monarchy led directly to the creation of modern Czech and Hungarian art based almost exclusively on French models.

The shift from northern European art to Paris was complete by the end of the first decade of this century. The last major Nordic influence was the 1905 Munch exhibition in Prague. The *Osma* painters, especially Filla and Procházka, were still quoting Munch in their paintings in 1907, but by 1910 their interest was directed towards the new art of Paris, to Cubism. Similarly, painters in Hungary had steadily moved away from Munich and flocked to Paris instead; the most dramatic *début* of the pre-war years was the first exhibition of the Hungarian 'Eight' in 1909 in Budapest; all the exhibitors were schooled in Paris, on Cézanne, Matisse and on the Fauves.

The exception is Vienna itself. Artists, ready to revolt against the *Secession*, were not fuelled by national aspirations, but by the need for the expression of the inner self, however violent, contorted, awkward or even explosive that might be. The art of Kokoschka, and later Schiele, and I mention only the most prominent painters of Austrian Expressionism, may be regarded as an indigenous development, which, especially in the case of Kokoschka, has more affinities with Austrian Baroque than with similar tendencies in other countries.

The choice facing the young artists of the Monarchy was indeed wide: they could have opted for one of the many prevalent and fashionable trends, including the more revolutionary brand of the *Secession* or the *plein-air* school, perhaps with a touch of Cézannism. They could have reacted against Art Nouveau by embracing the movements which emphasised the need for spiritual renewal: Symbolism or Expressionism. As patriots, they could have aspired to serve their country with their art in many ways: by maintaining links with the art of the 'glorious' past, or by formulating a new language or artistic expression based on the idioms of folk art. Or, conversely, they could have 'opened the doors to Europe', to seek out, study and bring home the new art of France, Germany, or indeed even of the United States and, thus, raise the level of the arts in their own countries to that of the international art movements.

The generation of the 1880s in the Monarchy chose French art. Almost without exception the young artists travelled to Paris and often endured great hardship in order to study modern French art at its source. Some artists of the first wave had settled in Paris and offered help, advice, even food and lodging to the newcomers. Through their network of contacts they introduced their compatriots to French art schools and artists, suggested visiting the prominent galleries and collections like the Pellerin, the Rosenberg and, first and foremost, the open house of Leo and Gertrude Stein in the rue de Fleuris. For example, the Hungarian sculptor József Csáky, friend of Archipenko, and the Hungarian painter Alfréd Réth exhibited with the first French Cubists while maintaining close links with the members of the Eight.[2] When the young János Kmetty visited Paris in 1911 they arranged accommodation for him, and acquainted him with the newest trends.[3]

Three observations may be made on the visits of Prague and Budapest artists to Paris. First, they revealed great individuality and eclecticism in their interests and studies: Kubišta, for example, was fascinated by Poussin's paintings in the Louvre; he even published an article on Poussin. János Kmetty was equally captivated by the Louvre's collection of Italian Renaissance sculpture and by the paintings of Courbet, Manet and Cézanne. Their overall open-mindedness did not prevent their realising the revolutionary nature of Cubism and did not deter them from absorbing what they could from its principles, however short their stays were. Kmetty writes in his autobiography: 'The spiritual luggage which I brought back from Paris *in* me and *with* me has set me up for life; I am still living from it. It was a new perception of Nature, a new way of painting and a new technique; it was Cubism'.[4]

Secondly, this conscious choice of what trend to follow reveals an attitude to adopt all too readily, an eagerness to imitate, which is in conflict with organic inner development. Although the chronology of the influence of African art on the development of early Cubism may remain unresolved, it is certain that Picasso did not consciously seek out primitive tribal art or prehistoric Iberian sculpture to build them into a new style. These art forms were coincidental in heightening his awareness of a radically new conceptual perception of Nature. In contrast, artists from central and eastern Europe arrived in Paris first and foremost with the aim of learning, of picking and choosing from hitherto unknown ideas and styles and taking them home almost as one takes home a souvenir from a trip abroad.

The third observation often made and then used as a mild rebuke of the artists of the Monarchy is that they were not schooled enough to discriminate between first and second-rate masters. Nor did the haste with which they adopted the new style allow them enough time to contemplate the relative merits of Picasso and Metzinger or Braque and Le Fauconnier. Nicholas Wadley in his preface to Miroslav Lamač's book on modern Czech painting blames this attitude on a superficial assimilation, on the over-eager acceptance of a ready-made Modernism, a 'pre-digested "instant" Cubism'.[5] It was indeed a danger born of the inexperience of youth and of an enthusiasm for what Paris offered. That criticism, however, could be glibly refuted by another generalisation namely, that what matters is not what is imitated but how the imitation is done: too faithful an imitation of the great masters of Cubism might have produced a series of second or third-rate Picassos with no hint of independent ideas. It may be safely assumed that Picasso himself did not prejudge the aesthetic quality of one African mask against that of another; he was concerned with the conception of representation in the masks and not in the finesse of execution. Similarly, central-European artists, after absorbing the principles of Cubism in Paris, from whichever artist they may have felt closest to themselves, interpreted them in an independent and individual manner on their return home.

Of the Hungarian 'Eight', it was only Lajos Tihanyi who was attracted to Cubism. A portrait painter *par excellence*, he exhibited in 1912 with the Eight a self-portrait in which the features of the face were broken up into angular shapes suggesting an attempt at Cubist analysis. The fragmentation of the facial planes was, however, neither thorough nor carried out in a cool, disengaged manner; it seemed as if an inner tension had distorted the features and an emotional intensity had squeezed them into a geometrical explosion. Cubist technique served Tihanyi only to heighten sensitivity; he wanted to express the spiritual, and it was no surprise that he was regarded by his contemporaries as the Hungarian Kokoschka.[6]

The Hungarian painter who had more than a brief encounter with Cubism was János Kmetty. Following his return from Paris in 1911, he painted a number of self-portraits conceived in a Cubist manner. They reveal a serious study of forms and their spatial relation, but the analysis never leads to fragmentation. Kmetty retains the unity of the head and the figure; he dissects only the details of the bone and muscle structure of the face and the folds of the shirt into Cubistic forms; other parts of the composition, for example, the hand holding an apple in the self-portrait of 1912, completely escape analysis. The structural lines may be overemphasised, suggesting fragmentation, but instead of shifting the planes to reveal new relations they keep relations firmly in place. Shading is retained to augment the appearance of unity.

This solidity, this almost sculptural quality, is the hallmark of Hungarian Cubism. Besides Kmetty, his friend and fellow-student, Peter Dobrović, painted a rather similar self-portrait in 1913 and his nude studies also show the same approach. A couple of years later the nude studies of József Nemes Lampérth are still indebted to Kmetty's interpretation of Cubism: although his use of colour is nearer to Fauvism, the heavy bands of pinks and beiges accentuate the forms of the solid, almost monumental, figures. Apart from portraits and nudes, Kmetty painted a series of landscapes with greatly simplified forms and prismatic colours (*Kecskemét*, 1912). The main feature of Cubism in Hungary is, nevertheless, the powerful presence and the immobility of the depicted object, a calm, imperturbable harmony which evokes Renaissance or neo-Classicist sculpture.

In contrast to the limited subject matter of Hungarian Cubist paintings, Czech Cubism presented a wide range of topics, including mythological, biblical and religious themes. Douglas Cooper in his succinct summary of Czech Cubism suggests that this thematic approach connects it with Expressionism and assumes that even a title may signify a deeper meaning, for example, Špála's painting, *The Song of the Countryside* (1914), which at first sight seems to be no more than a fine Cubist landscape.[7] Between 1911 and 1915, the years which roughly demarcate the Czech Cubist movement, the paintings of Filla, Procházka, Kubišta, Beneš, Špála and Josef Čapek and the sculpture of Otto Gutfreund stand out.

The first paintings of Emil Filla and Antonín Procházka, exhibited with the radical group of 'Eight' in 1907 in Prague, still show the influence of Munch but with more than a hint of some inherent movement. In Procházka's *Street* there is a gentle swaying of the shadowy figures which creates a slow rhythm. This is especially discernible in the pencil drawing of the same subject. In Filla's *Reader of Dostoyevsky* the composition of the swooning seated figure is based on the diagonal, although the window-frame in the upper right-hand field of the picture provides a strong balance and checks its diagonal thrust. Within three years both painters arrive at the threshold of Cubism without diminishing their interest in dynamic composition. The composition of both Filla's *Good Samaritan* and Procházka's

Prometheus are based on a strong, upward-moving zigzag line. The broken surfaces in Procházka's painting clearly indicate an attempt at introducing Cubist analysis, but the sheer force of the movement reduces it to a secondary, almost incidental feature. Another example is offered in Beneš's *Susanna in the Bath* (1910). It is only two years later than Filla's painting, *The Bathers* marries dynamism and Cubism successfully: this is perhaps the first example of an emerging national school. The dynamic composition stems directly from the Baroque; it is revealing that Filla shared with many of his colleagues a profound interest in the works of El Greco. Their source of the composition was, however, primarily the still vibrant tradition of Czech Baroque, imbued in the Czechs from childhood and fostered to conscious acceptance by patriotic aspirations which used the Baroque heritage to strengthen the awareness of national identity.

It is customary to equate this dynamism with Expressionism, that is to characterise Czech and Austrian Expressionism as the liberation of Self through empathy with Baroque vision. In contrast, in German Expressionism it is achieved through the expressive qualities of the medieval woodcuts. It is true that German Expressionism, especially the artists of *Die Brücke*, always maintained the primacy of spirituality in art and regarded the Gothic form as one of the chief vehicles of its expression. Kokoschka also regarded the spiritual, imaginary and visual experience of Baroque frescoes as of paramount importance. It may, however, be hazarded that the acceptance of Czech Baroque as the foremost national heritage played at least as equivalent a role in the creation of dynamic Cubism in Bohemia as it served as the vehicle to express the inner man. Spirituality is often associated with exaltation, even with tortured anguish; in Czech dynamic Cubism it may appear in the guise of pure joy. In Václav Špála's paintings the blue and red shapes seem to dance to some exuberant rhythm (*The Song of the Countryside*, 1914; *Washerwomen*, 1915). Moreover, his colour-harmonies owe more to Czech folk art than to Orphism; it was Špála's work that induced Nebeský in 1937 to describe Prague Cubism as a national movement.[8]

The later development of Czech Cubism may be summarised as a movement away from this unique form to a much closer adherence to the French analytical trend: by 1913–14 the fragmentation of the picture surface is complete; the construction is less agitated and calmness gains ground. When round forms are introduced (Procházka: *Coffee-pot*, 1913; *The Singer*, 1916), they counterbalance each other and the movement is no more than a surface ripple. In 1914 the Group of (avant-garde) Artists break up; Filla spends the war years in Holland, Gutfreund is caught in France and Kubišta dies in 1918. Nevertheless, Czech Cubism demonstrated that openness to external influences and eagerness to receive what is regarded as the latest trend in art do not result in mindless imitation. French Cubism in Bohemia, and to a lesser degree in Hungary, served as inspiration, a creative force in the formulation of an individual, independent modern art.

The artists of both countries shared a readiness to absorb trends which had originated elsewhere. This was a symptom common to most central-European cultures. Yet, when the same artists adhered to a movement and accepted a style, they transformed it and created an art which differed from country to country. I would be going beyond the scope of this chapter to try to examine the origins and components of the so-called national character in art. Central-European Cubism, nevertheless, might demonstrate that an approach to the study of the art of the Habsburg Monarchy from the angle of the 'geography of art', if I may use the expression employed by Nikolaus Pevsner in his pioneering work, *The Englishness of English Art*, would not be without its merits.

NOTES

1. Allan Janik and Stephen Toulmin, *Wittgenstein's Vienna*, London, 1973, pp. 94–8.
2. József Csáky, *Emlékek a modern mű vészet nagy évtizedéből*, Budapest, 1972, *passim*.
3. János Kmetty, *Őnéletrajz*, 1972. In Kmetty, *Festő voltam és vagyok: Kmetty János írásai*, Budapest, 1976, pp. 69–71.
4. Ibid., p. 73.
5. Miroslav Lamač, *Modern Czech Painting 1907–1917*, Prague, 1967, p. 9.
6. Lajos Fülep, *Lajos Tihanyi: The Portrait on its Painter*, 1918. In the catalogue *The Hungarian Avant-Garde: the Eight and the Activists*. Exhibition, Hayward Gallery, London, 1980, pp. 109–111.
7. Douglas Cooper. *The Cubist Epoch*, London, 1971, p. 152.
8. Václav Nebeský, *L'Art moderne tchécoslovaque*, Paris, 1937, p. 24.

10

The Self: Destruction or Synthesis, Two Problems of Czech Art at the Turn of the Century

PETR WITTLICH

In the Austro-Hungarian Empire at the turn of the century political problems inspired by the national question were on the increase. In particular the Language Ordinances pronounced by the Austrian Prime Minister, Casimir Badeni, led, in the years 1897–99, to an outburst of nationalist passion. Middle-class Czech politics represented by the Young Czech Party vacillated between vociferous obstruction and tacit support of the Vienna government. That Party's combination of militant patriotism and opportunism disgusted those young members of the Czech intelligentsia who had come to public notice as early as 1895 in the Manifesto of the Czech *Moderna*. Writers like F. X. Šalda, Antonín Sova, Otokar Březina or J. S. Machar demanded there that art be true to life and individual within the scope of a broadly conceived right to criticism. Humanity takes precedence over nationality. They replaced a demagogic idea of the unity of the nation with the demand for self-determination, for the free individuality they considered to be the only rational basis for a prosperous national collective.

This manifest contradiction between politics and culture was something new in the history of the Czech national movement. During the nineteenth century the two had been indivisibly linked. The new situation, when men of letters began standing on their own feet, even in the field of politics, was then connected with the crisis of the hitherto valid notion of a 'national art'.

In the fine arts this idea was successfully conceptualised as early as the 1860s by the painter Josef Mánes (1820–71). This late Romantic, who was fond of Raphael, used to paint for various Czech clubs and associations the then popular ceremonial banners. Among these the banner of the Říp Association (1864) excels in its brilliance of colour and the graphicness of the figures set in an ornament inspired by Romanesque illuminations. Mánes may, in many respects, be reminiscent of the pre-Raphaelites; especially in his combination of figures and ornament and in his interest in applied art, he prefigures the art style of the turn of the century.

Alphonse Mucha, who later in the 1890s participated in the development of the Paris Art Nouveau, consciously took up Mánes's initiative. Mucha saw the figure in a much more modern, flat way, thus attaining a higher degree of integration between the figure and its ornamental background. Later, this connection became, after Mucha's exhibition in Prague in 1897, the starting-point of artistically advanced Czech production, primarily in commercial art, but also in the stucco work of Prague urban architecture; thus it provided the impetus at the beginning of the century for a whole complex of environmental art. Prague Art Nouveau was, first, a fashionable and, later, a popular affair.

As early as Mánes the noble idealism of 'national art' would include a personal stratum of creativity. Something of that is evident in his drawing, *The Artist's Dream*. It was created as a privatissimum enclosed in the artist's letter to his patron, the industrialist, Lanna. The exhaustion of the dreaming artist indicates the immense sacrifices which lay behind his 'ideal art' and prefigured his sorrowful end. The replica of the banner of St George originated in the final stage of Manes's mental illness. In that work the relations between the figures are markedly changed. Comparison of the replica with the original suggests a psychoanalytical consideration of the loss of the supremacy of the super-ego at the price of the reversible identification of the ego – the knight with the liberated, demonised Id. There is no space in this chapter, however, for a detailed Freudian exposition.

The reason I have been speaking of Mánes is that he was accepted by the younger Czech artists as their potential model, as an artist with the highest of moral values. The *fin-de-siècle* generation named after him their artists' association which, in its creative as well as its organisational activities, laid the foundations of a truly Czech modern art.

Mánes's reputation had been slowly becoming established since the 1870s by Czech art critics, particularly by Miroslav Tyrš. Nevertheless Tyrš was keener on emphasising the neo-Classicist elements of Mánes's art, while the artists beginning in the 1870s, like the painter Mikoláš Aleš or the sculptor J. V. Myslbek, had understood Mánes's legacy in a more Romantic spirit. It was these two, the most productive, followers of Mánes who were in the end excluded from participating in the most prestigious 'cultural' undertaking of that time, the decoration of the National Theatre in Prague.[1]

They had to yield both to artists of a socially more conventional style and to painters who had gained their skills in Paris, having impressed the critics as well as the public by their craft. The difference in opinion on art may be best shown by comparing the coloured drawing *Žalov* by Aleš, a design through which he in vain applied for the right to carry out his cycle of *lunettes*, *The Myth of the Motherland*, in the foyer of the National Theatre, with the curtain which was eventually painted by Vojtěch Hynais in 1883. Aleš's drawing is highly emotional: from the artistic point of view, colour is submitted to line. Hynais's curtain (in Paris Hynais was the pupil of Gérôme) is socially effective especially because of its illusive form and its mastering of the whole in an elegant pinkish grey tone. This contradiction of idealistic stylisation, derived from Romanticism, and illusionistic colourism became the complex main element in Czech 'national art' at the end of the nineteenth century.

In the 1890s Hynais moved to Prague as professor in the Academy of Fine Arts. His illusionist Naturalism was considered the last word in modern art although his neo-Romantically minded colleagues used to make wicked jokes about the 'green reflexions' which could not be washed off the bodies of his models. He was, however, praised even by the ideologists of 'national art' for his 'noble sensualism' (Tyrš) as well as for his successes in international competitions.

Aleš, who at that time was living a wretched life, once drew a caricature of the mad Mánes as a gigantic figure with a burning candle in his hand crossing in daylight the Old Town Square in Prague and taking no notice of the petty-bourgeois crowd. Among the dwarfs at his feet we recognise Christian Ruben, the former German director of the Prague Academy, who had a fracas with Mánes as early as the 1840s, when he was introducing narrative historicism in the Düsseldorf manner to Prague.

It is notable that this drawing apparently inspired younger artists in 1900 as they tendered for the Jan Hus (John Huss) monument in Prague. The sculptor Stanislav Sucharda and the architect Kotěra submitted similar projects in which the gigantic figure of Hus contrasts with a tiny *staffage* at the foot of the monument.

The identification of Mánes with Hus, of the artist of genius with the great fifteenth-century religious and moral reformer and martyr, who was one of the primary figures for Czech historicism in the nineteenth century, indicated the striving for a (national) type replete in multifarious semantic content. The importance of this concentration on the typological is increased by the fact that as early as 1892 the sculptor František Bílek had made use of the compositional scheme of one large central figure and of several smaller figures in an expressively Naturalistic sculpture, *Tillage is the Punishment of our Guilt*, which constituted the grounds for the withdrawal of the scholarship previously granted to him to go to Paris by commission of the Prague Academy; this sculpture thus became the first major confrontation of the new generation with the art Establishment.

The common feature of Aleš's *Mánes*, Sucharda's and Kotěra's *Hus* and Bílek's *Christ* was the moral conflict between the self-sacrificing individual of high moral qualities and the mire of human pettiness. The conception almost programmatically comprised the suffering and death of the hero. (*Fin-de-siècle* culture had a great deal to do with dying, cf. the 'Conclusory Essay' to this volume.) The pathos of form which more or less rebuked the audience had considerable significance. Contrary to the self-conscious tone of the writers' Manifesto, the modern individualist problem has been treated here with a wingeing about moral deficiency and the conflict between ideal and reality.

The irritation and scepticism which dominated gained not only individualist but also absolutist status. That may be illustrated by comparing another of Bílek's sculptures, his *Jan Hus* of 1901, with Edvard Munch's *The Scream*, which may, in all probability, be considered the sculpture's model. *The Scream* was, in its lithographic version, reproduced by the leading Czech Decadents' journal, *Moderní revue*, in 1897. If we accept Munch's picture as an exemplary version of modern existential sensations, the sense of anxiety, we become, at the same time, aware that Bílek is attempting to establish an antithesis, to give an explanation that would, in also recalling the mystical tradition and native Baroque art, transfer the 'trauma' of this anxiety to the level of metaphysical hope.

Especially in the case of sculptors, who by the very nature of their work tended towards monumentality, we observe an endeavour to overcome the states of melancholy and existential stress that were strongly evident in the young Czech artists of the later 1890s; many of them had a compelling urge to commit suicide. Masaryk had written of suicide as a social phenomenon threatening European civilisation. Among Czech writers and artists the relation to Decadence (a discussion of the idea of Decadence took place in Prague in 1895) and to Symbolism became a key issue in anti-nationalist cosmopolitan pessimism. The newly discovered modern 'individual' fought against the sexual taboos of bourgeois liberal society and tried to resolve the social problems of contemporary industrial society by echoing anarchist doctrines (Karel Hlaváček, František Kupka). In trying to find symbols for their disgust at the 'mire' of social reality there developed something in the artistic imagination which I could call the sidereal complex.

It was becoming obvious in the frequent occurrence of cosmic themes philosophically based on the rediscovered neo-Platonic symbolics of light. Bílek, in a further reaction to Munch's 1905 Prague exhibition, cut down the more-than-life-size statue *The Amazement*, which had been inspired by an occultist vision of the beauties of the Universe. With Kupka the initial contradiction between Naturalism and idealism was, possibly, absolutised entirely unconventionally in his break-through into abstract art in *The Cosmic Spring*.

Yet another tendency was present, of a more synthetic character, a tendency which tried to solve the conflict between idealism and Naturalism in quite a different way, even as far as theme was concerned; it did that by plunging down to earth. Landscape painting acquired immeasurably more importance in Czech Modernism than it did, for example, in Viennese art. The typological concentration on landscape art was directed on the *motif* of the lake. The *motif* of the lake became the nucleus of typological concentration. This fact is clearly distinguished in a series of pictures: first, Otakar Lebeda's *Lake in the Giant Mountains* (1896), secondly Antonín Hudeček's *Evening Silence* (1900), thirdly Jan Preisler's *The Black Lake* (1904). Here the lake, viewed typically from above, serves as a symbol for the secrets of the Earth; at the same time it constitutes a pictorial parallel to the contemporaneous literary interest in man's unconscious and to the psychoanalytical problem of narcissism. It may well be observed within the series how the originally still Naturalist landscape has been combined with a human figure (Hudeček) and how in this way a typical thematic *motif* has been evoked, a *motif* which could potentially be further stylised and submitted to *motif* abstraction as, for example, in the case of Preisler. In Preisler that occurred with his immediate echo of *The Poor Fisherman* of Puvis de Chavannes.

Symbolism of this kind initiated a process of reform in Czech 'national art' and it did that in connection with fashionable ideas like, for example, Nietzsche's 'faithfulness to the Earth'. The first such synthesis of Naturalist and idealist views was Preisler's triptych, *Spring* (1900), characteristically destined for the rooms of the first truly modern Art Nouveau building in Prague, a building designed by Kotěra. By its very title this picture allegorised the epoch of the new blossoming of Czech art, which was to take place in the years to come.

The authenticity of this attitude may best be demonstrated by another series of three mutually connected pictures by Preisler. This first of them, *Landscape with Boulders*, originated in 1898 as a straightforward landscape sketch. The second, the pastel, *The Knight and the Fairy* (1901), was inspired by chivalrous symbolism which was at that time very much *à la mode*. The third, the final *Picture from a Larger Cycle* (1902), transfers the *motif* into a 'native' scenery. Preisler did not consciously establish a relationship between the first and the other two pictures, but the transformation of the two boulders into two figures took place as an organic process of imagination. Simultaneously there arose a synthesis between Naturalistically (the first case) and idealistically (the second) orientated imagination. The result was that the third large picture acquired quite new formal and contentual qualities. Still, because of its non-tonal conception of colour, it is considered the first really modern picture in Czech art.

Preisler's new synthesis of two at first sight particularly heterogeneous elements comprising not only the slogans of the day – Naturalism, idealism or Symbolism – but also the real integration of the sensual and intellectual abilities of creative man, has, because of the degree of formal unity attained, been ever since considered the new lasting value of Czech modern art. Such a unity must be constantly re-created picture after picture, individually, so that it can be perceived as something living.

When such a conception was to be transferred into the collective style-idiom, however, some problems surfaced in the form of decorativism or, later, neo-Classicism. Nature was then changing into a garden (as Schorske shows in his assessment of turn-of-the-century Vienna). The later generation of Expressionists protested, however, in the name of renewed contact with the fertile soil of the eternal struggle between idea and life. So even Czech art arrived at the formal shock caused by the Group of Eight, the leading representative of whom, Emil Filla, with his picture, *The Reader of Dostoyevsky* (1907), abruptly renewed the problem of Decadence; the theme of his picture may well be connected with the final passage of Huysmans's *A rebours*.

But in the consciousness of Czech artists there prevailed, even in this situation, the endeavour to grasp modern art collectively. Therefore in Bohemia before World War I Cubism was clearly understood as the problem of style uniting the work not only of the painter and sculptor, but also of the architect and designer.[2] The specific dynamic form of Czech Cubism, differing both from the analytical, and from the synthetical Paris formulae, shows that the notion of synthesis formulated earlier by Art Nouveau had once again become debatable. Any discussion of the extent to which the sidereal complex of Art Nouveau was projected into the crystallising of Czech Cubism, and how loyalty to the Earth in Art Nouveau transported its organic tension into Cubist dynamics would, however, go beyond the limits of this chapter.

The destruction of the object carried out by Cubism was outweighed by the new synthesis of style. So even here, in the preceding Art Nouveau, Czech developments confirmed the idea of the essential inner relationship between decay and innovation.

NOTES

1. Cf. Tomáš Vlček, 'National Sensualism: Czech *Fin-de-Siècle* Art', in László Péter and Robert B. Pynsent (Eds), *Intellectuals and the Future in the Habsburg Monarchy, 1890–1914*, London, 1988, p. 107 ff.
2. Cf. Magda Czigány's chapter in this volume.

11

The Significance of
Czech Fin-de-Siècle
Criticism

JIŘÍ KUDRNÁČ

This chapter focuses on the semantics of Czech *fin-de-siècle* literature by identifying keywords which link literary and extraliterary contexts. The concept 'criticism' constitutes the first fundamental keyword in the *fin-de-siècle* epistemology of art. The concept not only denotes a dominant literary genre but also describes the basic standpoint of the period. The second fundamental concept is the functional syncretism of Czech *fin-de-siècle* literature. The other keywords traced in this survey concern specific rather than general features.

Czech *fin-de-siècle* literature is predominantly the literature of the '1890s generation', the generation whose members began to publish mainly at the beginning of the 1890s and who formed a reasonably consistent unit from that time to the first decade of the twentieth century. The Czech *fin-de-siècle* atmosphere began, however, to be created as early as the late 1880s and was later preserved in a substantial part of literature as one of the dominant tendencies up to the beginning of the 1920s, when it possibly represented little but history for the new conceptions which were energetically thrusting themselves onto the scene. Czech *fin-de-siècle* literature was created by authors belonging to three generations, born between 1850 (T. G. Masaryk) and 1890 (Rudolf Medek). The basic features of *fin-de-siècle* literature were formed between the end of the 1880s and the end of the 1900s; after that its *raison d'être* began to be diminished, and any enrichment of its canon by younger authors, who persisted as its advocates, were exceptional (Otakar Theer, born 1880, Miloš Marten, born 1883, Arthur Breisky, born 1885).

The leading groups to create *fin-de-siècle* literature were formed in the late 1880s and early 1890s. A consciousness of identity appears very quickly, apparently as a result of similar attempts made before them, spontaneous, but unsuccessful attempts, in which major figures of true *fin-de-siècle* literature, F. X. Šalda, Vilém Mrštík, Antonín Sova and Hubert Gordon Schauer, had participated.[1]

The first of the groups among the creators of the Czech literary *fin-de-siècle* movement are the Realists, as they called themselves, comprising the theorists and critics T. G. Masaryk, Hubert Gordon Schauer, Jan Herben, Gustav Jaroš ('Gamma'), Jindřich Vodák and Josef Laichter. There is a justifiable view that the type of literary Realism propagated by these 'Realists' corresponds to contemporary Czech philosophical Positivism, which itself is influenced by the *fin-de-siècle* atmosphere.[2] The position of most of the Realist writers of the time, whose works correspond, to a certain extent, to the requirements voiced by these critics and the position of the critics themselves, were similarly transitory: besides the elements common to all *fin-de-siècle* literature, moralising utilitarianism or sentimental *genrisme* can be found on both sides. The most constructive elements of these theoretists' views led them to seek out and propagate the principles of 'modern' literature in works of such individual authors as the Russians Dostoyevsky and Tolstoy and the Czech Němcová. Not all the contemporary Czech literature these 'Realist' critics publicised actually belonged to the *Fin de siècle*; J. S. Machar and Petr Bezruč are exceptions.

The second group is represented by the *Česká moderna* or Czech *Moderna*, whose manifesto was signed by, among others, F. X. Šalda, F. V. Krejčí, Machar and Vilém Mrštík. The manifesto declared art to be subjectively experienced and original, without 'realistic, flat objectivity' and without any mechanical fulfilment of other, even the most fashionably artistic, programmes.[3] In fact, it stated the general principles of modern artistic creation; to a certain extent it echoed the conclusion of Šalda's earlier programmatic essay *Synthetism v novém umění* (Syntheticism in modern art). This group soon disintegrated, mainly for personal reasons. In fact all prose writers, poets and dramatists who did not actually create socially disorientating art and did not blatantly connect their art with a religious idea could fulfil the literary part of the *Moderna*'s programme. After the disintegration of this group, the problem of the interdependence of life and art was worked on by Šalda and Krejčí, each in his own manner; there was also Jan Vorel, who soon began gradually to disappear from literary consciousness.

The third group of writers was that concentrated around the periodical *Moderní revue*, founded in 1894. Its theorists were Arnošt Procházka, Jiří Karásek ze Lvovic and, later, Miloš Marten. This periodical came nearest of all to programmatic Decadence, Symbolism and aestheticism. The abilities of its critics were, however, by no means limited to a mere fulfilment of the standards demanded by fashionable trends. *Moderní revue* was the most prestigious of Czech *fin-de-siècle* journals and most innovative authors of the period published there.

The fourth group was given the name *Katolická moderna* (Roman Catholic *Moderna*); it adopted the programme published in the periodical, *Niva*, in 1895 by Sigismund Bouška, its leading critic. In 1896 the newly founded periodical, *Nový život*, became the organ of the *Katolická moderna*. The poet-ideologist of *Katolická moderna* was Xaver Dvořák.

Karel Dostál-Lutinov, a minor poet and polemicist, was editor of *Nový život*; he was, thanks to his many-sided practical activity and also to his effort to reach the widest possible public, called with enthusiastic exaggeration 'our Catholic Havlíček'.[4] The artistic programme of the Catholic *Moderna* was influenced by fashionable artistic trends, especially Symbolism and Impressionism, but it also followed the tenets of naive, traditional Realism. Subjectively strong Catholicism was a necessary condition for all artists belonging to this movement. The successful activation of Roman Catholicism which the Catholic *Moderna* managed to achieve also resulted from the aesthetic value of traditional Catholic ritual which was perceived at the end of the century to be artistically creative as well as receptive. The group had, besides its direct members, also culturally significant sympathisers like Julius Zeyer, Otokar Březina, and, later, Jiří Karásek.

The functional syncretism of Czech *fin-de-siècle* literature had its predecessor in the National Revival. The literature of the Revival expressed Czech interests both cultural and political (when Czech politicians actually did not exist): thus, it assisted in the constitution of both the Czech nation and Czech national policy. The fact of the existence of literature written in 'the national language' was of political significance, just as scholarly literature on Czech matters written at first in other languages was politically significant. From the 1840s onwards Czech national policy begins to develop fully and the period from the end of the 1840s to the mid-1850s is now generally understood as the period when the Czech literary Revival was consolidated. In that period the link between literature and politics reaches its firmest point. Leading politicians of various persuasions, conservatives, liberals and radical democrats, were major men of letters. Josef Jireček, Wácslav Wladivoj Tomek, František Palacký, Karel Havlíček, Josef Václav Frič and Emanuel Arnold. Nothing like that ever occurred again.[5]

After the constitution of an official Czech national policy, the question of the adequate assimilation of the cultural programme which existed (and which had been launched by the Jungmann school in the middle of the National Revival) with a practical political programme remained to be broached. The 1860s, 1870s and 1880s were marked by the penetration of political journalism into poetry[6] which then, however, communicated rather as journalism than as poetry. Fiction with its artistic devices was thus coming close to everyday politics at the cost of art, a fact for which Šalda rebuked even Neruda, whom he considered the noblest practitioner of literature in the previous three decades.[7] Other writers of the 1890s reproached their predecessors for the same thing. At the same time representatives of the *fin-de-siècle* movement criticised the usurping of the whole of Czech public opinion by predatory political journalism which, they said, had been prone to dilettantism,[8] and had imputed to culture the political tactics of so-called 'bittiness', the stage-by-stage politics which was pursued successively by the Old Czech and then the Young Czech Party.

In this situation *fin-de-siècle* literature was syncretic with a new vitality, as if it had returned to the original exploratory methods of the National Revival; it covered the whole of national life. The Literary criticism in magazines assumed fundamental constitutive importance and, necessarily, also a polemical character; it followed all aspects of national life. The *fin-de-siècle* movement rejected bad journalism, but by no means journalism as such. Journalism was, because of its comprehensiveness and complex authorial self-communication, 'a new literary form complying with the needs of the present time', as Masaryk said in praise of Dostoyevsky.[9]

From the end of the 1880s to the mid-1890s a number of analytical and programmatic articles appeared which deduce the *fin-de-siècle* literary programme from the contemporary state of society and culture in the Bohemian Lands and abroad. Generalising analyses are contained in reviews of individual works of fiction, verse and drama. It was mostly the journals, where the predominant part of *fin-de-siècle* literature was published, that were responsible for literary development. Journals dealing with fiction and art functioned, without exception, syncretically as did the book series founded along with them. It was in the periodicals that the reform of Czech scholarship was postulated and, in some of them, also effected; that was in programmatic connection with the reform of fiction. Czech *fin-de-siècle* journals thus serve as material of primary importance for literary history.

Literature was conceived as a phenomenon of general import and as an implement of change. Philosophical and political problems were discussed even in the works of writers who were later labelled practitioners of *l'art pour l'art*. In prose, the general and shallow, although topically motivated, emotionality of the *genre* Realists was superseded by thoughtful, original *fin-de-siècle* works: Viktor Dyk's political novels and short-stories, Karásek's *Gothická duše*, the short-stories and novels of Růžena Svobodová and Vilém Mrštík, and Březina's essays. The novel as such was conceived of as a genre with syncretic possibilities.[10] The same possibilities were found in the essay, which underwent a decisive development during the *Fin de siècle*.[11] Czech *fin-de-siècle* literature revives the imaginary conversation (Marten, Karásek, Dyk, Breisky) as well as the expression of emphatic personal moralities (J. K. Šlejhar, K. M. Čapek-Chod) and the closet drama. In contrast to the earlier neo-Revivalist allegorical style and journalistic generalisations, the new political poetry was both ideologically comprehensive and artistically concrete (Machar, Sova, Dyk, S. K. Neumann, Bezruč). Numerous collections of very hard-hitting, pointed political and literary satire were published by, apart from the authors I have mentioned, Jan Váňa, Ludvík Lošťák, Dostál-Lutinov and the members of the younger generation which is sometimes called the generation of Anarchists and Rebels.

Fin-de-siècle criticism is occasional, topical and comprehensive in its themes. Indeed, Czech *fin-de-siècle* critics were prolific authors. Features of journalism and impressionist, 'Dilettante', criticism combined with an aversion to all speculative systems. Artistic and journalistic sensitivity joined in an effort to introduce an empirical aesthetics. The criticism which thus grew from the treatment of individual works of art can also be characterised as a permanent striving for an unachievable methodology. Šalda considered himself to be an occasional critic; Karásek is said to have become a critic as a result of his hatred of bad books.[12] Krejčí's aim was the everyday work of spreading culture.[13] Vodák did not publish a real book during his life, while Bouška did not publish a single collection of his literary criticism. The more or less unknown critical work of Jan Vorel is forgotten in the journals of the period. Procházka and Masaryk's formulations are characteristic; they are painfully conscious of the apparent contradictoriness of occasional criticism and of the semantic fragmentariness of individual critical assessments in the context of their maximalist aims.[14]

Fin-de-siècle criticism thus perceived a pertinent aspect of any *Geisteswissenschaft*: its apparent fragmentariness, which was sensed by the authors themselves, should not be regarded as a squandering of talent.[15] *Fin-de-siècle* literary criticism in fact constitutes one of the strongest elements in modern Czech culture.

The whole decade of the formation of the *fin-de-siècle* literary movement initially appears to comprise little but ideological negativism. Instigations to such a classification originated in the young critics themselves, because of their own bitter condemnation of the national status quo. Jan Herben appears to support the view in his memoirs with the now all too familiar words: 'Later on I was frequently asked what kind of positive programme the journal *Čas* had. I do not know what to say. Our battle cry was: Castigate! Castigate everything that was dishonourable, false and rotten, in our opinion.'[16] This grand-sounding slogan shows one aspect of *Čas* and general *fin-de-siècle* activity. A second aspect consisted in a replacing or rebuilding of everything that was castigated. Thus the term 'revolutionary', which was frequently applied to literary and extraliterary activities in the *Fin de siècle* is justified.

The self-conscious claim to authenticity preceded and conditioned the formulation of the 'new beauty', which was born out of the *Fin de siècle*.[17] Creative authenticity was supposed to be a condition for the literary work's capacity of communication. Communication does not exclude disagreement (cf. the reception and rejection of Zola); on the other hand the propagation of some of the new authors and older authorities and practical empirical aesthetics, a distrustful attitude towards Herbart's aesthetics as well as a thoroughly negative attitude towards contemporary Czech politics, came to much the same thing. In a part of the generation the concepts 'authenticity' and 'morality' almost fused: literature is individually moral, provided it is authentic; thus it is not, even cannot be, moral in the previous, nondifferentiated sense, claimed Arnošt Procházka.[18] Hence the contemporary influence of Czech literature of the Wildean theory of lies and hence also the amount on self-stylisation; the latter fact was noticed, for example, by Šalda.[19] Authentic morality is a criterion typical of Masaryk and his friends and disciples, as well as of the growing artistically and ecclesiastically heretical tendencies of young clergymen and laymen in the Catholic *Moderna*. The entire activity of the writers linked with or coming near to Social Democracy constitutes a gradual formulation of a new, 'proletarian' morality.

The views of the *fin-de-siècle* movement are formulated within the contemporary and previous crises of Czech society and culture. *Fin-de-siècle* intellectuals laid the blame for these crises in the Bohemian Lands on liberalism, and liberalism's effect on the political practice of the Old Czech and the Young Czech Parties. In his works written at the end of the century, T. G. Masaryk repeatedly renounces the politics of national liberalism and sets it up as the opposite of his Realism. To him liberalism is 'belly-filling', pragmatic, morally 'indifferentist' and philosophically shallow. It reduces Masaryk's notion of a desirable continuity with the Reformation: 'we must regenerate above all morally – and it is this task that liberalism is not fit for.' 'The question is, either a true and profound conviction of the tasks set for a man's life or not; all other questions are subordinate to this.'[20]

Masaryk, predominantly a practical politician, at first wanted to regenerate the Old Czech as well as the Young Czech Party with his Realism; he did not, however, have much success. His contemporaries saw a similar topical political means in the manifesto of the Czech *Moderna*.[21] The part of the Manifesto devoted to politics aims sharp bolts at the Young Czech Party and, even approaches socialist ideas. Anarchism was the political confession of the Decadents.[22] The Catholic *Moderna* tended towards a certain 'liberalisation'. Nevertheless its first task, both artistic and political, was: 'That the Church, Roman Catholicism, should regain its leading role in Europe in culture and life, the role it had held in the Middle Ages.'[23] This group rejected any integration into a clerical political movement.[24]

F. V. Krejčí was a leading Social Democrat and the attitudes of Social Democracy were supported by other young writers by concrete action.[25] The aim was to embark on a practical policy which held fast to the goal, was self-confident and philosophically substantiated, did not embrace opportunism as a principle,[26] or strive for political power which its representatives could not make use of.[27] It was in the mid-1890s that a number of new political parties came into existence.[28] Most of these were interested in young writers, who actually joined in their activities, indeed sometimes assisted in their formation.

The general conditions and principles of original, modern creative activity were commonly postulated in the *fin-de-siècle* manifestos and declarations.

Young writers considered those Czech authors who had previously complied with the requirements put forward in the manifestos to be their legitimate predecessors. They agreed on Mácha, Němcová, Neruda, whom literary scholars of a hundred years later still tend to evaluate as the most 'modern' authors of their times.[29] On the other hand, *fin-de-siècle* men of letters felt it necessary to distance themselves from authors who had been overvalued.

Particularly in the polemics over Vrchlický, aesthetic and philosophical eclecticism was attacked, and with the same arguments which young critics had used to attack political liberalism.

The declaration of necessary requirements for artistic creation involved an emphasis on the works of those *fin-de-siècle* authors who were to realise these requirements, and did so from the beginning of their literary activity. Therefore contemporary criticism, when offering examples of the realisation of principles, besides the names of major foreign authors like Goethe, Baudelaire, Dostoyevsky, Verlaine, Balzac, Stendhal and Ibsen, and besides rare references to older Czech authors, also often quotes Czech *fin-de-siècle* authors, young writers and by no means always first-rate writers. These authors refused to accuse themselves of imitating their ideals; they considered themselves capable of realising the aims they held in common with their models.[30]

For *fin-de-siècle* authors liberalism and eclecticism were two faces of the same disappearing world. Their own aestheticism was intended to be of a different nature from Vrchlický's aesthetic eclecticism. It was considered a philosophically based, consistent observation from an aesthetic point of view and no longer the product of an epistemological vacuum.

In outlining and realising their cultural programme *fin-de-siècle* writers were 'intolerant'; they did not accept anyone who did not comply with their requirements. There is a similar degree of 'voluntarism' in that stance as there had been in the mid-Revival Jungmannian programme, which was suddenly building genuine 'artistic' literature and 'national' scholarship as if out of nothing.

The Czech *fin-de-siècle* cultural programme is willing to dispense with neither individual nor group requirements. The theorists of anarchism, socialism and communism, together with Nietzsche and other writers, outlined a new type of leading personality.[31] It overshadowed the surviving cult of national leaders, which had asserted itself in Czech public life over the previous fifty or so years, however autocratic and sentimentalist it was in the end.

The auras surrounding František Palacký, a 'father of the nation', and F. L. Rieger, the 'leader of the nation', were exceptional. Even for Jaroslav Goll, a sober historian, 'the joint names Palacký and Rieger had an inexpressible magic.'[32] Opposition journalists attacked the bearers of the cult rather than the cult itself.[33] The cult compensated the Czechs for the loss of a Czech king they could honour. The last but one Austrian Emperor was never crowned King of Bohemia. The nimbus of a king and a kingdom was a subject for historical sentimentalisation in almost all literature concerning Czech history.

Towards the end of the century regular constitutional demurrers put in by the Czech members of the Austrian parliament were also of a platonic nature. Czech politicians intended solving the Czech question within the Austro-Slav framework. In reality, before the *Fin de siècle* Czech historical sentimentalism could assert itself in fiction to an increasing degree (cf. the flourishing of Czech historical fiction in the second half of the century), whereas its continuation as a feature of actual life into the present gradually assumed grotesque features. The logical relation of clever writers from the period preceding the *Fin de siècle* to the actualisations of history was ambiguous, as can be seen from the contrast introduced in the historical writing of Svatopluk Čech, the way he measures the present against the past in *Nový epochální výlet pana Broučka, tentokrát do XV. století* (Mr Brouček's new epoch-making excursion, this time into the 15th century), and from the national allegorising and mysticising of two collections of political lyrics, both of which were greatly praised, *Písně otroka* (Slave songs) by Svatopluk Čech and *Zpěvy páteční* (Friday hymns) by Jan Neruda. One may see the alienation of history from real life in the sensitive historical dramas and poems of Jaroslav Vrchlický when one compares those with his political opinions and his inactivity in the Vienna Upper House. Finally, one can see it in the negativism of contemporary political life, which Julius Zeyer professed with conviction.

The cult of leaders wore itself out along with F. L. Rieger's retreat from fame. The illusion of national unity which the Young Czech party aimed at achieving after its victory in the elections had but a brief life. The democratic modesty of Karel Sladkovský (a radical democrat from the year of revolutions, 1848) was, as a matter of fact, exceptional at the initial stages of the Young Czech party.[34] Julius Grégr's brief path to the forefront of national politics was an attempt at prolonging autocracy in political leadership.[35] It was a result both of the adroit policy of his party against the 'Punctationen', or Czech-German Compromise of 1890, and of the inner decay of the Old Czech Party during the enforcement of the 'Punctationen'. The image of Karel Kramář as a national leader of the old type (he claimed to be such a leader long after the turn of the century) was only the pious hope of an unselfcritical, unrealistic politician and his partisans.[36]

Features of a leadership of a new type were obviously contained in the image of T. G. Masaryk, which had been constructed in the *Fin de siècle* and which were eventually canonised in the notion 'philosopher enthroned' by Karel Čapek.[37]

The representatives of *fin-de-siècle* culture were not seeking an autocratic leader, and where they saw tendencies to autocracy, even among their own generation, they tried to neutralise them. They promoted the notion of sovereign individuals collectively working on a programme for the emancipation of the rest. The process of integrating the Nietzschean personality into social revolution was shown, perhaps, most faithfully in the writings of Antonín Macek, that most cultured representative of contemporary 'worker' poetry; Macek might be compared with William Morris. The *fin-de-siècle* leader bears in himself the split personality of his transitional age and is seeking at least as frequently as he is finding. The characters of such leaders frequently form the subject matter of Czech *fin-de-siècle* writing. One is often reminded of Maeterlinck's *Les Aveugles*. Such leaders were systematically treated by Březina and, later, by Dyk and Šalda in drama.

The terms 'nation' and 'historicism' are of primary importance in determining the place of the Czech cultural programme in the *fin-de-siècle* movement. Hubert Gordon Schauer's article, 'Naše dvě otázky' (Our two questions), an introductory article in Vol. I, no. 1 of *Čas* (Time, 20 December, 1886), a heavily systematic opening to the Czech *fin-de-siècle*, adopts standpoints to both terms.

Schauer's 'Naše dvě otázky' poses questions regarding the meaning of Czech cultural life and its success up to 1886 and provocatively considers the possibility of the Czechs' joining the strong culture of the Germans and pursuing their intellectual task within the German cultural framework.[38] Journalistic and political attacks on the Realists followed its publication (the article was signed with only the cipher H. G.); they were labelled national nihilists, solemnly excommunicated from the nation and so forth.

What was new in Schauer was the drawing of conclusions, which was typical of the *Fin de siècle*, and the seriousness of his presentation. Three years earlier Eduard Grégr, a prominent Young Czech party man, had used nihilist rhetoric when he foisted Czech cultural nihilism onto the contemporary activities of the Old Czech leader, F. L. Rieger.[39] Grégr thundered on in the spirit of catastrophism, where Schauer contemplated rationally (although apparently only theoretically and academically). The problem was the same; Schauer was 'merely' courageous enough to be consistent. Some years later Jakub Arbes even claimed the possible spiritual paternity of 'Naše dvě otázky' by referring to a part of his novel *Kandidáti existence* (Candidates of existence), which was published in 1878.[40]

Schauer published the bases of what was amplified in the articles of further *fin-de-siècle* critics after his death (1892). The cheerless situation of the Czech nation, to which Schauer's article responded, led soon afterwards to the decline of the dominant Old Czech Party.

Witness is borne to the atmosphere of crisis in national culture and the need for that culture's enhancement, surprisingly enough in views expressed by two senior representatives of rival political parties, Eduard Grégr and F. L. Rieger. The former somehow considers digging Czech literature out of the earth by linguistically isolating it from the Germans; the latter would, with melancholic resignation, like to re-engender the atmosphere of the brief Czech-German cultural partnership which had existed at the beginning of 1848.[41]

On the other hand, the command 'be yourself and you will be Czech' was given without further specifications in the manifesto of the Czech *Moderna*.[42] The genuinely Czech nature of this new literature was felt to have arisen from the fact that international literary trends had found a creative response in Czech literature. Thus the authentic creative activity of Czech authors made Czech literature, not the authors' attempts at Czechness.[43] True writers when they open themselves to foreign stimuli need not fear for the 'Czech nature' of their work – in the opinion of the signatories of the Manifesto, and of other *fin-de-siècle* writers. The spirit of internationalism is a natural need of any literature which considers itself mature. It is not a matter of passive acquaintance with foreign literatures at any cost (for example, by means of inadequate translations), but of lively cooperation with these literatures on equal terms; neither literature loses or suppresses its identity. That is stated in Karel Hlaváček's essay 'Nacionalism a internacionalism'[44] and demonstrated in the foreign contacts of Czech *fin-de-siècle* literature, in the development of translation, in the reviewing of foreign books in Czech journals and so forth. The views of *fin-de-siècle* authors manifested themselves politically in their support of the Social Democrat workers who had been attacked for their internationalist programme.[45]

In looking for their ancestors, not only *fin-de-siècle* writers showed the sense of history typical of modern Czech literature and culture. Masaryk's interpretation of Czech history is based on connecting up remote phenomena. It was probably not so much historical as genuinely critical.[46] It was intended to prevent the observer from being sucked under by the currents of history; Masaryk called that historicism,[47] which he saw as the loss of an independent point of view on the part of an evaluating personality, i.e. the loss of the critical position itself.[48] Some of the theses of Masaryk's works were criticised by historians. Thus Masaryk and his opponents stirred up arguments about the meaning of Czech history, which contributed to systematic philosophical inquiries into Czech history and historiography, which were pursued by both historians and philosophers. Undoubtedly, Czech historiography derived much profit from the disputes.[49]

Prior to all this, similar arguments had occurred in literature and criticism. Again I have in mind works like Schauer's 'Naše dvě otázky', Zeyer's novel *Jan Maria Plojhar*, Čech's *Písně otroka* and the discussions which followed their publication.

Historicism, against which Masaryk fought, became anti-historicism. The relationship of the present to the past was not to be a dictate of history, but an independent, philosophically well-founded relationship, particularly with those significant predecessors, who had met the demands of what was judged authenticity.

Numerous articles by F. X. Šalda,[50] contemporary and later Czech socialist and Communist journalism,[51] and the politicising fiction of the Decadents (Karásek, Marten, Viktor Dyk) owe much to this atmosphere of historico-philosophical dispute.

The effort to create a systematic historical consciousness is manifested in the Catholic *Moderna*'s exploitation of the so-called Cyril and Methodius tradition, which intensified as work continued on the genealogy and interpretation of Roman Catholic culture in Czech history, in other words, in the creation of an ambitious parallel to an interpretation of Czech literature based on postulated liberal and Reformation traditions. The foundations of similar work on 'social' literature were laid by Rudolf Illový, a minor poet, but remarkable anthologist and journalist. The 'anti-quarianism' of the Decadents demonstrates the same type of communication with history, a type of communication which was later bolstered by their aestheticism.

The last two keywords which might be used in this scheme of the Czech *Fin de siècle* might be the 'justifiability' and the 'naturalness' of the movement. These concepts were used frequently in the writings of *fin-de-siècle* authors and of their opponents and they suggested an awareness of tradition and of novelty on both sides of the dispute. The significance of both notions for the *Fin de siècle* can be demonstrated by the fact that they comprise both an interpretation and a programme.

The vigour, indeed fieriness, of polemics in the period resulted from the fact that literary criticism had spread with considerable effect into the national culture in the broadest sense of the term. The whole activity of the Czech *Fin de siècle* was, in fact, a reassertion of the mid-Revival Jungmann school's empirical programme.

In the *Fin de siècle* the notion, 'national culture', was given evaluative meaning. That was most clearly the case with Schauer,[52] but other critics of the period shared his view. Perhaps that is the most significant consequence of the fact that criticism was taken as the starting point of the Czech *Fin de siècle*.

NOTES

1. Cf. F. X. Šalda, 'Kolem almanachu "Vpád barbarů".' *Kritické projevy, 13*, Prague, 1963, p. 275.

2. Jiřina Popelová, *Filosof František Krejčí*, Prague, 1942, p. 7; Jiří Cetl, *Český pozitivismus*, Brno, 1981, pp. 63–74.

3. The text of the manifesto in: F. X. Šalda, *Kritické projevy, 2*, Prague, 1950, pp. 361–3.

4. Karel Havlíček-Borovský was the leading ideologue of Czech radical patriotism in and after the year of revolutions, 1848. B. Stašek is the author of the statement. See Josef Hronek, *Katolická literatura česká přítomné doby*, Prague, 1924, p. 13.

5. It seems to hold good also for F. L. Rieger. His poems from his youth and his cooperation on

the opera libretti of his daughter Marie Červinková-Riegrová are well-known among Czech cognoscenti. Nevertheless he was more of a dilettante than a creative personality, unlike his predecessors. Cf. also the statements of A. Stašek, M. Švabinský and L. Šaloun about Rieger's relation to art in the miscellany, *Riegrův památník*, Semily, 1928.

6. Cf. for example, Josef Polák, *Josef Václav Sládek*, Prague, 1984, pp. 56–70, i.e. the chapter 'Charakter "ruchovského" období české litratury'.

7. See Šalda's essay 'Alej snů a meditace ku hrobu Jana Nerudy', in *Boje o zítřek*.

8. Cf. T. G. Masaryk, *Česká otázka* (Prague, 1895), *passim*; Jan Herben, *Kniha vzpomínek*, Prague, 1935, *passim*.

9. T. G. Masaryk, *Studie o Dostojevském*, Prague, 1932, p. 23.

10. Cf. Jan Vorel, *Román*, Prague – Vinohrady, 1895, and Eva Tasová, ' "Populární" esejista F. V. Krejčí', *Literární archiv*, 13 (1978), 14 (1979), 15 (1980), Prague, 1982.

11. Cf. Tasová, *op. cit.*

12. 'Psychologické poznámky k poznání generace let devadesátých,' *Rozpravy Aventina*, 6, 1930–31. Quoted from Jana Kostková, '*Kritik – básník, A chceš-li, vyslov jméno mé . . .*,' Prague, s.a., p. 15.

13. Cf. Karel Polák, 'F. V. Krejčí, typ kritika socialistického,' in *O českou literární kritiku*, Prague, 1940.

14. 'This book is only a fragment of the work . . . To the author, art and artistic problems were not a mere pleasant padding to conceal emptiness; art has been and is an equally inevitable and indispensable element of life, like every other fundamental and unsuppressible vital act or utterance. He issues a fragment when he would like to publish the whole, having been forced into this by circumstances of the book market. (*sic!*) Nevertheless he hopes that the basic idea will explicitly follow as well as the unified intellectual basis of these essays, the direction and route which took him to the present goal: individualist art on a traditional basis.' Arnošt Procházka, *Meditace*, Brno, 1921, p. 5. '*Česká otázka, Naše nynější krise* and also *Jan Hus* are only splinters from the workshop in which I work on certain philosophical tasks: I mean that literally and the intention of my words is that I am very well aware of a lack of symmetry here and there, of a certain fragmentary character, etc. . . . In arranging and binding together these various pieces I tried to present as much of the material as possible and to indicate various questions which should be, in my opinion, discussed and studied in greater detail. At the same time I write as concisely as I can, although I know that the commentary becomes more difficult. For example, right here in *Jan Hus*, I present Palacký's philosophy of history almost in its entirity in one small paragraph. I rectify just as concisely the usual interpretaton of Kollár, etc. In my works it is these things that are at stake, not the disputes of the everyday politics of various parties.' T. G. Masaryk, *Jan Hus*, Prague, 1923, p. 77.

15. See also J. S. Machar, *Knihy feuilletonů*, Prague, 1901, the foreword.

16. *Kniha vzpomínek*, p. 271.

17. Cf. Hana Hrzalová, *Proměny české prózy (1945–1985)*, Prague, 1985, p. 24.

18. Arnošt Procházka, *České kritiky*, Prague, 1912, pp. 158–9 (the essay on Josef K. Šlejhar).

19. The essay 'O básnické autostylisaci, zvláště u Bezruče', *Studie literárně historické a kritické*, Prague, 1937.

20. *Česká otázka*, Prague, 1969, pp. 129 and 127; *Jan Hus*, p. 82; *Česká otázka*, p. 127.

21. Antonín Pravoslav Veselý, *Omladina a pokrokové hnutí*, Prague, 1902, pp. 374 and 380–1. According to Jan Herben (*op. cit.*, p. 183), the manifesto of the Czech *Moderna* was 'a stimulus from a certain cartel of the younger generation directed against the Young Czech Party'.

22. See Robert B. Pynsent, *Julius Zeyer*, The Hague, Paris, 1973, p. 169, Karásek's wireless interview of May, 1937, and Arnošt Procházka, 'Sociální literatura', *Moderní revue*, 3, vol. V., 1896–97, p. 32.

23. Karel Dostál-Lutinov, 'Co chtěla Katolická moderna?', *Archiv literární*, vol. 1, Olomouc, 1919, p. 171.

24. Ibid.

25. It concerned the support of Social Democratic workers in connection with a performance in the National Theatre, Prague, which it was proposed to keep them out of for nationalistic reasons.

26. Cf. footnote 14 and other Masaryk formulations against making 'politics for politics' sake'.

27. This concerns the problem of the permanent opposition of the Young Czech Party. Jan Herben (*op. cit.*, p. 424) reproduces Grégr's statement of 1885 that the victory of the Young Czech Party in the elections would be a 'misfortune'.

28. Cf. Otto Urban, 'Otázka národní jednoty a politckého stranictví v Čechách na počátku šedesátých let 19. století,' *K dějinám českých politických stran v druhé polovině 19. a začátkem 20. století*, Prague, 1984, p. 27; and Otto Urban, *Česká společnost 1848–1918*, Prague, 1982.

29. Such topical re-evaluations continue as the 'search for predecessors of *fin-de-siècle* literature' as the period's prestige now grows in Czech literary historiography. Cf. Ivan Slavík (Ed.), Irma Geisslová, *Zraněný pták*, Königgrätz, 1978 and various other essays by Slavík.

30. 'We must attempt to become, you Molière or Byron, I Lessing or Belinsky, even if either you nor I could ever become any of them.' H. G. Schauer, 'O vzdělání spisovatelů, zvláště našich,' *Česká revue*, 1899, quoted by Vladimír Forst in 'Literárně kritické působení H. G. Schauera,' *Z dějin české literání kritiky*, Prague, 1965, p. 282. 'There does not exist a less just statement than that the Czech Decadence is running in the train of foreign models and living in servile dependence on them, especially on Baudelaire, Mallarmé and Verlaine, being satisfied with them, tapping their ideas and taking over what these poets gave. He who knows Baudelaire, Mallarmé and Verlaine also knows that it is absolutely impossible to be simultaneously Baudelaire and Mallarmé and Verlaine. And that anyone who succeeded in fusing these three highly distinctive artistic personalities, would be a miraculous and thus a supremely original artist.' Jiří Karásek ze Lvovic, *Chimerické výpravy*, Prague, 1927, p. 33. The same sense was contained also in Šalda's discovery of the Flaubertian features in the works of Růžena Svobodová and in the 'preparing of the ground for a Czech Dante' which was being carried out by the 'Catholic Modernists'.

31. Cf. for example Eva Taxová's study on F. V. Krejčí.

32. Jaroslav Goll, 'Z mých vzpomínek na Riegra', *Riegruv památník*, p. 44.

33. Cf. Eduard Grégr's political pamphlets.

34. Cf. Otto Urban, 'Otázka národní jednoty', p. 25.

35. Besides modern historical works, cf. Josef Holeček, *Tragédie Julia Grégra*, Prague, 1914, pp. 207–50 *passim*.

36. Among others cf. Zdeněk Nejedlý, *Dr Kramář*, Prague, 1920.

37. Jurij Křížek offers an evaluation of older Masaryk literature in his book *T. G. Masaryk a česká politika*, Prague, 1959, pp. 261–70 (the section 'Rozbor pramenů a literatury').

38. See H. G. Schauer, *Spisy*, Prague, 1917, p. 5–10.

39. See Edvard Grégr, *Slovo osudné*, Prague, 1883. The pamphlet was a reaction to a proposal of F. L. Rieger and other Old Czech Party politicians, which asserted that obligatory lessons in German at Czech schools should remain.

40. See Jan Herben, *op. cit.*, pp. 315–19.

41. 'If we could not speak German, we would buy our intellectual needs not on the German but on the Czech market and because the demand for Czech literary products would be greater, production would also be greater. In this proportion, however, our strength as writers and scholars would develop because our writers would find out that their works were not just a luxury subscribed to only because "one really ought to support Czech literature", but because they constitute a real need, a true necessity" for the spiritual development of the nation".' Grégr, *Slovo osudné,* p. 45. 'Because of when I was a young man, I belong to the period when quarrels among nationalities did not become as hot as, unfortunately, they do nowadays. I found myself on friendly terms with some German writers of that period, with my friend Meissner, with Uffo Horn and also with Ebert, a poet blessed by God. At that time our German countrymen were good, ardent partriots; they praised the glorious deeds of our ancestors with pride and enthusiasm; they mourned the decline of our culture and the glory of our country, and

I like to confess, and I am pleased that I can say here, how I received much inspiration, as did many other Czech countrymen, from these German men, and that they enhanced our national pride and our patriotism with their works. I regret the situation is today different; but I cannot relinquish the hope that happier times will return, that the waves of nationalist agitation will calm down and that unjustified suspicion of us will pass, especially when we do not intend to obstruct our German countrymen in their enjoyment of equal rights or to impose limitations on them in one way or another, since we consider with delight and satisfaction everything that benefits this country, everything that is done for education, for the scholarly and artistic progress of ths country.' Jan J. Langer (Ed.) *Politické výroky a zásady Frant. Lad. Riegra o poměrech a budoucnosti naší v Rakousku,* Prague, n.d., pp. 8–9.

43. The semantically empty, objectivistic depiction of the Czech countryside by a younger writer was judged unsuccessful. In his review of F.X. Svoboda's *Noví vesničané* Jiří Karásek wrote: 'We shall be Czech as soon as we are – Czech; such is the brief analysis of Mr Svoboda.' 'Nová česká poezie,' *Moderní revue,* III, 1895, p. 18. Quoted from Jiří Brabec, *Poezie na předělu doby,* Prague, 1964, p. 139.

44. *Moderní revue, V, 1896,* in book-form, *Dílo Karla Hlaváčka, III, Kritiky* (ed. Antonín Hartl), Prague, 1930, pp. 95–99. An analysis of Czech patriotism in the nineteenth century is presented by František Červinka in his book *Český nacionalismus v XIX. století* (Prague, 1965), where Hlaváček's essay is also referred to.

45. See note 25.

46. Cf. René Wellek, 'Reflections on my "History" ', *The Attack on Literature and Other Essays,* Chapel Hill, 1982.

47. Masaryk's own interpretation of Czech history showed a disastrously profound historicism. (Editor's note.)

48. *Česká otázka,* p. 171.

49. Cf. Tomáš Vojtěch, *Česká historiografie a pozitivismus,* Prague, 1984.

50. Cf. Otokar Fischer, *Šaldovo češství,* Prague, 1936.

51. Cf. Tomáš Vojtěch, *Česká historiografie.*

52. Cf. Dušan Jeřábek, 'Koncepce národní literatury u H.G. Schauera', *Sborník prací filozofické fakulty brnenske univerzity, D34,* Brno, 1987, pp. 17–24.

12

The Modern Occult
Revival in Vienna,
1880–1910*

NICHOLAS GOODRICK-CLARKE

The late nineteenth-century revival of interest in the occult in Vienna owed its inspiration to three foreign influences, all fostered and fashioned by specifically Austrian conditions. First was the contemporary craze for spiritualism and psychical research, which was stimulated by the arrival of travelling mediums from the United States and England. Their demonstrations and the ensuing controversy over seance phenomena fuelled scientific and philosophical debate concerning the mind-body problem at a time when materialist ideas were being challenged. Second was the strong appeal exercised by the ideas of Schopenhauer, Nietzsche and Wagner on student intellectuals impatient at the shortcomings of high liberalism in Austria during the 1870s. These German thinkers offered a radical critique of modernity, rationalism and self-seeking materialism, invoking myths and religious feeling to redeem the vitality of culture. Their Austrian disciples adopted a pietistic cult in this spirit and were receptive to similar idealist, utopian and occult ideas. The international theosophical movement, the third exotic influence, struck roots in this milieu of inspired cultural criticism and an illuminated rejection of liberalism, rationalism and atomistic individualism. This chapter presents a survey of the modern occult revival in Vienna between 1880 and 1910, with respect to both its sources and development.

The key figure in this modern occult revival was Friedrich Eckstein (1861–1939), the son of a Jewish paper manufacturer at Perchtoldsdorf. He read natural sciences at Vienna University and subsequently pursued a career as an industrial chemist and businessman, yet all the while cultivated an extraordinary range of interests in the arts, history, literature, religion and philosophy. The unofficial private secretary of Anton Bruckner in the 1880s and a close associate of such personalities as Hermann Bahr, Siegfried Lipiner, Gustav Mahler and Viktor Adler, Eckstein enjoyed the reputation of a brilliant polymath amongst his own generation.[1] His intellectual development is my central concern, for he successively avowed a pietistic Wagner cult, attended spiritualist seances and engaged in psychical research, and ultimately introduced theosophy to the Habsburg capital, becoming president of the Vienna Theosophical Society. To understand the origin of Eckstein's career in the modern occult revival, it is necessary to focus on the popularity of Nietzschean and Wagnerian ideas among students at Vienna.

In the late 1870s Eckstein came into contact with the Pernerstorfer circle, a group of young intellectuals who had clubbed together for the purpose of political and philosophical discussion a decade earlier. As early as 1867 Engelbert Pernerstorfer, Viktor Adler, Heinrich Friedjung and Max Gruber had, as pupils of the *Schottengymnasium*, formed the Telyn Society to discuss German folk nationalism, the social question and the failures of the contemporary liberal government in Austria. During their university studies these young men played a key intellectual role in the *Leseverein der deutschen Studenten Wiens* (1871–1878), a political society preoccupied with similar issues and the development of German nationalist consciousness among the students. The subsequent crises that beset the liberal government of the 1870s – the Franco-Prussian War, German unification under Prussia, the economic collapse of 1873 and the Ofenheim scandal – all served to deepen the disillusion of the Pernerstorfer circle with the self-seeking individualism and materialism of *laissez-faire* high liberalism in Austria.[2]

Between 1875 and 1878 the Pernerstorfer circle began to explore and expound the theories of Nietzsche and Wagner as an antidote to the cultural vicissitudes of liberalism. The early Nietzsche, represented by *Die Geburt der Tragödie* (The birth of tragedy, 1872) with its emphasis on Dionysian inspiration and the power of music in the revitalisation of culture, provided a coherent philosophical ideal opposed to the liberal faith in progress and scientific rationalism. With the emergence of Siegfried Lipiner as the circle's dominant intellectual force, Wagner was also widely accepted as the leader of the crusade for German cultural rebirth. From the mid-1870s until his death in 1883, Wagner had become increasingly involved in a new pietism, which was paralleled by an ambition to establish himself as the prophet of a new religion combining Schopenhauerian philosophy, musical theory and Christian mysticism. His programme called upon vegetarian associations, humane societies, temperance leagues, and the socialists to unite against the corrupt egoism of modern society. Although some members of the Pernerstorfer circle were eventually to follow Nietzsche in rejecting this development, the initial response to the new religious sect was highly favourable and the circle began to display the trappings of a religious cult. Richard von Kralik, Gustav Mahler, Hugo Wolf and Friedrich Eckstein joined the circle *c.* 1878 against this Wagnerian background.

After the government's dissolution of the *Leseverein* in December 1878, the Pernerstorfer circle patronised a vegetarian restaurant on the corner of Wallnerstrasse and Fahnengasse. Here the young intellectuals met in a gas-lit cellar to talk of Pythagoras, the Essenes, the therapeutics, the Neo-

Platonists, and the evils of meat-eating. Eckstein's autobiographical memoirs vividly record this bohemian scene: 'It was mostly young people who met there and took part in the collective exchange of views: students, teachers, artists and followers of the most diverse professions. Whilst I myself, like several friends, went summer and winter almost completely clad in linen, according to the theories of Pythagoras, others appeared clothed in hairy garments of natural colouring; and if you add to this that most of us had shoulder-length hair and full beards, our lunch table might have reminded the unselfconscious spectator not a little of Leonardo's Last Supper.'[3] To this circle belonged Hermann Bahr, Siegfried Lipiner, Gustav Mahler, Hugo Wolf, Viktor Adler and Friedrich Eckstein. The new cult of Wagner remained their paramount concern. Adler had visited Bayreuth as early as 1876 and an increasingly religious aura surrounded the accounts of members' later visits. A number of the circle attended the première of *Parsifal* at the Bayreuth festival in 1882. Eckstein demonstrated his Wagnerian piety by travelling the entire distance from Vienna on foot.[4]

In the late summer of 1880 Eckstein met Dr Oskar Simony (1852–1915), a reader at Vienna University and Professor of Mathematics and Physics at the Hochschule für Bodenkultur. Besides being a keen botanist and entomologist, Simony was a pure mathematician with a special interest in number theory and topology. He was concerned with the putative existence of higher mathematical dimensions and their possible relation to spiritual-istic phenomena. He studied the experiments of Friedrich Zöllner, Professor of Physics and Astronomy at Leipzig, who had interpreted the feats of the American medium Henry Slade in terms of spirits operating in a fourth dimension of space. Slade travelled on to Vienna in late 1878 and had seven seances with Lazar Hellenbach (1827–1887), a speculative meta-physician and the leading Austrian spiritualist. Simony was fascinated by the subject and persuaded Hellenbach to bring Slade to Vienna once again for investigations. Slade was to have stayed at Eckstein's house, but the project was abandoned when the medium suspiciously insisted on bringing an assistant.[5] Hellenbach continued to hold seances with travelling mediums, though with mixed results. Slade was said to have broken control but made a table disappear and Harry Bastian was unmasked as a fraud by Archduke Johann of Habsburg; the resulting furore was aired in a series of partisan brochures.[6]

Between 1880 and 1884 spiritualism enjoyed considerable popularity at Vienna. Hellenbach catered for the highest social circles and it is also recorded that Lipiner and other members of the Pernerstorfer circle frequented spiritualist seances in the early 1880s.[7] Eckstein and Simony had become close friends and jointly pursued their studies in spiritualism and psychical research, consuming the works of Sir William Crookes, Theodor Fechner and Sir Alfred Russel Wallace. Around 1884 they visited the distinguished British scientist Lord Rayleigh, then resident at Vienna.

Rayleigh told them that he had witnessed Indian ascetics moving objects at a distance, an achievement he regarded as the work of spirits.[8] Simony continued to attend seances, all the time hoping for a confirmation of the actuality of the supernatural phenomena. In due course he advanced a theory that mediums possessed abnormal muscular development and that the electrical energy in their peculiar muscular contractions could produce the phenomena attributed to the spirits.[9]

This involvement with spiritualism led Eckstein to theosophy, then in the earliest stages of its European dissemination. Begun in 1875 in New York by Helena Petrovna Blavatsky and Henry Steel Olcott for the purposes of studying spirit and other occult phenomena, theosophy subsequently developed into a new religious movement based on the ancient wisdom of Egypt, India and esoteric schools through the ages. Between 1879 and 1885 Blavatsky lived in Bombay and at Adyar near Madras, where the basis of an international sect was laid among Indians, expatriate English and other foreign visitors. Alfred Percy Sinnett, an English newspaper editor, generated widespread interest in theosophy with the publication of the *The Occult World* (1881), which contained numerous accounts of Blavatsky's 'miracles' and contacts with the mahatmas, and his *Esoteric Buddhism* (1883), which summarised the cosmological and religious ideas of theosophy for European readers. After his return from India in 1883, Sinnett became President of the London Lodge in the Theosophical Society in January 1885. Blavatsky and Olcott had visited Europe in summer 1884 to drum up support, and a German branch of the Theosophical Society was briefly established under the presidency of Wilhelm Hübbe-Schleiden in July 1884. Blavatsky finally returned to Europe in April 1885, together with Franz Hartmann, who was to play a prominent role in later German theosophy, and stayed at Naples (April–August 1885), Würzburg (August 1885–May 1886) and Ostend (July 1886–May 1887). She then came to London where she acted as a focus of theosophical activity until her death in 1891.[10]

Franz Hartmann had encountered spiritualism while working in the United States during the 1870s and then joined the theosophists at Madras between 1883 and 1885. Returning to Europe after an eighteen-year absence, Hartmann travelled on from Naples via his old home town Kempten to Vienna.[11] Here he encountered Friedrich Eckstein, who was greatly impressed by the expatriate's close association with the theosophists and invited him to lodge with him until his plans were settled. Hartmann offered Eckstein an introduction to Blavatsky, who was acting as a magnet to spiritual seekers on her slow tour across the continent. In late 1886 Eckstein visited Blavatsky at Ostend. Their meeting was cordial and their discussions enthusiastic, for Eckstein departed with sheaves of theosophical literature, an authorisation to found a Vienna branch of the Theosophical Society and a personal gift of a special Rosicrucian pendant. Back at Vienna, Eckstein and Simony graduated from spiritualism to theosophy, devouring

the works of Sinnett, Blavatsky's *Isis Unveiled* (1877) and Mabel Collins's
Light on the Path (1885).[12]

Eckstein was now the recognised local authority on theosophy, since
Hartmann had left to establish an alternative sanatorium for the treatment
of respiratory diseases at Hallein near Salzburg. He quickly attracted a circle
of theosophical novices and the Vienna lodge of the Theosophical Society
was founded in October 1887 with Eckstein as president, Dr Graevell as
Secretary and Franz Kanitzer as Treasurer. The group fused theosophical
precepts with the earlier Wagnerian pietism, with which there were
significant overlaps relating to anti-materialism and religious revival. A
bye-law of the lodge excluded from membership 'all users of flesh food or
spirituous liquors'. The same notice also described the circle as devoted
students of esoteric philosophy, a label justified by the catholic range of
Eckstein's occult interests, which included German and Spanish mysticism,
Palestrina's masses, the Templars and the Freemasons, Swedenborg,
vegetarianism and oriental religions.[13]

Through his close friend and fellow-lodger, Hugo Wolf, the Wagnerian
composer, Eckstein was introduced to Dr Edmund and Marie Lang in
November 1887. Their social circle included the brothers Julius and Karl
Mayreder, both architects, and the latter's wife Rosa Mayreder, the leading
feminist in Vienna. The friends often discussed religious subjects and
theosophy, which were close to Marie Lang's heart. In the summer of 1888
the group rented Schloss Bellevue at Grinzing for a summer colony, where
art, music and culture might flourish. Marie Lang cooked vegetarian meals;
Wolf composed *Lieder*; the main topic of conversation was theosophy,
whereby its elaborate cosmology, the 'miracles' and the mahatma letters
accompanied discussions of the social question from a 'progressive' standpoint. The group was joined by Count Karl zu Leiningen-Billigheim, a
young diplomat who had learned his theosophy from Eckstein and
subsequently became Secretary of the Vienna branch, and Franz Hartmann,
now well-known as the author of several books on theosophy. The Wagner
cult still prevailed, for Eckstein and Wolf broke their stay at the Schloss to
attend the annual Bayreuth festival.[14]

In 1889 Rudolf Steiner frequented the Lang circle. He had studied
literature at the Technische Hochschule under Professor Karl Julius Schroer,
who encouraged his interest in Goethe's symbolism. It was through Schroer
that Steiner met Eckstein. Steiner had read Sinnett's *Esoteric Buddhism*
soon after its German translation (1884) and asked Eckstein to explain the
secret doctrine. In due course Eckstein introduced Steiner to Rosa
Mayreder and the theosophical circle of Edmund and Marie Lang. Steiner
perceptively described them as 'homeless souls from Wagnerland', but nonetheless however, empathised with the subjective pietism of Marie Lang and
remained the life-long friend of Eckstein, who had shown him the occult key
to Goethe's symbolism. Under the influence of the circle, Steiner studied

oriental thought, medieval mysticism, Neo-Platonism and the Cabala. By the time Steiner left Vienna in 1890 to take up his post as editor of Geothe's scientific works at Weimar, his interest in both theosophy and German idealism was firmly established. In 1902 he became the General Secretary of a new German Section of the Theosophical Society, but subsequently broke away to form his own Anthroposophical Society in 1913.[15]

Eckstein's scientific and business interests took him to London in 1891. He stayed for several months and made the acquaintance of many leading theosophists, including Annie Besant, the successor of Blavatsky in London, Herbert Burrows, Edward Maitland, Henry Steel Olcott, Countess Constance Wachtmeister, and Alfred and Patience Sinnett. The First Annual Convention of the Theosophical Society in Europe was held on 9–10 July 1891 and Eckstein attended as the Austrian delegate. He subsequently accompanied the London theosophists on an Indian-vegetarian picnic held on the estate of Mrs Milbank near Maidenhead. A number of Indians were present and Mohan Mohini Chatterjee spoke about his recent studies of the *Bhagavad Gita*. Both Eckstein and Leiningen-Billingheim participated in the Second Annual Convention at London in July 1892. Although no Austrian delegates were present at succeeding Annual Conventions, the names of the Vienna Lodge officers were entered in their reports until 1897. Thanks to Eckstein's enthusiasm, Vienna must be considered the principal centre of German-speaking theosophy in its earliest European years.[16]

This pre-eminent position is demonstrated by the relationship between the Vienna Theosophical Society and the Blue Star Lodge at Prague, founded in 1891 by Baron de Leonhardi, a member of the Austrian parliament. The new theosophical lodge counted among its ten or so members Karel Weinfurter, A. Rimay de Gidofalva and Gustav Meyer (later Meyrink), who is best known for *Der Golem* (1915) and other occult novels.[17] The Blue Star Lodge pursued a variety of occult practices, including breathing and concentration exercises, magic, alchemy and tantric yoga. Meyrink actively corresponded with occult groups all over Europe, but retained the highest respect for Eckstein as an adept. The Prague group frequently sought advice from the Vienna theosophists regarding the wisdom, effectiveness or danger of their occult practices. They were generally counselled against magical invocations and Rimay's description of his success with visualization techniques was loftily dismissed. But Vienna still continued to give occult guidance to Prague. In the mid-1890s the Blue Star Lodge received a telegram from the Vienna theosophists, announcing that they were in contact with a new adept: 'Come at once, the way is open.'[18]

The Vienna group had evidently known the adept for several years. His name was Alois Mailänder (1844–1905) and he was the leader of a pietist group of weavers at Kempten, whom Wilhelm Hübbe-Schleiden, the German theosophist, had discovered around 1884. Some seven years earlier

Mailänder had gone through a religious experience, which transformed him into a Christian visionary. His simple teaching (both he and his weaver colleagues were illiterate) consisted in a primitive derivation of Jakob Boehme's theosophy combined with oracular biblical utterances. The Mailänder circle attracted many German and Austrian theosophists, including Franz Hartmann, the Gebhards, Friedrich Eckstein, Blasius von Schemua and Gustav Meyrink, who all made pilgrimages to Kempten. When Mailänder became ill through overwork, the leading theosophists raised funds so that he and his circle were able to retire and buy a farm near Darmstadt.[19]

Notwithstanding its initial lead in the 1880s and early 1890s Vienna was ultimately succeeded by Germany as the main focus of German-speaking theosophy. New lodges were founded in 1894 at Berlin and Munich, in 1898 at Hamburg and Hanover, in 1899 at Berlin-Charlottenburg, and in 1902 at Kassel, Düsseldorf, Leipzig and Stuttgart.[20] In 1902 Rudolf Steiner was appointed General Secretary of a new German Section of the Theosophical Society, which together with other national sections in France, Italy, Scandinavia and Holland replaced the former European Section. Under Steiner's leadership the Theosophical Society made strong progress in Germany with new publications, periodicals and an expanding member-ship.[21] A rival theosophical organisation, the German branch of the International Theosophical Brotherhood, deriving from the Judge schism of American theosophists in April 1895, had been founded at Leipzig in 1896 under Franz Hartmann's auspices and this national society remained distinct from the organisation under Steiner owing allegiance to the London theosophists.[22] These developments did not concern Vienna, where theosophical activities appear to have lapsed at the end of the century. After 1897 there was no further mention of the Vienna Lodge in the theosophical periodicals published at London.

Theosophy did experience a revival at Vienna, although in a different context from its initiation under Eckstein, Steiner and the Lang circle. After 1900 theosophical and occult ideas entered the *völkisch* ideology of German nationalism, racism and defensive political reaction. Around 1902 the elderly nationalist Guido von List, whose popular romances had described the ancient Teutons of the Austrian homeland, assimilated theosophical ideas to expound a new racist mysticism. In his 'Ario-Germanic' researches, published between 1908 and 1914, List celebrated the *Armanen*, ancient priest-kings of the Old Aryan religion, as the architects and governors of a Germanic golden age. These druidic hierophants had supposedly preached a gnostic religion based on occult notions and racial eugenics, with many borrowings from theosophy, including exalted masters, astrology, cabalism, Hindu cosmology and eccentric palaeogeographical theories. The List Society (est. March 1908) counted both prominent Vienna politicians and several German theosophists, including Franz Hartmann and Hugo Göring, and the Vienna Theosophical Society among its own supporters.

Close to List was another racist mystic, Jörg Lanz von Liebenfels, who combined occultism with pre-fascist political ideas in his magazine *Ostara* (1905–18), published to defend the interests of the master race against social inferiors and non-German nationalities in the Habsburg Empire. Lanz interpreted the grail as an electrical symbol relating to the supernatural powers of the pure-blooded Aryan race. Regarding the Templars' quest for the grail as a poetic metaphor for their supposed eugenic programme intended to breed a new caste of god-men, Lanz founded the Order of New Templars as the vanguard of his pan-Aryan racist movement in 1907. In 1915 he coined the term 'Ariosophy' to denote the twin sources of his doctrine in Social Darwinist racism and theosophy. Both List and Lanz von Liebenfels were associated with the Austrian Pan-German movement of Georg von Schönerer. Their abstruse theories demonstrate how theosophy and occultism were effectively quarried to buttress and legitimate, albeit in an esoteric sense with limited appeal, the burgeoning presence of German nationalism in the Habsburg Empire after 1905.[23]

Whereas the early Viennese theosophical movement (1885–*c.*1895) was defined by speculative parapsychology, a neo-gnosticism rooted in the Wagner cult and an intellectual rejection of liberalism, rationalism and materialism, the later ariosophical manifestation was explicitly linked to the mass political concerns of German nationalism and racism. The uses of theosophy for political purposes consisted in its universal and non-Christian perspective upon the cosmos, against which the sources of Teutonic belief, customs and folk-identity could be located. Indeed, the very structure of theosophical doctrine lent itself to *völkisch* thought. The implicit elitism of the mahatmas with superhuman wisdom corresponded to the whimsies of a master race; the notion of an occult gnosis in theosophy, notably its obscuration by Christian orthodoxy, accorded with the attempts to ascribe a long pedigree to German *völkisch* nationalism, especially in view of its really recent origins. The shift from liberalism towards the emergence of mass political movements, which increasingly threatened the precarious balance of the multi-national Habsburg Empire, favoured this changing perspective on theosophy at Vienna. While the modern occult revival had begun as an idealist and irrationalist reaction to the perceived failures of liberalism among a small intellectual circle in the 1880s, it ended by offering a religious mystique to a tide of illiberalism among the Austrian Pan-Germans by 1910.

NOTES

* This chapter is a slightly revised version of a paper printed in the *Durham University Journal* (vol. lxxx, no. 1), whose editors have kindly given me permission to publish the paper in this volume.

1. The principal source for Eckstein's life and interests is Friedrich Eckstein, '*Alte unnennbare Tage!*' *Erinnerungen aus siebzig Lehr- und Wanderjahren* Vienna, 1936.

2. The best available study of the Pernerstorfer circle and its intellectual rejection of liberalism is William J. McGrath, *Dionysian Art and Populist Politics in Austria* New Haven, 1974.

3. Eckstein, '*Alte unnennbare Tage*', p. 105f.

4. Ibid., pp. 110–12, 213–24.

5. Ibid., pp. 62–8. Lazar Hellenbach, *Mr Slade's Aufenthalt in Wien* Vienna, 1878.

6. Erzherzog Johann, *Einblicke in den Spiritismus* (Linz, 1884), and Lazar Hellenbach, *Die Logik der Thatsachen. Eine Entgegnung auf die Brochure 'Einblicke in den Spiritismus'* Leipzig, 1884.

7. McGrath, *Dionysian Art*, p. 94.

8. Eckstein, '*Alte unnennbare Tage*', p. 68f.

9. Oskar Simony, *Über spiritistische Manifestationen vom naturwissenschaftlichen Standpunkt* Vienna, 1884.

10. A survey of the early theosophical movement is contained in Howard Murphet, *When Daylight Comes: a Biography of Helena Petrovna Blavatsky* Wheaton, Ill., 1975.

11. Details of Hartmann's life and theosophical activities appear in Hugo Göring, *Dr Franz Hartmann, ein Vorkämpfer der Theosophie* Brunswick, 1895, and Franz Hartmann, *Denkwürdige Erinnerungen* Leipzig, 1898.

12. For Eckstein's earliest theosophical interest, see his '*Alte unnennbare Tage*', pp. 69ff. His meeting with Blavatsky is documented in Emil Bock, *Rudolf Steiner. Studien zu seinem Lebensgang und Lebenswerk*, Stuttgart, 1961, p. 79f and Charles Blech, *Contribution á l'histoire de la Société Théosophique en France*, Paris, 1933, p. 115.

13. Notice in *The Theosophist*, 9, 1888, Supplement, October–November, 1887, iv. References to Eckstein's esoteric interests in Eckstein, op. cit., pp. 194, 206f.

14. Details of the Lang circle and the summer colony at Schloss Bellevue in Eckstein, '*Alte unnennbare Tage*', pp. 183–6, 201–4.

15. Rudolf Steiner's involvement in Viennese theosophy is documented in Eckstein, '*Alte unnennbare Tage*', p. 130f; Bock, *Rudolf Steiner,* pp. 80–4; and Rudolf Steiner, *An Autobiography*, 2nd ed., New York, 1980, pp. 141–4.

16. Eckstein, '*Alte unnennbare Tage*', p. 260f. The Theosophical Society in Europe, *First Annual Convention. Report of Proceedings*, 9–10 July 1891, pp. 2, 17, and *Second Annual Convention. Report of Proceedings*, 14–15 July 1892, pp. 2, 15f, 33, 67, and subsequent annual convention reports, Reference Library, The Theosophical Society in England, London.

17. The inauguration of the Prague lodge is documented in *Lucifer* 10, No 55, 15 March 1892, p. 81 and *The Vahan* 1, No 9, 1 April 1892, p. 7.

18. An account of the activities of the Blue Star Lodge appears in Karel Weinfurter, *Man's Highest Purpose (The lost word regained)*, London, 1930, pp. 43–51, 152–4.

19. Alois Mailänder and his pietistic circle are documented in Hans-Jürgen Glowka, *Deutsche Okkultgruppen 1875–1937*, Munich, 1981, pp. 105–7.

20. Foundation dates of German theosophical lodges in The Theosophical Society (European Section), *Twelfth Annual Convention. Report of Proceedings*, 5–6 July 1902, p. 28.

21. *The Theosophical Review*, 32, No. 187 (15 March 1903), 83; *The Theosophical Review* 36, No. 213 (May 1905), 265–8.

22. Schwabe, 'Protokoll über die 1. Nationalkonvention der "Theosophischen Gesellschaft" in Europa (Deutschland)', *Metaphysische Rundschau* 1 (1896), 279–83. The origins of American theosophy are documented in Emmett A. Greenwalt, *California Utopia: Point Loma 1897–1942*, San Diego, 1978, pp. 1–34.

23. Nicholas Goodrick-Clarke, *The Occult Roots of Nazism: the Ariosophists of Austria and Germany 1980–1935* Wellingborough, 1985, presents a full documentary history of the racist mystical sects at Vienna and their links with Austrian Pan-Germanism.

13

Conclusory Essay:
Decadence, Decay and
Innovation

ROBERT B. PYNSENT

This conclusory essay attempts to outline the main elements of *fin-de-siècle* culture in Austria-Hungary on the background of contemporaneous English and French culture. The essay ends with a brief comparison between the *Fin de siècle* and the 'Sixties' as phenomena. I have borne that ending in mind while writing the preceding sections and that accounts for the large amount of space I devote to concepts like the decay of language, to images of the serpent, to occultism and the erotic. Those constitute the most evident links between the two periods.

Section II, 'The Historical Background', is also written with that ending in mind; because most of the lands in the Austrian sphere of influence in the 1890s are now socialist countries, I have to devote space, say, to the Balkans in an essay which purports to be concerned with central European urban culture. When I then turn to the three main cultural centres of the Monarchy at the turn of the century, I say little about Vienna, because this essay is concerned with cultural problems more than societies – not only because so much has been published in the last decade or so about Vienna 1900 and comparatively little about Prague and Budapest. Similarly, I can add little to our knowledge of the role of the Jews in Viennese culture (Beller makes new contributions in his essay in this volume), but I do try to compare the situations of Vienna Jews with that of Jews in the other two centres.

I devote a long section to a Hungarian who wrote German in Paris, Max Nordau, because he was a typical Monarchy Jew and a typical Monarchy 'artist'. Much has been written about his *Entartung* and so I devote my attention to his earlier and far more influential *Die conventionellen Lügen*. This work also expresses views which were to be central to general Austro-Hungarian cultural thinking at the turn of the century.

After Nordau, I define the term Decadence and then follow Wellek in rejecting the term Modernism except where it means a *fin-de-siècle* perception of the world which not only records the decay of civilisation, but also suggests a cure for that decay. That takes me on to the essential ambivalence of the Decadent mode. The Decadent was horrified at the impending doom of European civilisation, and luxuriated in that horror. That the doom was nigh was allegedly evident in the state of language, which had become bureaucratised and clichéd, and so the Decadents had to provide luxuriant decoration for doom-struck language. The cultivation of 'style' constituted much of that decoration. Outside language the same cultivation was evident in the concept of the dandy. I devote section X to that largely imaginary phenomenon.

The dandy embodied an attitude to woman which the Decadent strove for, but seldom achieved. Decadent man appeared to be frightened of the emancipation of women and so distorted the conception of the liberation of woman into a conception of the dominance of woman. For the *fin-de-siècle* man female sexuality became more and more an object of revulsion, but also fear. At the same time, however, men supported 'free love', votes for women and degrees for women at the universities. Having dealt briefly with attitudes to women and to love and sexuality, I turn to a central emblem of womanhood and of the superior knowledge which *fin-de-siècle* man strove for, the serpent. I point out how the use of the serpent in the plastic arts and in letters reflects the ambivalence of the Decadence and then go on to describe, in section XIV, the essential structural and linguistic device of Decadent art, the 'intermediate state'. That eventually leads me to a brief discussion of that part of the period's religion of art which is embodied in the idea of the fatal or magic book. That naturally introduces occultism as one of the results of what *fin-de-siècle* man saw as the decay or failure of religion.

The final chapter, the comparison of the *Fin de siècle* with the Sixties, sketches an idea by which Baudelaire's place is taken by Butor, the pre-Raphaelites' place is taken by the American Beat Generation, and Beardsley's by the political comic strip. This section suggests arguments, but goes into almost no detail about the lands once part of the Austro-Hungarian sphere of influence. Like the *Fin de siècle* the Sixties produced little or no great art (film buffs may disagree). The *Fin de siècle*, however, gave the impulse to the greatest art of the twentieth century. The Sixties is not yet over everywhere. Even in countries like Britain or Czechoslovakia, where it has been over for fifteen to twenty years, it is difficult to state precisely what cultural and social impact it has had. Certainly, however, moralist critics saw the Sixties as a period of decay and, equally certainly, the Sixties brought innovation.

I. DECAY AND INNOVATION

'Generally speaking,' writes Nietzsche, 'all progress must be preceded by a partial weakening.'[1] The Czech Decadent critic, Arnošt Procházka, takes Nietzsche's thought further and suggests an interpretation of the *Fin de siècle* in Austria-Hungary: 'An important chapter remains to be written on the relationship between progress and decay, about their close inter-connections, their inseparability. Once careful research has been carried out into the points of contact between evolution and decadence, it will be found . . . that they are synonyms.'[2] The fundamental idea of Yeats's essay, 'The Autumn of the Body', is that the Decadent period is a period in which art lies dormant, dreaming of a vivid future: in other words, the Decadence was a period of prefigurings and anticipations. But it was more than that. The writers and artists of particularly the 1880s to the 1910s (though Baudelaire, Nerval, Poe, Schopenhauer and so forth were perhaps part of the trend), were nervously or exultantly conscious of living in a period of general cultural decay. Verlaine expected his white barbarians to come to destroy European civilisation; Karásek aligned those barbarians with the Americans, and Hlaváček with the inner consciousness of European man. An American critic says of that consciousness, 'The decadent writers are right. Their society is dying. After the Great War Europe begins to assume the socialistic form foreshadowed in the nineteenth century and hardened into a scheme of values in our own day.'[3] All over turn-of-the-century Europe writers and artists, historians and sociologists, and possibly most of all, politicians, were consumed with the idea of impending catastrophe. Rapid industrialisation, political reform, the emancipation of members of non-established churches and religions, the growth of trade unions and mass political parties left everything in flux. No moral, social, or indeed, aesthetic standards seemed safe any longer. The 1890s were marked by 'a half-hushed uneasiness, a sense of social decline, a foreboding of death'.[4] Darwin and Darwinists had persuaded European man that evolution could lead to extinction and astronomers were claiming that every star and planet had its predetermined course and life-span; writers were claiming that contemporary world-weariness and spiritual nausea signalled the end of a civilisation.[5]

The Decadent mood was largely French in origin, though strong elements in it were Anglo-Saxon (Poe, Pater, Wilde), and it happened to spread to Austria-Hungary at just the time when the cultures of the Monarchy felt themselves to have 'caught up' with Western Europe. Or: the west-European Decadent mood was so attractive to Austrian Germans, Czechs, Galician Poles and Hungarians that they found themselves suddenly to have caught up with the rest of Europe. Whichever way round one understands the phenomenon, it still gave birth to one of the great stereotypes of cultural historiography: *fin-de-siècle* Austria-Hungary produced a series of thinkers and artists whose ideas shaped much of the thinking of twentieth-century European man. Freud, Schoenberg, Janáček, Bartók, Mach, Wittgenstein, Klimt, Mucha, Kafka, are the obvious names. Furthermore, the historian must be careful how he draws the cultural boundaries of Austria-Hungary at this time. On the one hand, Austrian German writers published in Munich and Leipzig rather than Vienna. On the other hand, the Monarchy was exporting its intelligentsia; Austrians, particularly Czechs, were responsible for setting up many of the grammar schools, breweries and libraries in the newly established Bulgaria in the last quarter of the nineteenth century. A Czech was the Bulgarian Minister of Culture and a Prague-educated Bulgarian was the first vice-chancellor of Sofia University. Alexander Battenberg of Bulgaria, when he lost heart as ruler, became an officer in the Austrian Army. Similarly, 'foxy' Ferdinand Coburg of Bulgaria had large estates in Hungary. Nearly all those areas which now form the non-Soviet socialist states of central and eastern Europe were at the turn of the century part of the Austrian cultural sphere.

The cliché that decaying Austria-Hungary constituted a remarkable centre of intellectual innovation is probably, like most clichés, true, but it is all too easy to forget that the *Fin de siècle* was a period of innovation over most of Europe. To overemphasise Austria-Hungary's role is to fall prey to the cultural relativism Gombrich warns against: 'the conclusion that cultures or life-forms are not only different, but incommensurable, that is that since there is no common denominator it is irrational to try to compare people of one country or one age with people of other times or nations.'[6] The first two-volume edition of Frazer's *The Golden Bough* appeared in 1890. Though, to be sure, one of the last products of the Monarchy's intellectual education, the Galician Malinowski's conception of anthropology turned Frazer's upside down, *The Golden Bough* remains the work of art. Frazer is still today the inspirer of amateurs, if Malinowski is the inspirer of scholars. In the same year (1890) Bahr published his ephemeral *Zur Kritik der Moderne* (Towards a criticism of the *Moderne*), but Ibsen published *Hedda Gabler* and Tolstoy *The Kreutzer Sonata*. Similarly in 1892 Hofmannsthal produced his *Der Tod des Tizian* (Titian's death), but Haeckel *Der Monismus* (Monism) and Shaw *Mrs Warren's Profession*. In 1899 Freud published his *Traumdeutung* (The Interpretation of Dreams), as Havelock Ellis in England was publishing the first volume of his *Studies in the Psychology of Sex.* In 1900 Schnitzler published *Reigen* (usually translated as 'La Ronde'), but outside Austria Thomas Mann published *Buddenbrooks* (dated 1901, published 1900) and Conrad *Lord Jim*. Finally, in 1914 František Gellner published *Cesta do hor* (A trip into the mountains), but James Joyce belatedly published *Dubliners* and Gide *Les Caves du Vatican*. Such comparisons are selective and possibly arbitrary, but they are instructive for those who have become bewitched by the concept of Vienna 1900.

II. THE HISTORICAL BACKGROUND

In the period all Europe had its share of crisis, but the Monarchy was truly in a state of unusual turmoil. Between 1875 and 1889 the Monarchy was internally fairly stable. External relations were strained because of the reemergence of the Bulgarian Question in 1885, which again emphasised the conflict of interests between Austria-Hungary and Russia. In December 1885 Austria-Hungary warned Bulgaria that if she proceeded any further into Serbia she would have to fight Austro-Hungarian as well as Serbian armies. This was a risky enterprise; indeed, Russian troops did begin to mass on the Galician frontier; the German Empire would not help the Monarchy in the Balkans: Bismarck's statement that Bulgaria was not worth the bones of a single Pomeranian grenadier still rankle in today's Bulgaria. Relationships between Russia and the Monarchy did not settle until the February 1903 programme.

The Great Defence Debate of 1889 weakened the Dualist system, which was further weakened by the crisis engendered by the language ordinances promulgated in May 1897 by the Galician premier of Cisleithania, Casimir Badeni, who clearly had little idea of the enmity obtaining between the Germans and Czechs of Bohemia, particularly of Prague. (For some years now Prague had ceased to be a German city; in the census of 1880, 120,000 Pragers declared themselves Czech and only 36,000 German.) Badeni's ordinances, which gave equal rights to Czech and German in internal governmental matters in Bohemia, apparently justified the Germans' worst fears. Bohemian Germans held mass demonstrations, also attended by citizens of Germany proper, in Aussig (now Ústí nad Labem) and Eger (now Cheb). The parliamentary conflict the ordinances inspired threatened the passing of the measures confirming the economic *Ausgleich* of 1867. One Moravian deputy, Lecher, stood up and delivered a twelve-hour speech against the *Ausgleich* and on 3 November 1897 the *Reichsrat* sitting turned into a common-or-garden brawl. Behaviour did not improve greatly in subsequent days and on 28 November Badeni resigned. Czech and German riots erupted in Prague, especially amongst students, and on 2 December martial law was declared for Prague and its surroundings. These were actually race riots. The Czechs were no longer concerned for the survival of their language as a vehicle of culture; the Charles-Ferdinand University in Prague had been split into German and Czech parts in 1882; a Bohemian Academy of Science and Arts had been founded in 1890 (a Hungarian Academy had been founded in Buda in 1830, a South Slav in Zagreb in 1867 and a Polish in Cracow in 1871) and most members of the young Czech intelligentsia were organised in various utterly cosmopolitan cultural groupings by the mid 1890s. The Austrian German intelligentsia was equally cosmopolitan. Of the period just before 1900 Robert Musil wrote, 'In those days one was international; one summarily rejected notions like state, nation, race, family, religion, for one was wary of all ready-forged links.'[7]

Between January and March 1900 there was a mass miners' strike in Cisleithania, but military matters were more important than industrial. 1903 saw the Army Crisis, when the military authorities were keeping in barracks a large number of men who should not have been there. A law had to be passed every year to allow Army units to be called up in Hungary. The military authorities kept, or threatened to keep, men in the Army for longer than the allotted period to keep numbers up, whenever the law was delayed. Sometimes they also called up men who had been enlistable in previous years but for some reason or other had not been called up. The military expected the deputies to pass the bill any moment, so that everything would settle down. Between the autumn of 1903 and October 1907 the Austrian and Hungarian chambers were in a state of bitter conflict. In Cisleithania, the premier Korber governed practically without parliament from January, 1903 to the end of December, 1904. On 15 September 1905 a large working-class and socialist demonstration in favour of universal suffrage was staged before the parliament building in Budapest, and similar demonstrations and strikes took place in Cisleithania in November. Finally a bill on electoral reform was passed by the lower house on 1 December 1906, by the upper house on 21 December, and it obtained the imperial and royal assent on 26 January 1907. By this law all men over twenty-four years of age had the right to vote in *Reichsrat* elections. The first general election under the new rules took place on 14 May and the result was an easy victory for the Social Democrats and Christian Socials. The Slav Congress in Prague of July 1908 led nowhere, as became clear when the Congress was re-convened in Sofia in 1910.

The Austro-Hungarian annexation of Bosnia and Herzegovina in October 1908 was a peaceful affair, which provoked an acute, prolonged international crisis. Foreign governments saw Austria disturbing the status quo, where Count Aehrenthal saw himself preserving the status quo in the Balkans. That status quo was further disturbed in 1912 when the Balkan League (Bulgaria, Serbia and Greece supported by Montenegro) defeated the Turks and succeeded in driving them out of all Europe except a small piece of eastern Thrace and the Gallipoli peninsula. But the Bulgarians were dissatisfied and on 30 June 1913 they opened the Second Balkan War with the Serbs and the Greeks. They lost, for Macedonia was split between Serbia and Greece and she had to return Adrianople to Turkey. After his victory over the Bulgarians at Kukush in July 1913 the Greek king, Constantine, was welcomed by his subjects in Athens with the sobriquet 'Bulgaroktonos' (killer of Bulgars), the name given to the Byzantine Emperor Basil, who had defeated the Bulgarians in 1014.

Apart from crises and disturbances and squabbles and racist court trials, the *Fin de siècle* in Austria Hungary felt the same *maladie du siècle* as the rest of Europe. It is easy to argue that it was felt all the more intensely in the Monarchy because of the racial and social tensions there and because of a feeling that the Empire was doomed to dissolution which was steadily growing through the first decade and a half of the twentieth century. Precious little by way of administrative or journalistic or literary documents would support that any such strong feeling existed – at least before 1915 and 1916.

The term *maladie du siècle* was coined by Musset (1836), and he gives it two partial delineations. (In this essay I retain Musset's term; I do not use the now more conventional *mal du siècle*.) The term is applied to a prostitute in a night-club:

> I suddenly realised that this wretched girl's face bore a fatal resemblance to my mistress's. The sight chilled me. There is a particular sort of shivering which takes a man by the roots of his hair; the common people say it is Death passing over your head but this was not Death passing over mine.
>
> It was the *maladie du siècle*, or rather this whore was the *maladie du siècle* and it was she who, with her pale, mocking features and husky voice, had just sat down before me.[8]

That establishes the seedy side to Decadent world-weariness, but more important for this conclusory essay is the political side:

> The whole present *maladie du siècle* has two causes; the people who has been through 1793 and 1814 bears two wounds in its heart. Everything there used to be is no longer; everything there will be is not yet. Do not search for the secret of our ills anywhere else.[9]

That expresses that sense of living in a transitional age which is essential to Decadent sensibility. According to Musset political and military defeat, the guillotining of Louis XVI and the abdication and banishment to Elba of Napoleon I, the fall of absolutism and the fall of empire, constituted the mainspring of that world-weariness, nihilistic scepticism and potentially destructive solipsism which make up the Decadent rejection of the notion of progress and the achievements of civilisation. Leaving aside Byron and Musset, Baudelaire is generally regarded as the first Decadent and after the failure of the 1848 revolution Baudelaire lost all his political enthusiasm and became the epitome of Decadence – especially of the Decadent approach to the two central means of male communication, women and language. The Decadent movement proper does not begin in France, however, until the 1880s, after the French defeat in the Franco-Prussian War and after the Commune.

The *Ausgleich* of 1867 appeared to leave the Austrians the losers. However unsatisfied some Hungarians may have been by the *Ausgleich*, on the whole they gained. It is true that their literature was left a little disconcerted by the *Ausgleich*, for writers had suddenly lost their major political target, the domination of Vienna. Thus, it seems, the Hungarians have almost no Decadent literature and those full-bloodedly Decadent works of such as Csáth or Balázs come too late to be called anything but derived. The same goes for the literature of the British Isles. Although Wilde had a considerable influence on late French Decadents and thence on Austrian Germans, Czechs and so forth, much of Wilde is derived. Nearly all English Decadent verse is derived (from the French) – unless one considers early Swinburne and Meredith Decadent, which one might . . . but then one would have to begin to think of the Indian Mutiny and even, possibly, the first two series of Reform Laws.

The imperial glamour of Vienna appeared to be diminished after the *Ausgleich* and certainly Germanness had lost to Magyarness. Moreover Vienna had suffered greatly in prestige as a result of the Austro-Prussian War – and particularly the loss of most of the Habsburg Italian territory. Notably, just as towards the end of the century French nationalism began to revive, so did German nationalism in Cisleithania. After 1867 German families had stopped sending their children to Czech schools in Prague and, as Prague became more and more Czech, so German nationalism there grew. On the whole, however, in Prague that nationalism remained below the surface until 1897. The Czechs lost far more than the Austrian Germans by the *Ausgleich*, for they had hoped and worked for a 'Trialism' rather than a Dualism, but their attempts had failed definitively in 1871. Still the Czechs, as inhabitants of the prosperous industrial centre of the Monarchy, initially appeared more or less to sit back and enjoy that prosperity. The political soil for the Czech Decadents was given manure by Gebauer and Masaryk's well-displayed demonstration that the Dvůr Králové (Königinhof) and Zelená Hora (Grüneberg) Manuscripts were early nineteenth-century forgeries and thus did not testify to a highly developed mid-mediaeval Czech culture. Their articles appeared in their own periodical, *Athenaeum*, in February 1886. The soil was further prepared by the Old Czechs' loss of their role as the leading Czech political force in the first two months of 1890; they were then thoroughly defeated in the *Reichsrat* elections of March 1891. The Young Czechs set themselves up in opposition to the government – and that is probably why they themselves eventually failed so miserably with the electorate. Also in 1891 the Czechs mounted their own Jubilee Exhibition where they showed off their technological advancedness. As a nationalist act it failed, however; the Emperor Francis Joseph visited it. The organ of the Czech Decadents, *Moderní revue*, was not founded until 1894, but by that time Decadent writing dominated the young literary scene (mainly in Moravian periodicals, but also in one or two well-established Prague periodicals). It may be sheer coincidence that the rise of Decadent literature and art in Europe appears to have a direct connection with political events, particularly with a sense of defeat, or with the need to ascertain new values after a defeat, but it may not.

III. VIENNA, PRAGUE, BUDAPEST

The urban intelligentsias of Austria-Hungary considered the Monarchy to be in a state of chaos and decadence. At the beginning of his first book, *The Future of Austria-Hungary* (1907), R. W. Seton-Watson writes that most British wrongly consider that the Monarchy is about to collapse. Nordau writes in 1883:

In Austria-Hungary ten nationalities face each other in pitched battle and attempt to do as much harm to their opponents as they possibly can. In every Crown Land, indeed in almost every village, the majorities have their boots on the minorities' breasts and the minorities, when they can resist no longer, feign a submission against which in their innermost hearts they furiously rebel. Indeed, against this submission they invoke the destruction of the Monarchy itself as their only possible salvation from an insufferable situation.[10]

The Czech Nineties critic, Šalda, gives a not unbiased, but lively picture of 1890s Vienna in his novel, *Loutky i dělníci boží* (Puppets and God's workers), although many of the critical pictures of Vienna were excised by the censor in the first and second (1918) editions. Vienna is a city in flux and a city which belongs nowhere: 'on the dividing lines between North and South, East and West, so that the forms of every type . . . had rubbed off on it, and it had never had the chance to crystallise'.[11] Vienna is a perverted city, and in the following Šalda appears to be flabbily emulating Schnitzler:

the ages of man were somehow inverted here: young men imitated old with their tiredness, wornness, *blague* and cynicism, whereas aged Fauns, Satyrs and Silenuses either sentimentally winked their paled eyes through their monocles or tried to invigorate their creased faces with a patronly understanding smile . . . hoping that paint had smoothed out their wrinkles and that their blackened moustaches and whiskers were set off to advantage by the well-placed rouge on their carefully tended, elderly complexions.[12]

The evocation of the general atmosphere is a trifle pat, and constitutes what a Czech of the time would expect to read: 'the *Alt-Wien* ditty of Girardi and the neurasthenic *Jung-Wien* poem by Hofmannsthal, the Jewishly witty column in a Liberal daily and the coarse geniality of an antisemitic election pamphlet . . . the last swing or slide in the "Wurstelprater" . . . all this fawned and flattered one.'[13] And:

Art and poetry were valid here as long as they were exhibitionism: a poem was a biographical riddle; a novel had to have *clefs* to its characters; a statue had to rouse interest because of who had modelled for it. Most important of all in Vienna were the actors . . . anyone who wanted any success had to learn from them, lover like husband, statesman like diplomat, writer like politician, the better class of whore like the *grande dame*.

They were all acting . . . they were not, however, acting a today but a dying image of the past, a shimmering reflection of the past on the stagnant, melancholic surface of dusk, while from the east was surging a night which extinguishes all colours and blurs all nuances.[14]

In this Vienna the Czech language is a subject of 'contemptuous songs' in the *cafés chantants* and a sensitive Czech walking through Viennese streets feels 'the wretchedness and humiliation of past ages gnawing at his body and burning on his breast'.[15] But an adoptive Vienesse like the Moravian German Schaukal felt much the same as Šalda; Vienna contained for him much of 'the irredeemable barbarism of this, the vulgarest of all historical epochs'.[16] (Still the petty official Schaukal allowed himself to be ennobled in the last year of the Monarchy.) The population types recruited for the dream realm of the Bohemian German Alfred Kubin's *Die andere Seite* (1909) constitute a satirical representation of Viennese *fin-de-siècle* types:

> The better among them were people of exaggeratedly refined sensitivity. Not yet rampant *idées fixes* like a mania for collecting, bibliophagy, possession by the demon of play, hyperreligiosity and all the thousand forms the more refined types of neurasthenia assumed were perfect for the dream state. Hysteria proved to be the most frequent manifestation in women. The masses were also chosen on the basis of abnormality or one-sided developments . . . hypochondriacs, spiritists, brash ruffians, blasé men in search of excitement, old adventurers in search of peace, conjurers, acrobats, political refugees, indeed even murderers who were being sought by foreign police, forgers and thieves. . . . In certain circumstances a particularly remarkable physical characteristic qualified a person to be called into the dream realm. Thus the many hundred-weight goitres, button noses, gigantic humps.[17]

This Vienna, which had grown from about 700,000 in 1880 to around two million in 1910, had lost its stability. More than half these two million were not Viennese by birth, and many of these were Czechs or Jews. According to Timms the instability of Vienna 'was caused by dynamic new forces which were undermining the traditional social order'.[18] The new Viennese non-Jewish middle-classes did not on the whole merge with the aristocracy, but remained as much outsiders as the Jews and so, as a 'substitute for the life of action, art became almost a religion; moreover, as the bourgeois sensed the slipping away of the world, he became increasingly occupied with his own psychic life'.[19] Hauser sees the same phenomena as Timms and Spector emerging for slightly different reasons. The culture of Vienna itself was old and tired and a lack of narrowly Austrian nationalism combined with the Jewish element in the new population to give Viennese art its 'subtle, passive character'. This art, created by 'rich sons of the bourgeoisie [who] are nervous and sad, tired and aimless, sceptical and self-ironic', evokes 'a feeling of passing away, of having missed something, and a consciousness of being unfit for life'.[20] Trakl's slightly Oriental sense of guilt seems to have something to do with that: 'Great is the guilt of the born. Woe, you golden tremblings of death, for the soul dreams cooler blossoms.'[21]

In a study of *fin-de-siècle* culture in Budapest, Prague and Vienna, Cohen asserts that 'public affairs and culture in Prague tended to be less innovative and less cosmopolitan than in Vienna or Budapest', that 'the Czech-German conflict tended not only to pervade much of the intellectual life [of Prague] but often to inhibit it as well' and that the 'many areas of Czech cultural life in Prague, as well as the German, were stodgier and more conservative' than in 'many other major European cities'.[22] At the turn of the century Prague may have been less innovative than Vienna in painting, but it hardly was in sculpture, graphic art or literature. Czech artists populated Paris, Munich and Dresden quite as much as Viennese or Hungarian. The main Prague literary periodical of the 1890s, *Moderní revue*, published in French and German as well as Czech and published translations from most European literatures and reproductions of works by artists of most European nationalities. Most serious literature in German or Czech virtually ignored the Czech-German conflict. Still, I would find it difficult to go quite to the lengths of Franz Kuna, who writes:

> Rooted in this kind of reactionary progressivism is the central paradox of the Vienna of these years: that whilst the city produced one of the most lively and important movements in modern art, music, and literature, it did not come up with a single major work of art. Works like *Ulysses, The Magic Mountain* and *The Waste Land* were not written there. The major, and truly modern, writers of the old Austria came from the less metropolitan city of Prague, which made far less noise about 'Modernism' than did Vienna.[23]

Kuna appears to be thinking mainly of Kafka, but he may also be thinking of Rilke. He points out that Rilke left Prague as early as 1896 and that by 1906 Meyrink and Camill Hoffmann had left; Werfel left in 1912 (as did Albert Einstein, who spent a year teaching at Prague University). The reason for the Prague German writers' leaving, Kuna suggests, was the 'drab atomization of life in their city'.[24] Like Cohen, Kuna does not know the Czech literature of the time, which certainly still in the 1890s and 1900s had old-fashioned historical and social novelists, but it also had Symbolist poets and novelists, attempts at Symbolist drama, full-blown Decadent and Naturalist works of considerable originality – as well as the Decadent, anarchist, more or less Existentialist philosopher, Ladislav Klíma. Some writers had turned from Decadence, Satanism and Symbolism to Expressionism or Vitalism before the Great War (S. K. Neumann, Šrámek). In art decorative Art Nouveau was being replaced by esoteric Symbolist art and Cubism and Expressionism. Indeed Czech literature and art were never to be as lively as from c. 1890 to 1914 again. The better known Avant-Garde from between the two World Wars relied a great deal on the art of the *Fin de siècle*. And the Czech intelligentsia of the period were far from taking themselves too seriously. One thinks of ironical poets like Hlaváček or Opolský or the sarcastic, satirical novelist, K. M. Čapek-Chod. Even the perhaps slightly too earnest Viennese professor of surgery and minor Czech poet, Eduard Albert, could write resignedly, but also ironically, 'In Bohemia we're immured in our fate. Czech art is understanding that.'[25] S. K. Neumann writes despairingly of Bohemia, '*caput regni* [Prague] is rotten, the whole *regnum* is rotten through,'[26] and Arnošt Procházka condemns the Czechs for a willingness always to search for compromise ever since the putting down of the Estates' Rebellion at the Battle of the White Mountain (1620): 'we have always tried to fuse noise and silence, battle and peace,

morning and evening, work and laziness into a single whole, into some
bastard harmony.'[27]

The picture of Prague and the Czechs which one obtains from contemporaneous English writers (if uninformed) is probably typical of the period and
of the English. Thus, for example, the English Decadent Arthur Symons
writes that the only worthwhile piece of Czech art is Comenius's *Labyrint
světa a Ráj srdce*:

> The Bohemians have produced nothing beautiful in any of the plastic arts; but in
> literature, for the most part given up to histories of piety and savagery, they have
> produced one book of genius, in whose hardness, quaintness, crudity, and
> vigorous, unbeautiful detail, I find all the characteristic qualities of the race,
> illuminated, here only, by that light which is imagination. The full title of the book
> is: 'The Labyrinth of the World and the Paradise of the Heart' . . . Like Rabelais,
> but with less intentional extravagance, Komensky will use ten synonyms for one
> statement; he writes all in verbs and nouns, which hammer on our ears with the
> clatter of the fighting peasants' flails.[28]

In the music of Smetana and Dvořák Symons sees a mixture of barbarism
and conventionality; Czech music lacks passion for him. On Czech women
he is rapturous; they manifest little of the *maladie du siècle*:

> They are often very blonde, at times very dark, and there is something a little wild,
> even in the soft beauty of blonde women, a fiery sweetness, a certain strangeness
> as of unfamiliar lights amid the shadows of still water; a little of the soft,
> unconscious savagery of the animals man has tamed, but which have never quite
> forgotten the forest. But they are not perilous, like the Hungarians; sly,
> sometimes, but simple. Children and young girls are often delicious, with their
> white skin and pale gold hair, which in some lights takes a faint shade of green, like
> the hair of a certain portrait of Palma Vecchio . . . in the gallery at Vienna.[29]

Symons has also heard that Czech-German rivalries are much in evidence. If
a Czech actress dares act in a German play, Czechs and Germans will brawl
over her in the street. Symons's assessment of contemporary Czech
patriotism reads like the writing of a Czech like Julius Zeyer in the 1880s. He
comments on the Czechs' blend of historicism and dreaminess (dreaminess
is something one normally links with a Slovak or Bulgarian rather than a
Czech):

> this new outbreak of national life is fed upon memories. The Bohemian still sees a
> phantom city, behind this city in which electric trams take him to the foot of the
> Vyšehrad, a city more real to him than even what remains of his national
> monuments. His memory is a memory of martyrs, of executions, of the savageries
> of religion and of political conflict, Catholics against Protestants, Germans against
> Czechs . . . to the Bohemian no stone that has been violently cast down is
> forgotten. Prague is still the epitome of this history of his country; he sees it as a
> man sees the woman whom he loves, with her first beauty, and he loves it as a man
> loves a woman, more for what she has suffered.[30]

Symons set down his impressions as a result of visits in the summer of 1897 and 1899. G. S. Street was there ten years later and he begins by describing Bohemia in terms which vaguely recall Symons's, though Street has a witty and Decadent tongue: 'she is less well known among us than she ought to be and like a woman may not be, inevitably, best pleased by an entirely secret devotion.'[31] Symons spoke about the Czechs' memories of their martyrs (and the Czech politician, T. G. Masaryk, had inveighed against their martyr complex in 1895), where Street speaks of their heroic sacrifice and patience. Street is impressed by the brooding spirit of Prague and, like Symons, he feels her history as he gazes at her:

> Prague is a very beautiful city, and would be still, though you took away its ancient glories; but the impression I had even then, and far more deeply when late at night I stood alone on Karlov Most [*sic*], was first of all, first and last, the sense of 'old, unhappy, far-off things'. The quotation is somewhat hackneyed, but it must be used of Prague if it is never used again . . . . dimly clairvoyant, I knew myself among the ghosts of the unhappy dead.[32]

Street mentions the fact that recently all German street names had been banished from Prague and he also speaks of the Czechs' apparently passionate love for their native language. He tells a typical story of a Prager's pleasure at his few Czech words and at his not being a German or speaking German. But this is an ordinary Prager, not a member of the intelligentsia. Street compares Bohemia with Ireland, an old idea, but his comparison is original:

> It is a rarely stimulating experience to be in a country which has a strong national feeling in it. In this Bohemia has been compared with Ireland; but the comparison is unjust, for the national feeling is far more thoroughly pervading in Bohemia, and – I would say it without offence – more profound and more sincere. It touches all classes, for one thing; it is based on a genuine racial difference. . . . The difference between England and Ireland is chiefly one of climate; a large class [of Irish] is indifferent, to say the least of it, to national feeling . . . There is, no doubt, a pro-German party in Bohemia, but it is a small and diminishing minority, and I am told that the Jews, who were of the German party, are now significantly inclined to fall into line.[33]

By the 1860s there was an established Czech as well as German middle class in Prague. Prague was essentially a bourgeois city. That is the major feature distinguishing Prague from Vienna and Budapest. After the *Ausgleich* a middle class was only beginning to be formed in Pest, and its members were 'Greeks', Jews and Germans from the old mining and trading towns of Hungary. Between 1867 and 1900, however, the population of Pest-Buda, then Budapest, trebled and the Jews joined the Magyar nationalist cause. The Millenium Exhibition of 1896 (a thousand years since the arrival of the Magyars in the area) represented the public manifestation of Hungary's (or at least Budapest's) cultural and technological adulthood.

Remnants of the strong anti-Magyar feeling the Exhibition roused in the non-Magyar intellectuals of Hungary is still occasionally perceptible today, among the Slovaks. Most of the Hungarian intelligentsia of the time were magyarised; there was no grammar schooling in Slovak or Roumanian or Ukrainian or Serbian. The discontent of the nationalities on the whole, however, remained gently bubbling under the surface before 1905. Thenceforth it frequently boiled over as in Černová in October 1907, when a Magyar, or magyarised, priest was sent to consecrate a church rather than the Slovak, Andrej Hlinka, who had collected the money for the building. (To be sure Hlinka was a trouble-maker.) The villagers started throwing stones and the gendarmerie became frightened and began shooting into the Slovak crowd; nine were killed on the spot and another six were fatally wounded. Hungary saw considerable organised social unrest during the *fin-de-siècle* period, especially the agricultural labourers' strike which began in the 1880s; then there was the five-week metal-workers' strike in May and June 1905, or Bloody Thursday, 23 May 1912, when nine socialists and workers were killed 'at the barricades' in Budapest.

Although signs of Decadent art were evident in Hungarian literature beforehand, in writers like Justh[34] and Komjáthy, Hungarian culture did not really enter the *Fin de siècle* until the 1900s, although József Kiss's periodical, *A Hét* (the week) which was founded in 1890, prepared the ground for Hungarian Modernism. *A Hét* was particularly important for its publication of translations of French verse, but nearly all the poets chosen between 1890 and 1901 were old fashioned, Hugo, Leconte de Lisle, Vigny, or conventional, Coppée, Ratisbonne; nevertheless Baudelaire and Bourget were each represented by four poems and the eccentric Decadent-cum-social poet Jean Richepin, who had a considerable impact on the Hungarian Ady and on the Czech Hlaváček, was represented by eight pieces. Karátson considers the publication in 1901 of a sizable anthology of nineteenth-century French verse in Hungarian a turning point in the Hungarian literary development.[35] (Similar anthologies in the 1880s had some impact in Bohemia.)

For non-Magyars Hungary outside Budapest was considered somewhat barbaric. Zeyer frequently referred to the Asiatic hordes who were oppressing the gentle Slavs. And Alfred Kubin writes ironically that 'from Budapest on a slight Asiatic element made itself felt. How? In the interests of this book I do not wish to insult Hungary.'[36] Arthur Symons also visited Budapest and also saw Hungary as the beginning of the Orient. What is most useful to us in his description is the comparison with Vienna:

> In Budapest there is nothing but what the people and a natural brightness in the air make of it. Here things are what they seem; atmosphere is everything, and the atmosphere is almost one of illusion. . . . Coming from Austria, you seem, since you have left Vienna, to have crossed more than a frontier. You are in another world, in which people live with a more vivid and a quite incalculable life: the East

has begun. . . . Some charm is in the air, and a scarcely definable sense of pleasure, which makes one glad to be there. One has been suddenly released from the broad spaces, empty heights, and tiring movement of Vienna, in which, to the stranger, there is only the mechanical part of gaiety and only the pretentious part of seriousness. Here, in Budapest, . . . idleness becomes active; there is no need for thought, and no inclination to think beyond the passing moment.[37]

The major Hungarian Symbolist, Endre Ady, certainly conceived of Hungary as in a state of decay (*Új versek*, New verse, 1906), 'The sad Hungarian Plain with its odour of death', but generally he regarded Hungary as fallow or scrub land – an uncultured desert.[38] In the figure of Ady one sees another difference between the Hungarian and the Austrian-German and Czech cultural functions of the *Fin de siècle*. Ady felt the need to shock his audience out of apathy with his 'unpoetic' language and Decadent poses. Schnitzler and Hofmannsthal expressed the interests of their own classes and, especially the former, analysed their mental state. Hofmannsthal's pose was not to shock, but to be aloof. The Czech Decadents around *Moderní revue* were an aggressive élite, who adopted the pose of not caring what anyone said about them or what impact they might have. The Viennese and the Hungarians and the Czechs did not like each other and knew very little about what was going on culturally in each other's territories. The artists of the three nations were more likely to meet each other in Munich or Paris than on Austro-Hungarian soil.

IV. THE JEWS

Another difference between the three separate but linked cultures lies in the roles played by the Jews. In 1900 23.4% of the total population of Budapest, 8.8% of Vienna and 6.7% of Prague were Jewish. The Jews of Budapest came from the Hungarian Lands, Russia and Galicia, those of Vienna from the same places but also from Moravia and, to a lesser extent, from Bohemia. The Jews of Prague, however, nearly all came from Bohemia (92%). Most Jews in Budapest were or quickly became Hungarian speakers; in Vienna they spoke German and in Prague, at least by the 1900 census, only 45% of the Jews declared German to be their language of social intercourse.[39] Czechs, in fact, still tended to consider Jews more or less automatically as Germans, however strong the Czech-Jewish movement and however many Jews attended Czech schools. The position of the Jews or people of Jewish descent in Vienna *fin-de-siècle* culture was central; they ran the daily and periodical press; they bought the pictures and statues (though there were very few Viennese Jewish plastic artists); they went to concerts – and they wrote music; Austrian-German Decadent literature was led by a Jew, Schnitzler, and a conscious quarter-Jew, Hofmannsthal; the new thought to come out of Vienna came from conscious Jews (Freud,

Wittgenstein). In Budapest the situation was similar except that all the cultural periodical press was founded and run by Jews. Two fifths of all Hungarian journalists were Jewish. New ideas came into Hungarian culture primarily through Jews. Jews had turned Budapest into the financial and industrial centre that it was at the turn of the century. Three fifths of Budapest's physicians and two fifths of her lawyers were Jewish.[40] Kiss was the most important Jewish Hungarian poet of the time, but his most significant contribution to Hungarian culture was the founding of *A Hét*, an apolitical journal with a 'snobbish disposition', and a 'mildly satirical tone' which was programmatically opposed to Establishment literature. Most of *A Hét*'s contributors were also Jewish (and the readership was largely Budapest middle-class, thus predominantly Jewish). According to Czigány, one contributor, Tamás Kóbor, was particularly important, not so much because he was an ardent assimilator, as because he urged the Jews themselves to oppose religious and racial prejudice.[41] In Prague the cultural role of the Jews was far smaller. Jews had a strong position in the Prague German press and the well-known Prague-German authors were Jewish: Werfel, Brod, Kafka. There were few Jewish impulses to Czech literary culture, though, to be sure, the prose-writer usually considered the founder of Czech science fiction, Jakub Arbes, was a baptised Jew, as was the most important precessor of the Decadents, a writer who became himself a Decadent, Julius Zeyer. Zeyer, furthermore, came from a German-speaking family and his Czech still had to be corrected by friends and editors when he was in his fifties in the 1890s. In the 1900s the liveliest of the Czech late Decadent and Anarchist satirist writers, František Gellner, was a Jew. Gellner contributed caricatures to *Cri de Paris* and *Rire* during his two prolonged stays in Paris. Jews had very little to do with the Czech press.

Where there are Jews there is antisemitism and one of the paradoxes of this period in Austria-Hungary lies in the fact that the Establishment's dependence on, even enjoyment of, Jewish culture did nothing to stem traditional prejudice. In Tiszaeszlar, eastern Hungary, in 1882 a group of Jews were tried for the ritual murder of the Christian girl, Eszter Solymosi; in the end the accused were acquitted. And an Antisemitic Party was founded in Hungary in 1883, though it lasted only a very few years.[42] Hungary produced one of Austria-Hungary's great racists, Stefan von Czobel. In his monumental *Der Genesis unserer Kultur* (1901–7) he categorises races or peoples according to whether they adhere to the aristocratic or the plutocratic principle. The Eygptians, west Europeans and Magyars adhere to the former where as Syrians, Arabs and Jews adhere to the latter. Naturally, the plutocratic is greatly inferior to the aristocratic principle.

In Prague, the one area of the Monarchy where there had been an almost continuous Jewish population, certainly since the ninth century, and where Jews had market rights before Germans, antisemitism arose in the nineteenth century, in the 1890s especially in the riots following the dismissal of the Badeni language ordinances (cf. Dyk's novels *Konec Hackenschmidův*, Hackenschmid's end, 1904, and *Prosinec*, December, 1906), when Jewish students were attacked as the most virulent German chauvinists. Antisemitic disturbances, mainly window-breaking, were aroused by the trial of the dimwitted rural Jew, Leopold Hilsner, for the ritual murder of the pure Czech gad-about, Anežka Hrůzová (1899). T. G. Masaryk brought more fame to himself by interceding in this trial, not to rescue Hilsner, but to express his revulsion at the ridiculous superstition of ritual murder (the blood libel). Masaryk earned himself political kudos; a song about Anežka Hrůzová still survives in the Czech oral tradition, and antisemitism continued.

Mainstream Czech literature was not antisemitic; Zeyer (who did not know he was wholly Jewish) and Vrchlický (who had a drop of Jewish blood but was not consciously Jewish) were particularly attracted to Jewish literary themes, in the 1880s. A signatory of the Czech *Moderne* manifesto, the liberal Vilém Mrškík, wrote in 1902 for the Russian *Novoye vremya* an article 'Semitism – Jesuitism' (which he published in Czech in 1903, *Moje sny*, II [My dreams]), where he speaks of an international Jewish conspiracy and hails the twentieth century as the century of the fight against Jews as the nineteenth century had been the century of the fight against the Jesuits. The Jews and Jesuits indulge in the same aggressive exclusivity which, Mrštík says, must be destroyed. To be sure the Decadent Karásek has a nasty Jewish usurer in his first novel, but soon he becomes a strongly Philosemitic writer – possibly largely for esoteric reasons. A writer belonging to a loose group of reform Catholic priests and writers known as the *Katolická moderna*, Catholic *Moderne*, Baar, saw the Jews as part of the scourge of ungodly capitalism threatening the idyll of Southern Bohemia. His still today extremely popular novel, *Jan Cimbura* (1908), contains the following typical piece of religion-based antisemitism, which looks forward to Czech Ruralist writers between the wars and Slovak nationalist writers of the 1970s and 1980s:

> the new Putim vicar heaved a sigh and said to his curate, 'Well, I am pleased. The village is virginal again.'
> 'What do you mean?'
> 'A virginal village is one where there isn't a Jew.'[43]

In Vienna antisemitism was formalised.[44] Political antisemitism arose from the conflict between liberalism and reform Catholicism. The Catholic reformers began speaking and writing of Judaeoliberalism and accused the Jews of intending to rise in rebellion against the Habsburgs as well as Mother Church. The initiator of Christian Social antisemitism was Carl von Vogelsang who, according to Moser, was responsible for inventing antisemitic political formulations like 'Judaism is capitalism'. Parallel to that political antisemitism, racial antisemitism grew, based on the ideas of Gobineau. In as early as 1878 the Libertas *Burschenschaft* introduced 'Aryan regulations', whereby Jewish students could not become members. Political and racial antisemitism united in Georg von Schönerer who, in his 1890 election platform, spoke of the Jews' control of national finances and the press, and in parliament in 1887 he declared antisemitism to be 'a foundation stone of nationalist thought, . . . one of the greatest achievements of this century'. The antisemitic political party which grew out of the 1888 fusion of the German Nationals and the Christian Socials was led by Karl Lueger, the man who is famous for referring to the Hungarians as the 'Judaeo-Magyars' and for phrases like 'I decide who's a Jew' and 'Where are my Jews?', and who later, in 1897, became the powerful Mayor of Vienna. Schorske has suggested that for Viennese Jews art became 'a refuge from the unpleasant world of increasingly threatening political reality'.[45] In 1894 Austrian German Decadent literature, especially its notional seedy side, its 'hectic-neuralgic verse written by hermaphrodites in whose literary organisms a mixture of morphium and *odeur de femmes* flows instead of blood', is derived by Ottokar Stauf von der March mainly from a Semitic influence: 'Most Decadents are Semites.'[46] The Jewish Otto Weininger extended this literary antisemitism into the anthropological, when he stated that Jews are 'saturated with femininity' and are, 'like women, wanting in personality'.[47]

V. MAX NORDAU

Nordau relates the following about Viennese Jews: 'when during matriculation the registrar of Vienna University asked the normal question about a potential undergraduate's religion and the student answered: "No religion", the registrar used to say with a genial smile, "Why didn't you say straightaway that you were a Jew?" '[48] On antisemitism he writes, perhaps optimistically:

> Here under the mask of antisemitism, a comfortable disguise for the expression of passions which would not be allowed to be seen under their real names, there appear, (i) among the ignorant and the poor, hatred of those who hold property, and (ii) among those who enjoy mediaeval privileges, the so-called privileged classes, the fear of gifted competitors for influence and power, and (iii) among confused idealistic young people, an unjustifiable, exaggerated form of patriotism, namely the unfulfillable demand for not only the political unity of the German fatherland, but also the ethnic unity of the German people.[49]

Max Simon Nordau (i.e. Südfeld) was born in Budapest in 1849, and he changed his name, Gsteiger suggests, to show his Prussian German inclinations. Nordau was an immensely popular cultural historical and cultural critic, 'a narrow-minded polemicist' and 'an intellectual of great talent and wide-ranging knowledge',[50] who, from 1880 onwards, lived and worked in Paris as a physician. Together with Theodor Herzl Nordau founded modern Zionism and in 1897 he became vice-president of the Zionist Congress. Nordau's fame rested and rests on his huge assessment of nineteenth-century literature based on the theories of Cesare Lombroso, *Entartung* (Degeneration, 1892–3; English and French translations followed immediately). The chief irony of this book is that another product of the Austro-Hungarian *Fin de siècle* who changed his name used the Jewish Nordau's terminology in pursuance of his persecution of modern art and Jews. Karl Kraus considered that a man who could find nearly all the significant figures of nineteenth-century literature mentally sick or deviant, must himself be suffering from some cerebral abnormality. Nordau uses the strident tones of totalitarian politicians.[51] And his book is silly and successfully appealed as a populist tract to those European minds who found high art beyond their intellectual reach. Nevertheless *Entartung* was the first attempt at a synthetic assessment of all modern European literary and, to a degree, philosophical trends. Praz's criticism of Nordau is no doubt well-judged (though Nordau had certainly read all he wrote about), but no one before Praz had had the courage to do what Nordau had tried to do. I doubt Praz is right about the Hungarian's insincerity: '*Degeneration* aims at being a literary nosology of the Decadent Movement, but it is completely discredited by its pseudo-erudition, its grossly positivist point of view, and its insincere moral tone.'[52] Wellek considers *Entartung* a satirical work and points out Nordau's influence on Tolstoy's *What is Art?*.[53] And Pierrot, who does not utterly condemn the work like Praz, claims that French Decadent writers had 'often amused themselves by deliberately leading poor Nordau up the garden path when he was researching his book in Paris'.[54] Still Nordau bears the responsibility for leading totalitarians and moralisers from that day to this automatically to link literary or artistic Decadence with social or moral or even aesthetic degeneracy.

In his own day his early work *Die conventionellen Lügen der Kultur-menschheit* (1883, The conventional lies of civilisation; English translation 1896), was far more popular. Particularly in the Monarchy it appeared to analyse truthfully the state of social decay and hypocrisy in which modern European man lived. It awakened in Austro-Hungarians that sense of living in a period of decay or transition which constitutes a prerequisite for Decadent art. As an art-object in itself it also represents a thoroughly Habsburg phenomenon: a work written in German by a Hungarian Jewish doctor living in Paris who has given himself a Prussian-sounding name. It is a messy work, but also a pithy and sometimes intelligent work. It is political, but it is neither conservative nor liberal. But nor is it anarchist, nor, strictly speaking populist: there is no room for scepticism or Nordau's form of irony in populism. T. G. Masaryk considered *Die conventionellen Lügen* a revolutionary work and even after the Great War Masaryk could not shake off Nordau's influence. In the 1890s Masaryk frequently wrote in the style of fifteenth-century Protestants about truth and living in truth and in Nordau he found phrases like: 'The lack of truth in our lives is beggaring us.'[55] Naturally, Nordau is more stentorophonic and hysterical than Masaryk ever was; in the opening paragraph of his book he presents a direly melodramatic picture: 'In spite of ever more favourable conditions for greater well-being, mankind is more excited, dissatisfied and restless than it has ever been. The civilised world is one monstrous hospital ward whose air is filled with oppressive moaning and on whose beds lies suffering in all its forms.'[56] As if he were writing in the 1980s he sees the rank growth of selfishness as the cause of social disintegration (in Nordau's anthropology man feels natural solidarity with his fellow men); he has no time for the individualism so highly praised by the contemporary British. The cult of individualism has made ordinary social intercourse a matter of a set of rules for shamming interest or concern. He dismisses totally modern philosophy:

> the fashionable current in philosophy is pessimism. Schopenhauer is God and Hartmann is his prophet. Auguste Comte's Positivism makes no progress as a doctrine, nor is it developing into sects, for even its adherents have realised that its method is too narrow and its goal – insufficiently elevated. French philosophers nowadays study almost only psychology or, to put it more accurately, psychophysiology. English philosophy can hardly be called metaphysics any longer since it has omitted to undertake metaphysics' most noble task, the search for a satisfactory worldview, and it now concerns itself only with second-rank practical questions. . . . Only Germany still has a metaphysics and this is a dour bleak metaphysics. . . . Hegelianism has turned into the lumber-room of worn-out systems and the world is being taken over by a philosophy whose tragic point is that the intolerable cosmos is to be led back to the nothingness by the will to the non-being of all creatures.[57]

Masaryk, too, had no time for pessimism, but at least in his early days he emulated Comte, though he soon rejected Positivism as well. Masaryk's conception of national consciousness closely approaches Nordau's conception of solidarity. And Masaryk was to become as suspicious of ready-made social institutions as Nordau is. For the latter the forms and expressions of modern social institutions are in a state of total disharmony. Men hold to conventions of respect which they know to be empty, so that every thinking individual becomes a clown who makes everyone else laugh but who is repelled and saddened by his own clowning. Nordau analyses the roots of modern pessimism, of what will later be labelled the Decadent worldview thus:

> As soon as one recognises that the institutions which have been handed down are empty, senseless mock forms, half scarecrows and half theatre scenery, one necessarily suffers the horror and indignation, thus disheartenment and attacks of black humour, which might be experienced by a living man locked up in a crypt of corpses, or a rational man living among lunatics who, in order not to sustain physical injuries, has to join in all the lunatics' crazy ideas.

This continuing contradiction between our views and all the forms of our culture, this need to live surrounded by institutions we consider lies, that is what makes us pessimists and sceptics. . . . In such unbearable discord we lose all our joy in existence and all our desire to try.[58]

Nordau's main 'lies' are religious, social (the roles of monarchs and aristocrats), political, economic and sexual. Nordau has no time for Christianity or the Christian morality. He claims that in teaching the love of one's neighbour Christianity had raised man's instinctual solidarity to the level of a command and thus supported the preservation of the species. On the other hand, it had condemned the sexual side of love and so ruined its own work. Chastity had once been necessary because early Christians had found gross promiscuity, but it had long become a torpid residual value and no longer had any place in Christian teaching. Anyway, he claims, the role of chastity had only ever been followed by those who suffered from religious mania, a disease which is nearly always accompanied by sexual dysfunction. (That myth is upheld in, for example, Karásek's *Gothická duše* [A Gothic soul, 1900].) When he avers religion is a lie he does not mean men's belief in some supernatural, extraterrestrial force, for he acknowledges that most of mankind genuinely believes in such forces. Such beliefs constitute a residue of humanity's childhood. (There, as often, Nordau's conceptions come close to those of occultists, who believe, say, that through meditation on specific ancient symbols a man may attain the blessed simple state of understanding enjoyed by man at the hub of 'humanity's childhood', when the given symbol was first constructed. Nordau is, naturally enough, anti-occultist, but perhaps there is a bit of the Cabala in his genes.) For Nordau religion is a lie insofar as it demands of civilised man the veneration of articles of faith, feastdays, ceremonies, symbols and priests. And when such religious lying is indulged in by a whole society it is far worse than if it is indulged in by a single individual. The state is lying when it ordains religious holidays, employs priests, makes princes of the Church members of its upper house. The modern priest is himself also lying when he allows himself to be paid for doing and saying things he knows perfectly well are nothing but superstitious jiggery-pokery. Nordau will not side with either Roman Catholicism or Protestantism: 'Catholicism is consistent, but Protestantism is arbitrary. Catholicism gives its head the right to declare what must be believed and forbids all criticism of such ordinances. Protestantism allows criticism of the faith on the basis of the Bible, but forbids criticism of the Bible itself.'[59]

Nordau has no time for constitutional monarchies, because they are neither flesh nor fowl. The archaic institution of the monarchy is sensible as long as it is fundamentally an autocracy. Thus he accepts the Russian and Turkish forms of monarchy. There is nothing hypocritical about absolutism, whereas 'constitutionalism' is an idiotic, deceitful comedy, resulting from an attempt to fuse two mutually exclusive political forms and *Weltanschauungen*. The constitutional monarch's powers are limited by the will of the people and yet he is monarch by the grace of God and thus he is in danger of blasphemously claiming to limit the will of God, argues Nordau. The idea of being monarch by the grace of God has become quite ridiculous, especially when one observes the way in the recent past new dynasties have made themselves at home by the grace of God in (the order is Nordau's) Sweden, Norway, Belgium, Serbia, Roumania, Greece and Bulgaria. A monarchy is unthinkable without faith in God.[60] The compromise of the constitutional monarchy manifests the unwillingness of ancient institutions to declare themselves for what they actually are; thus these institutions lay themselves open to mockery and risk the common people's beginning to cast doubt on their right to existence.

The survival of an hereditary aristocracy with titles and coats of arms is an absurd remnant of the days of absolutist monarchy. Still an aristocracy has an aesthetic value, since people born into such families tend to know how to behave gracefully. Nordau, in rejecting the rights of the aristocracy, is careful to point out that he holds no egalitarian views. Equality before the law is difficult enough, but social equality is unthinkable. Inequality is natural and thus to an extent hereditary aristocracy is natural. Aristocrats are more likely to behave honourably than non-aristocrats, because they are jealous of the family name, and thus they are useful to society as models. Family pride, not education, teaches noble behaviour; thus the aristocrat is a 'collective individual', someone who by nature conforms with Nordau's ideal of solidarity.

A true republic is acceptable as a notion, but that notion excludes all hereditary privileges, large capital and a hierarchy of state officials. The French Republic of 1870 or the Spanish of 1868 was nothing but a monarchy without a throne. No republican revolution is justified which merely changes the form of rule and fails to change the social, economic and philosophical assumptions which had obtained during the monarchy. The only rational sort of republic is a socialist republic. Nordau does not use the term socialist, but he describes a state where there is no capitalism, no class difference and where the form of government is based on a natural-scientific world view.[61] He does not advocate a 'socialist' republic, simply considers it the only logical conclusion to republican endeavour.

The chief curses of modern politics are fiscalism, a mentality bound to taxing citizens, and mandarinism, the bureaucratisation of everyday life. The limits the state imposes on the individual's action are disproportionate to the facilities the state offers him in exchange for limitation. All the rules the state establishes to control violence are futile since, except in war, nearly all violent acts are committed as a result of passion and no laws can control passion. Still there must be rules; anarchy is an illusion conjured up by confused minds.

Any group of men will naturally form a state organisation of some kind. Most states suffer from fiscalism, and fiscalism derives from the mediaeval conception of state, whereby the individual represents a forced labourer working to support the power and respectability of the state. The modern conception of the state, however, sees in the state an institution for the furtherance of individual well-being. Nordau considers parliamentary democracy a bastard institution which at least allows ambitious men to attain power by stepping on the shoulders of their fellow citizens. It allows the born ruler to maintain his individuality without threatening the state; thus parliamentary democracy functions as a safety-valve to prevent particularly strong personalities from causing explosions. The parliamentary system is 'the triumph, the apotheosis of egoism'.[62] The main political lie of the times thus consists in the fact that what looks like democracy is a cunning way of furthering certain individuals' ambition and egocentricity.

In his discussion of what he calls the economic lies of the civilised world Nordau appears to be influenced by Proudhon (although he disagrees with Proudhon's contention that property is theft). All politics at the end of the nineteenth century consists in the demand for bread, and everything else that goes on in parliaments and committees, exhibitions, wars and colonisations are just sideshows to the main spectacle of modern politics. Politics consists in persuading people they will be better off materially. The problem is that the majority of mankind had always been poor in comparison with an élite. What is new to the present superior, sick civilisation and totally alien to any natural state, is absolute poverty as a continuing phenomenon. Western Europe has succeeded in attaining a level of civilisation whereby a small minority lives in luxury and the majority can barely scrape an existence. It is indeed a decadent society when today's proletarian is more wretched than the slave in Antiquity; the only advantage he has over the slave is that he has the freedom to starve. Members of the proletariat have a life expectancy half, sometimes a third, of that a member of the well-heeled classes has. The proletarian's wage helps him not to die quickly. Another ill of modern society is speculation on the stock-exchange: Nordau calls that the most insufferable symptom of the diseased economic organism. The stock-exchange is a robbers' den where modern robber-barons gather and lie in wait so they can cut the throats of passers-by. Large-scale industrialists are almost as evil; Nordau enjoys the terms 'capitalist exploiter' and 'disinherited proletarians'[63] and he has no time for the Protestant praise of work (Masaryk had great faith in work). Rest and leisure comport far more closely with man's natural state than work, according to Nordau (cf. Marcuse in the 1950s). Work constitutes simply a troublesome necessity for the preservation of life. The idea of work as a virtue derives from the exploiters – who consider leisure among the working classes a vice. Capitalist society commends and honours work, but devolves that particular laud and honour only on lower mortals. Capitalist civilisation is a perversion of mediaeval culture when the nobles had leisure, for the nobles were the conquering class. In the Middle Ages manual work testified to the fact that one had been born into a family which had shown little courage on the battlefield. So, again, capitalism is *eo ipso* a manifestation of cultural decay. And the capitalist's dream is of an even more distorted form of consumer society:

> This will be the economists' golden age with unlimited production, uncontrolled consumption and industrial development without goal. In this golden age whole countries will be covered with factory chimneys as they now are with trees; people will nourish themselves with synthetic foods instead of bread and meat, work eighteen hours a day and die without knowing they have lived. . . . In that day the world will perhaps have the spectacle of a country where every shack contains a piano of the most recent design and where the whole population is dressed in the brand-new material, but has rickets, no blood in its veins and consumption in its lungs.[64]

Man's despoiling of Nature and of man will become a central theme of *fin-de-siècle* art.

Marriage, especially among the better-off, represents just such despolia-tion. Marriages have become purely economic arrangements with no moral or anthropological justification. Love may constitute merely the notional manifestation of the instinct to preserve the species, but the sexual act should be a sacred act; in the present day the sex drive has become an object of egoistical exploitation. Like Musset in his second characterisation of the *maladie du siècle* Nordau comes to the conclusion that 'woman is the immediate victim of the degeneration of civilised society'.[65] Love, he says, has been almost the only theme of literature ever since the beginnings of literary art; depictions of true love themselves become a lie when society has debased love, made it into a matter of economic agreement or of subjugation. Nordau's conception of sexual intercourse as the sublimest of human activities contradicts the mainstream Decadent conception of sexuality. Nordau has no time for sensuous hedonism in sex, nor for contraception. Both run counter to the elevatedness of the desire to procreate. In Nordau's understanding a degenerate man is one in whom sexual passion dominates his whole mental life. Such degenerates cannot suppress their desire for possession of the woman who has stimulated their sexuality and they are quite capable of perpetrating foolish or undignified deeds, where necessary even crimes, just in order to fulfil their particular sexual desires. There Nordau is closer to a Decadent view, albeit one could understand that view as a pretty ordinary description of being in love. Real love is rare at the end of the nineteenth century. What people take for love is actually 'an anxiety, half day-dreaming, half hysteria, a mixture of self-deception, reminiscence, acquired perception of something read in books or heard, diseased, sentimental imaginings, even straightforward mental disorder or madness, impulsiveness or melancholia'.[66] There are only two types of male-female relationships, those based on mutual attraction and directed towards procreation and those which are essentially prostitution, whatever they may appear to be on the outside. As far as that last category, the largest category in the grand European decay, is concerned, the common whore who sells her body to support a mother or a child is morally superior to the blushing virgin who copulates with a bag of gold on her wedding night. Nordau is a feminist. He bewails the lot of modern European middle-class woman who is trained by society to believe that her only life-fulfilment lies in marriage, that she can achieve her natural rights only through marriage. The only other freedom open to middle-class girls who have little money is the slavery of being governesses. As a feminist he has no time for the notion that emancipation is a panacea. Complete equality of men and women is a silly idea. He imagines that if women become equal to men in the matter of earning a living, women, because they are physically weaker, would soon go under; women's life would become even less bearable than it is at present. It would certainly come about that women would, then, be paid less than men for doing comparable work. Nordau's view on the consequences of women's emancipation accords, coincidentally, with a standard interpretation of antifeminism in *fin-de-siècle* art: 'Emancipation necessarily places man and woman in a relationship which is like that between a higher race and a lower race.'[67] Nordau is against marriage, indeed against monogamy altogether. He shares with Nietzsche the opinion that: 'Even concubinage has been corrupted: – by marriage.'[68] Monogamy, Nordau says, is not a natural state for man; it appears to have evolved because of a perceived need to place a guard over the freedom of the individual's sex-drive. It is good, he quips, that Romeo and Juliet died young and so their love lasted and the audience did not have to sit through the epilogue set in the divorce court. Nordau, then, proposes free love.

Among the other phenomena of social decay Nordau considers I would mention suicide. In Europe suicide is increasing hand in hand with alcoholism and drug addiction; all derive from a growing sense of bitterness among civilised men; the struggle for existence thus assumes wild, diabolical forms which had not existed in previous, pre-industrialist ages. Nordau makes the same connections as Masaryk, though Masaryk considered that contemporaneous 'suicidality' resulted from European man's loss of faith and that the likelihood of attempting suicide also depended on whether one was a Catholic or a Protestant. With the exceptions of the Anglo-Saxon lands, Masaryk claims in his *Der Selbstmord als sociale Massenerscheinung* (Suicide as a mass phenomenon, 1881) that a Protestant is more likely to commit suicide than a Catholic – just as a Catholic country is more likely to indulge in revolutions than a Protestant. Where Masaryk conceives of suicide as essentially the action of a mentally impaired person, Nordau, while admitting that is a possibility, says suicide normally demands a man/ woman of strong will. Nordau considers it a stupid act because it constitutes a futile attempt to protect life from threatening danger; one only kills oneself to avoid some mental or physical distress. 'Every suicide has something of the oft-observed action of the soldier who kills himself just before going into battle, because he is overcome by fear of the dangers of battle.'[69] Duelling is ridiculous, where suicide is futile. Duelling was a matter of concern to Austro-Hungarians altogether – as we know particularly from Schnitzler. The institution of the duel demonstrates that man's instinct for self-preservation is weaker than his herd instinct. The duel contradicts all the principles on which modern civilisation is based and constitutes another example of debased, decayed mediaeval values. Duelling performed a useful social function when disagreements between two collectives were settled by a duel between one member of each collective. Duelling was also justifiable when it had been simply a primitive manifestation of the individual's struggle for survival. Nordau blames 'militarism' for the continued existence of the duel in Europe, and the military code of honour which drives officers to duelling is empty.

Nordau constantly asserts that he abhors individualism, but he is a liberal individualist of a kind, and an elitist. His views combine those of an old reactionary and a 'progressivist'. And he is a Modernist in that he is fundamentally optimistic, however drastic the state of Europe. He defines freedom as a removal of obstacles to individuals' and social groups' exploitation of their natural strengths. Elsewhere he makes individualism and selfishness synonyms,[70] though he says he does perceive a slight growth in man's ability to identify his own interests with those of the group. That could be helped if one restricted as far as possible the inheritance of material possessions. He regrets men's cowardice, their unwillingness to be left to their own devices, to have to rely only on their individual strengths; the Christian religion has removed the positive side of individualism from ordinary men's horizons. But, like Nietzsche again, he accepts an élite of exceptional men, the conquerers, the shepherds of people, party leaders, 'but the great herd of mankind has nothing of this proud independence. Average individuals do not want to enter the struggle for survival as into single combat; they want a battle of massed armies with closed ranks.'[71] That is the same sort of individualism promulgated by the Decadents. Man, Nordau says, should strive towards the ideal of powerful independence, towards membership of the élite. In the élite the perception of its ultimate goal becomes consciousness (again a somewhat esoteric conceptualisation), whereas for ordinary human beings that perception remains a sort of vague longing for some sort of ideal. Consciousness is strength, longing sentimentalist hebetude. The élite is not necessarily concerned with leadership at all. The majority of mankind belongs to the herd. Herds have leaders, but those leaders necessarily accept, indeed condone, the herd and the herd mentality. A member of the élite, the conqueror type, cannot accept the herd or its mentality. Nordau's conqueror type is similar to Nietzsche's superman, and to the Decadent dandy. Nordau's conqueror type must reject communism, 'that foolish abortion of an imagination which surrenders itself to azure fantasies without paying any attention to the reality of the world or to human nature.'[72] The goal of civilisations would not be communism but a solidarity in which the fundamental moral principle is that one should do everything that furthers the wellbeing of humanity and nothing which brings humanity harm or pain. He imagines in the end a great, fraternal federation where everyone will be genuine, knowing, free and good.

Nordau's idealism is explicity based on the concept of a natural morality based on nature. Here again he concurs with Masaryk, but not with Masaryk's teacher and then friend, the Vienna professor of philosophy, Franz Brentano. Brentano, who declares himself an empiricist, denies all innate moral principles; he believes 'neither in the Baroque *ius naturae, i.e. quod natura ipsa omnia animalia docuit*, or in the *ius gentium*, a law acknowledged by the general agreement of nations as natural rational law, as Roman Law teachers conceived of it'.[73] Similarly Nordau notionally accepts the Kantian categorical imperative, while, logically enough, Brentano does not; he compares the concept with the sword Alexander used to cut the Gordian knot; for Brentano the categorical imperative is a sheer fiction. Brentano also appears to have a conception of human solidarity similar to Nordau's – and he is equally wary of the Judaeo-Christian idea of loving one's neighbour. Brentano considers that if one really cared for one's neighbour as much as for oneself one would do a great deal of damage to the common weal. He sees ideal man with moral knowledge and noble love serving an expanding collective goodness.[74]

Brentano is a more difficult thinker than the well-nigh popular Nordau and, some would consequently say, more of a materialist. Brentano initially describes the good as 'that which is to be loved with correct love, the lovable',[75] although we cannot recognise what is good on the basis of our recognition that such and such is or can be loved. For what appeals to us or not often depends on instincts or custom, habit. Brentano uses the concept 'correct' love to denote love of the morally preferable, in other words, an act of love which has been preceded by an individual or collective's moral judgement. We love correctly when we love knowledge/cognition (*Erkenntnis*), joy, correct love itself and so forth. On no account may the saying 'it's all a matter of taste' be applied to what is 'good, lovable.'[76] Since he is a man of his age, Brentano rejects hedonism (hedonism and pessimism walk hand in hand in Decadent art), but he admits there is a grain of truth in the hedonist doctrine: 'Pleasure in the bad is good in as much as it is pleasure, but simultaneously bad in as much as it is a wrongful mental act, and therefore, on the basis of this perverseness, it must be called something predominantly bad, but not something purely bad.'[77] Nordau considers hedonism a phenomenon typical of an age of decay. Nordau and Brentano share the same brand of feminism. Brentano hopes for an ennobling of man through the correcting of woman's social position. Furthermore, they both blame men's sexual ferity for woman's present position. Nordau was far more widely read than Brentano, but Brentano had a far greater influence on the Vienna, and then the whole Austro-Hungarian, intelligentsia. Brentano used such terms as 'current wrong in this state' and so forth, but he did not think in terms of decay like Nordau or Masaryk. Brentano was the sober mind in *fin-de-siècle* Austria-Hungary; he exercised a great influence on a whole generation of Austro-Hungarian bureaucrats. He did for them what the German trio, Schopenhauer, Stirner and Nietzsche, did for artists.

Nordau was also no historicist. He denies there ever has been or ever will be a golden age[78] (his brotherhood is a goal to be striven for, not a realisable golden age). He also makes no predictions. He does, however, accept that previous civilisations, like the Indian or Greek, had achieved greater intellectual and moral maturity than the modern industrial age. Being anti-historicist does not mean that one may not use history for comparison. The very notion of degeneration or decay is an historical notion, and a notion which is frequently used by historicists. The place of historicism in turn-of-the-century Austria-Hungary is most clearly visible in its architecture (sometimes its art is as telling, for example, Marold). In the architecture of redeveloped Vienna the golden age of the Habsburgs (the central Crown Lands), the Counter-Reformation, blends with the modern and therefore predicts further greatness. The Ringstrasse defies decay. More clearly still, the similar architecture of Pest, an unimportant, unhistoric little town before the last third of the century, was not based on a glorious past, but on a glorious future. It emblemised the equality of Budapest and Vienna. One could add that Pest architecture may also reflect an invented glorious past. The pseudo-Baroque of Austria-Hungary did to a degree constitute an invented tradition. Though one is stretching ideas a little, one might see the roots of Popper's anti-historicism in *fin-de-siècle* Vienna. He does state that his fundamental theses, 'that the belief in historical destiny is sheer superstition and that there can be no prediction of the course of human history', go back to 1919–20.[79] Popper's definition of historicism as 'an approach to the social sciences which assumes that *historical prediction* is their principle aim' and that one just has to discover the ' "laws" or the "trends" that underlie the evolution of history',[80] could be taken as a description of Masaryk's approach in deciding what the spirit of Czech history was and what the natural development of Czech history would be. Indeed historicism led Masaryk to believe he had found a spirit of Czech history. Popper objects to the nineteenth century's determination to explain human social behaviour in natural scientific terms as strongly as the Decadents objected to it (the Decadents objected mainly to socialist theory). Popper's 'Oedipus effect', in other words his description of the manner in which the predicted event is influenced by the prediction, may also be applied to Masaryk's bogus theory of the great evangelical Protestant force which moved Czech history (cf. the foundation of the Czechoslovak Church after the establishment of the Czechoslovak Republic). Masaryk's conception of Czech history also suffers from holism based on arbitrarily chosen details, an approach inherent in the historicist 'method'. 'If we wish to study a thing, we are bound to select certain aspects of it . . . since all description is selective' and 'all knowledge, whether intuitive or discursive, must be of abstract aspects' and 'we can never grasp the "concrete structure of social reality itself".'[81]

Nordau certainly sometimes approaches holism, but the only aspect of the Decadents' thinking which evinces the period tendency to holism is their attraction to the esoteric, to forms of thought which provide all-explaining systems. The Decadent approach to history was certainly not historicist. On the one hand it studies only details of history and, on the other, it is primarily concerned with the psychology of an historical individual (and hence to a limited extent also with a notional mass psychology in a given period which serves as a foil to the individual psychology). In Decadent writing an historical theme may be a psychological interpretation as in Pater's *Imaginary Portraits*, Marcel Schwob's *Vies imaginaires* or the Czech Breisky's *Triumf zla* (The triumph of evil, 1910), or history itself may serve essentially as an ornament, as in Hofmannsthal's playlets set in the Renaissance, or as in Karásek's *Sen o říši Krásy* (Dream of the Kingdom of Beauty). Hofmannsthal himself labels the latter use of history aestheticism:

> In some manner or other nearly all of us are in love with a past which has been seen through the eyes of, stylised by, the arts. It is, so to speak, our way of being in love with an ideal, or at least an idealised, life. That is aestheticism, in England, a great, renowned word, but in our culture generally a bloated, overgrown element which is as dangerous as opium.[82]

Decadents in Austria-Hungary were necessarily antihistoricist, because of the history-consciousness and historicism of the nationalist Establishments. The historical novel was the staple brain-fodder of the Vienna, Budapest or Prague citizen at the turn of the century. So antihistoricism was part of *épater le bourgeois*, part of the Decadent rejection of solid middle-class culture. But Decadents also had a conception of something akin to what is today labelled genetic memory, and that conception is antihistoricist. In a review of William Morris's poems Pater wrote as early as 1868: 'The composite experience of all the ages is part of each one of us: to deduct from that experience, to obliterate any part of it . . . as if the middle age, the Renaissance, the eighteenth century had not been, is as impossible as to become a little child, or to enter again into the womb and be born.'[83] Meyrink states the same idea in a more Austrian fashion:

> The circle of people emitting blue-tinted rays who were standing around you constituted the chain of inherited *Ichs* which every man of mother born drags around with him. The soul is nothing 'unique' – it will become unique later and that is called 'immortality'; your soul is still composed of many *Ichs* – as an ant colony is composed of many ants. You bear within your soul the remains of many thousand forebears – the chiefs of your line. It is the same with all beings. How

could a hen which had broken out of its egg in an artificial incubator immediately start looking for the right food if the experience had not been inside her for millions of years? – The presence of instinct manifests the presence of forebears in one's body and in one's soul.[84]

The conception of genetic memory is related to the idea of the unconscious which was popularised by Eduard von Hartmann, and which is to be found in Czech Decadent poets like Karásek and Březina. Indeed between 1870 and 1880 'the general idea of an unconscious mind had become a commonplace throughout Europe'.[85] Nordau links the unconscious with memory: 'Primal superstition continues to function in the sphere of the unconscious as a result of the laws of heredity. . . . Heredity is the memory of the species. In every individual the notions of his ancestors are alive.'[86] Such a conception implies an awareness of tradition physically within one and such an awareness must include a sense of responsibility. The apparent anarchism of many Decadent artists actually expressed a strong sense of responsibility to the history of one's race and to contemporaneous society.

VI. DECADENCE

Nordau has a programme, however woolly. Modernists may have programmes, but Decadents do not: although the unimportant short-lived French group which published the journal *Le Décadent* did declare they had a negative programme; this programme is self-ironising as well: 'L'avenir est au Décadisme. Nés du surblaséisme d'une civilisation schopenhaueresque les Décadents ne sont pas une école littéraire. Leur mission n'est pas de fonder. Ils n'ont qu'à détruir, à tomber les vieilleries et préparer les éléments foetutiens de la grande littérature nationale du XXe siécle' (1890).[87] The Decadence was a period. It was not just a series of techniques and approaches, a style. Stone accepts that when he writes jollily that 'before 1914 . . . self-contemplating decadence, in one form or another, became the dominant theme', and he defines the trend as 'a flight from the disintegrating intellectual world into hedonism, to amorality, to the nightmare world of an Oscar Wilde's *Salome*', and he goes on to maintain that by the turn of the century Decadence 'was being "aestheticized" into a world-weary, consciously *fin-de-siècle* "good taste" '. He takes Hofmannsthal's *Rosenkavalier* (1911) as an example of what happened when the Viennese found Decadence too dangerous.[88]

It is unfortunately not that easy to periodise the *Fin de siècle* and, even though styles might have changed, the ideologies of the period's cultural movements remained pretty stable. It is probably more common to call the age the Symbolist period, as Wellek suggests one should. Where, however, a Symbolist will be a Decadent, a Decadent does not have to use Symbolist symbols. Any definition of Symbolism will constitute at least a partial definition of Decadence. Symbolism sounds grander and bears no possible connotations of reprobacy. Especially for Hungarians and Czechs it was clearly better to be called a Symbolist than a Decadent, and the leading Czech Decadents, Hlaváček, Karásek and Procházka, all at some time or other denied they were Decadent. Vyacheslav Ivanov saw Symbolism as a recurrent type of literature, and Decadence as the final stage of Symbolism (Symons and others have seen Decadence as the initial stage of Symbolism, but that has historical reasons).[89] Ivanov sees Symbolism first in Classical times (presumably what we call the Latin Decadence), then in the Renaissance and, then in a degenerate form, in the *Fin de siècle*. The symptoms of this degeneration are, according to Ivanov, a preference for the artificial to the natural, a striving for the unusual and exotic, the overrating of form and underrating of truthfulness.[90] Hajek suggests that since one finds the terms Symbolism, Decadence, Subjectivism, Aestheticism and Neo-Romanticism so frequently used as synonyms, the term *Jugendstil* should be used, which would cover all those possible angles of vision.[91] That has no sense in any comparative approach; the English Art Nouveau is unusable in that sense, and *Sezession/secese/szecesszió* might work for Austro-Hungarian culture, but could not be used of French and British. Hauser uses Symbolism for the period up to about 1900, and thereafter up to the Great War, Impressionism. That is unhelpful.

What he says about the Mallarmé group's understanding of symbol, however, *does* help towards my definition of Decadence:

> Mallarmé's generation . . . recognised . . . that an allegory was nothing more than the translation of an abstract idea into the form of a concrete picture (image), where the idea remains to a certain extent independent of its pictorial expression, and that it could be expressed in another form. The symbol, on the other hand, brings the idea and the image into an inviolable unity, so that any change in the image also involves a change in the idea. In a word, the contents of a symbol cannot be translated into any other form; on the other hand, a symbol may be interpreted in many different ways and this inconstancy of interpretation, this apparent inexhaustible interpretability is the essence of the symbol.[92]

That does not quite explain the *fin-de-siècle* 'symbol'. Fundamentally basing oneself on Mukařovský's introduction to Hlaváček's posthumous collection, *Žalmy* (Psalms, 1934), one might say that a 'symbol' is essentially an image at two removes; it is an image of an image (hence its interpretability). An old-fashioned example is the following: the rose emblemises/ is an image for virginity and so becomes a symbol of the Blessed Virgin. Equally, however, the rose emblemises passion or consummated love and so becomes a symbol for the courtesan, but also for the Christ on the Cross. Wellek considers Symbolism to be the 'obvious'[93] term to denote the dominant style which followed Realism and dates it from Nerval and Baudelaire to Claudel and Valéry. He points out that Moréas had invented the label after there had been a journalistic attack on the Decadents in 1885;

Moréas published a Symbolist manifesto in 1886. Verlaine disliked the new label intensely, and Charles Morice spoke of synthesis (an alternative to 'symbol' later taken up by Bahr and Šalda in the notion 'synthetism'). Wellek defines the symbol as the reversal of the relationship between tenor and vehicle. Of the contents of Symbolist literature he writes:

> The utterance is divorced . . . from the situation; time and place, history and society, are played down. . . . One could say that the grammatical predicate has become the subject. Clearly such poetry can easily be justified by an occult view of the world. But this is not necessary: it might imply a feeling for analogy, for a web of correspondences, a rhetoric of metamorphoses in which everything reflects everything else. Hence the great role of synaesthesia . . . This characterization could be elaborated considerably if we bear in mind that style and world view go together and only together can define the character of a period or even of a single poet.[94]

Perhaps most important of all, Wellek points out that the Symbolists had a great 'distrust of inspiration, an enmity to nature'.[95] And that is indeed an essential characteristic of Decadence, marking the period off from Romanticism, as Wellek says, but also emphasising the precise studiedness with which the Decadent sought to work. Ady is enthusiastically confused about what a symbol and Symbolism are: Symbolism is the 'magnificent renewal of the old allegory' and 'the quintessential comprehension of life', where 'the world is a representation of the *Ich*. Only what the subject sees exists.'[96] Ady seems to be alluding to Berkeley's Illusionism, Stirner and Barrès as well as misunderstanding the Mallarmé aesthetic. He wrote these words after spending two years (1904–6) getting to know Baudelaire and Verlaine's verse.

A Definition of Decadence

Illusionism was certainly part of the Decadence; the world was an artifice and only the *Ich* definitely existed. Dowling argues that this world as an artifice is 'a world at one remove';[97] in other words, the whole world becomes an infinitely interpretable image. Decadent art is self-centred; gives the artist a special role; adopts particular stylistic poses; expresses an awareness or even a philosophy of decay; expresses also an awareness of existing in a period of transition; does not relay messages or express didactic opinions; but may strive to mock or shock or provoke the bourgeois or the Establishment.

The Self-centredness of Art

Of these seven points the first, the egocentricity of Decadent art, is the easiest to demonstrate. Psychoanalysis might not have been born in Vienna, had it not been for the Decadent concentration on *seine Majestät das Ich*. The sovereignty of the ego is counterbalanced by its irredeemability. As Timms writes: 'We may also recall the insistence of Ernst Mach that consciousness is such an unstable bundle of perceptions and impulses that one can no longer speak of a stable self: "Das Ich ist unrettbar". From Schnitzler and Hofmannsthal through to Kafka and Musil, this is indeed the central theme of Austrian literature: the instability of the self and the anguished attempt to construct an alternative identity.'[98] That goes for Czech Decadent literature as well. One notes how common it is to use a series of widely different autostylisations within not simply one collection of verse, but even one poem. And the self still dominates, is sovereignly unstable. A model autostylisation is sickness, usually consumptiveness, where the self's sickness represents both a rejection of the sick society and infection with that sickness. Meyrink comments on the seriousness with which writers considered their selves in flux: 'waiting for one's *Ich* to become king is waiting for the Messiah.'[99] That also has occult meaning; if one studies the Cabala seriously enough, one will remove the Veils and reach the essence, thus understand the cosmos and one's own soul. The earthly self and the astral self become united – or one becomes Buddha. (Meyrink mixes various esoteric traditions.) Before there was a hint of real Decadence in Hungary, the loner poet, Gyula Reviczky, assumed the illusionist approach, decided that 'The world is but a mood', and set about analysing the world by analysing his own changes of mood.[100] The approach foreshadows Yeats's gem of an essay, 'The Moods'. The self-centredness of Decadent art is epitomised by Vivian's words in 'The Decay of Lying': 'In a house we all feel of the proper proportions, everything is subordinated to us, fashioned for our use and our pleasure. Egotism itself, which is so necessary to a proper sense of human dignity, is entirely the result of indoor life. Out of doors one becomes abstract and impersonal.'

The Role of the Artist

That is also linked with the Decadent conception and portrayal of the artist, for Vivian's too often quoted words there do express the Decadent attitude to Nature (particularly shocking for the audience of Czech Decadent literature, since the Czechs either were 'peasants' or had been indoctrinated to believe that pure Czechness was pure 'peasanthood', and therefore good Czech literature must be 'peasantish'): 'My own experience is that the more we study Art, the less we care for Nature. What Art really reveals to us is Nature's lack of design, her curious crudities, her extraordinary monotony, her absolutely unfinished condition.' And: 'Life imitates Art far more than Art imitates Life.'[101] The literature of the Decadence was essentially art for artists. Some Decadents were widely read and that was not an awfully Decadent thing to be: Wilde in the Anglo-Saxon world, Huysmans or Zola in France, (Laforgue was initially more popular outside France than inside), Schnitzler in German Austria, and eventually Zeyer in Bohemia. Popularity did not necessarily entail understanding. The Decadent artist is a creator and experimenter. As Schaukal writes: 'when a great artist first uses some word, he fills it with the immense contents of his unique *Ich*. The way he places or juxtaposes that word immediately gives it a power which lives and creates of its own accord. The artist is lord of all the possibilities of this truly creative animation [*Beseelung*].'[102] That creativity, ideologically speaking, was intended to give a certain security; the created thing was a stable part of the unstable self. Even 'to savor the weariness of self, they [the Decadents] had had first to regard their own creative individuality as the one certain value in a disintegrating civilization'.[103] Rémy de Gourmont, himself once an adherent of the trend, characterises the period as 'an epoch when almost all sensitivity, almost all faith, almost all love have taken refuge in art'.[104] In Austria-Hungary it was most important that art now could and should express everything and be as subjective as possible about it, for through subjectivity one would achieve objectivity. The artist was no longer prophet or national teacher, but he was magician or high-priest, albeit in a more or less secret cult. The artist at once primarily wrote or painted for fellow adepts and could use his art to taunt the uninitiate.

There was something of infantile precocity in much Decadent sophistication (early Hofmannsthal or Karásek verse); the form of the aphorism, much beloved of the Decadents, tends to seduce to clever-cleverness rather than true sophistication or wisdom, unless employed by a great writer. The aphorism as a form also reflects the fragmentariness of the unstable self which dominates the period. Because the artist was seen to be in pursuit of the exquisite, brief forms characterise the literature of mainstream Decadence: the aphorism, the lyric poem, the short-story, the essay, the play (often brief one-acters), rather than the novel. *The Picture of Dorian Gray*, *A rebours*, Zeyer's *Jan Maria Plojhar*, Karásek's *Gothická duše* or Meyrink's *Der Golem* are exceptions: and it would be easy to extend the list of such exceptions. In the brief form the artist tries to express surprises; in this dull Victorian overindustrialised world, surprises, newnesses, may relieve the *taedium vitae*. Also, the surprise potentially constitutes a brief journey into the unknown or at least suggests something of the unknown. What has appeared to critics as the Decadent artist or Decadent hero's cerebral flight from reality is in fact an attempt to fly into the unknown, the uncertain. The unstable self seeks the certainty of uncertainty.[105] Only an élite was capable of that; the élite consisted in unstable selves whose instability was reflected in the interpretability of the symbols they used. Mallarmé conceived of a pure art which would be the possession of a charming, bizarre and sickly aristocracy who exist beyond the grimy democracy-minded, mob-minded world of the late nineteenth century.[106] The most consistent and strident promulgator of this aristocratism in Bohemia was Arnošt Procházka, though, before him, the aristocrat artist constituted a recurrent theme in the plays and prose of Zeyer. The Decadent artist or hero's apparent flight from reality may also take the form of pure aesthetic enjoyment (hedonism restricted to art itself), as Merkl suggests was the case with Samain. The pleasure of art becomes life and life the pleasure of art.[107] But, as 'a victim of abulia, the hero may or may not be aesthetically oriented . . . aesthetics . . . is merely a possibility'; whatever else may be true, however, Ridge continues, there must be 'a metaphysical aspect to the decadent'.[108]

Stylistic Poses

The third point in my description of Decadent art, that it adopts particular stylistic poses, is linked with Decadent metaphysicality or striving for metaphysicality. Depictions of total desolation may contain an implied metaphysical longing, or a statement on the lack of metaphysics in the modern capitalist world. That is clearest in a Hauptmann or Zola, but such a longing is also palpable in Ady and Hlaváček's depictions of deserts. Usually in the Decadent artist metaphysical longing is tempered by irony. Few Decadent writers are really funny, like Wilde, but they are often satiricial: Schnitzler, Dyk, Ady. Mainly, however, they are ironists. Irony may well serve chiefly as a shield for the unstable *Ich* in the world in flux. The French Decadent Rosicrucian painter, Alphonse Osbert, wrote: 'Art is a prayer, a rest from life, and it is certainly literary, since it translates emotions.'[109] Kugel's basic idea of how Decadent (Symbolist) art works, by 'frustrated allusions', by creating at least an illusion of withheld information, is particularly apt. It provides an explanation for appearances of metaphysicality as well as a method of expressing or appearing to express metaphysicality; it embraces artistocratism (the artist as initiate or elitist, withholding information because the audience is unworthy or because the only true audience is comprised of other artist aristocrats who know what that withheld information is); furthermore withholding information serves to protect the *Ich*, unstable or not (or at least that is what people think). Basing his analysis initially on Nerval, Kugel lists three categories of incomplete allusions implying withheld information: (i) name allusions, (ii) an apparent reference to an unknown story, (iii) incompatible-union phrases, usually oxymora (he actually quotes 'le soleil noir', an oxymoron used by, say, the Czech Březina, and one of the commonest dream-visions of schizophrenics).[110]

The typicality of these three categories can be best seen in the most important verse work in Czech Decadent literature, the ironic (and depressing) *Mstivá kantilena* (Cantilena of revenge, 1898). Hlaváček's first name allusion is to Manon (and Manon Lescaut was an archetypal vamp for *fin-de-siècle* man), but then the abbé himself appears to be her lover, not des Grieux. And so, where the first name allusion was clear to the reader, the second dislocates him and then, in linking those two with the Dutch Anabaptist rebels, the Gueux, the poet creates a semantic chaos, where interpersonal and temporal relationships are put into disarray or: given a new, symbolic pattern. On top of that Hlaváček speaks of the Gueux's kingdom, which is further confusing because it suggests Münster rather than the Low Countries. The white barbarians addressed in the prose interlude have no immediate meaning, even to a reader who knows Verlaine. *Mstivá kantilena*, a very brief work, contains three 'apparent references to an unknown story', a 'legend of the sin of the yellow roses', the 'legend of how the moon went blind through long weeping' and the 'beautiful legend of the dolphin'. As far as the 'incompatible-union phrases' are concerned, one need only look at the title of Hlaváček's cycle. A cantilena suggests plainsong and grace and probably Mediterranean summer; it suggests the opposite of the murky, petty or despairing concept, revenge. The central symbolic system is based on incompatibles: a call to a rebellion which must fail, bells which cannot ring, moons which shed no light, women and fields which are barren, and so forth. Hlaváček uses few brash oxymora. Březin, however, uses them brashly and in Březina the reader often feels that oxymora constitute simply a cheap, facile path to mysticism. Kugel also includes under incompatible union synaesthesia, the most popular rhetorical device of the whole Decadent period. Synaesthesia could be surprising, could reveal hidden links between disparate conceptual fields. Synaesthesia could become something like sensuous mystagogy. By his exploitation of both oxymoron and synaesthesia the writer evokes incomplete comprehension, for the phrase will suggest, connote, rather than denote and the audience will not be sure even of the connotations. In Decadence meaning, Kugel continues, may arise 'from nothing other than the disharmony of images'.[111] He also demonstrates how the Decadent poet may deliberately obfuscate grammar and syntax. If, he says, grammatical chaos or obscure word-order helps 'to make of the poem one blurred set of impressions in which it is not wholly clear which epithet applies to what, it is performing the act of fusion which is the poem's subject and theme'.[112]

Seeba maintains that comparison is the most characteristic linguistic device of Aesthetic man; the suggestion is that comparison means simile.[113] That is not wholly true; the symbol is essentially a metaphor; similes are used enormously – as long as one accepts a broad definition of simile, one like Christine Brooke-Rose's in her *Grammar of Metaphor*. If Seeba means that Decadent literature is literature which normally concentrates on imagery rather than unadorned emotion or action, then he is right. As Wellek said, the functions of tenor and vehicle tend to be reversed. A short-story may be essentially the description of a series of mental processes leading to a decision and concern only the inside of the narrator's or his subject's head. A novel may consist in an episodic series of impressions with virtually no action. Finally, as far as stylistic prose is concerned, the Decadent artist is not as condescending as he may sometimes appear; he is a colluder or, at least, an artist who aspires to collusion with the like-minded.

The Expression of Decay

There is a great deal of play in Decadence, which is part of the fourth point in my description of Decadent art: the artist's expression of an awareness of decay. In expressing his awareness he will usually be protesting (playing is a form of protest when one is in the midst of putrefaction). Decadents protest and reject, but they do not rebel; rebellions and revolutions are normally regarded as tasteless affairs, unless they can be seen as glorious either in their futility or in the ecstasy of their gore. And, like playing, ecstasy, the cultivation of ecstasy, forms very much part of 'the artist's protest against a spiritually bankrupt civilisation, his imagination striving for the unattainable to restore his wholeness'.[114] Though at the same time he may enjoy something like ecstasy, creative ecstasy, in the very act of existing amongst decay, as the *persona* does in the first stanza of Verlaine's 'Langueur' (1883), 'Je suis L'Empire à la fin de la décadence,/Qui regarde passer les grands Barbares blancs/En composant des acrostiches indolents/D'un style d'or où la langueur du soleil danse.'[115] Furthermore, these lines constitute an example of one of Kugel's 'incompatible unions', playful ecstasy. The Decadents protested against the contemporary decay of civilisation, but they also enjoyed protesting and thus enjoyed decay or the exploitation of decay. They are also pessimists. Strongly influenced by Darwin, Taine and Spencer, Decadent man saw himself the victim of merciless laws of heredity. In addition to that he saw himself as a desperate preserver of values in a society which was abandoning all taste, veracity and morality under the enormous weight of stultifying democratic forces which would inevitably lead to ochlocracy, even in the arts. For Austro-Hungarian Decadents this last point was particularly strongly felt, because they tended to think that the art of their country had largely been ochlocratic art before the *Fin de siècle*. The Decadents created their *paradis artificiels* in reaction to nineteenth-century ugliness. 'Contemptuous of contemporary reality, they were to turn their gaze backward toward certain favored and prestigious past eras, such as that of the Roman decadence or legendary Byzantium' (Péladan, Verlaine, Karásek, Breisky, Babits) 'or else . . . they were to proclaim their allegiance to the most spectacular aspects of modernity, such as . . . machinery'[116] (Huysmans, Karásek). This very modernity, however, has helped bring about the state of nervous exhaustion in which European man found himself. And this very modernity issued from the ugly, dreary industrial society the Decadents so condemned. The creation of *paradis artificiels* the Decadents, took from their main progenitor, Baudelaire, but, according to Pierrot, they were in debt to Flaubert for their:

> desire to escape the boredom of everyday life, their desire of a reconstitution of paradise by means of art alone in the distant realms of long-past eras characterized by titanic and barbaric architecture, an attraction mingled with dread for the woman-idol, a fascination with subtly refined pleasures and forbidden delights, the dizzying pull of sadism and cruelty.[117]

In fact, however, I would have said Flaubert's *Salammbô* and *La Tentation de saint Antoine* belonged to mainstream Decadence. Hauser defines the non-aesthetic aspect of the Decadence as a whole by enumerating much the same elements Pierrot asserts the Decadents owed to Flaubert:

> The concept Decadence contains . . . primarily the atmosphere of cultural decay and of crisis, in other words, a consciousness of standing at the end of a life-process, on the brink of the dissolution of a civilisation. Empathy with tired, old, over-refined cultures like that of Hellenism, late Roman times, the Rococo and with the 'impressionistic' late style of the Old Masters belongs to the essence of the sensation of Decadence.[118]

By those standards Kraus was also a Decadent, which J. P. Stern suggests when he writes that 'above all, Karl Kraus was deeply conscious of the decline and imminent dissolution of the culture he cherished, the Austro-Hungarian political accommodation he attacked without envisaging the means whereby to create an alternative'.[119] Although awareness of decay and the very term Decadence represent an acceptance of nineteenth-century concepts like evolution and progress, the Decadents did their best to reject the idea of Progress, which for them forms part of the philistine ideology. 'The mania for "progress",' writes Schaukal, 'tramples underfoot the nourishing roots of pasts'[120] and, a little more boisterously, 'Progress, the battle between the State and the Catholic Church [*Kulturkampf*], Freemasonry, the emancipation of women, etc.: the wretched conceit of deaf-mute "citizens of the world" who are able to "communicate" with each other only with a conventional language of gestures.'[121] The Russian Symbolists shared the same vision of a Europe in decay, a decay only destruction could stem. Valery Bryusov turns Verlaine's white barbarians into Huns in the poem, 'Gryadushchie Gunny' (The Coming Huns), and significantly enough, his Huns have certain occult qualities, for they will retain their innocence by perpetrating all manner of vileness in the temples of modern European culture. Where in Verlaine we saw an ecstasy of decay, in Bryusov we see an ecstasy of destruction (being destroyed). The British Decadents, Symons, Dowson, Johnson and Yeats were also waiting for an impending end;[122] expected destruction lured the Decadent mind to its exaggerated art. The Decadents 'produced the literature of a disaster – though it had not yet taken place'.[123]

The concept of cultural decay had a would-be Darwinist theory to support it, concocted in the Decadent period by the art historian, critic and, sometimes Parnassian, sometimes Decadent, poet J. A. Symonds. The essence of that theory (and the theory itself contains the sort of cultural catastrophism I have just been talking about) runs as follows:

> It often appears that the first impulse toward creativeness is some deep and serious emotion, some religious enthusiasm, or profound stirring of national conscious-ness. . . . In the earliest stages of expansion the artist becomes half a prophet, and

'sows with the whole sack' in the plenitude of superabundant inspiration. After the original passion for the ideas to be embodied in art has somewhat subsided . . ., there comes a second period. In this period art is studied more for art's sake, but the generative potency of the first founders is by no means exhausted. For a while, at this moment, the artist is priest, prophet, hierophant, and charmer all in one. . . . But now the initial impulse is declining; the cycle of animating ideas has been exhausted; the people has been educated. . . . Conceptions which had all the magic of novelty for the grandparents, become the intellectual patrimony of the grandchildren. . . . The type cannot be changed, because the type grew itself out of the very nature of the people, who are still existent. What then remains for the third generation of artists? . . . they . . . extract new motives from the perfected type, at the risk of impairing its strength and beauty, with the certainty of disintegrating its spiritual unity . . . the very artists who begin to decompose the type and to degrade it, and the public who applaud their ingenuity, and dote with love upon their variations from the primal theme, are alike unconscious that the decadence has already arrived. This, too, is inevitable and natural, because life is by no means exhausted when maturity is past, and the type still contains a wealth of parts to be eliminated . . . the artists of this third period are forced to go afield for striking situations, to strain sentiment and pathos, to accentuate realism, to subordinate the harmony of the whole to the melody of details, to sink the prophet in the artist, the hierophant in the charmer. There yet remains another stage of decadence, when even these resources latent in the perfect type have been exhausted. Then formality and affectation succeed to spontaneous and genial handling; technical skill declines; the meaning of the type, projected from the nation's heart and soul in its origin, comes to be forgotten. Art has fulfilled the round of its existence in the specific manifestation, and sinks into the dotage of decrepitude, the sleep of winter.[124]

Theorising along such lines would have been almost second nature to the educated *fin-de-siècle* man. Such is the root of another paradox of the Decadence. In their awareness or presumption of cultural decay the Decadents sought to deflect that decay by renewal, innovation.

The Decadent became at once gloomy at the inevitability of the end of art and made art into a religion or a secret society whose magic rituals had to be long studied. Cultural decay also suggests lack of life, and so the Decadents, for all their world-weariness, were great sensualists. And they learnt the ability to be sensualist about decay itself from Baudelaire. The Darwin manner of thinking also led them to regard men as animals (that was part of the general religious crisis Darwinism brought in its wake), and thus the artist acquired a new role, to demonstrate, with his ingenuity, how far man could 'deanimalise' himself. Many of the apparent affectations of the Decadents were in fact statements of an assertive humanity. A simple example of that consciousness is to be found in the speech 'Die Moderne', given at the inauguration of the 'Freie Bühne, Verein für moderne Literatur' (1891) by the Viennese journalist, Friedrich Michael Fels, whom Hofmannsthal, Salten and Schnitzler had chosen as the society's chairman. In this speech we find the following: 'The more one tears oneself away from the original animal in one, the more one becomes a true human being, the more one becomes a Decadent, for the more one loses originality of willing and acting, the more animal one becomes . . . In this sense Decadence has always existed everywhere. . . . We are Decadent.'[125] Art, then, is the only reliable expression of humanity. That idea is, again, linked with Mallarmé, who, as Wellek states, 'wants to express the mystery of the universe but feels that this mystery is not only insoluble and immensely dark but also hollow, empty, silent, Nothingness itself.' Wellek finds no reason to follow tradition and connect that with the contemporary interest in Buddhism and the impact of Schopenhauer and Wagner, though one should not exclude that Schopenhauer and Wagner were themselves greatly influenced by Indian thought. He continues: 'The atmosphere of nineteenth-century pessimism and the general Neoplatonic tradition in aesthetics suffice. Art searches for the Absolute but despairs of ever reaching it. The essence of the world is Nothingness, and the poet can only speak of this Nothingness. Art alone survives in the universe.'[126]

In Austria-Hungary the influence of Schopenhauer and Nietzsche was strong even before the Decadences of the individual lands really got underway. Thus it is strong in the Hungarian Jenő Komjáthy's one collection of verse (1895) and there it is combined with the influence of Spinoza's pantheism.[127] The same three thinkers had greatly influenced Julius Zeyer. Gyula Juhász recollects thus the reading matter of young intellectuals when he went up to Budapest University at the beginning of the twentieth century:

> those who exercised the greatest influence were all writers of quality like Schopenhauer, who expressed his ideas in a perfect form, or Nietzsche, who had the gift of a poet. Oscar Wilde was admired; translations of Poe were read, but they [undergraduates] were also enamoured of the ideas of Marx, Spencer and Stirner [who had become popular again because of John Henry Mackay], of pantheism *à la* Bruno Wille and of the moral doctrines of Tolstoy and Ibsen.[128]

The dying central character of Schnitzler's first prose-work to be published in book-form, *Sterben* (Dying, 1892), asks for Schopenhauer and Nietzsche to be brought to his sick bed. He starts to dip into them, but, now he has the heightened awareness of a man close to death, he soon puts them down, deciding he will henceforth read novels. The thinkers may be compulsive guides for the theorists of the dying century, but no longer say anything to the man, the dying individual. He considers them 'vile poseurs' and he adds, a little petulantly, 'Despising life when one is as healthy as a god, looking death straight in the face when one is holidaying in Italy and existence is blossoming all around one: I call that posing plain and simple. Let a gentleman like them be confined in a room, condemned to high fevers and breathlessness, tell him he'll be buried at some time between January 1st and February 1st next year and then let him perform one of his philosophical productions.'[129] As is so often the case, one cannot know where Schnitzler stands. Sometimes he appears to be an out-and-out Decadent; sometimes he appears to be satirising or parodying the Decadents, albeit that, too, would comport with the Decadent worldview.

Awareness of Transition

The Decadent artist's expression of an awareness of existing in a period of transition is closely related to his awareness and analysis of decay. It is, however, quite distinct. The awareness of decay suggests catastrophes and inevitable ends. The awareness of transition suggests an empty or confused temporal space between two definite points. Fels in his 'Die Moderne' demonstrates how optimistic the Decadent awareness of transition can be:

> I doubt there is any entirely modern writer in whose work the following thought is not expressed in some form or another: we are standing on the boundary-line between two worlds. What we do is only preparatory work for something great in the future, something that we do not know, that we barely have an inkling of. The day will come when we shall no longer be read. Let us look forward to the day when that comes to pass.
>
> That is the Decadent confession of a sinking, unstable race insecure in its activity.[130]

A strong influence on the central European Decadents and their immediate predecessors was the Swiss 'diarist', Amiel, and it is significant that Hofmannsthal describes him in terms of transitionality. 'Henri-Frédéric Amiel was born in . . . 1821, a time of transition . . . in Geneva, a city of transition, where the Alps sink down to the plain, where the elevated is extenuated into the graceful, where Germanic and Romance mingle, in Geneva, a half Calvinist, half Catholic city.'[131]

In his *Sokolské sonety* (Sokol sonnets, 1895; the Sokol was the Czech patriotic *Turnverein*), a collection which contains utterly unDecadent trifles, as well as a little Decadent verse, Hlaváček writes fairly pessimistically of living in 'a period of upheaval . . ., a period set whirling by an indefinite premonition . . ., a decadent period which is already intoxicated enough to fall into ruins'.[132] Most Decadently of all Karásek speaks of '*the horror of transition*, the uncertainty of the age which has cast out everything old but has not yet created anything of its own to replace it, an age with nothing to lean on, in which the anxieties of someone drowning are to be heard'.[133] It stands to reason that the Czechs should sense transition most strongly, since Czech politics was in a particularly perceptible state of transition at the time. Not long after the Old Czechs had lost their leading role, the Young Czechs lost theirs (c. 1895); no party of any power appeared to represent the views of the Czech intelligentsia. Czech nationalism was also in disarray. Most Czechs were loyal to the Habsburgs, but a tiny movement for independence was beginning to nag at the literary and artistic avant-garde. (The Decadent Dyk was among them.) Old-fashioned historicist nationalism had clearly had its day, though most Czech nationalists adhered to this brand of thinking. The Decadents and other young groups were generally critical patriots. The trouble was that criticism grew and grew until there was not much left about the Czechs for these young artists to be patriotic about.

Decadent Anti-Realism, the Purity of Art, Decadence and Naturalism

This critical patriotism is evident mainly in journalism, literary criticism (usually book reviews) and satire; it does not testify against the sixth point in my description of Decadent art, that art does not and should not relay messages or express didactic opinions. Generally speaking the Decadents took over Parnassian *l'art pour l'artisme*. Art was primarily to be beautiful – and useless. In fact the Decadents frequently failed in that endeavour. Wilde's *Dorian Gray*[134] is a profoundly moral novel and, as Thornton says, Huysmans's *A rebours* 'is not only the Bible of Decadence, but also one of its severest criticisms, a recognition from the first of its necessary failure'.[135] Still, the Decadents' aim was pure art. As the English precursor, Swinburne, wrote in his letter to *The Spectator* defending Meredith's *Modern Love* (1862): 'there are pulpits enough for all preachers in prose; the business of verse-writing is hardly to express convictions; and if some poetry, not without merit of its kind has at times dealt in dogmatic morality, it is all the worse and all the weaker for that.'[136] The difficulty over message-bearing and moralisation in the Decadence comes when one considers the relationship between Decadence and Naturalism. Pierrot points out that the conventional wisdom that Decadence replaced Naturalism is incorrect, since the two trends coexisted in periodicals, but he also notes in them a significant similarity: 'their starting points were basically one and the same: a fundamentally pessimistic conception of life.'[137] Typically of literary and art critics Hauser speaks of Symbolism (Decadence) as 'a sharp reaction against Naturalist and materialist impressionism'.[138] First, one acknowledges that there are major writers who wrote works of different natures which critics unanimously consider as either Naturalist or Symbolist (Decadent); Hauptmann provides two blatant examples (*Die Weber*, The Weavers, and *Die versunkene Glocke*, The sunken bell), and George Moore (*Esther Waters* and *Confessions*), but a similar apparent dichotomy might be suggested for Zola (*Germinal* and *Le Docteur Pascal*), even for Flaubert (*Madame Bovary* and *Salammbô*). Then in Czech literature there is a writer of what appears to be extreme Naturalist literature (a welter of cruelty to animals, wife-bashing, infanticide, and so on), who is essentially a Decadent in both style and in his metaphysical disquisitions on the nature of good and evil (in the same novels as his detailed gore), Šlejhar. Naturalism and Decadence are easily fused. One may distinguish them by describing them similarly. Both are pessimistic. Naturalism looks at a segment of material physical life under a microscope. Decadence looks at a segment of mental life under a microscope. Both trends indulge in detailed descriptions of material objects, though Naturalism generally prefers the ugly to the beautiful, where Decadence generally prefers the beautiful to the ugly. Both trends deliberately distort. Both are particularly concerned with heredity and the impact of environment. Naturalist heroes tend to be working or lower middle-class; Decadent heroes tend to be the last scions of a long aristocratic line. But a Czech Decadent hero can be of any class and is frequently poor or very poor. Naturalists and Decadents are concerned both with decay and with the part man has played in causing decay. As long as one is speaking about serious literature, and not popular imitations of Eugène Sue (Zoltán Ambrus) or Zola, I believe one will barely be able to distinguish between Naturalism and Decadence in Austria-Hungary. Except in one point: a Naturalist work will usually have a conscious message. Perhaps Naturalism is frequently little more than Decadence with a message.

The Art of Épater le Bourgeois

The seventh point in my description of Decadence, that Decadent art may strive to mock or shock or provoke the bourgeois, is only superficially connected with the sixth point. One cannot speak of *épater le bourgeois* as message-bearing. On the one hand, it is part of a stylistic pose; on the other, it constitutes a minor part of the general protest which comprises Decadent art. Even in semi-obscene Decadent jokes, like some of the drawings of Félicien Rops, the element of *épater le bourgeois* is only subsidiary. The whole idea that all art must be useless, starting with Gautier's preface to his *Mademoiselle de Maupin* and ending with the imitator Wilde's preface to *Dorian Gray*, does certainly mock Establishment bourgeois views, but the idea itself has a much more serious dimension than that; it is the kernel of Decadent aestheticism and it expresses the Decadent rejection of the glorious utilitarian and entrepreneurial morality which they in their youth had been taught to aspire to. Most Decadents in Austria-Hungary appear to have been either the children of rich Jews, who may or may not have earned money other than through their art, or to have been petty clerks. Useless, pure art could also be seen as something which would survive the general cultural decay. Arthur O'Shaugnessy wrote: 'What is eternal? What escapes decay?/A certain, faultless, matchless, deathless line/Curving consummate.'[139] The Decadents may frequently enjoy mocking the bourgeois, but they do it from above. There is nothing socialistic about this dislike of the bourgeoisie. For example, George Moore writes: 'Democratic Art! Art is the direct antithesis to democracy. . . . the mass can only appreciate simple and *naive* emotions, puerile prettiness, above all conventionalities.'[140] And Procházka writes: 'the mass, as a democratic multitude, as a whirling, confused teeming of utilitarian, materialist instincts and desires, has no interest, understanding or sensibility for art.'[141]

VII. MODERNISM, MODERN, AND MODERNE

There is no doubt that the Decadence made twentieth-century art possible, by freeing art from the strictures put upon it at least since the Renaissance: that art should attempt to be true to life, that art had a direct relationship with reality and that art should be instructive, even if in an entertaining manner. The Decadence also liberated art from the then fairly recent mythology concerning art's reflection of life. If the term Modernism means something like art freed of Dickensian Realism, then it seems reasonable to consider the Decadence as part of Modernism. But actually I am not sure that the now very widely employed term Modernism is of any use whatsoever to cultural historians, except either as an imprecise pejorative or as an equally imprecise term to describe those artists active during the Decadent period who proffered cures for the decay or who were otherwise artists whose work was message-laden, but formally clearly distinct from art in the preceding period. In other words, one would not call some pale imitator of Stendhal publishing in the 1890s a Modernist, but one might call Bernard Shaw a Modernist. I am not in this essay concerned with the South American conception of Modernism, particularly the Nicaraguan Rubén Darió's (1867–1916), since it had, practically speaking, no contemporary impact on the literature of Austria-Hungary.

By putting their anthology of essays together as they did Malcolm Bradbury and James McFarlane became the main proponents of the term. In their introductory essay, 'The Name and Nature of Modernism', they perhaps put an adequate case for the label. Sometimes, however, their own modernistic University of East Anglia language blurs their definition to a degree which is almost 'poetical', for example, and they are making an important point: 'Modernism . . . tends to have to do with the intersection of an apocalyptic and modern time, a timeless and transcendent symbol or a node of pure linguistic energy.'[142] Thus, Modernism is a product of or reflects transition, a characteristic better expressed by the term Decadence. The authors also claim that: 'One of the word's associations is with the coming of a new era of high aesthetic self-consciousness and non-representationalism, in which art turns from realism and humanistic representation towards style, technique and spatial form in pursuit of a deeper penetration of life.'[143] That also seems better expressed by the term Decadence – or Symbolism or, indeed, Aestheticism. The following reminds one of Thornton's comment on *A rebours* and constitutes a sound account of what happens in writers like Wilde, (early) Hofmannsthal, Przybyszewski, or Karásek: 'Modernism might mean not only a new mode or mannerism in the arts, but a certain magnificent disaster for them. In short, experimentalism does not simply suggest the presence of sophistication, difficulty and novelty in art; it also suggests bleakness, darkness, alienation, disintegration.'[144] Decadence, like Expressionism, may often be self-destructive; that is part of its internal irony. The authors' contention that Modernism contains the idea that the 'condition for the style of the work is a presumed absence of style for the age'[145] would seem to separate Decadence (Symbolism) from other cultural trends prior to World War I. Although the Decadent demands total individuality of style, the Decadent era does have certain stylistic hallmarks (lengthy periods; the use of exotic vocabulary . . . and settings; 'incomplete allusions'; the preference for connotation to denotation, and so forth), which would, say, align Wilde with Péladan and early Auředníček (i.e. writers who had not read each other at least when they began publishing, but who still have stylistic characteristics in common). The authors cannot put the Decadents in the same bracket as D. H. Lawrence and James Joyce, however strongly these two writers may be linked with the Decadence. Lawrence's sensualism forms his strongest link and Joyce's (after *Dubliners*) linguistic and emotional experimentation forms his strongest link. But there is not the similarity between Lawrence and Joyce (or Joyce and Breton) that there is between Wilde and Péladan. In other words, the more one attempts to place the *Fin de siècle* and the interwar Avant-Garde under one heading, the more confusing it will become. I do not deny there is a clearly perceptible continuity from the Decadence to the Avant-Garde, but that really is another matter. There is continuity between the Baroque and Romanticism.

Wellek objects to the term Modernism because, he says, it could be applied to any contemporary art. He also remarks that it obscures the dividing line between the Decadent period and such movements as Surrealism.[146] Ihab Hassan's term 'postmodernism' for what happens after 'Modernism', a term which describes art in a mood where the world is completely technologised and thus inhuman, is confusing and begs too many questions.

The concept 'modern' was used as a somewhat pejorative term in art before the advent of Decadence proper, and before the various manifestos and groupings who adopted some form of the word. In the title to his lyric epic, *Modern Love*, Meredith uses the word to signify faithless, disloyal, almost promiscuous. Modern love is a love where a woman deceives a man and then leaves him. For Meredith, then, modern denotes moral decay, the vanishing of honour. (He says there are only two choices, once a bond is made, Love or Vileness; the third choice is that apathetic resignation he calls petrifaction). For Arnold in his essay 'On the Modern Element in Literature' (1865) the characteristics of modernness are depression and *ennui*, which result from the fact that modern man is too keen on analysing himself and his relationships. Within the *fin-de-siècle* period the word modern becomes a word of abuse, because it has been previously debased by the middle classes.

It had been debased from the status it had achieved after Meredith and Arnold's day, in the form *Moderne*. The term *die Moderne* (i.e. *die* not *das*) first appears in an unsigned proclamation in the *Allgemeine Deutsche Universitäts-Zeitung* (1.1.1887), where it is put in opposition to *die Antike* (the culture of Antiquity, Classical ideals), but the first person to use it as a programmatic word was the Kiel literary historian and co-founder of the Berlin *Durch!* group, Eugen Wolff, who published his pamphlet *Die jüngste deutsche Literaturströmung und das Prinzip der Moderne* (The newest current in German literature and the principle of *die Moderne*) in Berlin in 1888. Hermann Bahr took the term from him for his declaration 'Die Moderne' (in the periodical *Moderne Dichtung*, 1.1.1890). Bahr's strident piece is on the one hand Decadent (that is the more original side of it in the context) and on the other little more than a condensed repetition of ideas in Nordau's *Die conventionellen Lügen*. Two paragraphs near the beginning manifest Bahr as a Decadent, but then also indicate the difference between Decadence and Modernism in the sense I have suggested. Modernism could be a useful term to describe those artists in the Decadent period who had messages, often cures):

> It may be that we are at the end, at the death of exhausted mankind and that we are experiencing mankind's last spasms. It may be that we are at the beginning, at the birth of a new humanity and that we are experiencing only the avalanches of spring. We are rising to the divine or plunging, plunging into night and destruction – but there is no standing still.
>
> The creed of *die Moderne* is that salvation will arise from pain and grace from despair, that a dawn will come after this horrific darkness and that will hold communion with man, that there will be a glorious, blessed resurrection.[147]

The biblical style of much of this manifesto suggests rebelliousness as well as pomposity. Bahr follows Nordau's main thought exactly. Present society is full of hypocrisy and lies, and the only cure for modern decay is a simple love of truth. Empty traditionalism is the curse on today's world. The only sentence which has no Nordau roots is the following, which sounds almost occultist: 'But the truth is threefold; life is threefold, and thus the vocation of the new art is threefold. One truth is in the body; one truth is in the feelings; one truth is in thought.'[148] As the Austrian *Moderne* manifesto largely followed Nordau, so the Czech *Moderna* manifesto (1895) largely followed Masaryk, and thus its authors are far more political than Bahr. It is as much a manifesto directed against the Young Czech Party and a pamphlet for universal suffrage as an invocation of a new non-nationalistic attitude to art, and a declaration of the equality of literary criticism with other arts. It is anti-nationalistic, but speaks of an essential 'national' art (as Wolff had in his pamphlet). The cultural parts of the manifesto emphasise individualism and originality:

> We want artists, not echoes of foreign tones, not eclectics or dilettanti. We have no respect for bright patchworks of second-hand thoughts and forms, rhymed political programmes, imitated folk songs or other versified folklore gewgaws, or dour flag-wagging or flat Realist objectivity.

> First and foremost individuality, lively, life-giving individuality. . . . We do not stress Czechness in any way: be yourself and you will be Czech. . . . We do not acknowledge ethnographical maps. We want art which is not a luxury object and which is not subject to the caprices of literary fashion. Our word 'modern' does not mean what is *à la mode*: the day before yesterday Realism, yesterday Naturalism, today Symbolism, Decadence, tomorrow Satanism, occultism – these ephemeral slogans which always level down and make uniform a series of literary works for a few weeks. . . . We want truth in art, not photographic truth, but that honourable truth which is the norm only of its bearer, the individual.[149]

So truth is there again, but in central Europe this was an age of deciding what was real and what only appearance. The signatories of the Czech manifesto included the mysticising Decadent Březina, the Naturalist Decadent Šlejhar as well as fundamentally Realist writers like Vilém Mrštík or Machar. As a grouping the Czech *Moderna* only lasted a few months and even then the links between the intellectuals concerned were pretty insubstantial.

Modernists may be artists of the Decadent period who proffer cures, but it is important that we add my proviso: as long as their works are formally distinct from the previous period, in other words, as long as they are clearly not latterday Realists. Furthermore the problems they treat will be similar or parallel to the subjects treated by Decadent literature. A crass example: where the Decadent has his scarlet *femme fatale*, the Modernist may, indeed, is likely, to discuss the double morality, total chastity for women, reasonable promiscuity for men. The essential subject is the same: human sexuality. Only because of the style, and even here I feel uncertain, can one claim that Nordau's *Die conventionellen Lügen* was not a Modernist work. (*Entartung* clearly is not; there Nordau has debased even his own strong points.) But Nordau does concern himself with double morality, the morality which demands 'unconditional fidelity from the woman but does not give her the right to demand the same from the man. If she forgets herself, she has committed a mortal sin . . .; if he does the same, he has allowed himself a charming peccadillo.'[150] This double morality is the theme of the Czech Hilbert's play *Vina* (Guilt, 1896; performed later in Polish, in 1898 and in Slovene, in 1911); here the young woman who is not betrothed to a sentimentalist poet had been seduced at the age of sixteen; it all comes out and, in the end, she kills herself. The fact that Austrian society openly expects a woman to be a virgin and tacitly expects a man not to be one, when they marry, is a theme of another play from the same year, Kvapil's *Bludička* (Will o' the wisp).

The most difficult problem, if one accepts the label Modernist in my narrower sense, is whether Freud was a Decadent or a Modernist. At least during the *Fin de siècle* he offered a cure for *fin-de-siècle* anxiety, and that was to release one's repressed childhood anxiety or trauma and thus, usually, one's repressed libido. Decadents do not offer cures, but, on the other hand, they do believe that ecstasy, sexual or not, is a release from anxiety. They also study the unconscious in man (usually woman) at moments of ecstasy. On the other hand, since sexuality was the main matter of intellectual discourse in *fin-de-siècle* Austria, one would expect Freud to seek clues to solving the human condition in sexuality, just as one would expect the Decadents, always searching as they were for the new, to explore hidden sexuality and sexual perversion. Even before the Decadent period two Austrians, Krafft-Ebing (*Psychopathia sexualis*) and K. H. Ulrichs (*Memnon, Ara Spei, Inclusa*), had excited the imaginations of writers (and the latter had helped claim that both male and female homosexuals were capable of a higher form of love than heterosexuals). Freud's interest in dreams and even the manner in which he interprets them has much in common with the Decadence. His style in his early works also manifests the language-consciousness one expects of a Decadent. Freud does, however, construct systems. He constructs a system, say, of infantile sexual development, a taxonomy of relationships between behaviour pecularities and excremental or sexual functions, also a system of more or less direct equivalents (going upstairs as an emblem of sexual desire); in other words, he did not have the Decadent understanding of or approach to symbol. The case of Freud argues for my narrow use of the label Modernist, but one can certainly accept that Freud belonged through and through to the Decadent period.

Hauser is keen to show that Nietzsche, Freud and Marx have much in common. He might have added Schopenhauer, for Freud's conception of the pleasure principle appears congenitally linked with Schopenhauer's notion that happiness is simply the momentary absence of unhappiness. He links Freud and Nietzsche by their common assessment that man's behaviour was deceptive or unnatural because certain elements in him had been repressed by distorting cultural forces (in Nietzsche's case the Christian Church). He links Freud and Marx by identifying Freud's notion of rationalisation with Marx and Engels's notions of false consciousness and ideology formation. Hauser makes that last link partly because he wishes fiercely to condemn Marxists' labelling of Freud as a Decadent (Hauser is confusing Decadent and decadent as Marxists deliberately did in the 1950s). Hauser's sardonic answer to the Marxists' label actually brings him unwillingly to the possible conclusion that Decadence might be a suitable designation for the whole period: 'If psychoanalysis is a decadent phenomenon, then so is the whole Naturalist novel and all Impressionist art, too, everything which is concerned with the discord of the nineteenth century.'[151]

Finally, the term Modernist is quite redundant if one is a sociological moralist critic like the chief inspirer of the Czech *Moderne*, Masaryk, who considered Engels a Decadent: 'The essence of Engels's Decadence lies in the facts that, just like all Decadents, he acknowledges the absoluteness of the sex drive and he judges all family relationships and intersexual contacts exclusively from that standpoint.'[152]

VIII. THE AMBIVALENCE OF DECADENCE

The true Decadent was a pessimist, but he had to try hard to be a pessimist, and he often failed – hence the frequent, indeed ubiquitous, ambivalence of Decadent art. The pessimist belongs to a tiny élite of the kind to which the Decadent aspired. The Decadent divided up society more or less in the same way as Arno Schmidt. Schmidt's analysis may easily function as an analysis of *fin-de-siècle* man's impressionistic perception of society. For that reason I shall reproduce it (with some adaptation and abbreviation) in detail.

A. 65% of society are optimists; their active imagination can be satisfied by a happy long walk: when these optimists judge the quality of something, they do so by contrasting; if they have imaginative impulses, they are more likely to be passive (dreams, etc) than active – the ratio posited is 3:1; their focus on their surroundings is blurred and subjective; their colour and consistency are pink and viscid. Their style of life-experience is tedious and respectable; their days consist in verbal blancmange; their erotic life is tempered by feelings of guilt; they tend to have (and perceive in others) indefinite, fluid faces; the rhythm of their days is undulating and flabby. Their typical roles in fiction could be a shopkeeper or lower middle-management or a sixthformer who always gets 'A's in German, or a Nobel prizewinner. A story about an optimist or optimists would have to end by running dry, or one would have to start repeating things.

B. 30% of society are suspicious (more or less sceptics); they are arguers and use argument as a therapeutic manner of becoming tired; when suspicious people (doubters) judge the quality of something they do so by drawing parallels; if they have imaginative impulses they are more likely to be passive than active, and the ratio posited is 2:1; their focus on their surroundings is sharp and subjective; their colour and consistency are grey and friable. Their style of life-experience is rhetorical and dialectical, nervous-wiry, wingeing-petty; they have the urge for tidiness and they have a rabbincial joy in the 'automobility of concepts'; they like using crumpled-silk types of words. Their typical roles in fiction could be someone in court (verbal battles and escape plans) or a policeman (conflicts with his superiors) or a bookkeeper *cum* envoy *cum* dictator of an imaginary power which conquers Frederick the Great. A story about a suspicious person might end after an exhausting journey to conviction of the certainty of such and such a phenomenon (long resolution). It might end also with a cavilling demonstration of his superiority: a retreat to catch his breath (Pyrrhic victory).

C. 5% of society are pessimists; they are prisoners like Prometheus with a tendency to lose themselves in (active) imaginings and with a capacity to remove mental pain; when pessimists judge the quality of something, they do so by extensive comparison, often comparison with general principles; their imaginative impulses are less likely to be passive than active, and the ratio posited is 1:2; their focus on their surroundings is sharp and objective; their colour and consistency are black and rugged. Their style of life-experience is complex; often passive (not only dreams), they are faced with dully horrific scenes perceived through dirt-clogged windows; because they are tormented their behaviour will often appear ill-tempered, but they are fundamentally decent; they are ruthless because they are themselves 'about to be pushed into the abyss'. Their typical roles in fiction could be a cripple in one of two express trains which are about to crash into each other or someone in prison or someone standing waiting for the firing squad in the Garden of Eden. A story about a pessimist will normally end with the end of his life as a passive experiencer, since he has such great imagination (not necessarily death, could be some mania, some total action, but he could also be saved or cured, or released).[153]

The Decadent liked at least to imagine himself living in one of two express trains about to crash, and general *fin-de-siècle* catastrophism helped him imagine that. Decadent literature was quintessentially a literature of the imagination, of *paradis artificiels* which were only rarely created by narcotics. That is a large part of the innovation of Decadence – that it does not use life but the fabrications of the mind as the stimulus for art. (The literature of the fantastic essentially originates in the 1890s as the new science-fiction originates in the 'Sixties'.) Decadents were interested in dreams, but they usually created those dreams themselves, did not use 'real dreams' as the Surrealists later pretended to do. In the case of painters like Simeon Sime or Edvard Munch one cannot tell the difference, but with Khnopff or Klimt or von Stuck or Délville or, indeed, Hlaváček the intellect always dominates, however sensualistic the picture. We might call that the first ambivalence of Decadence: the planned, studied, cerebral opposed by and combined with the sensualist. The sensualism very often lies only in their lexis or the use of a particular curve as the dominant visual image. The sensual ambivalence of Decadence is not general: a common phenomenon in Decadent works is an apparent contradiction between morbidity and life-affirmation even within one work (Zeyer, *Jan Maria Plojhar*, or Karásek's first collection of verse). Hajek, who uses the term *Jugendstil* for the period and its style, considers this apparent ambivalence actually to constitute simply two possible manners of expressing the mood of the times: 'the contradiction between Vitalism and Decadence (or the *Fin de siècle*) is not as great as the words imply. In any case catastrophists and epicureans of the "late" civilisation both use *Jugendstil*. Thus both concepts may be regarded as variants of consciousness within *Jugendstil*.'[154] Very much as in *Jan Maria Plojhar* the dying Felix in Schnitzler's *Sterben* at one moment is entirely indifferent to his dying and almost entirely indifferent to his woman, but then at the next he is determined to live the last piece of life left to him as fully as he can. That determination crystallises into: 'I can do without a year's life full of misery and anxiety; I do not want any more than a few weeks, a few days and nights. But I also want to *live* them; I do not want to deny myself anything at all, anything.'[155] Kubin gives satirical expression to this Decadent ambivalence when his narrator, just before devouring a large amount of ham and plumcake, says, 'I drank a black coffee and realised that I was incapable either of suicide or of living.'[156] What Beckson notes about Yeats, his aestheticism combined with Irish activism, is another facet of the same paradox. He points out that the combination was not uncommon: 'though some wrote of ennui, lassitude, disillusionment, and disengagement, at the same time they might praise the virtue of energy, the glory of nationalism, or the mystique of manhood. Few writers committed themselves to only one cause.'[157] Wilde entertained Parisian children on the occasion of Queen Victoria's birthday. Hlaváček would no doubt have remained an ardent gymnast in the patriotic Sokol club, had not tuberculosis overcome him. Leopold von Andrian was a diplomat and a great Habsburg patriot. The minor Czech Decadent, Vladimír Houdek, was an army officer – though he did have the Decadent decency to die in a lunatic asylum. The same paradox of Vitalism combined with Decadence or life-affirmation combined with nihilism, might be seen in the paradoxical linking of longing with scepticism in the Prologue's words in *Der Tod des Tizian*: 'full of precocious wisdom and early doubt, but still with a great yearning which enquires.'[158]

Praz points out the only apparently paradoxical link between lassitude and violence in the Decadence, a link which he considers essential to the formation of the trend. 'Ennui is only the most generic aspect of the *mal du siècle*; its specific aspect is – sadism.'[159] A frequent scene or emotion depicted in Decadent art is sensual pleasure derived from crime or the desire to be criminal. The topos is generally known as *bonheur dans le crime* after a story in Barbey d'Aurevilly's *Les Diaboliques*. One thinks of de Quincey's essay 'On Murder Considered as One of the Fine Arts' and of Wilde's 'Pen, Pencil and Poison'. In Zeyer's *Dům 'U tonoucí hvězdy'* (House at the sign of the sinking star, 1897) the Slovak main character Rojko (Slovak for 'dreamer') declares: 'A crime has something in common with a work of art; there is something in an artist as in a criminal which drives him to do what he does, drives him blindly – a mystery which no one has fathomed! Only a great artist is capable of as intense a sensation as a great criminal, or the other way round, if you will.'[160] One night the unaggressive Törless nearly attacks the salacious weakling minion Basini because 'such a murderous sensuality had been awoken in him after the torment of the empty-headed, dull-witted day'.[161] The scenes of this novel of Beineberg and Reiting's torturing of Basini may epitomise Decadent ambiguous sadism, especially since this sadism grows out of a mixture of privileged schoolboy indolence and sexual curiosity. The same scenes may also represent the moral decay of the Austrian privileged classes in the *Fin de siècle*. It is notable that the boys' parents appear to be on the whole more decent than the boys themselves. Hauser states that 'the Decadents were hedonists with a bad conscience',[162] and that is certainly true of these two Decadent creations, Zeyer's Rojko and Musil's Törless. Rojko is pursued by guilt throughout the novel. Törless is ashamed at his becoming sexually excited when he first experiences the other two boys' beating of the naked Basini.[163] That is reminiscent of the reaction of the victim in Kles's 'Eros' (1904), when the schoolmaster thrashes him, a thirteen-year-old alcoholic, in front of the class: 'The master went on and on flogging him – and then suddenly – in his tears, in his helplessness, fettered to the hard school bench, at the climax of pain – his sex moved for the first time. For years after that he was a "sad child", frightened, bemused.'[164]

The awareness that the erotic pervaded everything was a *fin-de-siècle* awareness, whose intensity infected the twentieth century with terminal disease. The sexualisation of not only art, but all human perception is directly inherited from Musset's *maladie du siècle* (the second characterisation). 'Love sits on the brain-pan of humanity,' writes Baudelaire,[165] and Nietzsche writes: 'The degree and nature of a human being's sexuality stretches right up into the last peak of his spirit.'[166] Two ironists of love. 'If the decadents discovered sexuality . . ., it was only for the most part to reject it, or at least to reject its normal forms.'[167] But Pierrot is simplifying matters by saying they rejected their sexuality. Here again we meet ambivalence. The Decadents re-created the old theme of *amor: dolor* in a hedonist materialist guise. Orgasm rules and orgasm is self-destruction and self-destruction is glorious but orgasm is vile because one is surrendering to the animal in one. But also: to love is to destroy. As Praz has pointed out, in the preliminaries to the Decadence during Romanticism, the man was the fatal creature and woman the victim: Byron loved and destroyed. 'The male, who at first tends towards sadism, inclines, at the end of the century towards masochism.'[168] The resolution of Wilde's *Salome* contains a more complex ambivalence than is at first apparent. The woman looks the sadist here, the ingenuous sadist and necrophiliac: 'Ah! I have kissed thy bitter taste on thy mouth, Jokanaan. I have kissed thy mouth. There was a bitter taste on thy lips. Was it the taste of blood. . . ? But perchance it is the taste of love . . . They say that love hath a bitter taste.'[169] Hajek points out that, actually, John the Baptist, by cursing Salome, had virtually committed suicide; he desires self-destruction. This is evident in the prefiguring of the words Salome utters at the end of the play:

SALOME: Let me kiss thy mouth.
JOKANAAN: Cursed be thou! Daughter of an incestuous mother, be thou accursed.
SALOME: I will kiss thy mouth, Jokanaan.

JOKANAAN: I do not wish to look at thee. I will not look at thee, thou art accursed, Salome, thou art accursed.[170]

Ady has a remarkable Decadent poem where masochism turns into narcissism, which is psychologically a thoroughly coherent interpretation of *fin-de-siècle* male masochism and of Austro-Hungarian catastrophism: 'Give me your eyes/Which kill, burn and desire,/Which always lend me beauty.//Give me your eyes,/In loving you I love myself,/And I am jealous of your eyes.'[171] Narcissism, homosexuality, necrophilia, sadomasochism, all have their role to play in Decadent literature. Much of it is accounted for by Pierrot's interpretation that, by 'exalting the abnormal, the decadent sensibility was encouraging or accelerating the self-destruction it more or less secretly longed for'.[172] The idea of beauty tainted by decay, which makes one think primarily of Baudelaire and Pater, forms part of this abnormality. One must not forget that the abnormal is 'new', surprising and potentially exciting artistically. The Medusa head, the Mona Lisa (as inspired by Pater's description of the picture), the nun, the corpse of a beautiful woman (see, for example, the Czech painter Jakub Schikaneder's *Drowned Girl* or *A Murder in the House*). Beauty tinged with decay represents their craving for love tinged with their fear of love. And that ambivalence is linked with the Decadent or 'modern' compulsion to self-analysis which was discussed by Arnold and Justh. That connection is made in the last stanza of Meredith's *Modern Love*: 'Their hearts held cravings for the buried day./Then each applied to each that fatal knife,/Deep questioning, which probes to endless dole.'[173] And perhaps the Baudelaire combination of the worship and the profanation of woman which runs through most of mainstream Decadence is also connected. One should not be surprised that Weininger could in the same work speak of 'the lowliest man standing immeasurably higher than the most elevated woman' and of the penis enslaving the woman, or that he should consider that man regards woman only as an object to be physically enjoyed.[174] That is a stock Decadent ambivalence, linked with 'the simultaneous recognition of the satanic and perverse nature of love, the contemptible nature of woman and the impossibility of doing without her'.[175] 'I am frightened of desiring,' writes Ady, 'consummation will come and dishonour me.'[176]

Quite apart from their cultivation of the artificial and the unusual one has to imagine that Decadent culture as urban culture was altogether wary of Nature. That is another point where it is difficult to fit the Hungarians into the Decadent context. Ady was as much a forerunner of the interwar urban avant-garde as he was of Hungarian ruralist literature. Hofmannsthal, Freud, Hlaváček or Březina were forerunners of the interwar avant-garde, but they had nothing in common with ruralism. Decadent writers certainly complained about the squalor of the new conurbations, but they also despised the vulgar countryside.

Artists in the Decadent period rarely adopted any party-political or political ideological stances. Decadent culture was largely apolitical. When it is touched by politics, the Decadent attitude is, again, ambivalent. They were anti-democratic but, because they abhorred the bourgeois, they often dabbled in socialism (Wilde, S. K. Neumann, Ady). They claimed to stand outside all accepted morality and more or less to be anarchists (or at least intellectual anarchists, bohemians), but actually they were conservative, even reactionary. Barrès, himself once a Decadent and later more or less a Fascist (like the Decadents D'Annunzio and Arnošt Procházka), called the Decadents the Boulangistes of literature.[177]

IX. THE DECAY OF LANGUAGE AND THE LANGUAGE OF DECADENCE

The Decadent period was greatly concerned with the aesthetic function of language. It was the period which created modern language experimentation; one thinks particularly of Rimbaud and Christian Morgenstern. But it was also in this period that de Saussure was lecturing and that Wittgenstein not only began to bring a heightened philosophical awareness of language to the educated public, but also, more than anyone else, perfected the Nietzschean skill of making philosophy literature. And many of the aphorisms of the *Tractatus* resound with the Nineties. 'What is thinkable is also possible' (3.02) is as Decadent a statement as 'The whole modern world view is based on the delusion that so-called natural laws are the explanations of natural phenomena' (6.371). The Decadents' own attitude to language constitutes one of the chief ambivalences of the trend. Seeba puts his explanation of the paradox between Decadents' scepticism about the communicative function and their verbal luxuriance elegantly: 'Purposeless verbal splendour is possible only because the possibility of linguistic communication has become questionable.'[178] In Austria-Hungary language-consciousness was particularly intense because of the dominant languages' problems with the nationalities and because, especially in Vienna, where several languages could always be heard simultaneously, speakers of individual languages were likely to feel that theirs was threatened, even if it was German.

Again, Nordau sees the decay of language as an essential element in the decay of European civilisation. The very title of his book 'conventional lies' concentrates the mind initially on language. Language is not his prime concern except insofar as it is part of the general subterfuge in which European capitalism is indulging. But since communication is primarily linguistic, language actually lies somewhere in the kernel of Nordau's assessment, for example:

> The form and content of our middle-class existence are mutually extremely exclusive. The problem of our official culture appears to be to find room for a cube

in a sphere of the same volume. Every word we speak, every action we perform is a lie against what we recognise in our souls as the truth. So we both parody ourselves and act out an eternal comedy which, however used to it we are, tires us, which demands of us a constant denial of our knowledge and convictions, and which, when we have time for introspection, cannot but fill us with contempt for ourselves and for the way of the world.[179]

The linguistic aesthete, the fine-chiseler, Hofmannsthal, also speaks about the decay of language in his 'Ein Brief' (The Chandos letter, 1902). Language decay appears to derive from *fin-de-siècle* catastrophism; if European civilisation is about to collapse, so is its main transmitter, or: a cause for the collapse of European civilisation is the decay of its main transmitter. It is significant that Hofmannsthal is in the following particularly concerned with the language of intellectuals' communication. The letter pretends to have been written in 1603, during the paradoxical Baroque period when civilisation was also seen to be collapsing and when the Habsburgs were consolidating their empire: 'The abstract words which the tongue naturally has to employ to formulate any sort of judgement, disintegrated in my mouth like mouldly mushrooms.'[180] The Decadent is again faced with his old problem. He has to decide whether it is he that is inadequate or contemporary institutions. The more frivolous brand of Decadent will always decide it is the institutions (in Hofmannsthal it is not so). Thus Schaukal's somewhat facetious definition of a poem blames language (at least partly) for cultural vacuousness: 'A poem [is] an arbitrary and evidently vain combination of inadequate words.' Elsewhere Schaukal equally facetiously suggests that literary success depends on the degree of linguistic distortion; 'One has only to spend a few years putting one's words in different positions from those imperiously demanded by syntax, and then one impresses the public. . . . One's bad behaviour will be imitated by numerous hacks and thus one will become a classic.'[181] Karl Kraus made a direct connection between language decay and moral decay. Linguistic banality reflected banality of character. Kraus frequently demonstrates that in his satires by exploiting, as Stern puts it, deconstructing, clichés. Stern points out that old clichés are not noticed at all because they have become part of the general store of dead metaphors which make up language, whereas if it 'is less old, and if therefore its constituent parts are easily recognised, the satirist will re-assess the saving in thought as thoughtlessness, and condemn the cliché as a sign of triteness, laziness, banality, as a sign of the enfeebled imagination that allows itself to be manipulated by euphemism and the artfully concealed lie.' Stern questions whether unthinkingness or banality are moral failings. He omits laziness, because laziness is commonly regarded as a moral failing. Stern also considers 'inadequate' and 'misleading' Hannah Arendt's apparent adherence to the Kraus view when she spoke of Eichmann as demonstrating 'the banality of evil' and Stern points out that Kraus had recurrently used the same type of

phrase about Hitler.[182] It was, indeed, not an uncommon approach to
Hitler, who represented all the petty bourgeois values the Decadent period
had been protesting against. The Silesian writer Alfred Kerr wrote about
Hitler as a feeble imitator; in other words, given the journalistic bent, he is
within the same semantic field as Arendt and Kraus: 'Hitler . . . is
Mussolenin at sale-price. He is the ochlocrat aping the "individualist". He is
brutality by imitation.'[183] Stern takes Kraus's view back to Schopenhauer's
'positing a firm and stable relationship between verbal slips and solecisms on
the one hand, and on the other the moral turpitude of those who commit the
solecisms and present them to the reading public.' And one can see how that
attitude can develop towards not only Kraus, but also Freud's concern with
the *lapsus linguae*. Stern's main point has two aspects: (i) that an evil act is an
evil act and the language used in connection with it has no bearing on that
fact, and (ii) 'it is simply not true to suggest, as writers inspired by Kraus
suggest, that the imagination acts as an infallible or even reliable moral
agent' and so 'Bringing order into the words does not bring justice into the
world.'[184] No one will disagree with Stern there. Just, however, as Kraus
wisely declared that bibliophile editions were an indicator of a decayed
society, so it is not unwise of him to make a parallel between linguistic and
moral putrefaction, as long as the Establishment is involved. The cliché is
particularly prevalent in morally corrupt societies, witness German newspapers or novels in the 1930s and 1940s or Czech or Hungarian newspapers
in the 1950s. Furthermore, though an evil act is an evil act, one does feel that
it is even more evil when it is accompanied by a cliché which seeks to justify
it. Honeyed words tend not to be mellifluous.

Views similar to Kraus's were held elsewhere. Henry Reeve writes in 'The
Literature and Language of the Age' (*Edinburgh Review*, 1889) that a
'corrupt and decaying language is an infallible sign of a corrupt and decaying
civilization. It is one of the gates by which barbarism may invade and
overpower the traditions of a great race.'[185] Reeve remarks that the overuse
of foreign words and 'barbarous terms' is a sure sign of linguistic decay. The
foreign word was particularly well liked by Decadents in France as in
Bohemia, in England as in the Austrian Lands. What the decay of language
actually entails is never quite clear. Ungrammatical, slipshod language,
malapropisms and so forth are the products of individual carelessness,
inability or lack of education. Language decay may simply be language
change and as a concept it doubtless belongs to a subjectivist element in
purism.

On the other hand there is no doubt that the period did feel frustrated by
language; writers of the period felt that language was an inadequate
expression of reality. Hence the spread of synaesthesia and 'foreign' words,
hence too, the adjectival burden of Decadent prose. The ambiguity of the
Decadent attitude to language is connected with an ambiguous attitude to
what is or is not reality and what is or is not truth – or falsehood. There is, as

Nietzsche puts it, little chance of a desire for truth anyway when man 'rests in the indifference of his not knowing at the same time as hanging on the back of a tiger dreaming'.[186] He doubts language is 'an adequate expression of all realities', and anyway: 'What is a word? The representation in sounds of a nervous stimulus.'[187] Nietzsche preempts most Decadent expressions of scepticism about language with his answer to Pontius Pilate's question:

> [Truth is a] mobile army of metaphors, metonymies, anthropomorphisms, in brief a sum of human relations which have been poetically and rhetorically enhanced, charged, adorned, and which, after a people has been using them for a long time, consider themselves stable, canonic and binding. Truths are illusions about which it has been forgotten that they are illusions, metaphors which have been worn out and have become semantically powerless, coins which have lost their emboss-ments and can now no longer be considered coins, but only pieces of metal. . . . to be truthful is to employ the usual metaphors or, to put it morally: out of duty to lie in accordance with a firm convention, to follow the herd and lie in a style which is obligatory for one and all.[188]

The *fin-de-siècle* approach to language has, in the end to be 'dialectical', as Hajek puts it. *Fin-de-siècle* man was a passionate believer in self-expression (for the élite) and was simultaneously convinced the linguistic instrument of his self-expression was inefficient. 'On the one hand,' Hajek writes, 'denominating things removes from those things their immediate being; naming thus weakens, creates *distance* and obstructs the identification of the denominator with the denominated, since the act of denominating interferes between the denominator and the denominated. On the other hand denominating is the unifying medium which makes the symbolising of universal unity possible in literature.'[189] Claudio in *Der Tor und der Tod* uses language to try to ensure that he will 'fix every vital experience for the future' and thus he destroys the experience. So too he uses 'associative comparisons which are meant to multiply unique experiences, but which likewise destroy them'. All 'linguistic expressions of human vitality appear to Claudio to be a lie'.[190] Hofmannsthal's Chandos finds that words are too poor to express the noble qualities that any object can suddenly assume. Language cannot express anything exceptional. The obverse of such unfruitful lucubration is to exploit the inadequacy of language, make a virtue of it. Thus Baudelaire exclaims 'let my heart become drunk with a *lie*'[191] and Wilde states that 'Lying, the telling of beautiful untrue things, is the proper aim of Art'.[192] Another manner of exploiting the inadequacy of conventional literary language is to explore dialect. The best known example of that in Austro-Hungarian Decadent literature is Schnitzler's *Leutnant Gustl* (1901). Stern notes that in the Vienna patois the author or his narrator uses the 'tendency towards a disarming domestication of the external world goes so far that, in order to express that which "mögen" expresses everywhere else, namely a distinct preference, the Viennese are reduced to saying "was ich nämlich mögen möcht . . .".' Schnitzler has

Gustl use this 'fluid, inchoate language' to indicate 'his mood of insinuation', his 'subjectiveness'.[193] A similar use of Prague and Chod dialects is to be found in novels and short-stories by Čapek-Chod and in the use of class register in the ironic tales of František Gellner.

It is possible to conceive of the whole Decadence as primarily concerned with the word, not the concept, as a trend which concentrates on the aesthetic rather than the informational function of language. Gautier in his introduction to Baudelaire (1868) describes the Decadence as a particular style: 'the style of decadence is the last word of the Word [Logos] summoned up to express everything and driven to extreme excess. In this connection one might remember the gamy language of the late Roman Empire, a language marbled with the greens of decomposition.'[194] And Symons writes of the word Decadent: 'the term is in its place only when applied to their style; to that ingenious deformation of the language, in Mallarmé, for instance, which can be compared with what we are accustomed to call the Greek and Latin of the Decadence.'[195] In *Der Fall Wagner* (The Wagner Case, 1888) Nietzsche characterises Decadence by the apparent autonomy of the word; language as an independent force takes over from meaning: 'The word becomes sovereign and springs out of the sentence; the sentence encroaches upon and obscures the sense of the page; the page achieves life at the expense of the whole – the whole is no longer whole. . . . Every Decadent style is an anarchy of atoms, a disintegration of the Will, in moral terms: "the freedom of the individual" – expanded to practical theory, "equal rights for all".'[196] Paul Bourget defines it similarly, 'a style where the unity of the book is decomposed to make room for the independence of the word.'[197] Mallarmé tried to create a language for verse which was entirely different from the language of everyday communication; 'language was given to become "real", language was to be magic, words were to become things.'[198] Hajek persuasively shows how in Beer-Hofmann's novel *Der Tod Georgs* (Georg's death, 1900) language has lost its communicative function, no longer tries to represent life; language 'is a completely autonomous formation which retains only an impression of life (just as in *Jugendstil* paintings; colours and lines, having become autonomous, rarely go in the direction of abstraction; they tend to retain the forms of life).'[199] In the Chandos letter Hofmannsthal has words separate themselves from everything and float individually around the writer, and in Meyrink's *Der Golem* words take on individual physical life. In Meyrink's case, if not seriously in Hofmannsthal's, one might see something of the Cabalist's approach to the word.

Dowling's conception of primarily the English Decadence as a language movement appears ultimately to derive from Gautier and Nietzsche. If one can accept her premises, it should not be too difficult to apply her suggestions to Austrian-German literature, but in the cases of Czech and Hungarian one would have to take the histories of the language into consideration. Both languages went through the purism and prettification of National Revival (in Hungary *Nyelvújtás*, language renewal); a process was set in motion to express the new ideas of Englightenment scholarship and to encourage these languages artistically to 'catch up' with the West, a process which was, practically, utterly unnecessary, but which was politically important, because of the Theresian and Josephine reforms which not only gave new powers to German but also involved a greater centralisation of the Monarchy and thus a sense of diminished importance for non-German nobles. By the time the Decadence began Czech was established in its new form, that is with many new archaic (mainly sixteenth-century) and non-Czech (i.e. other-Slavonic) elements, at least as a language of culture. Still Czech was not a politically established language at the beginning of the 1890s. Hungarian was also culturally established, but in our period it was also a dominant and dominating language. Unlike Czech, however, Hungarian had not really entered the realms of high culture. Serious opera in Hungarian began only in the Decadent period. Also it should be noted that the innovation at the beginning of that period in Hungarian literature was limited to verse. Hungarian was still felt to be a 'lyric' literature, perhaps unjustly, since that is normally the state with an undeveloped literary culture. So, in Austrian-German, Czech and Hungarian literature, there were reasons why a linguistic crisis of the sort Dowling posits for English literature could have existed. Indeed, there were a good deal more reasons for that crisis in Austria-Hungary than in Great Britain. I accept Dowling's notion, not because I am persuaded she is right, but because it provides useful spectacles for looking at Austro-Hungarian culture. In the three literary cultures I am concerned with a solidly established literary norm existed against which there could be a linguistic rebellion. Dowling's theory is that:

> the Decadence emerges . . . as a counterpoetics of disruption and parody and stylistic derangement, a critique not so much of Wordsworthian nature as of the metaphysics involved in any sentimental notion of a simple world of grass and trees and flowers. The world as it then survives in Decadent writing is by contrast a belated world, a place of hesitations and contrarities and exhaustions . . . Decadence . . . emerged from . . . a crisis in Victorian attitudes towards language brought about by the new comparative philology earlier imported from the Continent. For it was the new linguistic science . . . that raised the spectre of autonomous language – language as a system blindly obeying impersonal phonological rules in isolation from any world of human values and experience.[200]

Especially for Czechs and Hungarians of the Establishment, who very much believed in the sacrosanctity of language because language bore and mirrored the nation's wretched history as well as its true national or folk spirit, the language of Decadent writing was indeed sacrilegious, almost blasphemous. As was the subject matter. The use Dowling makes of Pater's *Marius the Epicurean* both to show Pater's elegant handling of English as a dead, Classical language and to point out what Pater says about language in the novel is coincidentally useful for any student of central European culture. The following quotation could be taken as an understated account of the Austrian-German, Czech and Hungarian linguistic situations:

> The popular speech was gradually departing from the form and rule of literary language, a language always and increasingly artificial. While the learned dialect was yearly becoming more and more barbarously pedantic, the colloquial idiom, on the other hand, offered a thousand chance-lost gems of racy or picturesque expression, rejected or at least ungathered by what claimed to be classical Latin.[201]

Dowling's contention that the autonomy of language in Decadent literature is 'invariably' described as something 'mysterious, disruptive, evil' is exaggerated. It clearly applies to Machen (who was popular among Czech Decadents) and to Meyrink, perhaps to *Dorian Gray* or *A rebours*. The audience of Decadent works may often have considered the performance of language disruptive and evil. And authors like Péladan, Bois, Ady and the Czech Marten no doubt intended to create with a seemingly autonomous language whose aesthetic effect should lie chiefly in its disruptiveness. Babits certainly had an attitude to Hungarian which was similar to Pater's attitude to English, and Babits was a connoisseur of English letters. Hofmannsthal also reacted to the mysterious autonomy and to Pater's words, when he is analysing Pater's critical method in *The Renaissance*: 'To grasp the mysterious processes, which could be compared only with the life of love, processes where the artist's soul endeavoured to express itself in symbolic ideas which have been deprived of conceptual expression, and where in dark urging these ideas remove their symbolic expression from outward life, to grasp these processes is to get as close as one can to the artist's idea.'[202]

The Decadents' attitude to language often also had something of their attitude to women. They worshipped this dead thing and profaned it to bring it alive. They liked to play with language. They played with it acoustically so that sometimes the sounds of words would contain more meaning than their denotations (Verlaine, Hlaváček). Březina, especially when he is still learning about spiritism and the esoteric arts and so has not yet elaborated a consistent set of emblems and symbols, uses sound to give meaning to the conceptual confusions of his verse. Dowling discusses at some length that Decadent work which most successfully indulges in linguistic play but also play in content and intertextuality, Beardsley's *Under the Hill*. She sees the book as a parody of what she calls 'antinomian or apocalyptic Decadence' as a whole, because of Beardsley's dismissal of moral regulation and his subversion of ideas of beauty and ugliness. It is, however, primarily in its style that *Under the Hill* is subversively playful – and playfully subversive. The author parodies throughout the techniques of withholding information which Kugel describes, especially with his references to non-existent works and stories. While *Under the Hill* is a parody of Decadence, it is also one of the most Decadent of Decadent works in European literature. In most parody parisitism dominates, but that is not so of this work, for it is also parodying itself. Hlaváček also parodies himself in several poems of his second collection, · *Pozdě k ránu* (Early in the morning, 1896). The Hungarian Dezső Kosztolányi, a devotee of Schopenhauer, whose first two collections of verse were published late in the period (1912 and 1916) combined 'big-city ennui' with straightforward pessimism and playfulness. He developed wordplay particularly during the Great War. But play was also a philosophical standpoint for him. In one poem he asks: 'Do you want to live, to live eternally,/Do you want to live in the game which has become reality?/To lie down on the ground amongst the flowers,/And do you want, do you want to play at death?'[204] It looks as if these lines allude to Millais's *Ophelia*. Certainly play has become a threat. It never becomes that in Ladislav Klíma, probably the only philosopher the Decadence produced. This Existentialist, whose thought was based mainly on Berkeley, Schopenhauer and Nietzsche, and himself, gave his philosophical ideas many names. One of them was ludibrionism. Klíma was also a novelist and both his novels were parodies, but, like Beardsley's novel, nonparasitical parodies. His philosophical writings are frequently in the form of aphorisms.

The cultivation of style in the Decadence concerns partly language and partly metalanguage. Sometimes the two cannot and should not be distinguished. The most celebrated discussion of style in the period is Pater's and Pater considers only artistic style. In his essay on style (1888) Pater also speaks of truth, and this is clearly the truth spoken of in the Czech *Moderna* manifesto: 'In the highest as in the lowliest literature . . . the one indispensable beauty is, after all, truth – truth to bare fact in the latter, and to some personal sense of fact, diverted somewhat from men's ordinary sense of it, in the former; truth there is accuracy; truth here is expression, that finest and most intimate form of truth, the *vraie verité*.'[205] All Pater actually demands of style is that it be characteristic or expressive, thus that it reveals that *vraie verité*. In this essay Pater also readopts his (and Mallarmé's) contention that all good art should aspire to music. Music, he says here, is 'the ideal of all art . . . because in music it is impossible to distinguish the form from the substance or matter, the subject from the expression'.[206] Music is also the highest art because it cannot be accurately described in any other art form and because it can theoretically describe anything. It was, thus, elitist from an aesthetician's point of view.

In literature style is the art of omission, according to Pater: 'the "one beauty" of all literary style is of its very essence, and independent, in prose and verse alike, of all removable decoration . . . in truth all art does but consist in the removal of surplusage.'[207] Very similarly to Pater, Symonds writes, 'the final end of all style is precision, veracity of utterance, truth to the thing to be presented.'[208] A little later he adds that good style demands beauty as well as precision. Symonds approaches Kraus's way of thinking, when he makes literary style an indicator of moral values. Style, he says, is 'the sign of personal qualities, specific to individuals, which constitute the genius of a man. Whatever a man utters from his heart and head is the index of his character.'[209] But perhaps that is also not far from Rémy de Gourmont's 'the thought is the man himself. Style is thought itself.'[210] Or from Schaukal's statement in his 1919 essay in memory of Peter Altenberg:

> Whatever sort of discourse it is, wordy or sparse, unpretentious or majestic, warm and swift or quiet and cool, ponderous and muffled or light and bright, clear or turbid, sweet or bitter, aggressive or modest: as long as soul breathes or flows out of it, as long as it works magic; without soul, without magic the discourse, even if composed by a master, will wither and fall to the ground.[211]

Miloš Marten follows Pater closely when he writes: 'Style lies in how the artist comes to terms with the material, how he re-forms, evaluates it. Style is form. . . . Form is the actual creative art of the artist. . . . there is no difference between material and form . . . the material disappears in the form.'[212] Machen's definition of style in *Hieroglyphics* (1902) is the most insinuatingly Decadent: style 'is the most outward sign of the burning grace within'.[213]

Style is also the man and period definitions of style tended to say more about an artist's appearance than his art. Thus Oscar Wilde's aphorism: 'In all unimportant matters, style, not sincerity, is the essential. In all important matters, style, not sincerity, is essential.'[214] Hence also the words of William Watson, who is better known as a patriotic poet than for the aesthete that he really was: 'Style always holds something back, never quite lets itself go. Probably passion *plus* self-restraint is the moral basis of the finest style.'[215] And Schaukal: 'Style rejects all compromise. Compromise destroys style.'[216]

X. THE DANDY

Richard Le Gallienne tried not to be a Decadent, but was one, perhaps especially when he was parodying Decadence in his verse. He also has an ambivalent attitude to dandyism. He expresses perceptively a commonly held view, which distinguishes between fine style and dandyism: 'literary self-consciousness is in danger of degenerating from the proper, controlled, and concealed self-consciousness of the artist into the absurd, self-parading self-consciousness of the dandy.'[217] Simultaneously, however, he expresses the attitudes the theorists of dandyism attributed to the mode, for example: 'It is they who despise fashion that lead it.'[218] The Decadent conception of the dandy is based on Barbey d'Aurevilly and Baudelaire. In *Du dandysme et de Georges Brummell* (Dandyism and Beau Brummell, 1843) Barbey describes dandyism as a way of life which can be achieved only in particularly civilised and old societies. In other words, dandyism is theoretically connected with exactly what Gautier and Baudelaire were to indicate as the necessary conditions for Decadent style. The key characteristic of dandyism, according to Barbey, is that it always surprises. It is the art of the unexpected. In *Mon Coeur mis à nu* (My heart laid bare, posth. 1887), Baudelaire writes that 'The Dandy should always aspire to be uninter-ruptedly sublime; he should live and sleep in front of the glass.' And just before that he points out what was to be an essential of dandyism, its indifference to sexuality; the dandy is the aristocrat of the spirit, the artist aristocrat, the contradiction, the annihilation, of the animal in man:

> The woman is the opposite of the dandy.
> Hence she ought to be horrifying.
> The woman is hungry and she wants to eat. Thirsty and she wants to drink.
> She is in rut and she wants to be fucked.
> Beautiful virtue!
> Woman is *natural*, in other words, abominable.
> Thus she is always vulgar, the opposite of the dandy.[219]

Nordau is not quite vulgar in his minor reaction to dandyism: 'Why do Brummell and Cartouche assemble such a court, like some great artist or scholar? . . . Because that satisfies the primal human herd-animal instinct of submissiveness to the leader of the herd.'[220] Indeed, followers of dandies might well be as animal as women, for they have no sense of individuality.

If Barbey were right that well-marinated, gamy civilisations produce dandies, one might have expected Austria to produce them. I do not think Altenberg or Roda Roda were dandies. Schaukal had a try. Only Bohemia produced a real dandy, Breisky, but just for a few months. He could not stand Austria, went to America, secured a job as a hospital porter and within a few weeks died in a lift accident. America was no place for a true dandy either. If one is to accept an historicist view that since London had its Wilde, Stenbock and so on, Paris its Montesquiou, Péladan and so on, Vienna ought also to have had real dandies; one may explain why Vienna did not by pointing to the fact that Vienna did not have a mature cultural background like London or Paris. Vienna was really all new. Prague had the cultural background but it was not a political power centre and so half the requisite cultural trappings was missing. Breisky was a freak. Budapest had recently become a power centre again but it had virtually no cultural tradition. Schaukal's monocled dandy asserts that the young Viennese's concern with art and artists was a sign of the *Unkultur* of Vienna (one is reminded of Broch's later label, *Unstil*). Schaukal's dandy describes *Unkultur* as the romantic, sentimental conception of art; behind the following is the idea that Vienna was basically banal:

> when someone sits at his desk or pulls himself up in bed beside a flickering candle

and with a dip-pen or crayon writes a poem on a scrap of paper, the back of an envelope, whether it is some tentative communication or a deliberate veiling of his emotions or immediate thoughts, that is *Unkultur*. And people who have done something like this often, and have received applause for it, grow used to regarding this as an extraordinarily remarkable thing and become famous: that is permanent *Unkultur*.[221]

The dandy is not necessarily the aesthete at all; he is more of an individualist than the aesthete Kraus satirises as 'capable out of world-weariness to take poison because it is green and to envy a baboon its red backside'.[222] Hauser sees the dandy as embodying a 'protest against the routine triviality of bourgeois life', and certainly the dandy does epitomise the Decadents' anti-democratic ideology. Hauser accepts Baudelaire's view of the dandy as a manifestation of heroism in an age of decay: 'the ideal of the completely useless, unmotivated, pointless existence.'[223]

Dandy combines with occultist and with homosexual in two of Karásek's novels, *Román Manfreda Macmillena* (The novel of Manfred Macmillen, 1907) and *Scarabaeus* (1908). The eponymous hero of the former defines dandyism as a mask behind which one hides the mysteries of one's inner life. Manfred is very much Karásek's adaptation of the Baudelairean dandy. He has a certain vanity which does not belong to the usual Decadent dandy, Breisky's, Marten's, or Schaukal's (the cult of youth in such as Karásek was mocked as degenerate by Ladislav Klíma):

His exterior immediately struck one, though there was nothing eccentric about him and although one sensed that he always avoided the eccentric, not because he was well-bred, but merely because it was not his style. His dress was distinguished, fashionable, but he did not wear anything that was the *dernier cri*, that one could buy in every shop in the Kärntnerstrasse. He was no longer particularly young, but he did his best to look pleasantly youthful. He deemed youth the only form in which one could appear in public. He wanted to differ from those who did not feel the indecency of being old by being eternally youthful . . . He refreshed himself by seeking the company only of his young friends. For he considered old age infectious . . . And he did not debase himself by having any contact with unattractive people. For the very sight of ugly people can make one hideous oneself. . . . The philosophy of dandyism teaches one how to be bored and thus how to be capable of living. The dandy should not be inspired by anything. But since that is practically unachievable, he is sometimes permitted inspiration, with one major exception; he may never admire the perfect; that is only for snobs. The dandy is inspired only by mediocrity. A bad theatre production provides him with illusion and bad love provides him with the sensation of being in love. The dandy should neither love nor despise people. He must merely be convinced that there are interesting people in the world and redundant people, and all those who are not interesting are redundant. Manfred lived in accordance with these rules. [He knew] that life had a point only if we are unconcerned about living . . . and that only Positivist knowledge made man stupid. . . . It was true that he read many recent books, but he only read them to confirm his opinion that today's literature contains nothing but utter folly.[224]

Manfred is homosexual and he loves another homosexual. Both know that homosexual love is superior to heterosexual (Karásek probably knew Ulrichs, and he certainly knew Edward Carpenter and de Joux). Heterosexual love is something for those people Manfred considered redundant, the uninteresting people, for it is nothing but animal passion. Heterosexual non-dandies (it seems from this novel that dandies have to be homosexual) are grey hypocrites who, even when they lie, utter only little lies; they have ruined vice; they fornicate and murder, but as cowards; they do it on the quiet, have no sense of the potential aesthetic glory of vice. In the view of Manfred's deadly lover, Francis, decency should be hidden away like a foul disease. The homosexual dandy of *Scarabaeus*, Marcel, is a slightly different type: he is an absolute solipsist; he lives to be alone but he is not wholly himself when he is alone, or: not the self his few acquaintances know. Marcel knows that everything which is beyond his self is trite and banal. He is also somewhat satanic, one of those figures possessed of evil which *fin-de-siècle* literature, following Baudelaire and, later, Huysmans, so delighted in. When Marcel closes his eyes it is as if he is locking them away in two silent coffins. He is a master of the esoteric arts and he lives only fictions, narcotic wildnesses which go far beyond even his everyday self. Marcel questions whether it is worth experiencing anything in life, since one can dream everything anyway. So Marcel's dandyism includes mysticised narcissism.

Karásek's conception of Marcel may be as influenced by Baudelaire's *Journaux intimes* (Intimate diaries) as Breisky's conception of the dandy. Though Breisky is a more original writer, at least on this subject. In the first section of the diaries, *Fusées*, Baudelaire states that 'the most perfect type of virile Beauty is *Satan* – in the manner of Milton.'[225] In the essay 'Quintessence dandysmu. Essai odpovědí na otázku Charlesa Baudelaira v Mon Coeur mis à nu: "Qu'est ce que le dandy?" ' (The quintessence of dandyism. An essay in answer to Baudelaire's question in *Mon Coeur mis à nu*: 'What is the dandy?' 1910), Breisky writes, 'The dandy is the spirit of rebellion, a relation of Milton's Satan.'[226] Baudelaire writes that 'in his life leisure had allowed him to grow, in sensitivity, meditation and the faculties of dandyism and dilettantism.' As a dandy he can compare himself favourably with other writers. 'For the most part other men of letters are base, very ignorant navvies.'[227] Breisky echoes that, perhaps, when he says that the tragedy of Oscar Wilde had been that a perpetual war between the poet and the dandy had been waged within him. Wilde may have been overcome by his own hedonism. The dandy avoids that: 'Dandies are hedonists who prepare themselves refined personal pleasures, but they may never permit themselves to be taken over by those pleasures. They are artists of mystification. . . . They never allow anyone to see inside their souls. If they speak about themselves, they never speak the truth. They are proud of the secrets of their intimate experience.'[228] Schaukal misunderstands the relationship between dandy and artist, or he satirises it, for Andreas von Balthesser is both a dandy dilettante and a parody of the type. Balthesser has written three works with decently Decadent titles, 'Perseus', 'The Androgyne' and 'The Corybants'. He is a ' "poet", a man with poetic talent, but otherwise a fellow man, a citizen of the world and child of the times with a more or less large brain of the world and more or less bright eyes of the times.'[229] Schaukal has no attitude to love, but the attitude of Breisky's dandy resembles Baudelaire's: 'Dandies are never natural, never yield to their feelings; they always control themselves brilliantly and never yield to strong, brutish emotional reactions like laughter, tears, despair or anger. They are prepared for everything; nothing can take them by surprise. They love the opal pallor of their boredom. . . . They know how to suffer with a smile and how to die with a smile. They are incapable of passion or love. Passion caricatures one and love is prostitution. And both wrest from one self-control, the basic qualification of the dandy.'[230] His attitude to woman also resembles Baudelaire's and is, anyway, typically Decadent: 'the dandy does not know love for woman. Sometimes he will respect her as a virtuoso on her instrument. But he is indifferent to her and despises her instinctuality. He looks down on her as a great actor looks down on the extra. The dandy judges her only with his eyes. He acknowledges only one genius in her: the genius of looks. And he can even find her amiable, if her beauty is sufficiently elegant and distinguished and if she knows how to surrender herself with grace. For the dandy making love with a woman is the same as smoking cigarettes or drinking champagne: a stimulant for the senses.'[231] Schaukal points out what may not have been obvious to his readers, that the clothes a dandy wears have very little to do with his dandyhood. Unlike Karásek's Manfred, Schaukal's dandy does not read modern books and journals; that is part of being outside fashion. Instead he reads *The Confessions* of St Augustine and a comparative grammar of the Romance languages. Then he goes 'to a club where there are pleasant sportsmen who leave their theatre-boxes empty when Wagner is being put on'.[232] Again the reader is not certain of how much that is parody, especially since Balthesser also does a lot of riding in the Prater. The relationship of Breisky's dandy to fashion is clearer: 'The dandy is never guided by fashion, but he is always imitated by it. Dandyism is inventiveness, imagination, newness, unusualness, individuality. Fashion is imitation, repetition, generalisation. . . . Dandyism begins where fashion ends. Fashion uniforms; dandyism disuniforms. The greatest enemy of fashion is the dandy. . . . The greatest ideal of the dandy is to be distinguishedly different.'[233] The extent to which Schaukal emphasises the role of the unforeseen in the dandy's way of life suggests he has been using Barbey d'Aurevilly. 'The essence of dandyism,' he writes, 'lies in the impromptu.' and 'I am a dandy not because I am well-bred, but because, with all my good breeding, I never neglect the impromptu.'[234] He defines this impromptu as 'the most fleeting, finest thing, one might say the hint of a statement. By statement I do not necessarily mean a verbal statement . . . the impromptu has respect for the moment. . . . *The dandy never misses the right moment.* He never emphasises that moment; *he never emphasises anything* (least of all his presence); he may even allow the moment to pass concealed, but he never fails to recognise it.'[235]

Because of his expectation of disaster and because of his enjoyment of that expectation the Decadent normally lives just for the moment. He cultivates moments, the sudden precious jewel in the pyrite flow of time. The dandy, then, naturally lives only for the present. A young writer in conversation with Balthesser is more of a dandy than Balthesser himself, for whom he has little respect. But he says he will try to live by Balthesser's rule that 'One never speaks of yesterday.'[236] Breisky writes that the dandy is 'the knight of todays; he closes his eyes indifferently to all tomorrows. A magical brightness shines out to meet him, the eyes of his Platonic mistress: *La Mort – la grand Consolatrice.* . . . His whole life is a triumph of the artificial – his end is probably never natural.'[237] Both Schaukal and Breisky feel the need to distinguish between the dandy and the gentleman. For example, the former maintains, '*The dandy has the best of manners.* The gentleman does not absolutely have to have good manners,' and at another point making a distinction particularly typical of the Decadents because the public used to consider fleshly Aesthetes immoral, ' "Dandy" is a concept of aesthetic and "gentleman" a concept of ethical evaluation.'[238] Breisky goes into more detail than Schaukal. Gentlemen, he avers, 'take life seriously, which dandies never do. A gentleman has a whole series of various interests in life, amongst them woman, but a dandy is not interested in anything except his own beauty. The gentleman endeavours to attain the ideal of a social charmer by adapting himself to society, by letting society forget his ego; the dandy, however, achieves his greatest effects by staging productions of his ego.'[239] For Baudelaire the dandy is 'eternally superior';[240] that is Schaukal's uncompromising elitist who 'ironises his consciousness' and who is '*completely unapproachable*' and can never be 'observed, watched'.[241]

Again here we note Decadent ambivalence, for the dandy is as typical a Decadent hero as other types, who are far from dandies, though some of them may be aristocrats in their resignation. But again, we cannot expect many dandies in Austria-Hungary. Schnitzler's Lt. Gustl is not even that. He is semi-educated, aggressive, indeed even vulgar – the very opposite of a dandy. Very many of Zeyer's main characters, including his two chief Decadent heroes, Jan Maria Plojhar and Rojko, are born sufferers. Felix, the main character in *Sterben* approaches that condition. For instance, he says to his doctor friend, 'I am not the sort of person miracles happen to.'[242] And in Karásek's *Scarabaeus* the homosexual Oreste, who is called an artist in life, looks like a dandy, but is not a dandy; he closely resembles one of

Zeyer's born sufferers. In fact, however, the born sufferer and the dandy are not so far removed from each other. The *carpe diem* life of the dandy is the life of a man who knows he is life's victim, and therefore puts on a show of controlling it. The dandy is an outsider in the Colin Wilson sense, for he is a knower. Williams interprets Baudelaire's dandyism, the dandyism which created central European dandyisms, as deriving from the poet's hypochondria, which was at the time regarded as the male equivalent of hysteria; dandyism was a manifestation of neurosis.[243] Whether it was a manifestation of or a reaction to the *maladie du siècle*, it certainly belongs to the attempts of the central European Decadents to express their rejection of their own middle-class society in a new, European way.

XI. FIN-DE-SIÈCLE ATTITUDES TO WOMAN

In *fin-de-siècle* Austria-Hungary Baudelairean antifeminism cohabited with an expanding feminist movement. The antifeminism was mostly a pose, part of the style of the times, but on the other hand men were put a little off balance by the phenomenon of the New Woman. Modern critics and historians have perhaps overemphasised the suddenness of feminism and the extent to which it had changed intellectuals' attitudes to woman. Earlier in the century George Sand and George Eliot had given themselves male names but so did the Irish Decadent George Egerton and the Czech Eduard Klas. Although middle-class women were in Austria-Hungary being allowed to take university degrees (first female Ph.D. in Bohemia, 1901) and so forth at the turn of the century, women's position there was similar to that in the rest of Europe. Middle-class women were essentially tied to sweet domesticity. They had no chance of attaining senior public positions and generally their clothing reflected their expected social function. It was cumbersome, though in a somewhat distorted fashion it emphasised female secondary sexual characteristics. The middle-class woman was there to look after her man and produce children and ensure their upbringing. Working-class women were employed. In Austria in 1890, 45% of employees were females, but of approximately six million middle-class women only 61,382 were gainfully employed.[244] Before the *Fin de siècle* really got underway middle-class women were in a social position which positively demanded the Decadent ambivalent attitude to them: they both were on a pedestal and excluded from serious participation in public life. It was as if man had put woman on a pedestal psychologically to compensate for the dreary embroidering in drawing rooms which society had allotted to her. But it was also as if the barren, wan devourers of Decadent dreams compensated for that awful woman of Victorian domesticity. However one looks at the situation the 'woman crisis' of turn of the century was, indeed, also, or primarily, a 'crisis of maleness'.[245] In philosophy there dominated the sense that sexual intercourse was demeaning for the man and anyway a rather ridiculous and obscene activity, and for both Schopenhauer and von Hartmann love was a delusion or trick, as for Nietzsche it was a series of little ruses. Kierkegaard saw women as reproduction-machines, Schopenhauer as man-catchers and Nietzsche as creatures whose only true function in life was to fight man's desire for them. Such views culminated in the *Fin de siècle* with the view that woman was primarily man's enemy. Thus Procházka, writing of the Polish-German sculptor Frančiszek Flaum, states, ironically but also with his whole heart: 'It was in the Jewish Eden that the enmity of man and woman was established, that the bitter, corrosive battle of the sexes began.'[246]

Through being banished from Eden man gained command over Nature, except the snake, and the snake was also woman. Woman was man's link with Nature or was, indeed, part of Nature. As Pierrot has pointed out clearly, for Decadent man, woman is particularly dangerous because she lures him to sexual intercourse where he attains 'that very state of nature it is the aim of all civilisation and culture to abolish'.[247] And one has to consider that also in the light of Decadent catastrophism. Unspiritual, Nature-bound woman could potentially destroy civilisation, while at the same time giving birth to barbarians. Destructive womanhood contains the germs of the destruction *fin-de-siècle* man expected, dreaded and delighted in. On the other hand, she contained the naturalness he abhorred. Woman threatened all the ideals of dandyism or any other aristocratism. In all her vulgarity, however, woman was still dangerous. Péladan declares: 'Passive, absolute, unjust, woman admires greatness only in the hope of having it sacrificed to her. She likes chaste men so that she can corrupt them, strong men so that she can enslave them, independent men to debase them.'[248]

The origin of the Decadent *femme fatale* is more complex than Praz would have, though Praz's running contention that the *femme fatale* appears to constitute the inversion of the fatal man of Romanticism is incontrovertible. In Romanticism woman was being put on a pedestal. In the Decadence she was generally being transfigured on that pedestal or torn down from it. The ubiquity of the *femme fatale* in the period certainly partly derives from man's sexual guilt. The Decadents' misogyny is mysophobic. Hauser, having spoken of the Decadents as essentially conscience-stricken, states that 'nowhere is this conscience more clearly expressed than in their approach to love'.[249] Sexuality was delightful but sullying, and woman comprised the desire to sully man, that is spoil his classical bourgeois beauty or offend against his aspirations to other beauty. The opisthotonus position Dijkstra observantly registers (but falsely interprets) in so many paintings of the period, a position where the woman's back is arched so far back as almost to make a bridge, does not constitute simply man's perception of woman as a creature only of orgasm; it expresses man's guilt that he is a creature only of orgasm, and his desire to make her such, and his fear that she may be such.

Part of the mythology of the times was that women were not as sexually perceptive as men, not as easily aroused (hence perhaps the interest in the *femme enfant*, e.g. Štursa's statute, *Puberty*). In *Differences in the Nervous Organisation of Man and Woman* (1891) Campbell writes, 'the sexual instinct in the civilised woman is, I believe, tending to atrophy.'[250] That notion meant that men felt that women were not as dependent on them as they imagined they were on women. Samain writes in his *Cahiers intimes*: 'Hardly 10% of women are truly sensual . . . The absence of sensuality in woman gives her an immense power to dominate man. . . . Flirting, which constitutes the foundation of female behaviour, results quite naturally from her unsensuality.'[251] This conception of women also meant that men had to demonstrate some greatness other than sexual attractiveness (all that was conventionally demanded of young middle-class women), in other words, that he had to comport with bourgeois standards of male propriety: man was to be dignified and publicly successful or worthy. The *femme fatale* is not a figure of Decadent male fantasy, but (i) an interpretation of his own sexual and philosophical insecurity; (ii) an expression of moral and aesthetic frustration and (iii) a product of a real intersexual situation in the middle classes (not the upper classes).

Ridge comes to a similar, but narrower, conclusion. For him the *femme fatale* is '*modern woman*', the replacement of '*natural woman*'; modern woman 'incarnates destruction rather than creation. She has lost her capacity to love, and with it her role as wife and mother. She is now a mistress, beautiful but profoundly unnatural.'[252] Pierrot links the *femme fatale*, 'woman as an idol, at once mysterious, inaccessible, and cruel', a woman 'whose cold and lascivious beauty lures men to their doom', with Schopenhauerian antifeminism.[253] Again one of the earliest conceptions of the *femme fatale* as 'modern woman' is in Meredith (Baudelaire is speaking of essential woman, not so Meredith):

> Her eyes were guilty gates, that let him in
> By shutting all too zealous for their sin:
> Each sucked a secret, and each wore a mask.
> But, oh, the bitter taste her beauty had!
> He sickened as at breath of poison-flowers:
> A languid humour stole among the hours
> And if their smiles encountered, he went mad.

and:

> She had no blush, but slanted down her eye.
> Shamed nature, then, confesses love can die:
> And most she punishes the tender fool
> Who will believe what honours her the most![254]

Classic *femmes fatales* are the Princesse d'Este in Péladan's *Le Vice suprême* or Isotta in Marten's *Cortigiana* (1911); the latter gives herself to all who long for her only when she realises she has the plague. The Princesse d'Este, having been raped by her first man like Isotta, decides to punish all manhood, though differently from Isotta, by total frigidity and by deliberately stimulating men's desire for her. The ideal *femme fatale* looks like a Gustave Moreau picture or the glisteningly artificial Harlot of Babylon (Queen of Lasciviousness) in Karásek's *Lásky absurdné* (Absurd loves, 1904).

Less classic (except under Moreau's brush), but equally Decadent is Salome. Mallarmé's 'Hérodiade' is based on Moreau's picture. His Salome's link with the moon appears to indicate Mallarmé's occult interests. In Flaubert's 'Hérodias' there is nothing cruel or perverted about Salome. She is simply the instrument of her mother's revenge. Wilde's Salome constitutes, however, a properly Decadent force of evil, although as a force of evil she is as artificial as John the Baptist is as a force of good. Wilde's Salome also embodies the two favourite types of the period: the *femme enfant* and the *femme fatale*.[255] She is beyond good and evil; she has one purpose, the fulfilment of her own erotic desire. She also has that beauty which the aesthetes considered of a higher kind; she combines extreme, almost boyish, slenderness with magic lunar beauty. Klimt's and Otto Friedrich's Salome is Moreau's and Wilde's. Salome gains tragic dimensions in Karásek's story (in *Posvátné ohně*, Sacred fires, 1911), where the ageing Salome loves an androgynous young huntsman. When her love is spurned she orders her head be cut off and has it sent on a silver charger to the huntsman – who is horrified.

The *femme fatale* side of Salome is that of the vampire. Though Salome is no calculating sap-sucker like the true vampire woman of the Decadence. The source is again Baudelaire (vampires tended to be male before him). In 'Les Metamorphoses du vampire' he depicts himself languidly turning to kiss a woman after she has sucked all the marrow from his bones. When he does turn, however, she has become a sticky-flanked, pus-filled vessel. That manifests the moral background to the Decadent conception of woman as vampire. Man is an illicit victim; man willingly partakes in the degeneracy of lovemaking with a monster called woman. Modern man is, then, weak. In Ridge's interpretation the sap-sucking *femme fatale* is an arachnid and man's love-making with her 'is a passionate death struggle in which the active female . . . destroys the passive male'.[256] For Pater the *Mona Lisa* is vampire woman, the *femme fatale* who also has superior knowledge to man's, which knowledge partly consists in the awareness of her own physical and psychological supremacy: 'Like the vampire she had been dead many times and learned the secrets of the grave.'[257] In Pater's version there is mental aristocratism in the vampire. That we discover in Hlaváček's poem 'The Vampire' also, though here the vampire is male, and the women who appear in the poem are feeble, sex-obsessed maidens longing to become victims of the aristocrat male.

Another female type of *fin-de-siècle* literature is the prostitute. And the Decadents' attitude to the prostitute contains their normal ambivalence: they may coldly depict her as the embodiment of female genitalia-centredness or they may express compassion with her (as an outcast like them, or because the Decadents were vaguely socially *engagés*). Again, the prostitute is an active female (like the vampire), and her client is more or less passive. That relationship is emphasised in, say, the Austrian Franz von Bayros's picture of a naked woman with greyhound and riding whip. The prostitute theme also derived from the role prostitutes played in the lives of postpubertal Austro-Hungarian middle-class (and in this case also sometimes upper-class) boys. The visit to the local brothel is a cliché of novels of growing up in the first decade or so of the twentieth century. In Musil's first novel the boarding schoolboys visit only an aged prostitute who is now demoted from the big city to a country pub. She is Czech (and peasant and small-town Czechs believed at the time that Czech girls were the most sought-after whores in the world). Törless's initiations with this ageing prostitute are painful for him, not a product of postpubertal curiosity: 'it seemed to him that Božena was a creature of immense baseness and the feelings he had to endure during his encounters with her were for him a cruel rite of self-sacrifice.'[258] So in Musil there is nothing of the Decadent compassion with prostitutes which constitutes part of their *épater le bourgeois* attitude, of the Decadent adoption of the *demi-monde* as allies against the bourgeoisie. The pre-Decadent Hungarian Gyula Reviczky, whose love poems have nothing 'sensual or erotic'[259] about them, found solidarity with prostitutes, because he was himself a social outcast. Trakl's compassion with them comports with his general compassion with all the poor and wretched of modern big city life. He writes of 'A whore who gives birth to a little dead child in icy showers: the walls of the tenement blocks there contrast with the silver mark of the spirit of evil and the horrific laughing of gold.'[260] The poverty-stricken prostitute who gives all the earnings she can make from drunkards to her indifferent soldier beloved in Zeyer's *Dům 'U tonoucí hvězdy'* is also primarily a victim of decayed urban society. The same is true of Kles's prostitute in 'Eros' (1904), though here decay has prog'ressed, for her livelihood derives from the dissolution of morality and of love in modern city life: 'Mostly sick, perverted men visited her and she liked to earn her money whatever was demanded of her; otherwise business suffered. It was also her ambition to acquire a deeper understanding of these wretched men who came running to her from their sweethearts or young, healthy, chaste wives.'[261] When Gellner identifies with Viennese whores, however, his anti-bourgeois solidarity with the *demi-monde* is amalgamated with a cynical enjoyment of the very decay of it all.

Salomes tended to be black-haired; ordinary bourgeois and upper-class sex-dominated women were blondes (cf. Samain, Schaukal), but the purest Decadent type was the titian or copper-haired woman. She is more recognisable in art than in literature. (Possibly Meyrink's shocking-red-haired prostitute Rosina is a parody of the Decadent copper-head.) The *fin-de-siècle* predilection for this colour of hair has three roots: its unusualness (outside the edges of Europe, Celtic countries, parts of Italy, Turkey); its former literary links with evil and, sometimes, Jewishness; its use by the pre-Raphaelites, particularly the colour of the hair of Rossetti's *Beata Beatrix* (though there is very slightly more red in that hair than will be in the typical Decadent copper colour, as there is in, say, his *La Ghirlandeta*). Beatrice (the saint, not Dante's Beatrice) is the archetypal virgin whore, i.e. she embodies a Decadent paradoxical attitude to woman. The fourth reason for the Decadent's liking for the colour probably comes later. It is an intermediate colour; it comes between the Salome black and the sexy blonde, and as we shall see shortly, *fin-de-siècle* man preferred intermediate states. This copper colour suggests the possibilities of both spiritual serenity and voracious sensuality – or an ideal blend of both. When combined with the slender, almost thin, bodies of some of its possessors the hair suggests otherworldliness, even asceticism. It is a secret and secretive colour. The colour is unnatural, but natural, might belong to a spirit or a *femme fatale*, just as it might belong to a mother or hearthrug woman. It clearly also connoted for *fin-de-siècle* man a certain unapproachability and ideal. The colour also appears to have had occult qualities. If one looks at Odilon Redon's *Astral Head* one notices that the emerging head is capped in scarlet, but what it emanates from is our copper-coloured hair. So too the halo of Redon's *Silent Christ* is that hair colour, but one must be careful not to lay too much store by that, since copper or old gold are the normal halo colours. Nevertheless the green impingements in the halo of Redon's *Christ* certainly suggest a mysticality of colour. Redon was deeply immersed in *fin-de-siècle* esoteric interests. Pinkness and the copper colour merge in his *The Birth of Venus*. It is, then, no coincidence that all seven (*sic*) women in Khnopff's *Memories* have copper-coloured hair – and pre-Raphaelite faces. Only one of the women in Maximilian Lenz's *The 'Sirk-Ecke' on the Ringstrasse* has our colour, but it is noticeable that she is the only woman with a personality in the picture and that she is secretive, and combines demureness with imperiousness. We notice that our copper colour completely dominates Egon Schiele's *Nude Girl* (the one inscribed 'Original-Skizze für das Panneaux in der Jagdausssstellung'). Klimt makes great use of the colour, and yet it remains special for him. In *The Hostile Forces* the most striking of the seven women, some of whom are hideous, is copper-haired and furthermore her hair could at any moment be transformed into a peacock's tail. One notes that this woman is sylphine as we expect copperheads to be, as the copperhead is in his *The Kiss*. Klimt sometimes appears to mock his own understanding of the colour, as in the moon-ringed, flabby-thighed *Danae*. The colour is parodied in *Red Fish*, where also the dominant feature of the woman is her buttocks, but then in the top-right hand corner the parody is rescued by the genuine copperhead with her expression of spiritual or sensual ecstasy. One cannot tell; so again we are back to that Decadent ideal of ambiguity. The Hungarian Symbolist József Rippl-Ronai's tapestry *Girl with Roses* has the hair, but her face lacks mystery and her posture threatens the opisthotonus. It is probably not coincidence that the Swiss Ferdinand Hodler uses a lanky copperhead for his *Dream* and that Munch's *Vampire*'s hair is either copper-coloured or is becoming copper-coloured as a result of her exertions at the rather decent-looking fellow's throat. The woman of Jan Preisler's *Spring* has the right hair and body, but her features are gross and the natural setting and, indeed, *motif* are unDecadent.

For all his misogyny *fin-de-siècle* man often did create women of a fragile, ethereal type, women who were more or less the equals of their creators, threatened neither to devour nor to fall as sacrificial victims – though there seems always to have to be a victim in *fin-de-siècle* art. The woman from the land of darkness in Przybyszewski's 'Sonnenopfer' (Sun sacrifice, 1897) is one of those fragile women – and she becomes a sacrifice not because of the king who loves her but because of the mob. Notably she has copper hair; she is 'as pale as our moonlit nights, with hair as if the sun had dripped smolten onto it and with a voice which seems to come from far away, as if with the wind were wafting a distant song over the sea at dusk.'[262] This frail woman has her double in Czech literature, Isema in Zeyer's 'Král Menkera' (King M. in *Báje Šošany*, Fables of Shoshana [Hebrew, white lily], 1880). The slender or thin woman who is beautiful and has power over men may end as victim as in these two stories or in Munch's *The Scream* (here beauty is presumed). But she may always suggest death, too, like Štursa's *Melancholy Girl* or Klimt's *Water Snakes*.

Woman can be victim in *fin-de-siècle* literature though rarely the victim Dijkstra frequently suggests: the fantasy victim of rape conjured up by male chauvinists. Woman may be envied by men, because she seems to be able to destroy and because she will survive the coming end of civilisation. She will, presumably, then indeed be raped by the white barbarians and then produce the new, fresh culture – Europe's rape by America or by the Slav East. Both those ideas were alive in the *Fin de siècle*. But in art generally what was also visible was a tendency to sadism towards women. In Hungarian literature we think primarily of Ady waking up in the night and tearing the flesh of his beloved. In Czech literature we find plenty of sadomasochistic frenzy in Karásek and Marten, and, indeed, Karel Sezima. Again the roots are probably to be found primarily in Baudelaire and Barbey d'Aurevilly, but one has to bear in mind the heightened awareness of sexual perversion among the middle classes since the publication of Krafft-Ebing.

In the crisis of maleness which was the *Fin de siècle* men feared the modern self-possessed, self-sufficient woman. They could turn her into a *femme fatale*, since that sort of woman was unnatural, or into a *femme enfant*, for that was not quite a woman (though she threatened womanhood). They could follow Nietzsche: 'If a woman has a tendency to learnedness, there is usually something wrong with her sexuality. Infertility predisposes to a certain maleness in taste; the man is, if you will permit me to say so, the "unfruitful animal".'[263] On the other hand they could follow the feminist cause. The feminist cause was a Modernist, not a Decadent trend, and it was supported by Modernists: Shaw, Carpenter, Ellis, Masaryk, Bahr, perhaps Machar, people who contributed little to the development of culture, but a great deal to the development of civilisation. Shaw may not have been dull, but most male feminists, because the women's movement was a moral cause, were rather dull. Still, it is a tenable notion that glitziness, an age of middle-class affluence and of hedonism, constitutes a necessary background for the success of what would be generally called serious social progress (not simply votes for women . . . eventually, but also universal manhood suffrage, the eight-hour working day, freedom of education for women, and so forth). Whether there actually is such a thing as social progress is another matter. It was a notion believed in at the time by nearly all except the most thorough-going Decadent pessimist. It is only since the 1940s that it has become more generally accepted by liberal-thinking Europeans that there is no such thing as social progress and that man is absolutely imperfectible.

The main Viennese female reaction to Decadent antifeminism was Rosa Mayreder's *Zur Kritik der Weiblichkeit* (Towards a critique of femaleness, 1905). What was clearly most felt in Austria-Hungary in the 1900s was that all this *maladie du siècle* could perhaps be cured by woman. The insecurity of living outside the standard ethical norms of good and evil might be disposed of by giving woman an equivalent social status to man. An anonymous writer in the Woman's Movement column of Masaryk's journal, *Naše doba*, describes the ideal emancipated woman as far as she could exist in Austria-Hungary in 1911. Before that he had described the generality of women, two types, (i) the woman who becomes too involved in public affairs, and (ii) the flirtatious dresser who wants to impress; even in public affairs she wants to impress with her dress; she is the equivalent of the notary's wife who is determined to have a better Sunday menu than the judge's wife. A third type, the existing ideal, comes very close to the artistic ideal we have just noticed in the fragile woman and, to a degree, in the copper-haired woman:

> There is another type of woman . . . Truly intelligent and intellectually independent women who have their ideal in their soul and who try to realise themselves in their everyday environment. These women turn away from the life which does not respond to them; they turn to themselves or they move in a small circle of friends in which they can apply and enjoy the beauty of their souls, in which they can protect their spiritual life from profanation. They avoid the public eye; they think independently. . . . These are the women who signal progress, change, a new direction in our life. These women are the quiet pathfinders of progress. It stands to reason that they protect their innermost self, for that is the most precious thing one can find in life.[264]

The writer goes on to say that the women's movement needs precisely such women to engage in public affairs, to gain true equality for women. The writer is unaware that this privateness is itself an expression of equality and of the intellectual quiet rebellion which characterises that elitism which was the Decadence.

XII. LOVE AND THE EROTIC

That same independent, private woman was considered to be the salvation for individuals and even European civilisation long before the *Naše doba* correspondent was writing and long before Bahr adopted feminism for its moral potential. According to the teachings of the unfrocked priest, Joseph-Antoine Boullan, who began preaching some form of Satanism in the 1850s and who also had close contacts with Vintrasian affairs, sexual intercourse was evil because material, but if performed with 'mystical', spiritual, intentions, it could cease to be evil. The occultist, Stanislas de Guaïta, wrote in connection with Boullan and others' ideas: 'It is through a culpable act of love that the Fall of Man in Eden took place; the Redemption of Man could and ought to be accomplished by acts of love.'[265] Jules Bois, another French Satanist, who certainly had some influence in the Bohemian Lands, distinguishes between the theatre of Melpomene and the Theatre of Hermes and Dionysos. The Theatre of Melpomene is that of the masses; passions and vulgarity win there. Women are bacchantes and 'their kisses are redolent of murder and luxury'.[266] This theatre deals with the base instincts of the masses. The bacchante is the typical vulgar priestess of modern times. The Theatre of Melpomene is concerned with the base half of our soul, where the Theatre of Hermes is noble, although for most men it is never felt except as a series of vague memories of the ideal. Here Psyche 'falls into the convulsive arms of Pluto-Sathan to save him by her caress which is redemption through love'.[267] Woman does not exactly save man; she gives him the opportunity for redemption. Bois links that with the law of the Tarot, for the law of love and salvation releases forces immobilised by the sword of the Tarot. Mary Magdalene had found the only way of immediate salvation. In Bois Christian love fuses with the act of love when he declares: 'what can be stated is that our salvation will come through Woman and Intuition. The Paraclete symbolically assumes feminine form.'[268] Bois conceives the notion of violent purity and lips which do not fear, for they have become spiritualised by the spiritual kiss that constitutes this act of love which consists mainly in its metaphysical intention. Bois sees his spiritualised sexual intercourse as a revolt against 'contemporary Anarchism with its brutish faith and its dilettante nihilism . . . the *taedium vitae* . . . which has invented the foolish epithet "fin de siècle".'[269] The living in Przybyszewski's 'Sonnenopfer' will also learn arcane secrets, the messages of the nerves and so forth, through woman. And in Komjáthy's *Eloa* love for woman redeems man. The idea, whether in its Satanist form or in Przybyszewski or Komjáthy's more or less neo-Romantic form ultimately echoes the Baroque notion of attaining heavenly love through earthly and possibly also mediaeval mystic eroticism. This conception of love, evident in the Czech Parnassian, Vrchlický, is important for the 1890s as an antidote to the despair of *fin-de-siècle* man. It might also provide a spurious philosophy for the growing movement for free love, produce a mystical justification for promiscuity among the middle classes.

As in the mediaeval conceptions of divine copulation or in the Baroque conception of Death as a lover, so in Decadent thought sex is associated with death, audible orgasm with the death-rattle. Eros and Thanatos are further linked by *fin-de-siècle* man, because of his existential anxiety, with the fact that copulation produces new victims of Death; thus copulation can be seen as a sarcastic comment on the facts that the two copulators are themselves dying, since they are living, and that they are so heedless as to wish to spread such oxymoronic existence. The ironic, melancholic Meredith speaks of his two main characters' 'marriage-tomb' in the first stanza of *Modern Love*, though that connection is a comment on the unspirituality of woman and on the pain of this particular marriage or love, rather than on the equivalence of love and death. Meredith is here essentially employing another old topos, *amor : dolor*. And the end of Schnitzler's *Frau Beate und ihr Sohn* (Beate and her son, 1913) comprises a mother at last achieving copulation with her son, Hugo; they are in a boat and her orgasm is accompanied by her dragging her son down into the water to drown with her. This is a fine piece of Decadent writing which appears to be an exposition of Freudian notions:

Now he let her keep hold of his hands and that soothed her. She drew him closer, pressed herself against him. A painful longing rose from the depths of her soul and darkly flooded over into his. . . . In a seductive premonition of eternal night they surrendered their dissolving lips to each other. . . . Beate felt as if she were kissing a man she had never known and who was her partner for the first time.

When she returned to full consciousness she still had enough spiritual strength not to awake entirely. Holding both Hugo's hands she threw herself over the rim of the boat. As it began to tip, Hugo's eyes opened to a sight in which a trembling of fear wanted to bind him to the common lot of man for the last time. Beate drew her death-devoted lover, her son, to her breast. Understanding, forgiving, redeemed, he shut his eyes; . . . before the tepid waves pressed between her eye-lids, her dying gaze drank the last shadows of the extinguished world.[270]

We notice that, there too, the notion of woman as redeemer appears briefly. Trakl's poem, 'Nahe des Todes' (The closeness of death) ends: 'Oh, the closeness of death. Let us pray. / In this night on tepid pillows / Yellowed by incense, dissolve the languid limbs of the lovers.'[271] Both Schnitzler's and Trakl's scenes incidentally also suggest a whole world (Austria) dissolving with the lovers. (Trakl's poem mainly concerns memories of childhood.)

The *fin-de-siècle* notion of ecstasy frequently combined love with death. Rudolf Kassner, in an essay on Swinburne (1898–99), speaking of *Salome* and the modern drama altogether writes that: 'To be music means to be in possession of one's fate, always means: the final act, maturity, sexual rapture and death all in one.' Having quoted that Hajek goes on to say that Kassner has thus enumerated the main elements in the method the *Fin de siècle* employed to overcome Time in drama. They lyricised time ('music'); they used one-acters ('final act') and erased development ('maturity').[272] The *Fin de siècle* was as time-conscious a period as the Baroque; that no doubt largely emerged from the sense of living in a period of transition. Ady combines erotic ecstasy and death with artistic inspiration,[273] which might be said to sentimentalise the theme philosophically, although one might spot Expressionist strength in it. In an incantation Trakl, purer than Ady can be because he is uncontaminated with the need for national criticism, addresses ecstasy thus: 'Oh, the orgasm of death. Oh, you children of a dark line. The evil flowers of blood shimmer silver on that brow, and the cold moon [shimmers] into its glazed eyes.'[274] The unsophisticated Hungarian novelist, Krúdy, who follows Freud and Robert Louis Stevenson, also frequently makes the connection between the ecstasy of love and the ecstasy of death. Most of the stories of Karásek's *Posvátné ohně* describe women or men attaining sexual ecstasy in death after a long period of frustration. The attention the *Fin de siècle* pays to ecstasy (its hedonism altogether) may well derive from cultural or social frustration, particularly in Austria-Hungary.

In Wilde's *Salome* orgasm appears to be achieved in the kiss (the heroine's kissing of Jokanaan's head), in which love and death are united in a brand of necrophilia. Otto Friedrich's Salome is approaching orgasm as she holds the severed head to kiss it. Beardsley's Salome will derive no pleasure from her kiss, except possibly that of the knowledge of having perpetrated something a trifle perverse. Lucien Lévy-Dhurmer's Salome has a kiss which combines the orgasmic with the perverse. Here the severed head is more orgasmic than Salome. The emblematic importance of the kiss in general in the period (represented most clearly by Rodin's and Klimt's versions of *The Kiss*), apart from its being a representation of sexual ecstasy as rebellion against bourgeois coyness, is that the kiss expresses (i) sexual equality and union, and (ii) beginning and end in one – the 'modern' pessimist cliché that the end of the love is contained in the first kiss (in other words the opposite of the pre-*fin-de-siècle* meaning, where the kiss was an oath). In French and Prague *fin-de-siècle* occultist circles there was another kiss, allegedly evoking spiritual ecstasy, where one kissed one's neighbour's anus at least in one's mind, for kissing the hindpart of evil or the material one was kissing the forepart (lips) of the divine. (That is also linked with the Templars' anus kiss; the would-be initiate was observed as he performed the act; the observers then decided whether he was capable of initiation.)

However strong free-love and anarchist and Vitalist movements may have been in the *Fin de siècle*, sexual activity remained fundamentally immoral in the Austro-Hungarian public consciousness unless it was designed to result in procreation. At the same time sexual desire was worshipped and publicly displayed in the culture of the period. Hlaváček depicts the apparent vicious circle of this twofold attitude in his drawing, *The Outlaw*. Here we have a man's head wrinkled, perhaps with age, perhaps with pain. The head itself evokes that of John the Baptist of Christ, for a circle surrounds it which resembles a halo. The man appears to be howling with mental or physical pain. His mouth is a vulva and his tongue a distended clitoris. The halo nearly touches the clitoris, passes through the lower reach of the vulva. Sexuality is outlawed and sanctified. Sexual excitement is pain. The work also depicts the period's celebration of erethism. The drawing repels aesthetically; its significance lies in its containing the pain and the irony (in this case perhaps sarcasm) the period evoked in the sensitive human being. In *Under the Hill* Beardsley is reacting to the same twofold attitude, but he reacts with parody – and pain is thus obliterated. As Dowling writes, 'the mock-heroic reductionism of Beardsley's tale is intent, not simply on reducing all behaviour to sexual behaviour – the premise of pornography – but on revealing all behaviour, including sex, as play.'[275] Freud was then, perhaps, essentially a pornographer.

Seeba claims, writing on our period, that the 'opposition of the aesthetic to the moral belongs to those dichotomous constructions in which the world resembles a Janus head, like the opposition of art to life or contemplation to action'.[276] He points out that Wilde had to suffer for the rest of the world's determination that the aesthetical was opposed to the moral. In fact art had and has nothing to do with morality, as Decadents like Karásek or Procházka constantly proclaimed. Though contemporaries like Kraus or Masaryk, let alone Nordau, disagreed.

The Decadent tried to conceal any moral attitude to the erotic or to fling apparently infantile indecencies into the national bourgeois reader's face. In fact within their aesthetics the Decadents assumed strong moral views – though one could not call them moralisers. Their views were fairly simple, too. Women were either Mary Magdalenes or Virgin Marys, or as Zeyer puts it in *Dobrodružství Madrány* (The adventures of Madrana, 1882), 'there are only two types of women, Delilahs and St Theresas.'[277] The *fin-de-siècle* artist was more concerned with the Delilahs or Magdalenes or Judiths or Salomes than with the Virgin Marys, and even when he delighted in the sheer lubricity or the luring beauty of such women, still they are usually felt primarily as a threat to man's well-being or as a force of evil. Those are moral standpoints.

XIII. THE SERPENT

An aspect of the period's moral attitudes is evident in their re-evaluation of the Old Testament and Talmudic link between woman and the serpent (Eve and Lilith). The image of the serpent or snake fascinated artists of the time either because of their knowledge of the occult or because of their concern with the unconscious or simply because they considered the snake a suitable instrument or vehicle for shocking their audiences. Woman as serpent is both *femme fatale* and the New Woman, but also both a force for good and a force for evil. Furthermore the serpent has a connection with the occult functions lent women by such as Bois.

The serpent may represent *fin-de-siècle* man's despair at the material and materialist world. It may express the horror of earth-boundness and unspirituality; its earthy energies are negative for the artist. The serpent also embodies the ambivalence with which the *fin-de-siècle* man regarded woman and sex. It embodies the activity and the passivity of woman, the unpredictability and the strength of an apparently weak creature.

The snake is creative: it is phallic, represents creativity, long life, pertinacity. The snake is also the Earth; it is fertility, and both nourisher and nourished. In European symbolic art the *Orbis Terrae* may be shown as a woman holding cornucopias and snakes in her hands; the Great Mother of the Christian and the Cabalistic tradition includes an enormous pink and green serpent and it makes no difference in iconography whether the Earth Goddess is depicted with snakes or serpents at her dugs.[278] The Oriental *kundalini* concept which found great favour in the Anglo-Saxon-Indian type of esoteric thought which spread to Austria in the 1880s had a less dynamic Occidental version which may have still been alive for the intellectuals of our period. It was believed that snakes were born out of the spinal marrow of the human corpse. Antigonus of Carystus states that little serpents are born of the decayed marrow of any men who have breathed in the smell of a dead snake before they die.[279] Anyway *fin-de-siècle* man still knew his Ovid and Pliny. *Kundalini* is coiled three and a half times at the root of the human backbone and when it is roused it 'resembles a vertical blue jet, emitting red flames from one side and yellow from the other. . . . (The red flames are usually to the left side in men on the right in women.) . . . the kundalini fire at last ignites sahasrara and . . . transforms that final chakra into the marriage bed of Shiva and Shakti, their divine ecstasy symbolic of our blissful release . . . into absolute being.'[280] Trakl's 'Sonja' appears to be a depiction of Sonja having attained *moksha*, 'blissful release'. I quote only the first nine lines (with no attempt at achieving Trakl's hypnotic rhythm): 'Evening comes into old garden; / Sonja's life, blue stillness. / Excursions of wild birds; / Bare tree in autumn and stillness. // Sunflower soft-bent / Over Sonja's white life. / Sore, red, never-revealed is let alive in dark rooms // Where blue bells ring.'[281] Eliphas Lévi, whose work Trakl probably knew and who was certainly known to the Czech Decadents, Zeyer and Karásek, writes in *Le Livre de splendeurs* (posth. 1894) that the serpent 'sometimes represents fire, sometimes the vital fluid, the flowing force of terrestrial life'.[282] In most cultures snakes were sacred and could emblemise immortality.

When we look at Klimt's *Water-Snakes* we do not immediately think of woman's being linked with the creative or nourishing force of the serpent. And women as water-snakes, as women rolled into waves in the sea, as near-fish (not mermaids) and with an undulatory litheness which might as well be that of a snake as of a fish, is one of the commonest images in *fin-de-siècle* painting and graphic art. The first connotation then as now was probably with the Old Serpent, the Tempter in the Garden of Eden – although *fin-de-siècle* man was a little less coarsely automatic than 1980s man. Lévi also describes the Devil, whom he characterises, in the style which would become true *fin-de-siècle* style, as the fatal magnetism of evil, the destructive force: 'It is the serpent of a thousand colours and coils; he guides his forked tongue and flattened head everywhere. He drools venom on all that is pure, tears down all that is beautiful, draws to himself all shame and ugliness. . . . He is more horrible than horror, more fearsome than fear, deadlier than death.'[283] The great serpent was one of the monsters representing destruction in pre-Judaic times, and in the later Judaic era, in Isaiah, Leviathan is called a 'piercing' and a 'crooked' serpent. That this serpent was Satan was apparently not explicitly stated before 50 BC, in the apocryphal Book of Wisdom,[284] though in the Apocalypse he quite firmly is so (Rev. 12:9). The serpent is frequently overcome by the bird, the eagle (iconographically). Here the eagle is the Son of Man, Christ, Light, the force of good – and the serpent is the Devil, Darkness, the force of evil. But the bird is also man and the serpent woman; hence the European dragon (a hybrid of snake and bird) may be the material world altogether – or, indeed, 'knowledge'. At Troy an eagle carrying a snake in its talons appeared to the Greek warriors, and this configuration, according to Rowland, 'symbolised the victory of the patriarchal principle over the female one of Troy, whose Asiatic goddess, Aphrodite, had induced Helen to break the bonds of her marriage under the masculine order of the Greeks and to select her own mate, Paris.'[285] Franz von Lenbach's picture of *The Snake Queen* inverts with Decadent naughtiness the standard relationship between woman and serpent. Here a woman looking into the heavens with an expression on her face which combines the leer with orgasmic glazing, stands one hip projected and arms spread as if crucified. A snake is coiled round her arms and shoulders. Woman herself has become the Tree of Knowledge. The Old Serpent is more or less her subject. Primarily, then, there is more evil in woman than the Devil. In Franz von Stuck's more famous, misogynous *Sensuality* the massive boa constrictor coiled between the woman's thighs and round her body is in undulating sympathy with her sexuality. Woman and Serpent are here equals. So they are in Gabriel Ferrier's earlier *Salammbô*, but that picture expresses sheer rapture; it has nothing of the obscenity of von Stuck's picture. Khnopff's *Istar* has snake-like tentacles penetrating the orgasmic goddess's vagina and abdomen; the tentacles are also roots coming from a gnarled tree which resembles a skeletal male terrified by the utter sex-boundness of woman.[286] In *Modern Love* Meredith appears to be linking modern (i.e. faithless) woman with serpents, though he is not quite consistent. Thus he speaks of the tears she sheds as a result of her adultery and wish further to betray her husband as snakes: 'the strange low sobs that shook their common bed. / Were called into her with a sharp surprise, / And strangled mute, like little gaping snakes, / Dreadfully venomous to him.' So too of what the barber can do with her hair he writes, 'The gold-eyed serpent dwelling in rich hair, / Awakes beneath his magic whisks and twirls.' On the other hand, he is as capable of as much venom as his wife, 'By stealth / Our eyes dart scrutinising snakes.'[287] The snake, like woman, is conventionally linked with treachery, cunning, with having evil errands in the back of its/her mind, and with ingratitude and envy. According to Lévi's mistakenly ascribed rabbinical text woman had been infected with the serpent's natural 'jealously and anger'.[288] The story of the snake the husbandman took in when he found it half frozen, and which had then eaten the husbandman's children – or messed up his house, depending which version you read, typifies the snake as the ungrateful one.[289] That is important for *fin-de-siècle* man's attitude to the New Woman. In all the male aggression of their antifeminism, males felt condescendingly hurt that women were beginning to jump off their pedestals onto their bicycles. The serpent also traditionally represents prudence, and Decadent man, rebelling as he was against Victorian prudence, no doubt distorted that a little into fear and contempt for feminine practicality.

Possibly the most important of the negative attitudes to woman as snake alive in the *Fin de siècle* was the attribution of woman to the brood of Lilith – or Lamia. The two are distinct but are not. First, it was possible to consider Eve as the Blessed Virgin and Lilith as Magdalene, so the very concept Lilith comported well with their attraction to ambivalence and oxymoron. Lilith, the A.V. screech-owl of Isaiah 34:14, is, according to the Talmudic tradition, Adam's first wife, who then became the Serpent who tempted Eve to knowledge, or gave Eve knowledge. That is why the Old Serpent often has a female human being's face – not only in mediaeval illuminations, but also, say, in Kenyon Cox's *Lilith* in the 1890s. The Vulgate translated the Hebrew Lilith as Lamia, i.e. a child's-blood-sucking nocturnal snake-witch. Lilith herself was feared as a succubus.[290] Dijkstra, if we can ignore his schoolboyish journalese, sensibly makes the Lamia concept an essential part of *fin-de-siècle* man's perception of modern woman: 'the lamia of myth was thought to have been a bisexual, masculinised cradle-robbing creature, and therefore to the men of the turn of the century perfectly representative of the

New Woman who, in their eyes, was seeking to arrogate to herself male privileges . . . and was intent upon destroying the heavenly harmony of feminine subordination in the family.'[291] Lamia was that version of the vamp which was so unnatural that she denied herself motherhood. Lévi reproduces the same view from his Rabbi Simeon and adopts it as his:

> Woman does not possess within herself strength and justice, these she must receive from man.
> She aspires after [*sic*] them with untellable thirst, but cannot receive them until she is entirely submissive.
> When she rules she brings about only revolt and violence.
> It is in this way that woman became man's overseer by drawing him into sin.
> In the incontinence of her desires she became a mother and gave birth to Cain.[292]

Even in the position of seductress (in the Romantic period man had been the seducer) her role is directly linked not only with Lilith, but with parallel myths about snakes or the Old Serpent itself. Snakes' breath was held to be infectious, for example. The lips of an attractive woman were like the breath of a snake. The snake's breath or Lilith's (then Eve's) words led to disobedience which led to pleasure and the Fall. The Fall was pleasure. And pleasure was punished by exile (cf. Hlaváček's *The Outlaw*, from a different point of view). The Old Serpent, if he is Satan, is actually not categorisable by terms like good and evil. So pleasure contains pain and pain (exile) contains pleasure – according to the *fin-de-siècle* esoteric mind. Following Philo, Klingender reminds us that the serpent embodies the pleasure principle, and here Klingender coincidentally makes very clear to us the moralising side of the Decadent attitude to woman: 'The creation of Eve . . . heralds the ascendancy which pleasure will gain over the intellect in man's soul, and thus his inevitable fall, for "since nothing in creation lasts for ever . . ., it was unavoidable that the first man should also undergo some disaster". And the serpent is the obvious symbol of the pleasure principle, because he "crawls on his belly with his face downward", just as the head of a man of pleasure is "weighed down and dragged down" by his intemperance.'[293] The serpent of Psalm 58 (Vulgate 57), 'their poison is like the poison of a serpent: they are like the dead adder that stoppeth her ear', is the sinner and his/her venom is his/her passions (the Vulgate word is not 'poison', but *furor*); nevertheless within the same symbol system the serpent may devour Lust;[294] the serpent may seduce to passion and then itself punish passion. That punishment was luring and then refusing (frustration), infidelity – or syphilis.

An analogous ambiguity is contained in the figure of the Medusa or Gorgon, which was also popular in *fin-de-siècle* art. Her snake-writhing head was, as Rowland points out. 'the pudendum, at once an attraction and symbol of castration to those who dreaded her power.'[295] That ambiguity is stated morbidly by Pater, on Leonardo's Medusa: 'What may be called the fascination of corruption penetrates in every touch its exquisitely finished beauty.'[296] In fact the Medusa head can be both phallic and vaginal; the snakes represent the destroyed manhoods the *femme fatale* has achieved and her lips are her vulva and her eyes are the fatal, serpentine attraction. The Medusa combines the two least trustful creatures in life, woman and the serpent.

But the serpent was also reviver and healer, and both male and female, and the force of reproduction (earth, water, fire, house, creativity). The healer aspect is clearly more important to the occult-inclined members of the *fin-de-siècle* generation than to the run-of-the-mill Decadent. On the other hand it constitutes a significant counterbalance to the serpent-woman-evil connection, a counterbalance which runs parallel to the conception of woman as redeemer. One of the most influential non-French writers on the Austro-Hungarian *Fin de siècle* was Swinburne and in his passionately sensualist 'Dolores' we read:

> But the worm shall revive thee with kisses,
>   Thou shalt change and transmute as a god,
> As the rod to a serpent that hisses,
>
> As the serpent again to a rod.
> Thy life shall not cease though thou doff it;
>   Thou shalt live until evil be slain,
> And good shall die first, said thy prophet,
>   Our Lady of Pain.[297]

The worm is death and the serpent. The serpent coiled around the rod could be Aesculapius's (that is also the emblem of Hygeia and Hippocrates). Lévi points out that the 'sacred serpent of Aesculapius has the same symbolic form as the serpents of Tisiphone [one of the Erinyes]; Moses himself, who tells us how a serpent introduced sin and death into the world, had erected the image of a bronze serpent to cure those victims mortally wounded by snake-bite in the desert.'[298] Moses's serpent also became a symbol for the Crucified Christ and a cross with a serpent coiled round it became a symbol of resurrection and then more important, of spiritual renewal or healing. The Cross and Serpent is the spiritual parallel to the material Aesculapian staff. On a third plane is the caduceus, 'two copulating serpents between the scepter or spear of dominion . . ., the adjunct of the man or god who had power over life.'[299] The caduceus was borne notably by Hermes, and Lévi speaks of a talisman consisting in 'the Goat of Mendes placed between two vipers analogous to the serpents of the caduceus'.[300] That symbol is said to represent the astral current which attracts and repels two poles. Lévi links the serpents of the caduceus itself with the 'fatal forces,' the magnetic powers of the Earth, and his caduceus has something in common with *kundalini*:

the two serpents of Hermes, one blue and the other red, entwined around a silver sceptre with a golden head.

These forces are the perpetual movement of the clock of centuries; when one serpent contracts, the other loosens its hold.

These forces break those who do not know how to direct them. They are the two snakes at the cradle of Hercules.

The child takes one in each hand, the red in the right and the blue in the left.

Thus they die and their power passes into the arms of Hercules.[301]

The uroboros, the serpent with its tail in its mouth, the serpent as circle, was originally the symbol of eternity and immortality, but was used, for example, by Samuel Richardson to symbolise 'ceaseless or self-consuming desire'.[302] Lévi tells us, having explained the caduceus, that the uroboros is the belt of Isis representing the tension between the current of love and the current of wrath which provides all movement and life. The uroboros may also denote erotic self-sufficiency and, once more, one is drawn to identifying the uroboros with the halo, and certainly one may identify it with the Magna Mater and thus the apparently eternal life-cycle of the Earth/Nature. Except, possibly, the halo, then, all its meanings could embody *fin-de-siècle* man's fear of the *femme fatale* or the New Woman. Dijkstra considers that the uroboros became one of the most frequent symbols of woman in *fin-de-siècle* art.[303] He links the number of round looking glasses held by women in the period with a male attack on female self-sufficient narcissism. He also interprets round pools and baths with women standing in them as the uroboros. He is no doubt partly right, but he under-interprets because he is consistently out of tune with the mysticising element in much turn-of-the-century symbolism. Even in the uroboros shape the snake may remain phallic and may, thus, also represent woman's obsession with sexuality and even woman's fear of male sufficiency. Uroboros as the belt of Isis, however, threatens total stagnation or decay, for it also stands for eternal self-cunnilingus or self-fellatio. There is another form of uroboros which is a version of the Cross and Serpent, and that is the serpent of initiation and wisdom with its tail in its mouth which is coiled round the Cabalistic Tree of Life. When Musil's Törless thinks of his friend Beineberg, whose occultist or theosophical father is serving in India, he thinks of 'snakes which are adepts at magic, in deep places'.[304] In the second of Trakl's 'Die Verfluchten' (The cursed ones) poems, the plague, represented in standard central-European imagery as a woman, is linked with thoroughly occult snakes (if I understand the poem correctly; it may have been inspired more by cocain than period occultist symbolism); 'A nest of scarlet snakes indolently rears up in her agitated lap.' The 'agitated lap', could be translated 'excited' or 'disturbed' or 'roused vagina'.[305] So we could be dealing with straight sexual emblems, except that she has been in the presence only of a child, and this child, whose hands had at one point run through her hair, has died. Still she could be deriving bored sexual excitement from killing once more. An occult interpretation would, however, be more satisfying. The plague's dress is blue (like Sonja's stillness), and blue is the colour of wisdom and mercy, inner glory and the phallus (the phallus essentially in the sense of dominion or fertility, not in the Positivist Freudian sense). The red serpent (*draco rufus et magnus*) is the force of destruction (so here female sexuality as destruction), though the red serpent may also be a seraph. The snakes are also wisdom, knowledge (of death and of sexuality – which the child will never have) and her lap or vagina is the force or life which is also the force of death, the Magna Mater or great sea. So the poem is a life-cycle poem. Life or death embodied in the plague is without compassion, is even cruel. She is not moved by the child of life's tears. In the Czech Březina's poem 'Doupata hadů' (Dens of snakes, in *Stavitelé chrámu*. Builders of the temple, 1899) beds of flowers turn into dens or lairs of snakes: 'They reared up before my footsteps, hissing poisonous flames in the darkness, / Their monstrous heads blossomed on stems which were tossed by the storm of the depths; / they grew into my body [cf. the Khnopff picture of Istar], bound my will with their evil serpentine suggestiveness / And from their motionless eyes they shot livid light into my eyes.'[306] These are mainly sexual emblems, where human passions invade the spiritual calm represented by the garden. But the snakes are also knowledge. Their suggestiveness implies that they charm instead of being charmed (as in, say, our Psalm 58). They represent the forces of evil and the elements of material knowledge which constantly arise before us to obstruct our path to purity of spirit.

The serpent, then, expresses the essential, unstable ambivalence which characterises Decadent thinking. The uroboros devours itself to sustain itself. Like Saturn it brings into life as the giver of death: innovation and decay.

XIV. THE INTERMEDIATE STATE

That ambivalence, combined with the intensely felt perception of living in an age of transition, is represented by intermediate states which are expressed by both form and iconography.[307] The type of intermediate state that could be used was defined by the Decadent's catastrophism (for example, not all seasons are suitable settings), their cultivation of moods and moments, their anti-Positivist desire to communicate suggestions of material or abstract objects, not definite objects, and their intensive cultivation and analysis of the self. For, whatever William James and occultists and mysticisers might say, one's own self is less *knowable* than another's self, and so one's impression of another will be far more definite than one's impression of oneself. At the turn of the century the Austrians (Viennese) felt the intermediate state of a crumbling social system (immensely fast-growing bourgeoisie); the Hungarians (Budapestis) felt the intermediate state of growing into something but not quite being anything; the Czechs (Pragers) felt the intermediate state of looking like something, but not being anything (a capital city without a state to be capital of). It is no coincidence that when Baudelaire wanted to publish his collection of verse in 1848, he decided to call it *Les Limbes* (Limbo), a title which reflects just such a spiritual intermediate state as was afflicting the young artists of Austria-Hungary in the 1890s and 1900s.[308] Karásek depicts the pressure felt while living an intermediate existence: 'Nothing thorough. Not even thorough passion, thorough emotion, indeed not even thorough boredom. Everything semi-emotion, semi-passion, semi-boredom. . . . Nothing but foolishness, nothing but torment for the sake of unobtainable chimeras.'[309]

Synaesthesia expressed the intermediate state; sweet-scented music is neither music nor fragrance; the mauve taste of her soul is neither taste nor coloured nor concrete nor abstract. The essence of the symbol. Words meaning vague or indefinite are the clichés or the touchstones of *fin-de-siècle* art; they indicate an intermediate state of communication. It is false communication too, narcissism, whose vagueness only may communicate something. The classic *fin-de-siècle* definition of literature as semi-communication is Mallarmé's in his 1894 Oxford lecture: 'Avec véracité, qu'est-ce, les Lettres, que cette mentale poursuite, menée, en tant que le discours, afin de définir ou de faire, à l'égard de soi-même, preuve que le spectacle repond à une imaginative compréhension, il est vrai, dans l'espoir de s'y mirer.'[310] Hajek suggests that *fin-de-siècle* literature was concerned only with states of consciousness: 'That dream and reality, things seen, things read, things thought, are all equally valid and indistinguishable, confirms the thesis that it is only a matter of states of consciousness.'[311] Hence the vagueness, the blurred boundaries and uncertain footholds and points of view of this art. Hence also the rich soil for the germination of political extremism. A world of no answers beyond the self suddenly demands answers. That is the double insecurity of the intermediate state.

Meyrink's *Der Golem* typifies the intermediate state. The action is nearly all dream or vision and nearly all took place thirty-three years (*sic*) before it does take place. Everything, including words, becomes embodied and then disembodied. The reader also finds himself hanging in his comprehension between irony and mysticality. Everything that happens in the novel, all objects tend suddenly or slowly to fade or to disappear or to be extinguished. As Hajek says and as magicians aver: it is all a matter of states of consciousness. Meyrink put it as follows:

> When people rise from their beds they imagine they have shaken off sleep, and they do not know that they are falling prey to their senses, that they are becoming victims of a new, far deeper sleep than the sleep they have just fled. There is only one true waking state and that is the state you are now approaching. If you spoke to people about it, they would say you were sick, for they are incapable of understanding you. Therefore it is pointless and cruel to speak to them about it.
> You will flow forward like a river –

And are as if asleep.
Like a blade of grass which will soon fade –
Which will be hewn down in the evening and will wither.[312]

Parallel to that is the conception of living for or in impressions or of trusting only impressions. Total impressionability is a mental intermediate state which rejects Positivist analysis as evidently, if not as 'mystically', as Meyrink's river-dream state. The impression lies somewhere between knowing and non-knowing; it is a state of consciousness where there is no striving for analysis, or where the analysis takes place in the subconscious or unconscious. Impressionability approaches mental or intellectual passivity although the determination to believe only impressions is spiritually active. Again this notion reflects the *fin-de-siècle* doubting of communication. The organist in Hlaváček's *Mstivá kantilena* is an incarnation of the intermediate state, of the impression. He is red-headed (carrot red, not the titian of the Decadent ambivalent woman) – anger, villain; he is a brawler with hirsute brawler's hands. He is referred to vaguely as *kdosi*, someone (or other). He conceals tears behind his tousled, probably frightening, exterior. When his loutish hands touch the keys they play 'a very soft impromptu, an anxious impromptu'.[313] The organist poem incorporates that essential part of Decadent irony which comes close to the Romantic, for not only is there a tension in the action of the poem itself (the result, the impromptu, is unexpected, almost bathetic), but also in the man described. The ruffian organist is actually a dandy.

As far as Decadent themes are concerned, the central intermediate state is dying, the narrative of dying, of the intermediate state between being and non-being. It would be facile to suggest that was because these artists knew Austria-Hungary was dying, but they certainly did know the century was dying and that established social relationships were dying. Industry was also killing the countryside as cultural collectivism was threatening individualism. It is no exaggeration to say that nearly all Czech mainstream Decadent prose fiction consists in stories of dying. But, again, Schnitzler has a work about living in dying, *Die letzten Masken* (The last masks, 1901) where, as Stern Baroquely puts it, what 'silences Rademacher is the annihilating truth of his own imminent death. In the face of that total extinction, which is the only truth he knows, all is vanity and nonsense.'[314] The play itself has as part of its opening dialogue: 'FLORIAN: Heavens, I thought he had already died. NURSE: It will go on for a bit yet.'[315] And one has to think only of the titles of works I have already mentioned when treating other aspects of the period: Hofmannsthal's *Der Tod Tizians* and *Der Tor und der Tod*, Beer-Hofmann's *Der Tod Georgs* and, most evidently of all Schnitzler's *Sterben*. The dying man in this novel is not always Decadently resigned; he can be aggressive about his dying, for example: 'What he hated most mortally was walking there before him. A piece of what would still be here when *he* would no longer be here, something that would still be young and full of life, something that would laugh, when he would no longer be able to laugh or cry.' Although that apparently, and only apparently, contradicts what the narrator has two pages later: 'Truly, death held no more horror for him. He was quite indifferent to everything.'[316] In Czech prose[317] the concentration is, generally speaking, on heightened sensitivity rather than morbidity, though that morbidity which Pater claimed characterised the age is not lacking. In a work on dying by Auředníček, 'Fantom slávy' (The phantom of fame), the dying artist Josef 'went on and on painting with the relentless pertinacity of the consumptive, whose every passion has a pathological force'.[318] And in Sezima's sadomasochistic *Passiflora* (1903): 'Her fading hair with its languid lustre of warm gossamer flowed over the pillow and exuded the frail fragrance of dried mint. / Feverish weakness lay in the features of her face, in her eyes, in her beautiful hands which were folded droopingly on her lap.'[319] Decadents also liked to use human dying in similes for natural phenomena. Hlaváček compares a sunset with Christ's Passion (thus also possibly echoing the twilight of the gods/idols topos of the period) and Ružena Jesenská addresses the setting sun as a ruby in its death-agony. Rutte writes of thoughts which 'fall asleep like sick dancing girls'.[320] Sometimes such images clearly reflect the Decadents' Baroque preoccupation with the transitoriness of everything in the world. A typical example of that, which echoes Blake and the Romantic Mácha whom the Decadents were the first to understand, arises in Breisky's imaginary portrait, 'Tiberův konec na Capri' (Tiberius's end on Capri): 'When he looked at a rose, he could not but imagine its fading; he had a picture in his mind of it withered, with no leaves on the bush. When he saw the beautiful skin of a pomegranate, he imagined it eaten away inside by worms.'[321]

Dying may be called an extended state of consciousness, but the equally typical period state of consciousness is the mood. The mood is an intermediate state *per se*. It is an emotional reaction, but a reaction which is not firmly connected either with its apparent immediate stimulus or with whatever or whosoever suffers under the given mood. The mood expresses a temporary, unstable intermediate state of the individual; it does not express the individual. Indeed the expression of moods may be interpreted as an expression of a mask (the Decadent concealing his self) or of a pose (the Decadent playing with his audience). Hlaváček writes in his posthumously published *Žalmy*: 'between individual words there are sometimes dark, sometimes yellow-glowing chasms, deep gulleys and treacherous inlets which one has to make navigable to express the delicateness of moods.'[322]

The Decadents' descriptions of putrefaction express the notional awareness of the decay of European civilisation. It looks like a parody of Decadence when Auředníček writes of 'a surge of words permeated with the hot exhalations of some diseased but alluring passion'.[323] Marten's description of the sense of decay in the period is more studied and melodramatic: 'She was approaching as if she had come from invisible miasmata, from an atmosphere poisoned by the breath of decay rising from the drenched earth, from the dying vegetation through whose fibre sap had ceased to flow, from the hopeless death-agony of everything.'[324] Karásek initially uses images of the intermediate state of putrefaction to transmit a sense of social alienation, in other words, aristocratism; this brand of aristocratism derives from the artist's superior awareness of the degeneration of society, perhaps the whole of humanity. Karásek, however, repeats statements like the following so often that they soon lose their emotional impact, become simply deadwood in the Decadent code: 'The stench of decomposition can be smelt everywhere; / Ruin is pouring its corrosive poison on everything, / Even the strangely crimson sun is rotting . . . / Torrid blood is evaporating in my veins, / And, weakening, my body awaits the end / Of its death-agony, the end of everything.'[325]

Sickness is also an intermediate state. It may come between two periods of health or between a period of health and a period of dying. When a man is sick he is alive, but cannot live fully, and so, for the Decadent, sickness can be a metaphor for the nihilist's longing for a vital strong life, a metaphor for the kernel ambivalence of the Decadent *Weltanschauung*. Sickness is meant to produce clearness of vision or the wild artificial paradises of delirium. Whichever it is, man becomes hypersensitive. In Hlaváček's *Mstivá kantilena* the sickness of the passionately barren women and the gaunt rebels is transferred onto the church bells and the moon and the surrounding countryside. Convalescence, the state between sickness and health, when one is characterised by an interesting pallor, is the subject of Hlaváček's acoustically most effective representation of the intermediate state. Convalescence is also the subject of Arnošt Procházka's short-story, 'Vrah' (A murderer). Another form of sickness is the degeneracy or hypersensitivity of the last of a long noble line. That topos of European literature appears to be a straightforward emblem of the end of an old order, or of European civilisation.

Decay or degeneration in Nature is another Decadent topos; it constitutes a reaction against the sentimentalisation of Nature in previous periods; it further expresses the Decadents' fear of the natural, which is the same thing as their fear of the unnatural. Thus we find wildernesses and deserts representing the political and cultural desert the Czechs or Hungarians felt was theirs at the turn of the century. The desert could also represent the burnt-out soul, a common autostylisation for the period. The desert in Nature may be reflected by crumbling buildings as well. Crumbling buildings may suggest the futility of human endeavour, but they also suggest the joyless natural sequence of generations. Take the following description of Prague in Karásek's *Stojaté vody* (Stagnant waters, 1895):

> The oppressive breath of age wafted around him, like the stench of crypts and tombs. It was the torpid, motionless, dead mood of old, decrepit, run-down

streets . . ., dour houses . . . blackened and ponderous, cloaked in the magic that is the property of everything which is soon to perish. . . . Again he sank his eyes into all these forms, forms which had been seen by so many before him, so many deceased and disintegrated lives of long lost ages. He felt their being scattered all over these damp walls, which were exuding a pungent smell of fungus.[326]

The most common example of decay in buildings consists in descriptions of Venice. Decaying Venice is one of the great topoi of the European Decadence. Venice is where 'beauty pines away in the imminent shadow of death'.[327] But also it was a city which the new technological inventions had not and often could not penetrate. It is a city of many isolations and much decay. It is a city and not urban; it is land and it is water; it is the past in the present. Altogether a fine intermediate state. In his poem 'In Venedig' ('In Venice') Trakl speaks of those isolations rather than the decay, but the intermediate state constituted by the city is brought out by a shadow disappearing by a canal, the sickly smile of a homeless child, and by the crepuscular nature of the whole description. Auředníček's evocation of the Vendramini Palace typifies Decadent descriptions:

No other splendid building of Venice manifests so profoundly the grief of perishing, the combination of a glittering past with a hopeless future. The corridors and halls were lined with crumbling statues, veiled pictures, and here was a broken looking-glass, there tattered, yellowed damask. I can still clearly remember a small cradle which was a little masterpiece. . . . What children had this sad remnant of past maternal tenderness rocked? . . . Death breathed from all this splendour.[328]

Arthur Symons, who also wrote Decadent descriptions of Venice, chose quite a different city as representative of a complex intermediate state. That is Sofia, the most distant capital in Austria-Hungary's sphere of influence. The description is dated 1902.

There is something dry, hot, and fierce in this place, which is at once ordinary, sordid, and almost startling. It is a place at once violent and sullen, in which everything is dusty and dingy and half-used or half-finished. Stones and building materials lie strewn in the streets, houses are being made and houses are falling into ruins; everything is crude, sordid, with a crudity and sordidness which are half-western and half-eastern, and made of the worst elements of both. . . . Men stared about at the street corners in rags of all colours, sewn together in all fashions; there is something sordid and savage in these brutal faces, these huddled figures, this slouching gait, in this boisterous language with its jerks and splutters, in the barbarous clash of costumes, in all this idleness, suspicion, this mingling of elements that do not unite, this hostility of races, seen in the mere coming and going of the people; together with an odd sense of provinciality, as you meet processions with bands, carrying coloured flags, like friendly societies in England, and walking through the streets in step, singing solemn tunes like hymn-tunes.

On Sunday, Sofia takes on something preposterously like the aspect of an English Sunday. . . . At night Sofia returns to itself, or to what is more dubious and unfamiliar in itself. . . . The *danse du ventre*, done by a Greek in a kind of uniform covered with gold lace and wearing a long ivory-handled sword, and by an Armenian girl in a white vest and green trousers, was the most elaborate pantomine of sex that I have ever seen; it made a kind of art of obscenity. . . . In that dance I realised the whole difference between the consciousness of the East and what seems to us most like the Eastern point of view among Western nations. . . . What is so disquieting in Sofia is that it lies between two civilisations, and that it is a kind of rag-heap for the refuse of both. The main street of Sofia is the most horrible street in Europe. You see first of all mere European frippery . . . 'fancy articles', none personal to the place; rows of second-hand books and pamphlets, mostly in Russian . . ., and along with them, strung upon upright boards by strings, cheap photographs of actresses . . ., then stalls of fruit, powdered thick with dust, dust-covered loaves of bread, which looked like great stones, crescents of sausages, coloured greenish red . . .; but above all meat: carcasses stripped of the hide, with their tails still hanging, the horns and hide lying outside in the gutter . . .; everywhere yellow meat hanging from chains; all smells and all colours, as of the refuse of a slaughter-house. . . . And there is a continual coming and going of peasants in ragged and coloured clothes, women and girls with negress-like faces, wearing Turkish trousers under a sort of apron, half-naked gipsy children darting hither and thither, merchants, casual Europeans, in bowlers and overcoats; and all the time, the rattle of electric trams in the street as they pass to and fro, with their mockery of progress, through the city of dust and rags.[330]

That is the intermediate state of modernising decay in contrast to the almost natural decay of the past in Karásek's picture of Prague or Auředníček's of Venice.

Sofia's intermediacy is its scruffy puberty. Human puberty is a minor theme of Decadent literature and art, mainly because puberty is a period of frustration and hypersensitivity, but also because *fin-de-siècle* man was particularly concerned with sexual awareness. One might say that puberty is the time when *seine Majestät das Ich* has its first inklings of its majesty or first tries to establish its majesty. Puberty is a time of insecurity as well as of transition. Furthermore it is a time when a human being has adult characteristics, but is still a child; a parallel between that and the states of the Hungarian and Czech arts, perhaps even the Austrian German, may be drawn. Certainly the Austrian-German Decadence did not grow out of a satedness with life and culture like the French, any more than did the Hungarian or Czech. Musil may well be making the cultural parallel in his initial description of pubertal Törless, when he speaks of 'the dangerously soft spiritual ground of these years . . . when one has to signify to oneself and yet one is far too incomplete a person actually to signify anything. . . . danger lies in this age of transition. If one made clear to such a young man the ridiculousness of his person, the ground would fall away from under his feet, or he would plunge like a sleepwalker who has been awakened and who suddenly sees nothing but emptiness. . . . He seemed at that time to have no personality whatsoever.'[331] Karásek picks on the futile defiance as well as the frustration of puberty: 'Oh, torment of puberty, which seeks satisfaction /And rebels in vain and enervates itself in vain!'[332] S. K. Neumann's use of the topos in *Satanova sláva mezi námi* (Satan's glory among us, 1897) has broader significance; it appears to refer to the Czech sociopolitical desert as well as to cultural immaturity: 'In the tepid region / Where the air tastes / Of flowering hospital gardens, / And where in selenic nights / Vegetations of unborn colours / Exhale faintly; / Sources in the tepid region / In the uncertainties of puberty.'[333] Depictions of female puberty are of a different nature. The *femme enfant* constituted a threat to manhood as well as purity that was essentially impure (because it was female) and a statement on the irredeemability of woman once she had grown beyond puberty.

Puberty is an intermediate state which looks more forward than anything else; it is dynamic intermediacy, thus a striving out of intermediacy into adulthood, whereas homosexuality is a static intermediate state. Carpenter refers to homosexuals as 'the intermediate sex'; he understands homo-sexuals thus, following K. H. Ulrichs: 'belonging distinctly to one sex as far as their bodies are concerned they may be said to belong *mentally* and *emotionally* to the other.'[334] It has been pointed out that the period's misogyny helped make homosexuality an attractive model or goal or situation for intellectuals.[335] The very non-creativity, non-reproductivity of homosexuality was attractive because it was anti-Nature, non-animal. Furthermore, the homosexual could flout the love of women without having to pose. The homosexual was not dependent on women and therefore did not fear the New Woman. Homosexuality seems to have been particularly prevalent among British Decadent writers, for example, Symonds, Wilde, Douglas, the Estonian Stenbock – and the English Decadent of Czech noble family, Theodore Wratislaw. The Great Beast, Edward Alexander Crowley, who changed his name to Aleister Crowley because he considered that to become famous one had to have a name consisting of a dactyl followed by a spondee,[336] combined homosexuality with occultism, like the characters of some of Karásek's novels, but he was essentially a hetero-sexual. Crowley's influence on central-European literature came mainly, however, after World War I. Crowley, as a young man at least, had the basic Decadent view that women were a contamination of one's body as well as one's intellect.[337] French Decadent literature had Verlaine and, if you can call him a Decadent, Gide, but otherwise entirely minor writers like Achille Bécasse and Jacques d'Adelsward Fersen. The Czech Decadents' outrage at the Oscar Wilde trial was marked by a special issue of *Moderní revue* and Karásek has as his motto to *Sexus necans* Lord Alfred Douglas's words 'I love a love, but not as other men'. In this collection he calls homosexuals the 'vyhnanci lásky', love's exiles or disinherited which, presumably, echoes Otto de Joux's favourable study on homosexual love, *Die Enterbten des*

Liebesglückes (The disinherited from love's happiness, Leipzig, 1893). Karásek imagines a world of homosexual love which combines Symonds's ideas of Greek or Arcadian Love with Nietzsche's superman: 'It will be a world which gives birth to rugged men / Bronzed gymnasts with giant, muscular bodies. // It will be a world of love as . . . mighty as a battle and as ardent as heavenly fire. // It will be an embracing of bodies like coils of pythons, / The rapture of limbs crackling like whole slums on fire.'[338] In this collection and in *Sodoma* Karásek's homosexual love is often sado-masochistic, and sadomasochism is another intermediate state: it combines two apparent opposites, pain and ecstasy. Jaroslav Maria in his 'Renaissance fresco' drama *Michelangelo Buonarroti* (1912) treats a Nietzschean superman homosexual, glorious, proud in his depravity; he has a life of homosexual one-night stands, but then suddenly conceives a passion for a woman. In fact, in Maria homosexuality goes beyond the intermediate state and just becomes the expression of Renaissance power. One might see in Maria, who frequently depicts sexual extravagance in his prose and drama, a typical representative of the Decadent tendency to express a longing for chastity by describing passion unbridled. And Maria did have occultist leanings.

The androgyne, which Praz calls the 'obsession' of 'the whole Decadent movement',[339] is not necessarily linked with homosexuality. Beardsley's androgynes or indeed the pre-raphaelites' probably have nothing to do with it. Still the androgyne (like the gynander) is nothing if not an intermediate state. The *Fin de siècle* questions conventional sexual roles and the bourgeoisie's ideals of male handsomeness and female beauty. Such sexual ambiguity probably enters the Decadent consciousness through Gautier's *Mademoiselle de Maupin* (1835), which linked that ambiguity with those Roman Emperors who were particularly attractive to the Decadents. 'Satiation follows pleasure. . . . I have experienced all the prodigious feats of Sardanapalos, but still my life has looked too chaste and calm: it is wrong to believe that position constitutes the only path to satiation. One attains that by desire also; abstinence is more wearing than excess. . . . Tiberius, Caligula, Nero . . . I too should like to build a bridge on the sea and pave the waves; I have dreamed of setting fire to towns to provide light for my parties; I wanted to be a woman to know new aspects of voluptuousness.'[340] The young men of Hofmannsthal's plays appear androgynous. In Bohuslav Knoesl's first collection of verse, *Martyrium touhy* (Martyrdom of desire, 1896), 'a young man of maidenly beauty is slumbering with a stem of white lilies in his hand. And now I stand here penetrated by poison spikes of unsatisfied desire.'[341]

The androgyne is not to be confused with the hermaphrodite, who also has his/her place in Decadent literature. The intermediate state of hermaphro-ditism, however, is linked with the need for sexlessness or for a state in which sexual desire will not interfere with the mind and spirit. Thus the hermaphrodite will appear in parody (Beardsley) and occultist (Meyrink) works. Each of the sephiroth on the Cabalistic Tree is bi-sexual; in its relationship to its predecessor the sephira is feminine (negative) and to its successor masculine (positive). The sephira Hod, which represents the pelvic region, but not the genitals, has the hermaphrodite as its sign and its colours are the Decadent colours of purple and russet or orange (the titian-haired woman). In Meyrink's Ibbur book one of the letters on which the narrator fixes his thoughts (the twenty-two letters of the Hebrew alphabet can represent the twenty-two paths of the Cabala Tree) stands for destructive woman and the other '*the hermaphrodite on the mother-of-pearl throne, on its head a crown of red wood.*'[342] Later on Meyrink describes an hermaphrodite in connection with the Egyptian cult of Osiris: 'the magic union in human form of male and female, a union as demigod. The goal of existence! – No, not the goal, but the beginning of a new way, which is eternal – has *no* end.'[343] The occultist or mystic's search has no end, if he is searching for knowledge, not revelation. The search itself is an intermediate state between the mundane and knowerdom; that search is represented by the hermaphrodite.

A natural phenomenon of occultist importance which is a key Decadent intermediate state is the moon or moonlight. (The impact of Chinese art on the period was considerable, and no doubt that influenced the Decadents' use of moonlight.) Moonlight is only reflected light; it is light and not light. Furthermore it casts an 'unreal' light on any townscape or landscape, a light which evokes vague figures, dim outlines, shades – and one thinks of the black-and-white drawings of the period. Moon was the unattainable woman (cf. Mallarmé's Pierrot etc.). Moon was also woman in general and woman's narcissism and sterility. Laforgue, like Auředníček, even describes women's breasts as moons.[344] The ring around the moon, indeed even the disk of the moon, is also reminiscent of the uroboros, of sexual self-sufficiency and wisdom. As Pierrot points out, the moon could also represent the astral body, actually the astral corpse the world was likely soon to become, according to Decadent catastrophism, 'a macabre Damoclean reminder forever hanging over mankind's head'.[345] In comparing Mallarmé's Hérodias with Flaubert's Salammbô, Praz points out that both women are, so to speak, astral; the moon is Hérodias's sister as it is Salammbô's mother.[346] For the occultists the moon is, obviously enough, linked with reproduction (woman's menstrual cycle . . . as against man's alleged solar cycle). Moonlight is naturally deceptive like woman; and it gives what it covers a colour of decay: the moon embodies the destructive and reproductive aspects of woman. It also embodies woman's destruction of man and the heightened etheric sensitivity she can awaken in him. Lunar energy is meant to provide man with the powers to practise the esoteric arts, if he knows how to find those powers. The moon is Diana, unassailable virginity, who has men torn up if they approach her beauty too closely (but also Diana, Artemis, of Ephesus, the goddess of reproduction, fertility) and

Hecate (Asonya) the goddess of witchcraft. The *fin-de-siècle* mind is probably most impressed by the moon's sick, threatening pallor, but also by the fact that its colour is sometimes the green of poison or absinthe, sometimes the red of blood, and also by its role as accompanist for the artificial night-work of the Decadent in his study. The moon is also the only obvious natural element which can always penetrate the Decadent's anti-natural urbanity. It has little of the sentimental moon of Romanticism and Realism, and when it retains something of that, it accompanies sickness, as in Schnitzler's *Sterben*: 'the blue moonlit night flowed in soft waves. . . . It was not necessary to light a lamp; a bright strip of silver moonlight lay on the floor.'[347] It may be linked with the narcotic state as in Trakl's 'Verklärung' (Transfiguration): 'On your lips / Dwells quietly the autumn moon / Dark singing drunk with poppy juice.'[348] The moon is linked with dreaming and occult energy in the opening of Meyrink's *Der Golem*; it is linked with intermediate mental states:

> The moonlight falls on the foot of my bed and lies there like a large, flat, bright stone.
>
> When the full moon's form begins to shrivel and its right side begins to collapse – as a face approaching old age first shows wrinkles on one cheek and becomes thin –, at such times in the night a turbid, painful unease overtakes me.
>
> I neither sleep nor wake and in my half-dream the experienced and the read and heard mingle in my soul as rivers of different colours and different clarities flow into one.[349]

Meyrink does not lose his occultist imperviousness there either, for he soon compares that bright stone with a lump of grease. Later, when the narrator is in prison, the light of the full moon is compared with glistening oil. In this light he becomes aware of the hermaphrodite character Mirjam-Hillel.[350] When Zeyer's Jan Maria Plojhar falls from his horse, in his semi-consciousness he mistakes the moon for the face of Christ.[351]

Before the night and the moon comes another intermediate state beloved of the Decadents, the evening. (Day is vulgar.) The evening is dying day and may also be emblematic of the dying century or the dying civilisation – the twilight of the idols. In the evening forms and colours become indistinct. Schnitzler's *Sterben* begins with twilight. The pubertal Törless is particularly sensitive to the intermediate state of evening:

> He thought he could hear the rustling of the withered leaves which the wind brought together. Then came that moment of most intense quietness which always precedes the falling of complete darkness. All forms, which were becoming ever more deeply embedded in the twilight, and all colours, which were dissolving, seemed to remain still for some seconds, to draw in their breath . . .[352]

The evening assumes 'mystical' and erotic functions in Jesenská's 'Noc divně světlá' (Strangely bright night): 'I shall give everything with which my sunset burns; / You understand the causes of all fires; / You are child of the moon-bright Sea of seas, / My Love of love, my sigh of sweet Sighs.'[353] However one interprets these lines, a godhead is being addressed. The Sea of seas sounds like the Virgin Mary or the Great Sea of the Cabala, the superior mother, Binah, thus also Aphrodite Anadyomene. The moon, Diana, is virgin, and has no child. The Virgin Mary is also the Mother of Sighs, and Levanah, the moon.

Parallel to evening as an intermediate state is the very early morning, the time of mists, and again indistinct colours and forms. Early morning is linked primarily with fear and despair – it is the great time of suicides, and of the fitful dreams of waking, and, indeed, the time one remembers dreams. The early morning gives hope to Felix's Marie in Schnitzler's *Sterben*, for she is an optimist, an idolater, has nothing in common with the *fin-de-siècle* élite. Hlaváček calls his second collection of verse *Pozdě k ránu* (The Early morning) and in the poem 'Upír' (Vampire) there he describes early morning as the time when any member of the élite has to prepare himself for entry into the drudgery of common life; the early morning brings fear of banality. The creative soul has to return to its workaday body, which in the early morning is still 'intoxicated / By a mystic orgy – / It wakes up inside an everyday parasite, / Which will once more trudge through the day in the profane din of the street, / As it had had to on the cursed day before / And as it would have to on the repellent day after . . .'[354]

The approximate equivalent of evening among the seasons is autumn, which, as the season of decay, naturally attracted *fin-de-siècle* man. As the Romantic *homme fatale* turned into the Decadent *femme fatale*, so Romantic spring turned into Decadent autumn. Spring was vulgar and false for the Decadent. Summer was equally vulgar, except when the heat was oppressive and so could emblemise the oppression he felt in his soul. Like evening, autumn could stand for the twilight of civilisation. It was also the season which saw Nature at her artistically most creative. The colours were often like that of the titian hair of the *fin-de-siècle* woman. As one would expect, one finds an early statement of the Decadent attitude in Baudelaire: 'I prefer your fruits, autumn, / to the banal flowers of spring.'[355] And one finds autumn in, obviously enough, Verlaine's 'Art poétique', but also in , say, Mallarmé's 'Soupir'. And autumn is frequently used to describe a soul-scape, a *paysage de l'âme* in Decadent literature altogether. Autumn may contain fear of an end, as it does in Trakl, even though it is apparently a time of riches; there are not only the reds and autumnal pale blue of the sky, but there is also the wine. Still 'a skeletal horror attacks / When the dew drops blackly from the bare willows' and all around is 'black putrefaction'.[356] A distillation of the Decadent autumn is to be found in the beginning of Sezima's prose piece, 'Autumn scents' (1898):

A paling, not yet senilely shivering, but a somehow youthfully debauched autumn without warmth.

A barely perceptible fragrance floats from the forest into air which is as clear as the water of a lake. A matt silky tone of decay flows into one's nerves.

And quietness. A sullenly cold calm over the earth, over the languid glint of grey grass and purple fields; over the chilled-blue forest and over the violet contours of the clouds.

Deadness.[357]

The fogs of autumn are a topos of the period. They created visual and auditory intermediate states and an atmosphere where one expects the unexpected.

The fog scene comes conceptually close to the subaquine scene, another period topos. The submerged landscape or man-made object (most commonly a ringing bell as in Gerhart Hauptmann's *Die versunkene Glocke* [The sunken bell] or Jesenská's *Estera*) is mysteriously oneiric. Like fog, water blurs contours. Furthermore it renders the real unreal or incomprehensible. Colours and sounds are distorted, become like the colours and sounds of a dream. Water is the element of fruitfulness, reproduction, sexuality, but it is also the provider of mirrors and the element which causes decay. It is female in its natural destructiveness and creativeness, and the frequency of boat imagery in Decadent verse (for example, Rimbaud, Ady, Karásek) suggests the sexual activity of the male in his aggression (the phallic keel) and his fundamental powerlessness (the storms, waves, undertows of femaleness). Water connotes also narcissism. If one looks into a mirror one is, theoretically, attempting 'to discover the truth about oneself, to reach the permanent self behind the multiple flux of the consciousness'.[358] Thus the subaquine scene may be considered also a *paysage de l'âme*. Rodenbach asks why one should 'descend into the submarine soul' and warns that 'the deep waters of the soul are perfidious'.[359] Redon's painting *Seahorses in a Submarine Landscape* (sometime before 1904) is essentially occultist; the eye of God and the eye of the soul look out, watched by nearly bisexual sea-horses and the serpent of wisdom is hinted at and only faintly red on the sea's bottom; astral selves try to glimmer through the greens and blues. In *fin-de-siècle* art the underwater landscape can also represent the vanity of human endeavour and the unattainability of beauty. The underwater scene as a depiction of the unconscious is to be found in Březina and Hlaváček.

Waiting is another intermediate state frequently used by Hlaváček, only occasionally by Březina. Waiting is pendant between past and future, an expectancy based on an arrangement, but waiting also connotes uncertainty, sometimes even insecurity. For waiting implies some dependency which the aristocratic tries to avoid. It can also imply hope, 'waiting for a miracle', as it does for Mirjam in Meyrink's *Der Golem*. And hope is contrary to the *fin-de-siècle* ethos. Miracles are for the naive and for those who do not know one has to study and refine before one can attain new perception, new consciousness. The waiting in Rutte's 'Píseň čekajícího' (Song of a waiting man, *Smutečni slavnosti srdci*), set by the gates of a silent, metaphorical park in a starless metaphorical night, is dominated by fear. In Austrian-German literature Hofmannsthal's *Die Frau im Fenster* (The woman at the window, 1897) epitomises the topos. The window in the same author's 'Der Jüngling und die Spinne' ('The young man and the spider') provides the youth with fear and a vision of death, when he had previously been drunk with his own amorous success. Claudio in *Der Tor und der Tod* also sits at the window. Seeba interprets this window as the Decadent's study-window, his false link with the real world from which he has cut himself off: 'the window, an anthropological spatial symbol, barred the way into life for Claudio. He had always stood at the window, just looking at the world, excluded from it by himself. As aesthetic man, i.e. as "observing" man, he had always seen life framed in a window and . . . instead of experiencing life he had "interpreted" and "comprehended" life as a framed picture.'[360]

Fear or anxiety is the most common mental intermediate state of the *Fin de siècle* – indeed the English language adopted the word *angst* from the *fin-de-siècle* state. Fear is a state based on the past, real, imagined or second-hand (for example, from reading) experience projected into the future. It constitutes an intense consciousness of selfness. It may also, as Pierrot says, 'have no basis in reason, it may be inexplicable, but it is nevertheless fully experienced. . . . it appears as a more or less cyclic crisis which the human consciousness undergoes in its relation with the real.'[361] In *Liebelei* Schnitzler presents 'fear as an *aesthetic* value, as the sure sign of a man's sensitiveness, as though it were the only possible alternative to the heedless enjoyment of material and erotic pleasures.'[362] That is the fear of death – in the same opposition as Hofmannsthal's 'Der Jüngling und die Spinne'. Fear renders the women of Hlaváček's *Mstivá kantilena* barren. When religion fails, life and death may become opposites, but death also may become meaningless and so fear itself may become something like a cult. The object of that fear may cease to be death and become the 'black gorge of emptiness' as it does in Houdek's sonnet, 'Strach temný . . .' (Dark fear . . .).[363] In Hlaváček's cycle the fear is existential and vague, however concrete its effects. It appears to derive from an awareness of futility. The state is linked with Decadent catastrophism and its ambivalence, the Decadent's fear and enjoyment of the approaching end.

The same goes for the dance of death. The obvious example of this particular form of ecstasy is Salome's dance in Wilde's play, except that in Wilde, and here I am persuaded by Hajek's interpretation, Salome is all body and Jokanaan all spirit. The two characters are themselves symbols of dualism. Salome's dance is 'a symbol of immediate, ecstatic life removed from mental control', but simultaneously a symbol of the body's removal from time, in other words of a suspended state.[364] In Karásek on the other hand the ageing Salome's dance before the huntsman she is incapable of seducing, while still representing a suspended state (she loses her wrinkles and silicosis and she becomes as youthful and lithe as she had been years before when dancing for the Baptist), is not removed from mental control. She deliberately manipulates time and body. The result in the Wilde case is not 'the fruit of a quickened, multiplied consciousness',[365] as it is in Karásek. The dance of death, like other intermediate states, may well emblemise the ending of a civilisation. In Karásek's play, *Apollonius z Tyany* (Apollonius of Tyana, 1905), the Gnostic philosopher turns out to be homosexual and he and his *confidant* Damides are in love. Apollonius, who has hitherto not aged, suddenly has a crisis of self-confidence (European culture's crisis) and he loses his magic powers. At the end of the play both he and Damides are dead and the coarse masses have taken over civilisation. The woman who had loved Damides, Tarsie, has gone mad and she performs an ecstatic dance of death. In her dance of death the body is removed from mental control, but the spirit is alive in her. The Eternal Spirit is alive in a body which is unnatural in its madness and its apparently purely physical ecstasy. Her eyes are dilated, her features drawn and pale and her nipples take on an intense red hue as if they were wells of blood. Finally she howls with demonic laughter and falls onto Damides's corpse, having lost all her human features. Love is a destroyer of civilisation – as in Musset's second delineation of the *maladie du siècle*. In Sezima's *Passiflora*, after her sadist husband has killed himself, having first caused two trains to crash in an ecstasy of sadism, Klára dances a frenetic dance of death. Her dance is a purification of the body, though it had started as an apotheosis of the animal in woman. When it is over she spends the rest of her tubercular life becoming more and more the victim of hallucinations. Her life becomes one of spiritual sensualism, which consists mainly in spiritual self-flagellation. There is in her only the inner pain of the saint.

Klára's hallucinations and dreams reflect the earlier Decadent preoccupation with oneiric writing, the writing of dreams, often the narcotic-induced dreams one links with de Quincey and Baudelaire. The intermediate state of the dream, where proportions and relations were free to be apparently quite independent of the bourgeois Realist world, attracted *fin-de-siècle* man. In a dream one has a true experience which is not a true experience: the reality of unreality. Dream reality is also spiritually and aesthetically more inspiring than the world of society or the streets or the poky little office in which one spends most of one's working life. Dreams as a subject of art were to acquire their own sub-genre, the *poème en prose*, and the main inspiration of the avant-garde of turn-of-the-century painting and graphic art (for example, Munch, Redon, Hlaváček, Váchal) is dream; indeed it is arguable that Cubism, as an analytical trend, was a reaction against prior anti-analytical, spiritual trends in art. For dreams demanded new forms or gave new meanings to old forms. Dreams appealed to the irrationalists, occultists as well as 'mystics', and in them were sought the expression of universal spirit. Then by the time of such as James Sully and Paul Chabeneix and, finally,

Freud in dreams was sought the expression of the self and selfness. Certainly it appeared in the *Fin de siècle* that dreams either were more important than accepted reality or provided the key to reality. Rachilde, Maeterlinck, Rodenbach, all saw in dreams a higher reality, as did in Bohemia before them Zeyer. For Mallarmé and his disciples dreams were to provide 'one of the means of divining that higher and ideal reality whose existence was guaranteed by the theory of symbols'.[366] Oskar Kokoschka, significantly enough, dedicates his dream *poème en prose*, 'Die träumenden Knaben' (The dreaming boys, 1908), to Gustav Klimt. In this work the intermediate state of puberty is the subject of the intermediate state of dream. Blue, the colour of dreams, as in Trakl, dominates. Exotic freedoms of social (sexual) behaviour fuse with exotic vegetation and exotic sounds; the end, however, is not facile pubertal eroticism, but a higher ideal of the self as the lover of everything, the embodiment of cosmic love. Notably, water in this dream world is characterised as the end of all being. Trakl's dream *poèmes en prose* contain more violence and sexuality and decay but they form a path to death and higher being – like the poem of a Baroque mystic. Dreams appear to contain a spiritual erethism to match the physical erethism of much *fin-de-siècle* graphic and verbal art. However artificial it might seem, the young Hofmannsthal's poem, 'Ein Traum von grosser Magie' (A dream of great magic), contains much of the higher reality the Decadents were seeking, for example: 'In dream he felt the lot of all mankind, / As he felt his own limbs. / Nothing was near or far for him, nothing small or large.'[367] Kubin ironises the Decadent dream cult in *Die andere Seite* – while also partly adhering to it – and so the chapter entitled 'The confusion of dream' begins: 'that night I went to sleep with great thoughts. My dream was less grand.'[368] The dream is actually a series of grotesque pictures. Meyrink's *Der Golem* is a dream novel about the self in flux.

In a world where imagination seemed to have been limited by the natural sciences and capital, where what counted as achievements were the Eiffel Tower or Tower Bridge or underground railways, *fin-de-siècle* man sought manners of thinking unbound by the laws of science. Science seemed a superficial, crude, mass business. 'The more room a thought has for the spreading of dream's wings, the more twilights it has which can be shone through with light, the greater the thought will be.'[369]

XV. THE MAGIC OR SACRED BOOK

In the self-centred, study-bound culture of the *Fin de siècle*, where the Church has lost its power as a haven for the mystically minded, there was a marked tendency for the cultivated man or woman to seek inspiration for dreams, a depiction of a higher reality, or instructions on how to progress to a higher reality, in a book. The Bible had been worn out by conventional,

Establishment Christianity. This was the period of the discovery of William Blake. The most immediately graspable representation of the search for the Book is Jean Délville's *Portrait of Mrs Stuart-Merrill*, also entitled *Mysteriosa*. Mrs Stuart-Merrill's chin rests on a large leather-bound book with a simple triangle on its cover. Her hair, the Decadent titian colour, is blown out as if by a spiritual mind. Her lips are sealed in almost child-like concentration but the pupils of her grey-green eyes are cast up as if in rapture, though that rapture either is cleansed of sexuality or summons some mystic sexuality. The triangle has standard mystical and occult meaning. Primarily, perhaps, its two base points represent the physical and the mental self, where the apex represents the soul or Supernal Being, the essential Soul which is universal and eternal. The two base points are being (the dualism of being) and the apex higher being, if I use the terms I used when speaking of dreams and the *danse macabre*. The superior six Sephiroth in the Cabalists' Tree are also conventionally described as forming two triangles. The triangle may also express the Supreme Being, as the triad or trinity which may represent the Godhead, as it does in the shape of three young men in the Old Testament and then in the Trinity of Christian doctrine. The pyramids, perceived on the horizon as triangles, are said to represent the striving of man's eternal spirit or soul to the state of illumination within the Great Spirit or to Knowledge, as the materialist occultists put it. Occultists tend to think dialectically or rather within ideas of fusions of opposites (which are not opposites, except to the banal mind); the triangle is the opposite of and includes the inverted triangle, the *mons Veneris*.

If the essence of the world is the nothingness, as it is for Mallarmé and his contemporaries elsewhere in Europe who were disciples of Schopenhauer and the Indians, then art can supersede that nothingness. Where Baudelaire, Wellek suggests, uses his poetry to transform Nature, to extract flowers from evil, Mallarmé cuts Nature completely off from Nature. 'The work or, in Mallarmé's terms, the Book is suspended over the Void, the silent godless Nothingness.'[370] As high-priests of culture *fin-de-siècle* men like Mallarmé were, probably, consciously attempting to restore the book to the position it had had in ancient civilisations. For the Greeks, the Egyptian god Thot, the lord of Magic, had invented writing. In Curtius's view it was not until Jacob Grimm, the Victorians and their equivalents, that the book lost it sacred function and symbolic value.[371] So again one may see the Decadent conception of the magic or sacred book as a direct, reasoned rejection of Victorian values.

Dowling links the concept of the fatal or magic book with the Decadents' liberating of language from its accepted bourgeois constrictions, from set meanings. She discusses Wilde's 'The Portrait of Mr W.H.' (1889) as a predecessor (*sic*) of the notion of the fatal book in English Decadence. She writes about the obsession of Wilde's characters with the secret of a book, i.e. of Shakespeare's sonnets: 'For like the very syntactic elements of

Decadent style itself ("the page is decomposed to give place to the
independence of the phrase, and the phrase to give place to the independence of the word"), Cyril and Erskine in their early excitement and
subsequent deaths are first discomposed and then decomposed by the
"secret" of the text.'[372] Her conception of the fatal book is a narrower
conception than Mallarmé's sacred book or Mme Blavatsky and her
followers' conception of the magic and sacred book, her own *The Secret
Doctrine* (1888) or *Isis Unveiled* (1877): 'The fatal book *is* fatal . . ., not
because of its power to kill outright, but because of its power decisively to
change an individual life.'[373] Dowling cites as her first example the effect
The Golden Ass has on Marius and Flavian in Pater's *Marius, the Epicurean*
(1885). She also cites the effect Gautier's *Mademoiselle de Maupin* had on
the narrator in Moore's *Confessions of a Young Man*. For Wilde's Dorian
Gray, Huysmans's *A rebours* is just such a fatal book. In Czech literature
one thinks immediately of the impact of de Quincey's Levana essay on the
main character of Zeyer's *Dům "U tonoucí hvězdy"*. In Austrian-German
literature one thinks of the impact of the Ibbur book on the narrator of
Meyrink's *Der Golem*.

Dowling spends some time on what has been called 'the most decadent
book in English literature',[374] Arthur Machen's semi-occultist *The Hill of
Dreams* (1907). She points out that the cult of books practised by the main
character Lucian, 'like the orthodox cult of the Bible on which it is modelled,
is doomed to fail without revealing what faith could possibly succeed it.'[375]
But that is the cult of the book as a model of style or language, not the cult of
the magic or sacred book, the book which might offer a key to the higher
reality. If the book serves any ultimate purpose to Lucian that seems to be
sexual gratification derived from the beautiful bodies of words.

The extent to which the Decadents sought to replace reality with a book,
with fiction, may be seen in Claudio's perception of his own life in
Hofmannsthal's *Der Tor und der Tod*, in the initial soliloquy: 'I have always
toiled under the enigmatic curse / . . . Of experiencing my life like a book, /
Which one half does not yet understand and half understands no longer.'[376]
That is as frustrating for Claudio as it was to be for Machen's Lucian. If one
seeks life or the interpretation of life in a book or books, one is likely to miss
life itself. On the other hand, if life itself is so dreary and philistine, one is
limited to book experience. So here again we have the Decadent paradox of
joy in death combined with life-affirmation, except that Hofmannsthal does
label Claudio a fool.

Beineberg's father in *Törless* has an attitude to books which is Oriental
and Cabalistic; he also indulges in bibliomancy. He reads neither novelists
nor Western philosophers. In other words, he represents the occultist trend
in *fin-de-siècle* Austria:

> When he read he did not want to meditate on opinions and arguments, but in the
> very act of opening a book he sought to enter the midst of exquisite knowledge as if

through a secret gate. They had to be books whose very possession was like the sign of a secret order and like the guarantee of superterrestrial revelations. And he found that sort of thing only in books of Indian philosophy, which he did not consider mere books, but revelations, reality-key works like mediaeval books of alchemy and magic.

He used to lock himself away with them . . . normally towards evening. Then he chose a passage at random and wondered whether the most secret meaning of that passage might not that day be solved for him. And he was not disappointed, however often he must have realised that he had not penetrated further than the forecourt of the consecrated temple.

Thus an aura of something like sacred mystery floated around this tanned, sinewy outdoor man. . . . His eyes were not dreamy, but calm and hard. Their expression had been formed by reading in books in which no word could be dislodged from its place without disturbing a secret meaning; their expression had been formed by a careful, reverent weighing up of every sentence for its meaning and double meaning.[377]

A similar type of reading is described by the narrator of *Der Golem* as he reads the chapter Ibbur (the impregnation of the soul):

The book spoke to me as a dream speaks, only more clearly and much more plainly and it touched my heart like a question.

Words flowed from invisible lips, came alive and surged towards me. They turned about and transformed themselves before me like colourfully-clad slave-girls. . . . Each hoped for a while that I would choose her and would not let my eyes stray to the rest. . . . Then they brought me a woman who was quite naked and massive, like a metal colossus.

For a second she stood still in front of me and then she bowed down before me.

Her eyelashes were as long as my whole body and she pointed mutely to the pulse of her left hand.

It beat like an earthquake and I felt that the life of a whole world was within her. . . . And I read the book right to the end and then sat holding it in my hand; then it was if I had been searching through the pages of my brain, not of a book!

All my life I had born within me everything the voice had said to me; it had just been hidden and forgotten and till today, had kept itself hidden from my thinking.[378]

One sacred book which was to be mentioned or alluded to over and over again in the occult wing of the Decadence was Joachim of Fiore's 'Eternal Evangel'. The Vintrasian sect in France, which was at the foundation of much Decadent occultist musing, believed that the New Testament Reign of the Son was about to come to an end and the Third Reign, the Reign of the Holy Spirit, the Paraclete, was nigh.[379] Initially this may be interpreted as a positive, optimistic interpretation of Decadent catastrophism. In Joachim's (c. 1135–1202) thinking the Third Reign was not to be accompanied by a third Testament; the Church would not be superseded but translated into a new spiritual plane.[380] Joachim wrote nothing called the 'Eternal Evangel', but, according to Reeves and Gould, his *Liber Concordiae* would have given nineteenth-century men an exposition of his 'distinctive Trinitarian division of history into three stages', but, because of its apocalyptic nature, the equally difficult *Expositio in Apocalypsim* was the work they were more likely to have read.[381] It is not at all certain that Vintras, who was not an educated man, had read any Joachim, however close his ideas may sometimes have apparently been. Joachite ideas may well, however, have reached Bohemia through the Vintrasian sect. Joseph-Antoine Boullan, a friend of Huysmans's, who took over a Lyons-based sect which once had Vintras as its pope,[382] probably knew Julius Zeyer. But the Eternal Evangel idea did not come to Bohemia in the form of a 'spiritual rationalisation' of free love, which is what it was eventually reduced to in France. Its main literary manifestation was Vrchlický's poem, 'Věčné evangelium' (The Eternal Evangel), in *Fresky a gobeliny* (Frescos and tapestries, 1891), where the poet has the Third Reign as the coming 'kingdom of Eternal Love'.[383] This kingdom is appearing from the East in the tradition of much Decadent and neo-Revivalist writing, and it is a kingdom of Love largely because such a concept comports with the poet's notion that love is the only salvation for the nineteenth century and (ii) the narcotic, intoxicating inspirer of great art. It is significant that Vrchlický characterises the Third Reign as a walking on roses, and the Second (or First and Second) as walking on nettles. This may be a mistake, but it is probably automatic symbolism on Vrchlický's part – the rose as love or love consummated. Joachim had characterised the three *status* of history as 'nettles, roses and lilies respectively.[384] The rose signifies earthly love and its astral manifestation is the lily and so the lily would be appropriate for the third stage if Vrchlický had been anything of a Decadent occultist. Right at the end of the period, in 1913, Janáček began setting the poem to music; his cantata was first performed in 1917.

XVI. THE OCCULT, THE MYSTICAL AND THE MALADIE DU SIÈCLE

The French Revolution and the notion spread by Romanticism that the individual could change and improve society, the spread of the industrial revolution and the consequent growth of religious indifference amongst the urban lower classes all contributed to the disarray in which the Roman Catholic Church found itself in the nineteenth century. This was particularly significant in Austria-Hungary, where Catholicism was the state religion; a concordat between Vienna and the Vatican was signed in 1855. The Jesuits were re-admitted to Austria. The Church fought its palpably diminishing influence: the dogma of the Immaculate Conception was proclaimed in 1854 and the Vatican Council of 1870 introduced the doctrine that the Pope was infallible when he spoke *ex cathedra*. Neither of those proclamations accorded with the age which produced Darwinism and materialist socialism.

And yet that discord aptly epitomises the ever more perceptible dualism which occultist sects, movements like theosophy and, much later, Steiner's anthroposophy, indeed the Catholic reform movement itself and the various philosophies of messianic racism, sought to confront. Durtal in Huysmans's *Là-bas* (1891) speaks of 'the decomposition of ideas in the period'.[385] Out of this religious crisis, Mallarmé submits, there could arise a new religion in France but this would be 'a thousandfold amplification of the instinct of heaven in everyone'; at the moment, however, literature and music contain the 'Mystery'; the conflict is, he says, simple to see: 'Everything is summarised in Aesthetics and Political Economy.'[386] For Mallarmé there is no hope for conventional religion, but Huysmans soon returned to the bosom of Mother Church. Indeed even British Decadents like Wilde and Beardsley became Catholic.

For Catholic Decadents the draw of spiritism or spiritualism, occultism or a form of more or less Christian mystical teaching was strong. Probably that resulted from their sense of the ambivalence of the world – not only from their dislike of the clear black and white morality of the *embourgeoisé* Church. They were attracted by the 'great axiom of occult philosophy – harmony results from the analogy of opposites'.[387] For occultists the term Positivist was as pejorative as it was for Decadents and Modernists. The occultists are also elitists; Papus writes in his appendix to Lévi: 'One must be daring to gain supremacy over the phantom of the imagination and the worries of the mind; one must be daring to think differently from the vulgar, opposing the immutable reason of the wise to the ever-changing incoherence of the common crowd.'[388] The Cabalists' minute readings of their texts evince an attitude to language not far removed from the attitude Dowling attributes to the Decadents. The antifeminism often manifest in occultism contrasts with the worship of woman as saviour in some sects – the same contrast we find in *fin-de-siècle* writers who had little or nothing to do with occultism. Both occultism and Decadence expressed a profound mistrust of the nineteenth-century worship of the natural sciences. Marcel in Karásek's *Scarabaeus* cannot see that natural sciences have advanced anything except the vulgarisation of esoteric truths. In 'mysticism' and occultism nothing is definite; the individual strives to enter a different state of consciousness like the true Decadent artist; esoteric thinkers and practitioners think of intermediate states. The obvious example is the Bardo state, when the soul judges itself immediately after death by choosing the after-life it is to have. This state is described in Tibetan scriptures, a corner-stone of much late nineteenth-century esoteric thought.

In this 'crisis of religion' some *fin-de-siècle* men truly sought mystical experience – even if, like William James, they had to resort to nitrous oxide to achieve it. Most of such seekers turned to aspects of occultism. They were, however, essentially experimenters rather than idealists and so their use of the occult might well appear to be a distortion to the 'believing' occultist.

Occultism was, however, only an influence on the mainstream of the *Fin de siècle*. Decadent man was fundamentally anti-historicist. Popper has pointed that out: 'Historicism is a very old movement. Its oldest forms, such as the doctrines of the life-cycles of cities and races, actually precede the primitive technological view that there are hidden purposes behind the apparently blind decrees of fate. . . . Every version of historicism expresses the feeling of being swept into the future by irresistible forces.'[389] It is, incidentally, easy to see how occultism and 'mysticism' can appeal so directly to today's young intellectuals in countries like Czechoslovakia and Bulgaria. One historicist system is replaced by another. Decadents did not like systems, for systems bridled individualism. McFarlane has pointed out how the interest in, then investigation of, occultist thought, resulted from the period's 'growing interest in the nature and development of the individual personality or ego' and, like Goodrick-Clarke in his chapter in this volume, he sees the sources as primarily Anglo-Saxon, omits the French beginnings – which were equally important, at least for the Bohemian Lands. Certainly McFarlane is right when he sees much of the occultist interest lying in a direct reaction to the impact of Herbert Spencer's *Principles of Psychology* (1865) and *Synthetic Philosophy* (tenth volume completed in 1896), and his 'sweeping formulations of his faith in rational progress and in the efficacy of scientific method'. And for some of the nineteenth-century investigators of the esoteric individual 'rather than social change' was, indeed, seen as 'the key to human advancement'.[390] Most Decadents were not concerned with human advancement or claimed not to be. Modernists (in my narrow sense, again) certainly were. When the arch-Decadent Karásek was turning to occultism, he denied he had ever been a Decadent. Occultists believe in progress, at least the progress of the individual. They also met in lodges and gathered in orders as they do today; it constituted a social privacy, not an individualist intimacy such as that the true Decadent fostered. Still any true *fin-de-siècle* man would have agreed with their contemporary, the French occultist, Edouard Schuré's, words in his preface to the *Grands initiés*: 'Never has the human soul had a profounder sense of the inadequacy, the misery, the unreality of present life. Never has that soul so ardently aspired to the invisible beyond without succeeding in believing in it.'[391] That in itself constituted a necessary part of man's making himself god unto himself. Stirner's notion of 'der Einzige' like Nietzsche's of the superman belonged essentially to the same manner of thinking which inspired the Decadence and the occult revival.

One could argue that we are not dealing so much with an occult revival in Austria-Hungary as with an undercurrent of thinking which culminates in the *fin-de-siècle* period. If we ignore mediaeval mysticism and the alleged esoteric Jewish school in Prague in the mid-Middle Ages, one might see the beginning of occultism in the baptised Jew, Pavel Žídek (1413–71) – also known as Paulerinus and Paulus de Praga. In Pilsen in the 1450s he compiled his encyclopaedia of modern knowledge, *Liber viginti artium* (or *Libri magni*). One incomplete manuscript of 359 large pages survives in the Jagellonian Library in Cracow. It is said that Poles considered it the book of mysteries of their version of the Faustus figure, Twardowski. Then, the court of Emperor Rudolph II was the major European centre of occult activities. Both John Dee and Edward Kelley spent some time there. (Karásek wrote a play about that.) Legend has it that Rudolph was friendly with the Cabalist Rabbi Jehuda Löw ben Bezalel, the creator of the Golem (which produced in our period a play in Czech by Vrchlický, a German *novella* by Rudolph Lothar and a Czech novel by Karásek). Löw, a native of Worms, who was rabbi first in Mikulov (Moravia), then Poznań and, finally from 1573 onwards, in Prague, was certainly one of the most learned Jewish scholars of his time.[392] Half a century later the emigré scholar, publicist and esoteric thinker, Comenius (Komenský), introduced the ideas of the Rosicrucians into English Freemasonry. The Freemasons themselves were strong in the Austrian, Bohemian and Hungarian Lands during the Enlightenment and the early part of the National Revivals. Then in the late Czech Revival, Amerling, in planning his model school and model curriculum was guided by astrological principles. It may not be pure chance that the Czech *fin-de-siècle* literary investigation of occultism was begun by a Jew who was brought up as an ardent Catholic, Julius Zeyer.

The Church itself was aware that occultism was a direct result of its inadequacy to the age. In 1870 Pius IX declared that 'at this time particularly numerous terrible, evil demons' are inhabiting Europe. 'The only cure,' he said, was 'to invoke Jesus Christ who was hung on the Cross to purify the air, *ut naturam purgaret.*'[393] The occultist movement proper began in France as in Austria-Hungary under the strong influence of Swedenborg (cf. particularly Gautier, Baudelaire, Karásek). Baudelaire's sonnet 'Correspondances', which shaped so much of Decadent imagery, was written, as Beckson points out, directly under the influence of Swedenborg's 'Platonic idea of the universal analogy between the natural and spiritual worlds and [his] belief that forms, numbers, colours, and perfumes in both worlds were reciprocal'.[394] Swedenborg's teaching on evil spirits would have attracted writers with a satanist bent, although it did not comport with the teaching of a true occultist, who cannot wholly accept that good and evil are opposites, because he thinks in analogies. For Swedenborg 'the Devil means the hell which is at the back, and where the very worst dwell, called evil *genii*; and Satan denotes the hell which is in front, where dwell the less wicked who are called evil spirits; and Lucifer denotes those who are of Babel or Babylon.'[395] Swedenborg also had a strong impact on the thought of one of the most influential occultists, Eliphas Lévi. Pierrot sensibly simplifies the development of esoteric trends in nineteenth-century France as three more or less consecutive movements, magetism, spiritism (and spiritualism) and occultism (which would include the Rosicrucians).[396]

The first trend, which, according to Pierrot, was largely maintained by one Henri Delage, is of little interest for students of the Austro-Hungarian *Fin de siècle*, although concepts like 'magnetic' and 'fluid' do retain an esoteric meaning in some Decadent writers (Marten, Meyrink, Karásek). The theories of magnetism had little impact. They just became part of the fashionable terminology for expressing relations of influence between individuals.

Spiritualism and spiritism were more important. Spiritism appeared on the Continent from the Anglo-Saxon lands in the mid-1840s. Pierrot states that Allan Kardec had been its most influential proponent during the first ten years of the Second Empire. Goodrick-Clarke gives an account of its spread in the Austrian Lands, particularly in its occultist manifestation under the influence of the Theosophists. It seems to have been Zeyer, who was a student of Western and Eastern occultism, who brought the movement to Prague from Paris, in 1871. The spiritists he became interested in, the school of Paul Gibier, were on the side of natural science against Christianity and all religion.[397] The spiritualist movement grew particularly quickly amongst the peasantry of the Monarchy. It had a strong following in the Tyrol, Upper Austria and Northern Bohemia. This form of spiritualism (rappings and *séances*) began in the United States on 31 March, 1848 in Hydesville near Arcadia, N.Y., when two young girls were one night found by their parents talking with spirits.[398] Writers did become involved in this spiritualism in its early stages in France, for example, Catulle Mendès or Villiers de l'Isle Adam, but it does not appear that they took it very seriously.

Occultism proper, however, was often taken very seriously. The French occultists disliked Blavatsky's theosophy, and sought the elements of arcane knowledge in Western thought (including Assyria, Egypt and Israel) and did not, like Blavatsky (and Zeyer), try to combine Western and Oriental thought, to find the Perennial Philosophy. Lévi and his disciples asserted that there was an unbroken Western tradition of secret thought; they held to the Platonic principle of universal analogy; they, like the spiritists, sought to re-establish a harmony between religion and the natural sciences, in other words, were consciously reacting to the failure of religion; they were intent on learning the art of white magic. Lévi's main occultist interest was in the Cabala, but he also taught the Tarot. His follower, Stanslas de Guaïta, together with Péladan, founded the new Cabalistic order of the Rosy Cross. When Boullan died, Huysmans believed that Péladan and de Guaïta had killed him by black magic.[399] The most thorough exponent of occultism in Czech *fin-de-siècle* literature was Lešehrad.

The far earlier Vintrasians, who represent the 'mystical' rather than occultist trend, were connected with Boullan and the Decadents, especially through the fact that Huysmans had a Vintrasian priestess as his house-keeper. According to Huysmans the Vintrasians promised a 'reign of liberty, goodness and love' before the Second Coming of Christ.[400] The

Vintrasians celebrated a Mass of Melchizedek (Sacrifice de Gloire de Melchissédech) which was meant to be the Mass of the future, a Mass which would be offered up to for God for a regenerate mankind. This mass served to destroy evil spirits while glorifying the God of the Holy Ghost and Love. The working-class Pierre-Michel Vintras's visions, an account of which is given in his *Le Livre d'or: revelations de l'archange saint Michel* (The golden book: revelations from the Archangel St Michael, 1849), commanded him to found a sect to prepare for the coming of the Paraclete, which he duly did. The sect spread and in 1852 the Vintrasians, who adopted complex Hebrew names, were accused of heresy and went into exile in Belgium and England. The ideas of the Vintrasians had no great impact on the *Fin de siècle*, but they came to form part of the general occultist background like the ideas of magnetism. Because Vintrasian beliefs were influenced by the Gnostics, they did appeal to the elitism of the period: higher knowledge is not acquirable by the intellect, but only by enlightenment.[401] Their anti-intellectualism perhaps appealed to *fin-de-siècle* man just because he was so cerebral.

The Vintrasians' development into Valentinism, the belief that salvation would come through Woman also appealed to the Decadents' ambivalent attitude to woman. Valentinism was a form of gnosticism by which Wisdom (Sophia) had fallen from the realm of light into the realm of matter. Sophia was uncreated wisdom which had fallen into the realm of created wisdom, but she, as the Virgin Mary, retained a duality. On earth Sophia was a mixture of spirit and matter and the intercessor between the realm of dark (the world) and the realm of light (the other world, or heaven or supernal knowledge). It was on account of their attitude to Woman and of the participation of women in their rites that charges of indulging in obscene orgies were levelled against the Vintrasians.[402] It is possible that this aspect of Vintrasian teaching influenced Vrchlický and Borecký. In early Březina the idea of attaining god or unity with the Supreme Being through woman may be linked with Vintrasian thought, but equally well it could derive from the Baroque notion of attaining spiritual love through material love.

Péladan's and de Guaïta's new Cabalist Rosicrucian order, established in 1888, was not directly linked with the Rosicrucianism which had continued to exist fitfully in Europe for some two centuries. The bank-clerk Péladan appears to have gained his 'mystical' leanings from his elder brother, Adrien, a Cabalist and homeopathic physician, who had been initiated into a Rosicrucian group in Toulouse in 1858.[403] De Guaïta, a schoolfriend of Maurice Barrès's, was of noble origins, unlike his future fellow, Péladan. De Guaïta began as a macabre poet. He was introduced to occultism by Catulle Mendès who told him to read Lévi. The most important member of Péladan and de Guaïta's order was Papus, the man who continued Lévi's work. Because of his fervent Catholicism, Péladan broke with the order in 1890 and founded another called the Order of the Catholic Rosy Cross, the

Temple and the Grail. The aim of this order was to carry out works of mercy in preparation for the Reign of the Holy Ghost. In *L'Art ochlocratique* Péladan wrote that the artist should be a knight in armour waging perpetual war on the bourgeoisie. The artist was also engaged in the symbolic search for the Holy Grail. (That last notion appears frequently in Zeyer's works.) In 1892 Péladan held his first Salon de la Rose-Croix for spiritual art; in the five years these salons existed painters of such importance as Moreau, Puvis de Chavanes, Redon, Délville and Rops exhibited there.[404] The rules of the Salons were as follows, and here again we notice the Decadents' self-conception as the overcomers of the French Revolution:

> The Rosicrucians seek to destroy Realism. They reject all military, patriotic, anecdotal, oriental, rustic and sporting scenes. On the contrary, the Order encourages subjects drawn from Roman Catholic dogma, the interpretation of Oriental theogenies, decorative allegories and the purified nude. The word 'foreign' has no meaning for the Rosicrucians. As far as architecture goes, since this art was destroyed in 1789, the Salon will accept only restorations or projects for fairytale palaces. Finally, the last 'magic rule', no woman shall ever exhibit among the Rosicrucians.[405]

Among the hangers-on of the Péladan set was the young homosexual poet, Edouard Dubus, of whom Karásek was an ardent admirer. Dubus died of an overdose of morphine.[406] The Dutch Decadent painter, Jan Toorop, was also strongly influenced by Rosicrucianism.[407]

The Blue Star Lodge founded in Prague in 1891 by the Austrian deputy Baron de Leonhardi, whose history Goodrick-Clarke outlines, was linked with the Rosicrucians. The Lodge became affiliated with an old weaver who had allegedly been initiated into the Rosicrucians.[408] Meyrink was an active member. Of the occult tidbits concerning Prague in *Der Golem* probably the most interesting is the tale of a house up by the Castle which is visible only in fog. In daylight all one sees there is a grey stone. The narrator's informant continues:

> A great treasure is meant to be buried under that stone and the stone itself is meant to have been laid as the foundation-stone for a house by the order of 'Asiatic Brethren', who allegedly founded Prague. At the end of days a man will live in that house; actually I should not say a man, but a hermaphrodite, a creature made of a combination of man and woman. And he will hear the image of a hare on his coat of arms. By the way, the hare was the symbol of Osiris – and that is probably the *origin* of the custom of Easter bunnies.[409]

Meyrink's novel contains references to the Cabala and many to the Tarot. More interesting than that for the Decadence in general are his references to the divided self. Selfness is to be diminished as far as possible according to most esoteric teaching. Meyrink describes the attempt to suppress this selfness:

After all I was standing only at the beginning of the path.
Did I not have any right to happiness?
Is mysticism synonymous with being free of desire?
I overemphasised the 'Ja' in me: let me dream just an hour longer, a minute, a
brief human existence!

And I dreamt with my eyes open:

The gems on the table grew and grew and surrounded me from all sides with
coloured waterfalls. Opal trees stood together in groups and projected the
beams of the sky's light-waves; the sky glistened blue like the wing of a gigantic
tropical butterfly; the beams sprayed sparks over unbounded meadows full of
hot summer air.

I felt thirsty and coiled my limbs in the icy foam of the brooks which
bubbled over rocks of shimmering mother of pearl.[410]

In Zeyer's *Dum "U tonoucí hvězdy"* the division of self is more complex.
Most clearly one has the astral self of the main character, Rojko, but then,
by the end of the novel, one realises that Rojko and the narrator are two
halves of the same person. Rojko is pure impression, feeling, intuition, and
the narrator is the scientist. At the end, after the apparent death of Rojko,
he and the narrator are fused: mysticality and science are fused. The
Hungarian esoteric Decadent writer, Viktor Cholnoky, has a story called 'A
köver ember' (The fat man), where the unattractive narrator relates the
story of a murder of which he himself is the victim.[411] Krúdy's story of split
personality in *A vörös postakocsi* (The red postchase, 1917), however
blatantly Freudian, could also be interpreted as an esoteric description of
the divided self. (It is sometimes difficult to distinguish between Freud and
esoteric thought – though it was his erstwhile friend and colleague, Jung,
who eventually openly took the esoteric path.)

The esoteric use of symbols is often very close to the Decadent
(Symbolist) use of symbols. When he is discussing Papus, Pierrot describes
the occultist theory of symbols as a system, 'whereby, as a result of vertical
correspondences, each object in the perceptible world becomes the material
clue to an invisible reality.'[412] It may be cheating, but if one takes one of the
poems Kugel selects for analysis, Saint-Pol-Roux's 'Liminaire' (1893),[413]
the difficulty of distinguishing between the occultist system and Decadent
non-system of symbols becomes clear. The poem pretends to be addressed
to an adolescent poet, but actually describes that adolescent poet. At one
point he speaks of a pink clock of existence evoking the poet's phantom at a
table of fools. The phantom is the astral self, and the 'table of fools' does
suggest a ritual, as Kugel suggests. It also, however, recalls Arthurian
legend as well as the concept fools in Christ or holy fools. Then the pink or
rosy clock of existence assumes fuller meaning as does the mention two lines
later of the 'the faith of sunflowers'. Kugel points out that the sunflowers
imply faith connected with the unending rising and setting of the sun, cyclical
time. They also imply, however, passing through light and darkness. Only in

the day can the sunflower follow the sun, and so rosy existence is not so rosy. And the rose is the Cross of Christ, and so on. Some of Trakl's verse reads like distilled Saint-Pol-Roux.

The symbol as used by Saint-Pol-Roux or, more so, Mallarmé is only interpretable by the initiate. The true Symbolist poem has either to be studied like the Cabala or has to be allowed to well over one like waves of musical impressions. The most banal things in banal reality may hide symbols or be made into symbols. An easy example of that is Mallarmé's little poem on the seller of garlic and onions. Meyrink is positively didactic about the Czech card game played in pubs, *taroky* (i.e., about its link with the Tarot, the Hebrew alphabet – 22 –, the Hebrew Torah and the Egyptian word for 'the one who is asked'); after the didactic passage Meyrink writes: 'under the words there opened an abyss of ever new meaning.'[414] The occultist's new meanings are virtually infinite; the Decadent's, however, are generally finite. Though, again, one might make an exception of a Mallarmé or Hlaváček.

Occultist linguistic elitism is, however, based on words or letters which are learnable, for which one needs no imagination. Their existential elitism is different. One of the most important Ancient thinkers for them was the leading neo-Platonist, Plotinus, who writes, for example, 'Gold is degraded when it is mixed with earthly particles; if these be worked out, the gold itself is left and is beautiful . . . And so the soul; let it be but cleared of the desires that came by its too intimate converse with the body, emancipated from the passions.'[415] The eponymous heroine of Marten's *Cortigiana* is reading Plotinus as a girl when she is raped. Thus she has been forced not to abide by asceticism externally, though she abides by it internally for the rest of her life. She becomes the most celebrated courtesan and she practises her asceticism in her mockery of her own body, mocking men's bodies by providing them with sensual pleasure, the 'pleasure' of darkness. Her self-control begins to slacken when she realises she has contracted the plague and she begins to be morbid about the fact that her beauty will soon putrefy. She soon restores that self-control, however, by providing death for the many men to whom she pretends to give herself that night.

The elitism of occultism often is or appears arrogant. The occultists' denial of a disunity of good and evil is as arrogant as the Decadents' cult of evil, but the occultists were not generally aware of being artificial, however many charlatans there were among them. Buckley writes of Decadent 'evil' as it appeared in art as 'actually for the most part, like Decadent style, an artificial growth, the calculated product of a curious sensibility; and as such it reflected not the terrors of the objective world but the spiritual isolation of the artist, striving too deliberately to transcend the moral values of a middle-class convention.'[416] The Decadent may put his cultivation of dreams to the same use as the occultist who tries to liberate his imagination into meaningful dreams. Pierrot gives the example of Villiers de l'Isle Adam who developed his oneiric faculties as a 'means of demonstrating the primacy of the internal universe over the external world'.[417] The occultist would express internal and external thus: the primacy of the macrocosm (the universal mind, the hidden forces) over the microcosm (man, selfness). The danger for both the Decadent and the occultist is that he may end up with little but 'sterilising abstractions'.[418] Beineberg in *Törless* puts the occultist stance arrogantly: 'people like Basini . . . signify nothing; they are an empty, chance form. Real human beings are those who are able to penetrate themselves, cosmic human beings who are capable of submerging themselves until they reach their correspondence with the great global process.'[419]

The most obvious forms of occultism in true Decadent or preDecadent literature are Luciferism and Satanism. In Luciferism, because of his name and his connection with Venus (light-bearer, morning star), Lucifer is seen as the principle of light, even the Holy Ghost. Léon Bloy has been considered a conscious Luciferist because of 'aspects of his symbolic view of history and his belief in the mission of the outcast'.[420] Before Bloy, Nerval had given the exile an occultist meaning; he conceives of a race of outcasts who, 'by their rebellion against the demiurge who rules the world, are the expression of truth and freedom'.[421] In his notion of the great place suffering will have in the redemption of the world, Bloy saw a great role for the poor and for the outcast race, the Jews (cf. his *Le Salut par les Juifs*). Lucifer, is, then, the archetype of the outcast. What the Czech poet, S. K. Neumann, suggests is his own Satanism, is in fact Luciferism. In *Satanova sláva mezi námi* Satan is the saviour of mankind who will relieve modern man of the suffocating burden laid upon him by Christ's teaching. Christ had betrayed Satan. Satan is a rebel and a friend of all rebels. He is a beautiful, pale Adonis with darkly glowing eyes. He is also the sun and the summoner to sun-worship. Luciferism fuses with Satanism in Neumann, when, in the poems 'Credo' and 'Ad te clamamus' he claims that mankind has been reborn through women's sexual passion; male sperm is the baptismal agent for this rebirth and Satan's Real Presence is in that sperm.

Stock Satanism consists in an inversion of Christian rituals, in Black Masses, and the cult of unchastity, such as it is described in Huysmans's *Là-bas*. Boullan's practices seem to have been Satanist. Griffiths informs us that 'among the healing methods which he used some of the least horrifying appear to have been the mixtures of consecrated host, urine and faecal matter which he applied to the nuns of [his] Order when they were ill.'[422] Stanislas de Guaïta published an account of some of Boullan's doctrines in *Le Temple de Satan* (1891). Bois's Satan declares that he is 'Man, Life and Death', and: 'I shall purify my black father, the Abyss, / The stones of evil will build the Truth.'[423] Satan had traditionally been linked with sex. In the Middle Ages, when Satan and the Devil were usually synonyms, the Devil was depicted with 'a snake-like sexual organ. It was hard and exceptionally large, and because it was forked like a serpent's tongue, he was able to perform coition and buggery simultaneously.'[424] Satan or the Devil was also traditionally linked with forbidden knowledge (not only carnal, cf. Flaubert's *La Tentation de saint Antoine*), and since the occultists were generally striving for superior knowledge they were likely to be lured towards Satanism. Even if in literature that was usually little more than a gesture, as was the case with Karásek's few Satanist poems. In 'Setkání' (Meeting, *Sexus necans*), the *persona*'s altar is said to be covered with excretions of wine from orgies and crumbs of the Host which had been used in a Black Mass. That is really only a matter of shocking the bourgeois like, say, the ending of Baudelaire's 'Le Possédé' (The possessed one) where the *persona* declares that every fibre of his quivering body is calling out that it loves Beelzebub. Pierrot suggests that the reemergence of Satan as a literary subject in the Decadents manifested an 'exacerbation of [. . .] religion-orientated anxiety'; a feeling of guilt in these artists, he suggests, increased 'the consciousness of evil and sin' and so the Devil or Satan became near automatic expressions or reflections of that consciousness.[425] Jullian agrees with the Decadent Lorrain that cultural snobbery had a great deal to do with the spread of Satanism in *fin-de-siècle* Paris.[426] For the non-Satanist occultist Lévi, 'The Devil is the beast, or rather, the beastliness, the stupidity which governs the multitudes; he is *the attraction, the fatal magnetism of evil.* / This magnetism of evil . . . leads astray the pagans, these persecutors of the Christians, as well as the Christians themselves, persecutors of free thought.'[427] Actually that conception of the Devil is close to orthodox Christian.

Charles Morice averred that 'Every true poet is instinctively an initiate', i.e. of the occult.[428] That is a worthless statement, factually, but it does demonstrate how widespread occultism was perceived to be and how much it was considered part of literary sensibility in the *Fin de siècle*.[429]

XVII. THE FIN DE SIÈCLE, ITS AFTERMATH AND THE 'SIXTIES'

The Decadence did not die with World War I; indeed, during that war Decadent playfulness attained one of its zeniths in Dadaism and in Apollinaire. Movements like Proletarian Poetry in the 1920s appeared to constitute the antithesis of the Decadence – though even there one will find Decadent imagery, particularly liturgical imagery. Still, however, influential individual Decadent artists (Lautréamont, Rimbaud, Březina) may have been in the 1920s, it was not until the pessimistic 1930s that the Decadence could have its first revival, indeed its only real revival. Wilhelm Reich's writing on sexuality may be seen as the 1930s continuation of the Decadence. Fear dominated the 1930s in central and eastern Europe and that fear was an intense form of Decadent catastrophism. The artists of the 1930s were almost automatically politically *engagés*, unlike those of the *Fin de siècle*, but as the 1930s proceeded, so did nihilism.

The preoccupations of the 1930s intelligentsia were similar to those of the *fin-de-siècle* intelligentsia, free love, the role of woman, the destruction of form, dreams (Surrealism), magic and the occult (especially astrology) and artistic cosmopolitanism. In the 1930s Paris also played a cultural role similar to that it had played in the Belle Epoque. Then, in the 1940s, there was again no time for the Decadence.

The 'Sixties' saw its resurgence. Nevertheless, where in the *Fin de siècle* the Decadence was elitist and the Decadents were marginal to society, in the Sixties Decadence became a mass movement. One might say that the Sixties saw the vulgarisation of elitism.

The *Fin de siècle* bears a striking political, social and artistic resemblance to the Sixties. It is also as vague a delineation of time. In Britain the Sixties probably begins in 1963 with the Beatles and ends in 1972 or 1973, with all the strikes and the fall of Edward Heath. In Britain the Sixties was, significantly enough, heralded by mass-produced reproductions of graphic art by Beardsley and Alphonse Mucha. In France the dates are similar, but in West Germany it began later, perhaps not much before the student riots, though again the period was over by 1973. In Austria the position was similar to that of West Germany though one could say that the period continued until far later in the 1970s, at least in the arts. In Czechoslovakia the period began in 1963 with the first Havel play, but then was halted by the fall of Dubček in April, 1969. In Slovakia it actually probably continued until the mid 1970s, though there were a few hiccups around 1970–1. In Yugoslavia it began around 1965, but then stopped with the quelling of the second round of student riots in 1972. In Hungary the period began possibly in 1965 with Jancsó's film, *The Round-Up*, but probably with the artistic and economic relaxation perceptible in 1968, and at the moment (1988) the Sixties atmosphere seems to be still alive. In Bulgaria it began in 1968 with the beginning of political theatre and the Czechoslovakia Youth Organisation and British Young Liberal fringe activities at the World Youth Festival and ended either in 1977–8 (the 'spy-mania') or, after the Lydmila Zhivkova period, at the beginning of the 1980s with the internal results of the alleged Bulgarian involvement in the attempted assassination of the Pope, the umbrellaing to death of an emigré journalist on Waterloo Bridge, the annihilation of the national identity of a million or so Turkish inhabitants of Bulgaria, and so on.[430] Like the *Fin de siècle* the Sixties soon acquired mythic status.

In none of the cultural areas I am primarily concerned with did the Sixties begin without a cultural and political prelude. That was the same with the *Fin de siècle*. As far as the Sixties is concerned, the first cultural impulses came from the emergence of rock 'n' roll and of the Beat Generation in

America, and the writings of Ionesco and Camus in France. (The British Angry Young Men probably gave a small stimulus to the European Sixties, in that they did question social norms, at least in some measure.) The *nouveau roman* also helped pave the way for the analytical aspect of the Sixties; and for the Sixties suspicion of 'received reality'. It also consciously attempted to create new relationships between reader, author, narrator and depicted character (Butor). Moreover the practitioners of the *nouveau roman* were doubters of meaning and of the panaceas imposed on the world in the East and West by politicians and thinkers after World War II. Robbe-Grillet wrote (more or less like a Decadent): 'the function of art is never to illustrate a truth – or even a questioning – which is previously known, but to proffer questionings (and perhaps also, in time, answers) which do not yet know themselves.'[431] The main politicophilosophical preparers for the Sixties were Erich Fromm and Wilhelm Reich, and then late Sartre and Herbert Marcuse.

The *Fin de siècle* was a period of affluence for the middle classes. The Sixties was a period of affluence for the lower classes, too. The producers of art remained and will always remain the middle classes (a writer or academic has material and spiritual aspirations which are closer to those of the middle than those of the lower classes; whatever the writer's social origins, the middle classes provide the norms of his or her behaviour). The Sixties was a largely male period – women had almost no active role in the 'counter-culture'. In the 1950s fashion (clothes, the new pop-music) was, for the first time in the history of Europe, set predominantly by the lower classes. The Sixties saw the gradual embourgeoisement of working-class impulses. At the end of the 1960s in Britain, and then France, the working class re-asserted itself with the appearance of skinheads. For some time they managed to survive alongside hippies and Flower People. The skinheads eventually 'won', for, at the end of the Sixties, their descendants, practitioners of punk, funk and the rest, took over. In most of the socialist Europe, punk belongs to the Sixties, but that is because pop-music and the culture surrounding it is largely a preserve of the young intelligentsia in socialist Europe. Working-class protest or barbarism in the West becomes middle-class protest or barbarism in the East.

In the second section of this Conclusory Essay I suggested that one might find political circumstances in individual geographical areas which were favourable to decadence (e.g. France, Bohemia) or unfavourable (Hungary, Britain). Previous to the Sixties the political situation of most cultures of the northern hemisphere were comparable with each other and with the cultures of France, Bohemia or the Austrian Lands in the *Fin de siècle*. Most of those who experienced the affluence and were involved in Sixties culture had known some brand of welfare state for all or most of their socially conscious lives. They had also known austerity, economic and political (McCarthyism, Stalinism – but no economic austerity in America).

The Korean war also remained a sobering reminder of where the Cold War could lead. They had experienced the beginning of the large-scale decolonisation (in the British and French Empires) which would be more or less completed during the Sixties. In America, Germany, France and, largely, in Czechoslovakia and Hungary, the Sixties was predominantly a middle-class movement. The British, who were to become the leaders of fashion and pop-music in the Sixties, had also experienced political abandonment by the Americans in Palestine and then in 1956, in Egypt, again by the Americans, who were, initially at least, the leaders of the mass political movements of youth in the Sixties. (The Viet-Nam War in the western Sixties became the main subject of political *engagement*, after the civil-rights issues had been more or less solved in America.) The same year as the Anglo-French invasion of Egypt witnessed the Soviet quelling of the Hungarian anti-Communist Uprising and the XXth Congress of the Soviet Communist Party, which officially introduced de-Stalinisation. To compare such events with the political events leading up to the *Fin de siècle* might show that I lack a sense of proportion, if one ignores the fact that for the nineteenth century I have been dealing only with middle-class trends and middle-class reactions.

Although the *Fin de siècle* was dominantly pessimist and the Sixties dominantly optimist, the roots of the pessimism and the optimism were at least analogous. *Fin-de-siècle* man imagined he was witnessing the failure of science and liberalism (notions like progress, the perfectability of man, the common weal improvable by science). Sixties man imagined he was witnessing the failure of technology and of socialism (notions like progress, 'engineering the human soul', social equality). That in the West forms of New Left socialist thinking (Marcuse, the crazes for Castro, Mao, Trotsky, Che Guevara and so forth) apparently dominated the little magazines and student rebellions, testifies to the virtual end of all belief in the possibility or desirability of bringing anything like Soviet-style socialism to the West. *Fin-de-siècle* man imagined he saw the failure of conventional religion, as did Sixties man. The Sixties marked the beginning of a godless age, but also of liberation theology, guitars in European churches and charismatic Christianity. It also marked another occult revival. The Sixties revival was marked by apparently insignificant phenomena like pop-festivals and massed-hippy streaking in 'mystical' places like Stonehenge and Glastonbury, and the arrival of Indian gurus. The study of Indian philosophy was far more widespread than it had been in the *Fin de siècle*. Vegetarianism and yoga ceased to be the exclusive preserve of cranks. At the end of the 1960s horoscopes even penetrated the pages of the Czech Socialist Party weekly, *Ahoj na sobotu*. The investigation of esoteric science has increased ever since, particularly in Bulgaria and Czechoslovakia, among intellectuals as much as, if not more than, among ordinary petty bourgeois.[432] In his popular product of the Sixties, *The Occult* (1971), Colin Wilson expresses himself very much like a *fin-de-siècle* man desirous of expanding his consciousness. In his Preface he writes:

> Man's consciousness is as powerful as a microscope; it can grasp and analyse experience in a way no animal can achieve. But microscopic vision is narrow vision. We need to develop another kind of consciousness that is the equivalent of the telescope.
>
> This is Faculty X. And the paradox is that *we already possess it to a large degree*, but are unconscious of possessing it. It lies at the heart of all so-called occult experience.[433]

He unknowingly echoes Morice's words about the relationship between the poet and the occult: 'the poet is a man in whom Faculty X is naturally more developed than in most people.'[434]

The Sixties interest in the occult and in non-European religions went hand in hand with drug-taking,[435] and narcotics had been providers of *paradis artificels* for *fin-de-siècle* man. In the Sixties Aldous Huxley was most revered for his experiments with hallucinogenic fungus, but he made a more significant contribution to the period with his *The Perennial Philosophy* (1946), whose first paperback edition appeared notably in 1958. Huxley's 'anthology' is a reaction to despair at the world's lack of spirituality, at modern man's concentration on selfness. He promotes spiritual liberation through contemplation and spiritual love. The spiritually liberated man is one who is able 'to meet all, even the most trivial circumstances of daily living, without malice, greed, self-assertion or voluntary ignorance, but consistently with love and understanding'. He cites, for example, St Bernard: 'Love seeks no cause beyond itself and no fruit; it is its own fruit, its own enjoyment. I love because I love; I love in order that I may love . . .', or Fénelon: 'all this restless dwelling on self is very far from the peace and freedom of real love'.[436] The Sixties, however, debased such conceptions of love in the period's very optimism. Love became a facile answer to economic, class and political problems. That is exemplified in ludicrous slogans and mottoes like 'Make love, not war' in America or 'socialism with a human face' in Czechoslovakia. The Beatles song which states that 'all you need is love,' helped debase a high ideal; love became utterly materialised.

The Sixties was the age of the contraceptive pill. That and the coil succeeded in providing generally the free love Nordau and the Modernists of the *Fin de siècle*, then the 1930s intelligentsia were demanding. The Sixties turned Huxley's ideals into *Playboy*, groupies and drinks parties all doomed to end with black masses of collective copulation. Marcuse in his 'Political Preface 1966' to *Eros and Civilization* (1955) makes another link with *Fin de siècle*: 'The new bohême, the beatniks and hipsters, the peace creeps – all these "decadents" now have become what decadence probably always was: poor refuge of defamed humanity.'[437] Those who had imagined they were fighting against one-dimensional man became one-dimensional man. With sadness Marcuse writes of the failure of his own notions, that man could avoid the fate of a Welfare-Through-Warfare State only by achieving a new starting point where he could reconstruct the productive apparatus without that 'innerworldly asceticism' which provided the mental basis for domination and exploitation. This image of man was the determinate negation of Nietzsche's superman: man intelligent enough and healthy enough to dispense with all heroes and heroic virtues, man without the impulse to live dangerously, to meet the challenge; man with the good conscience to make life an end-in-itself, to live in joy, a life without fear. 'Polymorphous sexuality' was the term which I used to indicate that the new direction of progress would depend completely on the opportunity to activate repressed or arrested *organic*, biological needs: to make the human body an instrument of pleasure rather than labor.[438]

One needs to forget the word 'progress', but otherwise these words cannot fail to remind one of *fin-de-siècle* hedonism, the rejection of the 'Protestant work ethic', so fostered by such as T. G. Masaryk; Marcuse's desire was to *épater le bourgeois* in a more vehement and effective manner than Nietzsche and the Decadents had been able to. Marcuse's polymorphous sexuality is inseparable from the Cult of the Orgasm inspired by Reich, whom he now rejects. With his *Essay on Liberation* (1969) Marcuse enthusiastically embraces the Sixties youth culture, however.

In what remains perhaps the most perceptive essay on the Sixties, 'The New Mutants' (*Partisan Review*, 1965), Leslie Fiedler (who himself joined in the 1968 anti-Viet-Nam tax rebellion) describes the young's perception of Reich and his idea of full genitality: 'Young men and women eager to be delivered of traditional ideologies of love find especially congenial the belief that not union or relationship (much less offspring) but physical release is the end of the sexual act; and that, therefore, it is a matter of indifference with whom or by what method one pursues the therapeutic climax, so long as that climax is total and repeated frequently.'[439] The permissive society, as long as that means the promiscuous society, reached socialist countries before it reached western Europe, though by a different route. That appears to have been a result of the social engineering of the Fifties, of the officially avowed desire to rid society of 'residual bourgeois values'. The 1930s and then Sixties Reichian Cult of the Orgasm may be compared with the Decadent cult of ecstasy. The theoretical intentions were similar, the liberation of the individual from the strictures of received values and institutions, the liberation of self. But again the Sixties ended in debasement. The individual became part of a mass individualism. Oppressive optimism made orgasm a goal which if unachieved left the individual 'unfulfilled' – a Sixties term which was as hollow as the hollowest Decadent cliché. Frustration was as close to the centre of Sixties culture as of Decadent. The Decadent search for a true self freed of Victorian bourgeois ideals was replicated in the Sixties in the Eriksonian 'identity crisis'. Again, the Sixties formalised, where, generally speaking, the *Fin de siècle* was still searching. The Sixties had solutions. The Sixties saw itself as a new age, where the *Fin de siècle* saw itself as an age of transition.

That does not mean, however, that the Sixties was not just as much a period of flux as the *Fin de siècle*. That was more so in America and socialist Europe than in western Europe. Of course there were the occupations of the London School of Economics, the burning down of the Garden House Hotel in Cambridge, the self-righteous stubbing out of cigarettes on horses' flanks in Grosvenor Square (the Sixties, very unlike the 1890s was a period of self-righteousness), the white-biked Provos in the Netherlands, the *évènements* of May 1968 in Paris, the riots in West Berlin, the sit-ins, sleep-ins, teach-ins in Cologne, Mainz and so on, 'anti-authoritarian' education movements in Scandinavia and West Germany, but these were little more than expressions of euphoric violence. Undergraduates still danced in white tie and tails in the Pitt Club where the main function of the psychedelic lighting seemed to be to pick out the scurf on their shoulders. So too, in Japan successful firms conscientiously recruited particularly bellicose student protestors. In America and, to a degree, in Northern Ireland, the Sixties did involve a serious restructuring of social institutions, bussing, and the emancipation of the Blacks, in Ulster the emancipation of the Roman Catholics. In socialist Europe, the Sixties meant economic reform (attempts at the decentralisation and 'debureaucratisation' of industry), the rehabilitation of a number of politicians and intellectuals and, primarily, a certain liberalisation of the arts. Liberalisation often initially meant the return to a concentration on the individual from a concentration on the collective. The new dominance of the *Ich-Form* in fiction epitomised that. Furthermore, again at least initially, the Sixties in socialist Europe involved a looking backwards (it involved a looking forwards in the West). There was a reckoning with the Fifties, with 'the mistakes of the Personality Cult' and, in Hungary, with 1956 (for example, Déri). Directions in the socialist European Sixties remained vague and were usually subsumed in the catch-all term 'democracy'. Only two of the socialist contries had had a tradition of anything like Western democracy, East Germany and Czechoslovakia. The leading roles of Communist Parties were never seriously challenged. Hence the vagueness of direction.

One of the characteristic signs of the *Fin de siècle* as a period of flux lay in its attitude to gender, in the figure of the androgyne, and in the treatment of homosexuality. That is paralleled in the Sixties. First, we have so-called sexual liberation which was a 'male chauvinist' debauching of woman (cf. the vulgarity of periodicals like *Blow-Job*). Instead of the New Woman, the Sixties apparently conceived of a New Man. Again Fiedler is perceptive. He sees the young men of particularly the Anglo-Saxon world trying to assimilate themselves with the two sections of society from which they are definitely different, women and Blacks. (This is going on parallel to the cross, sadistic sexual-liberation movement.) He connects the non-sexing of the male with Whitman, a poet who had an immense impact on European *Fin de siècle* (cf. the essays of J. A. Symonds, Havelock Ellis and Karásek):

'It is not absolutely required that the antimale antihero be impotent or homosexual or both (though this helps, as we remember remembering Walt Whitman), merely that he be more seduced than seducing, more passive than active.' He further links Sixties culture with antisemitism and the sacred or fatal book: 'the posthumanist, post-male, post-white, post-heroic world is a post-Jewish world by the same token, anti-Semitism is inextricably woven into it as into the movement for Negro rights; and its scriptural books are necessarily *goyish*, not least of all William Burroughs's *The Naked Lunch.*'[440] (Other sacred books were, for example *Last Exit to Brooklyn*, de Beauvoir's *Le deuxième Sexe*, Greer's *The Female Eunuch*, but also the *Kama Sutra*, *The Perfumed Garden* and Joyce's *Ulysses*.) In homosexual writers like Ginsberg or Harry Mathews Fiedler sees clues to the new attitude to sex and sexuality. Ginsberg's visit to Czechoslovakia was one of the starting-points of the Sixties there (he was crowned King of May in Prague in 1965 and then expelled). In the early Sixties Fiedler sees anti-female bias (Albee's *Who's Afraid of Virginia Woolf?*) Later in the Sixties and particularly immediately as 'Sixties' we have radical women's lib, with conflagrations of brassières. But the Sixties was the period of first the sex-emphasising miniskirt and then the sex-diminishing maxi. It was the period of the artificial beehive hairstyle and the long straight locks. Long straight locks were for males and females, but the males also had pseudo-guru beards redolent of hitchhiking trips to Afghanistan and Nepal. Males wanted to be called beautiful and that was indeed linked, at the time of Fiedler's essay, with the Beatles hair-cut, 'high-heels, jeans tight over the buttocks' and the 'retreat from masculine aggressiveness to female allure'.[441] Later in the Sixties the two sexes became united in non-aggressiveness and a superficial non-sexedness emblemised by long embroidered overcoats and a cultivated dirtiness. What started as a rebellion against bourgeois uniformity became an imposer of a new bourgeois uniformity. A few years after Fiedler, Melly writes that 'there has sprung up a tolerance of bisexuality so powerful as to constitute an ideal. Fashion photography has sold unisex on the widest possible front, and not only within the context of the sophisticated magazines.'[442] The Sixties also led to a cultivation of sexual perversion, which Melly rightly sees in the sadomasochism and fetishism of the early James Bond films. And of a parody of James Bond films he writes, 'You can laugh with an erection, and the overtly camp sadism of *Modesty Blaise* – in particular the breaking of the clown's neck between the legs of a glamorous redhead – is nastier and more effectively sado-masochistic than anything in Bond.'[443] In the run-up to the Sixties Melly also notices necrophilia, a not infrequent subject of Decadent literature (for example, Baudelaire or Zeyer); indeed the origins he suggests for this necrophilia remind one immediately of the *fin-de-siècle* cult of youth: 'There are also a whole list of pop numbers of a necrophiliac tinge, e.g. "Tell Laura I Love Her" and "Teen-Angel", all of which push the idea that a sudden and violent death is a pop happening because it prevents its victim from growing older.'[444] One thinks, too, of the ending of the film, *Bonny and Clyde*.

The so-called sexual revolution of the Sixties had some impact on socialist Europe. Homosexuality was to a degree tolerated. Even the *fin-de-siècle* Czech combination of homosexuality and an inclination to occultism reoccurred in one of the most respected Czech writers of the Sixties and after, Ladislav Fuks (cf. his homosexual depiction of the Communist hero, Fučík, and his occult novel, *Oslovení ze tmy* (1973). But Eastern-Bloc countries had to conduct their own sexual revolution in the arts, because it constituted a part of the reaction against Stalinism, one of whose character-istics was prudery (perhaps: decency) in the arts. Anti-prudery, however, soon became formalised, a semantically void ritual. The most obvious example of that was the obligatory full-frontal naked woman in Hungarian films. The same formalisation had taken place in the West, notably with the musical *Hair*, Melly's facetiousness is justified:

> The final irony is *Hair*, the negation of pop, a completely traditional theatrical presentation sailing under false colours. Here everything, including the invasion of the audience, has been rehearsed with the precision of a military parade. The four-letter words and the famous naked scene are minutely adjusted to shock nobody. The middle-class audience sit bathed in a self-congratulatory glow at its own tolerance.[445]

The main four-letter word of the period, 'fuck', very much represents the emptiness of Sixties liberation, but it also indicates the Sixties fascination with language. Furthermore the trial at the end of 1960 concerning *Lady Chatterley's Lover* may be loosely compared with the trials of Oscar Wilde in the 1890s. These trials all represent art standing up against authority. (The Ruskin and Whistler trial is another example, as, possibly, is the *Oz* trial.) All these trials were equally ludicrous. But so was the propagating of 'fuck'. In the American Sixties 'not only radical protest, but even the attempt to formulate, to articulate, to give word to protest assume a childlike, ridiculous immaturity. Thus it is ridiculous and perhaps "logical" that the Free Speech Movement at Berkeley terminated in the row caused by the appearance of a sign with the four-letter word.'[446] Michael McClure's essay '*Phi Upsilon Kappa*' (1963) and his contemporary 'Fuck Ode' are other examples. For Fiedler they epitomise the Sixties young's attack on language itself, 'the very counters of logical discourse. They seek an antilanguage of protest as inevitably as they seek antipoems and antinovels'; 'fuck', he suggests, ends as 'the ultimate antiword'.[447] But still it could be used with effect by older artists, as it was by W. H. Auden in the last line of his poem in protest at the Warsaw Pact intervention in Czechoslovakia, a poem he declaimed in Great St Mary's, in Cambridge, early in 1969. 'Fuck' penetrated Anglicanism. The Sixties was just as concerned about communi-cation as the *Fin de siècle* had been. That is exemplified by one of the most transitory gurus of the age, Marshall McLuhan, whose *Understanding Media* (1964) became one of the sacred books. That was a typical Sixties irony, since it prophesies the impending final demise of the written word as a form of communication. McLuhan conceives of man in the new age as a gatherer of information, sees the end of man as a contemplative: 'Man the food-gatherer reappears incongruously as information-gatherer. In this role, electronic man is no less a nomad than his paleolithic ancestors.'[448] In his trendy collage sequel, *The Medium is the Massage* (1967; the tital puns on his own refrain in *Understanding Media*, that the medium is the message), he created one of the ludic catchphrases of the Sixties: 'The family circle has widened. The worldpool of information fathered by electric media – movies, Telstar, flight – far surpasses any possible influence mom and dad can now bring to bear. Character no longer is shaped by only two earnest, fumbling experts. Now all the world's a sage.'[449] The belief in the global communicability of everything by the orgasmic grunt was reflected by concrete poetry (something which had actually been invented simultaneously in Switzerland and Brazil before the Sixties). Concrete poetry was often 'written' by natural scientists. The last Czech concrete-verse happening appeared some time after the Sixties was over in Czechoslovakia, and it was not produced by dissidents or emigrés.[450]

Concrete poetry dispensed with language as well as standard poetic form. It was a joke as well as a serious attempt at immediate, simple communication. In prose, too, for one of the bywords of the Sixties declared the death of the novel; form was disrupted. Just form in the Hungarian Őrkény or Czech Páral, form and language in the Hungarian Esterházy or Czech Linhartová. And the reasons were the same as the reasons for the disruption of form in the *Fin de siècle*. As Austrian-German literature was the dominant German Decadent literature, so Austrian literature was usually the most innovative German literature of the Sixties. It was centred on the Vienna Group, one of whose members, H. C. Artmann's, Decadent manifesto was proclaimed in 1953, many years before the Sixties came to Austria. It is a statement of an attitude, not a programme:

1) the poetic act is that writing [*dichtung*] which rejects all second-hand reproduction, that is, every communication transmitted by the spoken or written word, or by music.

2) the poetic act is writing purely for writing's sake; it is pure writing, free of all ambition of recognition, praise or criticism.

3) a poetic act will perhaps be transmitted to the public only by chance. But that will be only in a hundred cases. Out of every respect for its beauty and purity it should never intend becoming public, for it is an act of the heart and of pagan modesty.

4) the poetic act is strongly consciously extempore and is anything but a mere poetic situation, which has no need of the writer [*dichters*]. Any old fool can enter a poetic situation without ever being aware of it.

5) the poetic act is the noblest form of pose, free of all vanity and full of merry modesty.

6) we count among the most venerable masters of the poetic act in the first place the satanistic-elegaic Claudius Drusus Nero and above all [*sic*] our lord, the philosophical-human Don Quixote.

7) the poetic act is entirely worthless materially and thus can never conceal the bacillus of prostitution. Its very execution is simply noble.

8) the executed poetic act recorded in our memory is one of the very few riches we can really take with us without its being expropriated.

The writers whom the Vienna Group first adopted as models and recited in their demonstrative procession were linked with the Decadence: Baudelaire, Poe, Nerval, Trakl and Ramón Gómez de la Serna.[451] The Vienna Group was as concerned with performance (particularly cabaret) as with the composing of texts. Two contrasting but representative prose products of the Group are Konrad Bayer's macabre short novel about the epileptic Bering, *Der Kopf des Vitus Bering* (1965, Vitus Bering's head) and Oswald Wiener's *Die Verbesserung von Mitteleuropa* (1969, The improvement of central Europe), a usually deadly serious cynical, misanthropic work, which does frequently reveal humour. In Bayer's novel, syntax and meaning are almost grotesquely disrupted, for example, 'when or more accurately the heralds entered the gardens garden, the clock while struck the in the number in the clocktower striking in the following hours has no influence on the sequence of the events.'[452] Wiener employs a different sort of disruption, that of analysis, so that the reader's perception is concentrated on form rather than action, for example:

> b) *the guests introduce each other*
> noun table! how do you do, noun being
> noun sensation! noun brown
> verb sit! noun thinking
> pronoun I! a pleasure! adjective hard![453]

That sort of writing reflects the way in which art became something of a religion in the Sixties as it had done in the *Fin de siècle*. The mockery or disruption of recognised form is in itself a recognition of form. That goes for the Campbell's soup tins and Marilyn Monroes as much as for the prose of the Vienna Group. George Melly, himself becoming transfixed by the grand generalisations of the Sixties, not only recognises the religiousness of the teeny-bopper fans, but imagines them yearning for spiritual experience as much as the Berkeley, Woodstock and Stonehenge junkies:

> The teenage furies didn't make their idols; they accepted them as idols ready-made. . . . the love and fury is not resentment as such, but something much more primitive; a religious impulse; the need to sacrifice the Godhead in order to elevate it above temporal considerations. And just because the overt emphasis is sexual rather than spiritual [that] in no way invalidates this argument. Throughout history religious enthusiasm at this level is frequently indistinguishable from sexual hysteria.[454]

The popstars themselves, those who did not die of an overdose or who were not particularly ephemeral phenomena, became also the buyers of art. By the late Sixties they had something of the function of the Jews in Vienna at the turn of the century. The Institute of Contemporary Art was founded in the heart of traditional regal London as a temple to Sixties artistic rebellion. Rebellion became ritualised, and became hedonistic.

Hedonism may be a form of pessimism, but hedonism can be ritualised, as part of oppressive optimism. Still Nietzsche's point is valid, and helps to explain Barthes's own high Sixties sensualist hedonism, as it is explicit in *Le Plaisir du texte* (1973):

> for Nietzsche himself hedonism is a form of pessimism. *Plaisir* is ceaselessly deceived, reduced, deflated, to the profit of strong, noble values; Truth, Death, Progress, Struggle, Joy, etc. Its victorious rival is Desire: we are always being told about Desire, never *Plaisir*; Desire is said to have an epistemic dignity but not *Plaisir*. It is said that society (our society) rejects (and ends by not knowing) *jouissance* so much that it can produce only epistemologies of the Law (and of the contestation of the Law), never of its absence, or better still: of its nullity. . . . (A rather crass, but still noteworthy presumption of proof: what is 'popular' does not know Desire, knows nothing but *plaisirs*.)[455]

Barthes's sensualism is altogether reminiscent of the Decadents'. It is anti-positivist: 'We shall be scientific for want of subtlety.'[456] And it thus contains an essentially synaesthetic approach. From the point of view of *jouissance* writing seeks 'pulsional incidents; it is language papered with skin, a text where one can hear the texture of the throat, the patina of the consonants, the voluptuousness of the vowels, a whole stereophony of deep flesh: the articulation of the body, of the *langue*, not that of sense, of the *language*.'[457] Like a Decadent he imagines that fear might be the same thing as *jouissance*; he rejects the idea that fear is an unpleasant emotion, but suggests that one is slow to identify fear with *jouissance*, because there is something mediocre and undignified about fear.[458] In Barthes's sensualist taxonomy the *plaisir* of the text lies in the classics, in 'culture (the more culture there is, the greater, the more diverse the *plaisir*). Intelligence. Irony. Delicateness, Euphoria. . . . The *plaisir* of the text can be defined by, say, time and place of reading.' Texts of *jouissance* are '*plaisir* in pieces; language in pieces; culture in pieces. They are perverse in that they are outside all imaginable finality – *even that of* plaisir (*jouissance* does not compel *plaisir*; it can even be apparently boring.' The *plaisir* of a text is not stable. One can never be sure it will please a second time round; it is 'precarious'. With Decadently suggestive abandon he continues: 'the *jouissance* of the text is not precarious; it is worse: *precocious*; it does not come in its time; it does not depend on any maturation. All is ravished at once.'[459]

Barthes had always been concerned with language and considered that modern literature's primary concern had been with language since the *Fin de siècle*. It is not by chance that linguistics flourished so rankly in the Sixties. It is almost a Sixties academic subject. Like comparative literature or sociology. The cult of art in the Sixties brought with it its vulgarisation. Even in European universities the Sixties introduced the examination of literature by multiple-choice questions. The arts became culture, just what the artists of the *Fin de siècle* were striving against, and just what Aldous Huxley observed with horror was happening long before the Sixties began and long before the United Kingdom bowed to the vulgar European notion of a Minister for the Arts:

> Because it was German and spelt with a *K, Kultur* was an object, during the First World War, of derisive contempt.[460] All this has now been changed. . . . the cult of Culture [is not] confined to the Soviet Union. It is practised by a majority of intellectuals in the capitalist democracies . . . With an earnestness and enthusiasm that are, in circumstances, unutterably ludicrous, [clever, hard-boiled journalists] invite us to share their positively religious emotions in the face of High Art . . .; they insist that so long as Mrs X goes on writing her inimitable novels and Mr Y his more than Coleridgean criticism, the world, in spite of all appearances to the contrary, makes sense. The over-valuation of Culture [. . . has] even invaded the schools and colleges. Among 'advanced' educationists there are many people who seem to think that all will be well so long as adolescents are permitted to 'express themselves', and small children are encouraged to be 'creative' in the art class.[461]

The Sixties brought this 'self-expression' and 'creativeness' to fruition and thus debased the creative aristocratism of the *Fin-de-siècle*. All the world became an artist, or so they thought. The Sixties saw mass individualism. *Seine Majestät das Ich* became *ihre Majestät das Wir*. At least by the end the Sixties was a sort of middle-class ochlocracy. Where in the *Fin de siècle* art suggested, in the Sixties it bullied.

Fin-de-siècle decadence was halted by the Great War, 1930s decadence by the World War, but the Sixties was halted (where it has been halted) by yobbocracy in western and socialist Europe. The western European yuppie has his equivalent in Czechoslovakia, Hungary and recently even in Bulgaria. And socialist-bloc yuppies are by no means necessarily members of the Communist Party.

NOTES

1. Freidrich Nietzsche, *Menschliches, Allzumenschliches. Ein Buch für freie Geister* (1878–9), Vol. I, Munich, 1960, p. 190.
2. Arnošt Procházka, *Francouzští autoři a jiné studie*, Prague, 1912, p. 109.
3. George Ross Ridge, *The Hero in French Decadent Literature*, Athens, Georgia, 1961, p. 176.
4. Jerome Hamilton Buckley, *The Victorian Temper. A Study in Literary Culture*, 2nd ed., Cambridge, Mass., 1969, p. 228.
5. Cf. Jean Pierrot, *The Decadent Imagination, 1880–1900*, translated by Derek Coltman, Chicago and London, 1981, p. 47.
6. Sir Ernst Gombrich, ' "Sind eben alles Menschen gewesen." Zum Kulturrelativismus in den

Geisteswissenschaften'. A lecture given to the International Association for Germanic Language and Literature Studies at Göttingen in August, 1985, TS, p. 2.

7. In 'Der deutsche Mensch als Symptom' (1923), quoted by Edelgard Hajek, *Literarischer Jugendstil. Vergleichende Studien zur Dichtung und Malerei um 1900*, Düsseldorf, 1971, p. 18.

8. Alfred de Musset, *La Confession d'un enfant du siècle*, Paris, 1973, pp. 82–3.

9. Ibid., p. 36.

10. Max Nordau, *Die conventionellen Lügen der Kulturmenschheit*, 14th ed., Leipzig, 1889, pp. 2–3.

11. F. X. Šalda, *Loutky i dělníci boží. Román milostný o dvou dílech*, [1917], 3rd ed., Prague, 1920, Vol. II, p. 34.

12. Ibid., II, pp. 35–6.

13. Ibid., II, pp. 36–7.

14. Ibid., II, pp. 42–3.

15. Ibid., II, p. 56.

16. Richard Schaukal, *Leben und Meinungen des Herrn Andreas von Balthesser, eines Dandy und Dilettanten*, Munich and Leipzig, 1907, p. 166.

17. Alfred Kubin, *Die andere Seite. Phantastischer Roman*, Munich, 1962, p. 40.

18. Edward Timms, 'Peter Altenberg – Authenticity or Pose?' in G. J. Carr and Eda Sagarra (Eds.), *Fin-de-Siècle Vienna. Proceedings of the Second Irish Symposium in Austrian Studies*, Dublin, 1985, p. 129.

19. Jack J. Spector, *The Aesthetics of Freud. A Study in Psychoanalysis and Art*, London, 1972, pp. 20–1.

20. Arnold Hauser, *Sozialgeschichte der Kunst und Literatur* [1953], Munich, 1967, p. 971.

21. Georg Trakl, 'Anif', *Gedichte* (ed. Hans Szklenar), Frankfurt on Main and Hamburg, 1964, p. 56.

22. Gary B. Cohen, 'Society and Culture in Prague, Vienna and Budapest in the Late Nineteenth Century', *East European Quarterly*, XX, 4 (January 1987), pp. 468, 479, 480.

23. Franz Kuna, 'Vienna and Prague 1890–1928', Malcolm Bradbury and James McFarlane (Eds.), *Modernism 1890–1930*, Harmondsworth, 1976, p. 124.

24. Ibid., p. 130.

25. 'Jsme v Čechách do osudu zazděni. / To pochopit – je české umění.' 'České umění' in the posthumous collection of verse edited by the leading Czech Parnassist, a poet without whom the Czech Decadence would probably not have thrived so well, Jaroslav Vrchlický, *Na zemi a na nebi*, Prague, 1900, p. 16.

26. 'Píseň nenárodní', *Apostrofy hrdé a vášnivé* [1896], *Básně I*, Prague, 1962, p. 127.

27. *Literární silhouetty a studie*, Vinohrady, 1912, p. 16.

28. *Cities*, London and New York, 1903, pp. 140–2.

29. Ibid., p. 150.

30. Ibid., pp. 153–4. Describing Prague as a woman: a queen or a whore, was a frequent topos of Czech *fin-de-siècle* literature.

31. G. S. Street, *People and Questions*, London, 1910, p. 276.

32. Ibid., p. 286.

33. Ibid., pp. 299–300.

34. Cf. Viola Finn, 'Zsigmond Justh: In Search of a New Nobility', in László Péter and Robert B. Pynsent (Eds.), *Intellectuals and the Future in the Habsburg Monarchy 1890–1914*, Basingstoke and London, 1988, p. 129 ff.

35. André Karátson, *Le Symbolisme en Hongrie. L'influence des poétiques françaises sur la poésie hongroise dans le premier quart du XXième siècle*, Paris, 1969, pp. 39–41.

36. *Die andere Seite*, p. 24.

37. *Cities*, pp. 189–91.

38. Cf. Karátson, *Le Symbolisme en Hongrie*, pp. 55, 68, 69.

39. Cf. Cohen, 'Society and Culture in Prague, Vienna and Budapest', pp. 470 and 479.

40. Cf. Lórant Czigány, *The Oxford History of Hungarian Literature From the Earliest Times to*

the Present, Oxford, 1984, p. 264.

41. Ibid., pp. 279–80.

42. Karátson, *Le Symbolisme en Hongrie*, p. 14.

43. J. Š. Baar, *Jan Cimbura. Jihočeská idyla*, 14th ed., Prague, 1940, p. 363.

44. In the following remarks I largely follow the excellent brief survey of Jonny Moser, 'Antisemitismus und Zionismus im Wien des Fin de Siècle', in the catalogue to the 1985 Vienna exhibition, *Traum und Wirklichkeit, Wien 1870–1930*, p. 260 ff.

45. Quoted by Spector, *The Aesthetics of Freud*, p. 21.

46. Quoted by Hinrich C. Seeba, *Kritik des aesthetischen Menschen. Hermeneutik und Moral in Hofmannsthals 'Der Tor und der Tod'*, Bad Homburg, Berlin, Zurich, 1970, p. 33.

47. Quoted by Bram Dijkstra, *Idols of Perversity, Fantasies of Feminine Evil in Fin-de-Siècle Culture*, New York and Oxford, 1986, pp. 220–1. This wild, usually unintelligent, narrow-mindedly feminist, uninformed work on mainly French, English and German art is often useful for snippets of information and for illustrations not usually found in works on the Decadence. No student, not even the most radical feminist, should, however, take it too seriously.

48. *Die conventionellen Lügen*, p. 34.

49. Ibid., p. 2.

50. Manfred Gsteiger, *Französische Symbolisten in der deutschen Literatur der Jahrhundert-wende (1869–1914)*, Berne and Munich, 1971, p. 55.

51. Cf. Seeba, *Kritik des aesthetischen Menschen*, p. 34.

52. Mario Praz, *The Romantic Agony*, translated from the Italian by Angus Davidson [1933], London, 1962, p. ix.

53. René Wellek, 'The Term and Concept of Symbolism in Literary History', *Discriminations: Further Concepts of Criticism*, New Haven and London, 1970, p. 108.

54. Pierrot, *The Decadent Imagination*, p. 55.

55. Nordau, *Die conventionellen Lügen*, p. 342.

56. Ibid., p. 1.

57. Ibid., pp. 12–13.

58. Ibid., pp. 29–30.

59. Ibid., pp. 76–7.

60. Ibid., p. 69.

61. Ibid., p. 83.

62. Ibid., p. 172.

63. For example, ibid., pp. 208, 214, 241.

64. Ibid., pp. 240–1.

65. Ibid., p. 277.

66. Ibid., p. 260.

67. Ibid., p. 308.

68. Friedrich Nietzsche, *Jenseits von Gut und Böse. Vorspiel einer Philosophie der Zukunft* [1886], Munich, 1981, p. 68. Perhaps less witty, but on the same theme, a popular *fin-de-siècle* Austro-Hungarian columnist Roda Roda (Sandor Friedrich Rosenfeld) wrote 'Marriage is grounds for divorce'. Elsbeth Roda Roda, *Das grosse Roda Roda Buch*, Berlin, Darmstadt, Vienna, n.d. [1970], p. 330.

69. Nordau, *Die conventionellen Lügen*, pp. 47–8.

70. For example, ibid., pp. 121, 254, 337.

71. Ibid., p. 50.

72. Ibid., p. 242.

73. Franz Brentano, *Vom Ursprung sittlicher Erkenntnis*, [1889], Hamburg, 1969, pp. 7–8.

74. Ibid., pp. 31 and 91. Both Nordau and Brentano base their thoughts on a misunderstanding of the O.T. and N.T. command. What is actually meant is that anyone who does not respect, love himself first cannot possibly respect, love his neighbour. It is a perfectly rational command.

75. Ibid., p. 19.

76. 'Vom Lieben und Hassen' [1907], Ibid., pp. 151–2.

77. Ibid., p. 85.
78. *Die conventionellen Lügen*, p. 17.
79. Karl R. Popper, *The Poverty of Historicism* [1957], London, Melbourne and Henley, 1979, p. iv.
80. Ibid., p. 3.
81. Ibid., p. 78.
82. Hugo von Hofmannsthal, 'Walter Pater', *Ausgewählte Werke in zwei Bänden, II, Erzählungen und Aufsätze*, Frankfurt on Main, 1957, pp. 304–5.
83. Quoted by Linda Dowling, *Language and Decadence in the Victorian Fin de Siècle*, Princeton and Guildford, 1986, p. 112.
84. Gustav Meyrink, *Der Golem. Roman* [1915], Munich, 1970, p. 189.
85. Pierrot, *The Decadent Imagination*, p. 120.
86. *Die conventionellen Lügen*, p. 49.
87. Quoted by Philippe Jullian, *Esthètes et magiciens. L'art fin de siècle*, Paris, 1969, p. 335.
88. Norman Stone, *Europe Transformed 1878–1919*, Glasgow, 1983, pp. 402–3.
89. Arthur Symons, *The Symbolist Movement in Literature* [1889, 1908, 1919], New York, 1958, p. 4.
90. Cf. Fedor Stepun, *Mystische Weltschau. Fünf Gestalten des russischen Symbolismus*, Munich, 1964, p. 230.
91. Hajek, *Literarischer Jungendstil*, pp. 14–15.
92. *Sozialgeschichte der Kunst und Literatur*, p. 958.
93. *Discriminations*, p. 93.
94. Ibid., p. 113.
95. Ibid., p. 118.
96. Quoted by Karátson, *Le Symbolisme en Hongrie*, p. 135.
97. *Language and Decadence*, p. xi.
98. 'Peter Altenberg, Authenticity or Pose?', p. 128.
99. *Der Golem*, p. 192.
100. Cf. Czigány, *Oxford History of Hungarian Literature*, p. 253.
101. Oscar Wilde, *The Works*, London and Glasgow, 1948, pp. 909 and 931.
102. Richard von Schaukal, 'Wilhelm Busch' [1904], *Über Dichter*, Munich and Vienna, 1966, p. 41.
103. Buckley, *The Victorian Temper*, p. 229.
104. Rémy de Gourmont, 'Une religion d'art', *La Culture des idées* [1900], Paris, 1964, p. 111.
105. Cf. Hauser, *Sozialgeschichte der Kunst und Literatur*, p. 952.
106. Ibid., p. 962.
107. Heinrich Merkl, *Ein Kult der Frau und der Schönheit. Interpretationen zur französischen, italienischen und spanischen Lyrik des Fin de siècle*, Heidelberg, 1981, p. 203.
108. Ridge, *The Hero in French Decadent Literature*, p. 48.
109. Quoted by Jullian, *Esthètes et magiciens*, p. 96.
110. James L. Kugel, *The Techniques of Strangeness in Symbolist Poetry*, New Haven and London, 1971, p. 44.
111. Ibid., p. 46.
112. Ibid., p. 61.
113. Seeba, *Kritik des aesthetischen Menschen*, pp. 106–7.
114. Karl Beckson, 'Preface to the First Edition', *Aesthetes and Decadents of the 1890s. An Anthology of British Poetry and Prose*, rev. ed., Chicago, 1981, p. xi.
115. Paul Verlaine, *Choix de poésies*, Paris, 1898, p. 253.
116. Pierrot, *The Decadent Imagination*, p. 10.
117. Ibid., p. 40.
118. Hauser, *Sozialgeschichte der Kunst und Literatur*, p. 948.
119. 'Karl Kraus: Language and Experience', Sigurd Paul Scheichl and Edward Timms (Eds.), *Karl Kraus in neuer Sicht. Londoner Kraus-Symposium*, Munich, 1986, p. 25.

120. *Andreas von Balthesser*, p. 156.
121. Ibid., p. 163.
122. Cf. Dowling, *Language and Decadence*, p. 245.
123. A. E. Carter, *The Idea of Decadence in French Literature 1830–1900*, Toronto, 1958, p. viii.
124. John Addington Symonds, 'On the Application of Evolutionary Principles to Art and Literature', *Essays Speculative and Suggestive* [1890], 3rd ed., London, 1907, pp. 31–3.
125. Gotthart Wunberg (Ed.), *Die literarische Moderne. Dokumente zum Selbstverständnis der Literatur um die Jahrhundertwende*, Frankfurt on Main, 1971, p. 74.
126. Wellek, *Discriminations*, pp. 115–16.
127. Cf. Czigány, *The Oxford History of Hungarian Literature*, p. 255.
128. Quoted by Karátson, *Le Symbolisme en Hongrie*, p. 59.
129. Arthur Schnitzler, *Erzählende Schriften, I. Novellen*, Berlin, n.d., pp. 71–2.
130. Wunberg, *Die literarische Moderne*, p. 73.
131. *Ausgewählte Werke, II*, p. 272.
132. Karel Hlaváček, *Dílo, I, Sokolské básně a studie*, Prague, 1930, p. 9.
133. Jiří Karásek ze Lvovic, *Renaissanční touhy v umění. Kritické studie*, Vinohrady, n.d. [1902], p. 165.
134. Cf. David Daiches, *Some Late Victorian Attitudes*, London, 1969, pp. 40–1.
135. R. K. R. Thornton, *The Decadent Dilemma*, London, 1983, p. 21. Gourmont himself calls *A rebours* a didactic novel. *La Culture des idées*. p. 111.
136. Richard Aldington (Ed.), *The Religion of Beauty. Selections from the Aesthetes*, London, Melbourne, Toronto, 1950, p. 131.
137. Pierrot, *The Decadent Imagination*, p. 8.
138. Hauser, *Sozialgeschichte der Kunst und Literatur*, p. 957.
139. Beckson, *Aesthetes and Decadents*, p. 24.
140. George Moore, *Confessions of a Young Man* [1886], London, 1929, p. 100.
141. Arnošt Procházka, *Meditace*, Prague, 1912, p. 10.
142. *Modernism*, p. 50.
143. Ibid., p. 25.
144. Ibid., p. 26.
145. Ibid., p. 29.
146. *Discriminations*, pp. 91–2. Wellek also rejects the use of the term *die Moderne* here, which is inadmissable because various groups of writers from the 1880s (Germany), turn of the century (Vienna, Prague, Zagreb) and even after the Great War (Bratislava) called themselves the *Moderne*. This term is then precise as a label for a group, even though it may be imprecise in the sense that various members of individual *Moderne* groups may have had various ideas of what *Moderne* meant.
147. Wunberg, *Die literarische Moderne*, p. 52.
148. Ibid., p. 54.
149. F. V. Krejčí *et al.*, 'Česká Moderna', *Rozhledy sociální, politické a literární*, 1896–6, pp. 1–2.
150. Nordau, *Die conventionellen Lügen*, p. 300.
151. Hauser, *Sozialgeschichte der Kunst und Literatur*, pp. 986–7.
152. T. G. Masaryk, *Otázka sociální. Základy marxismu filosofické a sociologické*, 3rd ed., Prague, 1946, Vol. II, p. 91.
153. Arno Schmidt, 'Berechnungen II. Ein Werkstattbericht', *Texte und Zeichen*, 2 (1956), p. 100.
154. *Literarischer Jugendstil*, p. 14.
155. Cf. *Erzählende Schriften*, I. pp. 57, 58, 60.
156. *Die andere Seite*, p. 97.
157. *Aesthetes and Decadents*, p. xxxviii.
158. Hugo von Hofmannsthal, *Die Gedichte und kleinen Dramen*, 2nd ed., Leipzig, 1912, p. 42.

159. *The Romantic Agony*, p. 161.
160. Julius Zeyer, *Spisy*, Vol. XXIV, Prague, 1907, p. 190.
161. Robert Musil, *Die Verwirrungen des Zöglings Törless* [1906], Hamburg, 1959, p. 102.
162. Hauser, *Sozialgeschichte der Kunst und Literatur*, p. 950.
163. Musil, *Törless*, p. 74.
164. Petr Kles, *Pozůstalé spisy prózou i veršem*, Prague, 1931, p. 197.
165. Charles Baudelaire, 'L'Amour et le crâne', *Les Fleurs du mal* [1857, 1861], Paris, 1919, p. 231.
166. *Jenseits von Gut und Böse*, p. 63.
167. Pierrot, *The Decadent Imagination*, p. 123.
168. *The Romantic Agony*, p. 232.
169. *The Works*, p. 560.
170. Ibid., p. 545. Cf. Hajek, *Literarischer Jugendstil*, pp. 56–7.
171. 'Add nekem a szemeidet', quoted by Karátson, *Le Symbolisme en Hongrie*, p. 111.
172. *The Decadent Imagination*, p. 134.
173. George Meredith, *Poems*, Vol. I, Westminster, 1898, p. 52.
174. Cf. P. Labanyi ' "Die Gefahr des Körpers". A Reading of Otto Weininger's *Geschlecht und Charakter*', Carr and Sagarra, *Fin de Siècle Vienna*, p. 162.
175. Pierrot, *The Decadent Imagination*, p. 124.
176. Quoted by Karátson, *Le Symbolisme en Hongrie*, p. 112.
177. Quoted by Hauser, *Sozialgeschichte der Kunst und Literatur*, p. 963.
178. *Kritik des aesthetischen Menschen*, p. 109.
179. *Die conventionellen Lügen*, pp. 28–9.
180. *Ausgewählte Werke*, II, p. 342.
181. *Andreas von Balthesser*, pp. 8 and 65.
182. Stern, 'Karl Kraus: Language and Experience', p. 26.
183. Alfred Kerr, 'Die Diktatur des Hausknechts' [1933], *Die Welt im Licht*, Cologne and Berlin, 1961, p. 385.
184. Stern, 'Karl Kraus: Language and Experience', pp. 23 and 27.
185. Quoted by Dowling, *Language and Decadence*, p. 87.
186. Friedrich Nietzsche, 'Über Wahrheit und Lüge im aussermoralischen Sinne' [1873], *Unzeitgemässe Betrachtugen*, Stuttgart, 1955, p. 607.
187. Ibid., p. 608.
188. Ibid., p. 611.
189. *Literarischer Jugendstil*, pp. 85–6.
190. Seeba, *Kritik des aesthetischen Menschen*, p. 118.
191. 'Semper eadem', *Les Fleurs du mal*, p. 75.
192. *The Works*, p. 931.
193. J. P. Stern, 'Introduction', Arthur Schnitzler, *Liebelei, Leutnant Gustl, Die letzten Masken*, Cambridge, 1966, pp. 35–6.
194. Théophile Gautier, *Portraits et souvenirs littéraires*, Paris, 1875, p. 172.
195. *The Symbolist Movement in Literature*, p. 4.
196. Quoted by Seeba, *Kritik des aesthetischen Menschen*, pp. 36–7.
197. Quoted by Carter, *The Idea of Decadence*, p. 134.
198. Wellek, *Discriminations*, p. 114.
199. *Literarischer Jugendstil*, p. 83.
200. *Language and Decadence*, pp. x–xii.
201. Ibid., p. 119.
202. *Ausgewählte Werke*, II, p. 303.
203. *Language and Decadence*, p. 146.
204. Karátson, *Le Symbolisme en Hongrie*, p. 148.
205. Walter Pater, *Appreciations with an Essay on Style*, Library edition, London, 1924, p. 34.
206. Ibid., p. 37.

207. Ibid., p. 19.
208. 'The Art of Style', *Essays Speculative and Suggestive*, p. 224.
209. 'Personal Style', ibid., p. 217.
210. Rémy de Gourmont, *Selections*, chosen and translated by Richard Aldington, London, 1944, p. 109.
211. *Über Dichter*, p. 85.
212. Miloš Marten, *Styl a stylisace*, Prague, 1906, pp. 16–19.
213. Quoted by Dowling, *Language and Decadence*, p. 39.
214. 'Phrases and Philosphies for the Use of the Young' [1894], *The Works*, p. 1113.
215. 'The Mystery of Style', *Excursions in Criticism*, London, 1893, p. 107.
216. *Andreas von Balthesser*, p. 99.
217. *Retrospective Reviews, Vol. II, 1893–1895*, London and New York, 1896, p. 160.
218. Ibid., p. 185.
219. Charles Baudelaire, *Journaux intimes. Fusées. Mon Coeur mis à nu. Carnet*, edited by J. Crepet and G. Blin, Paris, 1949, pp. 53–4.
220. *Die conventionellen Lügen*, p. 107.
221. *Andreas von Balthesser*, p. 12.
222. 'Der Fall Kerr', *Literatur und Lüge*, Munich, 1958, p. 187.
223. *Sozialgeschichte der Kunst und Literatur*, pp. 966–7.
224. Jiří Karásek ze Lvovic, *Román Manfreda Macmillena*, 3rd ed., Prague, 1924, pp. 13–15.
225. *Journaux intimes*, p. 22.
226. Arthur Breisky, *Střepy zrcadel. Essaie*, edited by Jarmil Krecar, Prague, 1928, p. 95.
227. *Journaux intimes*, p. 87.
228. *Střepy zrcadel*, p. 95.
229. *Andreas von Balthesser*, p. 121.
230. *Střepy zrcadel*, p. 94.
231. Ibid., pp. 97–8.
232. *Andreas von Balthesser*, p. 14.
233. *Střepy zrcadel*, pp. 95–6.
234. *Andreas von Balthesser*, pp. 24 and 25.
235. Ibid., pp. 30–1.
236. Ibid., p. 74.
237. *Střepy zrcadel*, p. 100.
238. *Andreas von Balthesser*, pp. 29 and 31.
239. *Střepy zrcadel*, p. 100.
240. *Journaux intimes*, p. 60.
241. *Andreas von Balthesser*, p. 25.
242. Schnitzler, *Erzählende Schriften*, I, p. 22.
243. Roger L. Williams, *The Horror of Life*, London, 1980, pp. 10 and 17.
244. Cf. František K. Bakule, *Žena a její kouzlo*, Prague, n.d. [1902], pp. 84–5.
245. Labanyi, 'Die Gefahr des Körpers', p. 164.
246. Arnošt Procházka, *Cesta krásy*, Prague, 1906, p. 34.
247. *The Decadent Imagination*, p. 130.
248. Quoted by Ridge, *The Hero in French Decadent Literature*, p. 148.
249. Hauser, *Sozialgeschichte der Kunst und Literatur*, p. 950.
250. Quoted by Dijkstra, *Idols of Perversity*, p. 119.
251. Quoted by Merkl, *Ein Kult der Frau*, p. 354.
252. *The Hero in French Decadent Literature*, pp. 142–3.
253. *The Decadent Imagination*, p. 38.
254. *Modern Love, Poems*, I, pp. 4 and 8.
255. Hajek, *Literarischer Jugendstil*, p. 40.
256. *The Hero in French Decadent Literature*, p. 141.
257. Walter Pater, *The Renaissance. Studies in Art and Poetry* [1873], London, 1912, p. 109.

258. Musil, *Törless*, p. 31.
259. Czigány, *The Oxford History of Hungarian Literature*, p. 254.
260. 'An die Verstummten', *Gedichte*, p. 67.
261. *Pozůstalé spisy*, pp. 195–6.
262. Stanislaw Przybyszewski, 'Sonnenopfer', in Jürg Mathes (Ed.) *Prosa des Jugendstils*, Stuttgart, 1982, p. 147.
263. *Jenseits von Gut und Böse*, p. 71.
264. 'Ženské hnutí', *Naše doba. Revue pro vědu, umění a život sociální*, XIX (1911–12), p. 155.
265. Quoted by Richard Griffiths, *The Reactionary Revolution. The Catholic Revival in French Literature, 1870–1914*, London, 1966, p. 135.
266. Jules Bois, 'Le Symbolisme des Noces de Sathan et le drame esotérique' in *Les Noces de Sathan. Drame esotérique*, Paris, 1892, p. 4.
267. Ibid., p. 7.
268. Ibid., p. 8–9.
269. Ibid., p. 10.
270. Arthur Schnitzler, *Erzählende Schriften*, Vol. IV, Berlin, 1922, p. 106.
271. *Gedichte*, p. 15.
272. Hajek, *Literarischer Jugendstil*, p. 71.
273. Cf. Czigány, *The Oxford History of Hungarian Literature*, p. 293.
274. 'O des verfluchten Geschlechts', *Gedichte*, pp. 93–4.
275. *Language and Decadence*, p. 145.
276. *Kritik des aesthetischen Menschen*, p. 7.
277. *Spisy*, IV, p. 68.
278. Cf. Francis Klingender, *Animals in Art and Thought to the End of the Middle Ages*, London, 1971, pp. 179, 247, 302.
279. P. Ansell Robin, *Animal Lore in English Literature*, London, 1932, p. 143.
280. David Conway, *Secret Wisdom. The Occult Universe Explored* [1985], Wellingborough, 1987, p. 127.
281. *Gedichte*, p. 50.
282. Eliphas Lévi, *The Book of Splendours*. Appendix by Papus. Foreword by R. A. Gilbert, Wellingborough, 1981, pp. 78–9.
283. Ibid., p. 80.
284. Klingender, *Animals in Art*, p. 210.
285. Beryl Rowland, *Animals with Human Faces. A Guide to Animal Symbolism*, London, 1974, p. 143. There Rowland also points out that in Mexico the supreme deity, the Sun, took the shape of the eagle and killed the snake and the rabbit, symbols of the night sky and the moon. Klingender, in *Animals in Art*, reproduces an eleventh-century marble relief from Byzantium where eagles also have a serpent and hares (rabbits) in their talons, p. 272.
286. All four of these pictures are reproduced in Dijkstra, *Idols of Perversity*, pp. 308–12.
287. *Poems*, I, pp. 3, 9 and 36.
288. *The Book of Splendours*, p. 59.
289. Rowland derives this story from the *Gesta Romanorum*. In fact it is in the Phaedrus version of 'Aesop', i.e. long before the *Gesta* was compiled. *Animals with Human Faces*, p. 146.
290. Klingender, *Animals in Art*, p. 214.
291. *Idols of Perversity*, p. 309.
292. *The Book of Splendours*, p. 59.
293. *Animals in Art*, p. 150.
294. Ibid., pp. 330 and 302.
295. *Animals with Human Faces*, p. 143.
296. *The Renaissance*, p. 130.
297. Algernon Charles Swinburne, *Poems and Ballads*, [First Series]. A new edition, London, 1903, p. 189.

298. *The Book of Splendours*, p. 81.

299. Rowland, *Animals with Human Faces*, p. 145.

300. *The Book of Splendours*, p. 137.

301. Ibid., pp. 60–161.

302. Rowland, *Animals with Human Faces*, p. 145.

303. *Idols of Perversity*, p. 127 ff.

304. *Törless*, p. 65.

305. *Gedichte*, p. 48.

306. Otokar Březina, *Básnické spisy*, 2nd ed., Prague, 1942, p. 143.

307. A more detailed and less interpretative study by Robert Pynsent of the intermediate state, of interstatuality, devoted entirely to Czech Decadent literature has appeared in *Česká literatura*, 36 (1988), 2, pp. 168–181.

308. Cf. Williams, *The Horror of Life*, p. 16.

309. Jiří Karásek ze Lvovic, *Gotická duše. Román* [1900], 3rd ed., Prague, 1921, p. 47.

310. 'La Musique et les Lettres' in *Studies in European Literature being the Taylorian Lectures 1889–1899*, Oxford, 1900, p. 138.

311. *Literarischer Jugendstil*, p. 80.

312. *Der Golem*, pp. 56–7.

313. Karel Hlaváček, *Dílo, II, Básně*, Prague, 1930, p. 61.

314. 'Introduction', Arthur Schnitzler, *Liebelei . . .*, p. 42.

315. Ibid., p. 149.

316. *Erzählende Schriften*, I, pp. 55 and 57.

317. Major Czech Decadent works of prose fiction whose action consists in dying are Zeyer, *Jan Maria Plojhar* and *Dům 'U tonoucí hvězdy'*; Šlejhar, *Kuře melancholik*; Kamínek, *Dies irae*; Wojkowicz, *Mizení . . .*; V. Mrštík, *Santa Lucia*; Karásek, *Gothická duše, Sen o říši Krásy* and *Posvátné ohně*.

318. Otokar Auředníček, *Malířské novelly*, Prague, n.d. [1892], p. 166.

319. Karel Sezima, *Passiflora. Román*, 3rd rev. ed., Prague, 1927, p. 40.

320. Mirko Rutte, *Smuteční slavnosti srdcí*, Prague, 1911, p. 37.

321. Arthur Briesky, *Triumf zla* [1910], Königgrätz, 1970, p. 18.

322. Karel Hlaváček, *Žalmy*, Prague, 1934, p. 52.

323. *Malířské novelly*, p. 107.

324. Miloš Marten, *Cyklus rozkoše a smrti*, Prague, 1907, p. 30.

325. Jiří Karásek, *Sexus necans. Kniha pohanská*, Prague, 1897, p. 16.

326. Jiří Karásek, *Stojaté vody*, Prague, 1895, p. 29.

327. Praz, *The Romantic Agony*, p. 397.

328. *Malířské novelly*, p. 14. For Decadent depictions of Venice, see Christiane Schenk, *Venedig im Spiegel der Decadence-Literatur des Fin de siècle*, Frankfurt on Main, Berne, New York, 1987.

329. *Cities*, p. 65.

330. Ibid., pp. 204–10.

331. *Törless*, p. 13.

332. *Sexus necans*, p. 24.

333. S. K. Neumann, *Básně*, I, Prague, 1962, p. 166.

334. Edward Carpenter, *Love's Coming-of-Age. A Series of Papers on the Relations of the Sexes* [1896] 7th ed., London and Manchester, 1911, p. 117.

335. Dijkstra, *Idols of Perversity*, p. 206.

336. Timothy d'Arch Smith, *Love in Earnest, Some Notes on the Lives and Writings of English 'Uranian' Poets from 1889 to 1930, London, 1970, p. 95*.

337. For homosexuality in English literature of the period see also Brian Reade (Ed.), *Sexual Heretics: Male Homosexuality in English Literature from 1850 to 1900*, London, 1970.

338. 'Bacchanal', *Sexus necans*, p. 10.

339. *The Romantic Agony*, p. 366.

340. Théophile Gautier, *Mademoiselle de Maupin*, Paris, 1955, pp. 140–1f.
341. 'Improvisace snu', *Martyrium touhy. Básně*, Prague, 1896, p. 12.
342. *Der Golem*, p. 61.
343. Ibid., p. 134.
344. Dijkstra, *Idols of Perversity*, p. 127.
345. *The Decadent Imagination*, p. 47.
346. *The Romantic Agony*, p. 339.
347. *Erzählende Schriften*, I, p. 59.
348. *Gedichte*, p. 63.
349. *Der Golem*, p. 5.
350. Ibid., pp. 183–4.
351. Julius Zeyer, *Jan Maria Plojhar* [1891], Prague, 1964, p. 224.
352. Musil, *Törless*, p. 24.
353. Růžena Jesenská, *Rudé západy*, Prague, 1904, p. 34.
354. *Dílo*, II, p. 47.
355. *Les Fleurs du mal*, p. 307.
356. 'Der Herbst des Einsamen' and 'Ruh und Schweigen', *Gedichte*, pp. 54–5.
357. Karel Sezima, *Za přeludem. Tři prózy*, 3rd ed., Prague, 1927, p. 69.
358. Pierrot, *The Decadent Imagination*, p. 209.
359. Georges Rodenbach, 'L'Ame sous-marine, III', [1896] *Choix des poésies*, Paris, 1949, p. 186.
360. *Kritik des aesthetischen Menschen*, p. 101.
361. *The Decadent Imagination*, p. 151.
362. Stern, Arthur Schnitzler, *Liebelei . . .*, p. 12.
363. Vladimír Houdek, *Vykvetly blíny*, Prague, 1889, p. 54.
364. Hajek, *Literarischer Jugendstil*, pp. 55 and 68.
365. Pater, *The Renaissance*, p. 252.
336. Pierrot, *The Decadent Imagination*, p. 183.
367. *Die Gedichte . . .*, p. 17.
368. *Die andere Seite*, p. 106.
369. Otokar Březina, *Hudba pramenů*, Prague, n.d. [1903], p. 40.
370. *Discriminations*, p. 116.
371. Ernst Robert Curtius, *Europäische Literatur und lateinisches Mittelalter*, 7th ed., Berne and Munich, 1969, p. 329.
372. *Language and Decadence*, p. 163.
373. Ibid., p. 164.
374. Praz, *The Romantic Agony*, p. 376.
375. Dowling, *Language and Decadence*, p. 159.
376. *Die Gedichte . . .*, p. 116.
377. Musil, *Törless*, pp. 19–20.
378. Meyrink, *Der Golem*, pp. 15–17.
379. Cf. also Griffiths, *The Reactionary Revolution*, p. 127.
380. Marjorie Reeves and Warwick Gould, *Joachim of Fiore and the Myth of the Eternal Evangel in the Nineteenth Century*, Oxford, 1987, p. 8.
381. Ibid., p. 5.
382. Ibid., p. 189.
383. Ibid., p. 292 ff. There are Joachimist manuscripts in Prague, though it seems to me unlikely that Vrchlický would have known them. Cf. Ibid., p. 297.
384. Ibid., p. 24.
385. Ibid., p. 186.
386. 'La Musique et les Lettres', pp. 159–60.
387. Lévi, *Book of Splendours*, p. 96.
388. Ibid., p. 167.

389. *The Poverty of Historicism*, pp. 159–60.

390. 'The Mind of Modernism', Bradbury and McFarlane, *Modernism*, pp. 75–6.

391. Quoted by Jullian, *Esthètes et magiciens*, p. 334.

392. For an account of Löw and of literary representations of the rabbi, see Angelo Maria Ripellino, *Praga magica*, Turin, 1973, p. 157 ff. For a popular account of the legends surrounding him, see Adolf Wenig, *Staré pověsti pražské*, 4th ed., Prague, 1972, p. 169 ff.

393. Quoted by Rémy de Gourmont, *La Culture des idées*, p. 140.

394. *Aesthetes and Decadents*, p. xxix.

395. Emanuel Swedenborg, *Heaven and its Wonders, and Hell: From Things Heard and Seen*, London and New York, n.d. (Everyman), p. 302.

396. *The Decadent Imagination*, p. 97. See also pp. 79, 92, 101 and 112.

397. Jan Voborník, *Julius Zeyer*, Prague, 1907, p. 30.

398. Cf. Conway, *Secret Wisdom*, pp. 101–2.

399. Griffiths, *The Reactionary Revolution*, p. 136.

400. Cf. Reeves and Gould, *Joachim of Fiore*, pp. 191–5.

401. Cf. Griffiths, *The Reactionary Revolution*, p. 123 ff.

402. Ibid., pp. 126–9.

403. Christopher McIntosh, *The Rosicrucians. The History and Mythology of an Occult Order*, 2nd revised ed., Wellingborough, 1987, p. 105.

404. Ibid., pp. 107–8.

405. Quoted by Jullian, *Esthètes et magiciens*, p. 339.

406. Griffiths, *The Reactionary Revolution*, p. 137.

407. Cf. Dijkstra, *Idols of Perversity*, pp. 326–8.

408. McIntosh, *The Rosicrucians*, p. 146.

409. *Der Golem*, p. 144.

410. Ibid., p. 118.

411. Czigány, *The Oxford History of Hungarian Literature*, p. 285.

412. *The Decadent Imagination*, p. 116.

413. *The Techniques of Strangeness*, p. 45 ff.

414. *Der Golem*, p. 88.

415. Quoted by McIntosh, *The Rosicrucians*, p. 28.

416. *The Victorian Temper*, p. 232.

417. *The Decadent Imagination*, p. 75.

418. Ibid., p. 77.

419. Musil, *Törless*, p. 62.

420. Griffiths, *The Reactionary Revolution*, p. 125.

421. Ibid., p. 143.

422. Ibid., p. 131.

423. *Les Noces de Sathan*, pp. 34–5.

424. Rowland, *Animals with Human Faces*, p. 143.

425. *The Decadent Imagination*, p. 90.

426. *Esthètes et magiciens*, p. 107.

427. *The Book of Splendours*, p. 80.

428. Quoted by Jullian, *Esthètes et magiciens*, p. 106.

429. Occultism remained very much alive in Czech literary circles after World War I. Two Decadents, Karásek and Lešehrad, continued to write occultist works. The former also edited a serious occultist periodical. Váchal continued to do occultist paintings and drawings. Younger artists also showed occult leanings, among the important writers: Richard Weiner and Jan Bartoš. Freemasonry also flourished; the minister of foreign affairs, Edvard Beneš, was also leader of Czechoslovak Freemasonry.

430. Any historian would be justified in labelling these dates impressionistic. They are based on discussions with colleagues and friends from all the countries concerned. I omit Poland and Roumania deliberately, since those two countries' political and artistic trends have little

chronologically or factually in common with those of the rest of 'socialist' Europe. I by no means wish to deny the originality, particularly of Polish culture, or its contribution to modern thought (Mrozek, Kolakowski, Milosz, and so on).

431. Alain Robbe-Grillet, *Pour un nouveau Roman*, Paris, 1963, pp. 12–13.

432. This occultism is thoroughly disapproved of by the authorities. It is difficult to find out just how widespread it is. We find an indication of its importance in Havel's *Pokousení* (Temptation, 1987, so far published only out. Czechoslovakia), and there is a Bulgarian admiral who is reputed to be one of the best astrologers in the country. Bulgaria is, however, a special case because of its rich conventional and folk religious history.

433. Colin Wilson, *The Occult*, London, Glasgow, Toronto . . ., 1979, p. 14.

434. Ibid., p. 113.

435. For an occultist's dismissal of the Sixties occult revival and its connection with drugs, see Conway, *Secret Wisdom*, pp. 110–11.

436. Aldous Huxley, *The Perennial Philosophy*, London and Glasgow, 1948, pp. 55, 94, 123.

437. *Eros and Civilisation. A Philosophical Inquiry into Freud*, Boston, 1974, p. xxi.

438. Ibid., pp. xiv–xv.

439. In Richard Kostelanetz (Ed.), *The Avant-Garde Tradition in Literature*, Buffalo, 1982, p. 277.

440. Ibid., p. 276.

441. Ibid., p. 279.

442. George Melly, *Revolt into Style. The Pop Arts in Britain*, London, 1970, p. 143.

443. Ibid., p. 173.

444. Ibid., p. 32–3.

445. Ibid., p. 202.

446. Marcuse, *Eros and Civilisation*, p. xxi.

447. 'The New Mutants', p. 273.

448. Marshall McLuhan, *Understanding Media. The Extensions of Man*, London, 1967, p. 302.

449. Marshall McLuhan and Quentin Fiore, *The Medium is the Massage*, Harmondsworth, 1967, p. 14.

450. Jirí Valoch and B. P. Nichol (Eds.) *The Pipe. Recent Czech Concrete Poetry*, Toronto, 1973.

451. Gerhard Rühm (Ed.), *Die Wiener Gruppe*, Reinbek, 1967, pp. 10–11.

452. Konrad Bayer, *Der Kopf des Vitus Bering*, Frankfurt on Main, 1970, p. 19.

453. Oswald Wiener, *Die Verbesserung von Mitteleuropa, Roman*, Reinbek, 1969, p. xc. (The novel is paginated in Roman numerals throughout.)

454. *Revolt into Style*, p. 41.

455. Roland Barthes, *Le Plaisir du texte*, Paris, 1973, pp. 91–2.

456. Ibid., p. 96.

457. Ibid., p. 105.

458. Ibid., p. 77.

459. Ibid., pp. 82–4.

460. Actually, in England it still retained its contemptuous meaning well into the 1950s.

461. *The Perennial Philosophy*, p. 119.

Index